Dialogue, Connect, Engage

Also by John E. C. Cooper from Centennial College Press

Crisis Communications in Canada: A Practical Approach
(2nd edition, 2016)

Dialogue, Connect, Engage

Cross-cultural and Diversity Awareness in Canadian
Communications Environments

John E. C. Cooper, EdD

CENTENNIAL COLLEGE PRESS
TORONTO, ONTARIO
2025

CENTENNIAL COLLEGE

Centennial College Press
951 Carlaw Avenue
Toronto, ON M4K 3M2

Mailing address
Centennial College Press
P.O. Box 631, Station A
Toronto, ON M1K 5E9

https://centennialcollegepress.com/

Dedicated to my grandchildren,
Charles and Eleanor Cooper

LAND ACKNOWLEDGEMENT

I respectfully acknowledge that this book was researched and written on traditional lands inhabited for thousands of years by the Michi Saagiig Anishinaabeg. I acknowledge the importance of these lands to the Michi Saagiig Anishinaabeg and the important role they play as our communities continue to learn from Indigenous knowledge and values and build greater opportunities for collaboration. In respecting and recognizing Indigenous Peoples as both the rights holders and stewards of the waters and lands on which I have had the privilege to live and work, I also acknowledge that these are the traditional and treaty territories, covered under the Williams Treaties, of the Mississaugas of Scugog Island First Nation, Alderville First Nation, Hiawatha First Nation, Curve Lake First Nation and the Chippewa Nations of Georgina Island, Beausoleil and Rama.

Contents

Chapters include objectives, a case study, profile, "Let's Check In!" self-assessment exercises, lists of key terms, questions, research/writing exercises and references. Not all these elements are included in every chapter.

Foreword

Finally, a textbook for the ages! Dr. John Cooper's remarkable insights into diversity, equity and power lay the foundation for *Dialogue, Connect, Engage*, a groundbreaking exploration of social inequities. Drawing upon his extensive expertise in critical analysis of power and privilege, Dr. Cooper seamlessly blends scholarly rigour with a profound commitment to social justice.

When I first encountered John during our doctoral studies program, his keen intellect and unwavering dedication to challenging the status quo immediately stood out. His brilliant analyses of global issues highlighted the complexities of power dynamics that underpin systemic inequalities. However, what truly distinguished John was his fearless willingness to confront uncomfortable truths and expose the stark realities of injustice—a trait that earned him the reputation of a true social justice warrior.

In *Dialogue, Connect, Engage*, Dr. Cooper's steadfast commitment to fighting inequities shines through on every page. This book is more than just a scholarly endeavour; it is a testament to his convictions and his relentless pursuit of a more just and equitable future. Through extensive research and thoughtful reflection, Dr. Cooper invites readers to join him on an academic exploration—one that challenges preconceptions, disrupts entrenched biases, and fosters genuine connections across the intersections of power, privilege, and understanding.

Dialogue, Connect, Engage offers invaluable guidance for practitioners seeking to explore the nuances of power dynamics, marginalization, and discrimination. By weaving together insights from industry professionals, practical strategies, and authentic case studies, Dr. Cooper equips readers with the tools and mindset needed to move toward a collective consciousness of change.

In essence, *Dialogue, Connect, Engage* is more than just a textbook—it is a call to action for students and practitioners alike. It challenges us to confront our privilege, interrogate our biases, and work towards a future where equity, diversity, and inclusion are not just ideals but lived realities.

—Sharmaine Itwaru, EdD
(she/her)
Professor, George Brown College
Adjunct Faculty, Brock University

Introduction

John E. C. Cooper's new book, his eighth, has never been needed more than now for our public relations profession.

Whether we are emerging practitioners or seasoned veterans, professional communicators must guide our relationships wisely in this intertwined, multicultural world, a global village so interconnected that the simplest of messaging errors can cause immense hurt and damage. This new book addresses these issues and more.

Cooper has a doctorate in education, more than 35 years of public relations experience and teaching, focusing on issues and crisis management, writing and planning, and has taught three generations of PR students.

I first met John more than a decade ago when we were asked to help develop a Bachelor of Public Relations Management program at one of our country's top polytechnics. We were also honoured to have chapters on our specialties included in the ground-breaking book helmed by the late William Wray Carney, *Fundamentals of Public Relations and Marketing Communications* (University of Alberta Press, 2015). Carney's criteria for authors to write a chapter in his book included balanced components of teaching experience, published works, and recognition as a leader in a PR discipline.

It was indeed an honour for me to be included with such company, including John's, since his textbook, *Crisis Communications in Canada: A Practical Approach* (the second edition of which was published by Centennial College Press in 2016) is so highly regarded.

This new book reflects his vast experience in that it is readable, teachable, impeccably researched and pedagogically designed.

The latest brilliant generation in our PR classrooms will love this book. And it will be embraced by those teaching PR, since each chapter is relevant and contains effective case studies, questions, and exercises. It covers communicating with Indigenous and 2SLGBTQI+ communities, the challenges facing the policing environment, and the need to communicate sensitively during disasters, pandemics and in racialized situations.

Our profession keeps evolving, and this book will help PR practitioners of all levels continue to secure our important role in the organizational engine room.

—Mark Hunter LaVigne, M.A., APR, FCPRS, LM

CHAPTER ONE

Engineering Consent: The Social Power of Communications

OBJECTIVES OF THIS CHAPTER

This chapter is designed to help advance an understanding of ideas regarding effective cross-cultural communications through the following:

- A discussion of Edward Bernays and the history of modern public relations, as well as the emergence of the concept of "engineering consent";
- An examination of ethical guidelines in public relations, both Canadian and American;
- An understanding of key messages and communications planning;
- Defining race and culture, and understanding systemic and overt discrimination;
- Developing an understanding of ethnocentrism, cultural relativism, intercultural empathy and intercultural awareness; and
- An interview with a public relations teaching practitioner, and through it, an understanding of technology and its use in bridging cultures.

BERNAYS AND THE INFLUENCE OF A GENERATION

Earlier generations had movie stars, pop stars and rock stars, and today we have social media celebrities and influencers.

If we go back further, we find the father of modern public relations, Edward L. Bernays (1891–1995), nephew of the famed psychoanalyst Sigmund Freud, creating a niche for himself as a growing social influencer *sans* social media sites. For Bernays, the site of his social media was the milieu of human interaction itself, the tableau of American society. A prolific writer, author and public speaker, Bernays was at home making ideas work in the very granular world of promotion in the early 20th century, helping to shape the zeitgeist of his era by figuring out the means to change human behaviour.

In the late 1920s Bernays was working for the American Tobacco Company on ways to encourage more women to smoke in public. He was changing a hidden-at-home habit into a public one by kindling a link between the idea of cigarette smoking and notions of freedom and social power using a slogan, "Torches of Freedom," and hiring young women to smoke openly in a New York City parade (Malharek, 2017). Viewed from our perspective in the 21st century, getting more women to smoke was not a good thing, but it opened the door to understanding human behaviour. Bernays saw seemingly limitless power in the expansion of communications opportunities being generated by the growing numbers of newspapers, magazines, books, radio, motion pictures—"all these media provide open doors to the public mind ... the world's most penetrating and effective apparatus for the transmission of ideas" (Bernays, 1947, p. 113).

By the time Bernays was active in the nascent 20th century public relations industry, agents of change like filmmaker D.W. Griffith were already understanding (and exercising) the power of mass media as a social influencer: Griffith's 1915 motion picture *The Birth of a Nation* would galvanize white Americans against their African American fellow citizens and reignite interest in the hate-mongering Ku Klux Klan; it was a movie that "stole from, coerced, and outwitted its own audiences. For *The Birth of a Nation* is arguably history's most successful failure, a film whose narrative heights are matched only by its ethical depths" (Blakemore, E., 2015, February 4).

By contrast, Bernays believed fervently in the cause of equal rights, and would work with organizations like the National Association for the Advancement of Colored People (NAACP) to generate nationwide publicity for its 1920 regional convention in Atlanta, Georgia. Bernays (and his client group) knew the anger that holding the convention in a hotspot of the Deep South would engender. However, despite intimidations that ranged from disruption of the event to death threats against the organizers, Bernays persisted in laying out the themes of the conference (the economic importance of Black workers in the south; the development of more tolerant attitudes towards African Americans; the desire to induce southern social leaders to support the cause of the NAACP), and the event was a success (Museum of Public Relations, 2020).

North of the border, Canadian public relations of a sort had been well established for decades. Canadian journalism in the 19th and early 20th century was often a mixed bag that combined elements of news reporting, marketing and public relations. The cost to print newspapers, magazines, flyers and other printed products became more reasonable in the 19th century, ushering in an era of independent publishers, whose daily and weekly newspapers were often allied with specific political and social causes, such as William Lyon Mackenzie's *Colonial Advocate*, Joseph Howe's *Novascotian*, Mary Ann Shadd's *The Provincial Freeman*, the Japanese Canadian newspaper *Tairiku Nippō* (created in 1907 and shut down following the internment of Japanese Canadians during World War II) and the long-running *The Chinese Times* (Yarhi and Walkom, 2017, October 24). These publications served a growing class of literate Canadians, increasing in tandem with the Dominion's focus on providing the schooling necessary to meet the growing demand for workers with strengths in reading, writing and numeracy. It was all about growth: in literacy, population, a booming capitalist economy, and an audience willing to listen. For example, there were significant opportunities to promote, through marketing and public relations, the further "opening up" of western Canada to immigrants (we will talk about the effect of this policy on Indigenous Peoples in Chapter 3). In 1910, the magazine *Canada West: The Last Best West,* in a blend of marketing and public relations under the guise of journalism, promised to its readers free land and education, sunny skies, cheap living and clean air. It targeted immigrants as well as eastern Canadians. *Canada West* was colourful—it provided idyllic images of prairie skies of robin's-egg blue, honey-gold grain crops in expansive, verdant fields, and a wealth of smiling, friendly faces; there were tips for the newcomer and focused success stories, and in contrast to

> our modern world of empty advertising spin, and though *Canada West* had purely promotional ambitions, its success hinged on providing practical information.... *Canada West* contained everything the Canadian government thought the prospective farm owner needed to know. Issues repackaged the same message, often running the same kinds of articles every year: statistics on farm yields; information on railways, telephones, immigration, homesteading, schools, building materials, climate, cattle, and hog prices; river and lake access; land and customs regulations; different church denominations; freight rates; and much more, as part of an initiative, begun in the mid-1890s by Prime Minister Wilfrid Lauri-

er's government, to sell 100 million acres of prime farmland (Chandler, 2016, September 7).

Laurier's immigration campaign, headed by Minister of the Interior Clifford Sifton, involved saturating the U.S. and Europe with pamphlets and advertisements that extolled Canada's virtues and doling out free trips to American editors and British MPs; all told, it "has been heralded as one of the greatest and most successful PR efforts in Canadian history.... The campaign was a massive success, and played a significant role in the 2 million new immigrants who entered Canada from 1896 to 1911" (Goldman Communications, 2016, August 17).

While today public relations is defined as "the strategic management of relationships between an organization and its diverse publics, through the use of communication, to achieve mutual understanding, realize organizational goals and serve the public interest" (Canadian Public Relations Society, 2020a), in the days of Sifton and Bernays it was still largely considered propaganda, and hampered by the stigma of potentially untrue, misleading or biased influence.

By the time Bernays sent a dozen or so young women puffing away onto the streets of the Big Apple nine years after the NAACP conference, he already had an established track record of "creating circumstances" that helped the organizations that hired him to generate "earned media" (free publicity through news stories). Bernays successfully linked feminism with the exercise of societal freedom, at the same time helping to engender an environment by which his tobacco-producing client would earn more money through the creation of a new market demographic (Malharek, 2017).

Bernays had already hit on the kernel of truth that would drive public relations: change people's viewpoint by changing their behaviour. His work was less that of "a Svengali and more the product of a talented and experienced press agent who'd also served as a propagandist for the U.S. Committee on Public Information during World War I" (Malharek, 2017). In fact, Bernays would write glowingly of the committee's work in impacting the public conscience with a "war of words (that helped to) build the morale of our own [American] people, to win over the neutrals, and to disrupt the enemy" (Bernays, 1947, p. 115).

Bernays' ideas were consistent with his time, which was (with the exception of the Depression) characterized by dynamic, sometimes hyperactive economic growth. He at once linked many of his ideas to the American ideals of patriotism and free speech, and to the capitalism to which they were bound. For Bernays, the dissemination of ideas and influence was a natural outflow of good leadership, accomplishing "purposefully and scientifically what we have termed 'the engineering of consent' … action based only on thorough knowledge of the situation and on the application of scientific principles and tried practices to the task of getting people to support ideas and programs" (Bernays, 1947, p. 114).

Bernays' view was of "the public as primarily emotional and irrational.… [T]his basic insight was sufficient for him to create circumstances favorable to his clients" (Malharek, 2017), although Bernays also saw the responsibility of public relations practitioners to "push only those ideas he [the practitioner] can respect, and not to promote causes or accept assignments for clients he considers antisocial" (Bernays, 1947, p. 116).

Bernays created the template for much of public relations work for the next half-century; today, the norm of social media monitoring underscores Bernays' exhortation to conduct "research of the public to learn why and how it acts, both individually and as a group.… What are their present attitudes.… What are the impulses which govern these attitudes.… What ideas are the people ready to absorb?" (Bernays, pp. 116–117). Today, researchers look for the opportunity to incentivize market-driven data collection to create "total knowledge" platforms where surveillance capitalism makes all things known and used—habits, behaviours, attitudes—and social learning is engrained as an exercise where "people imitate one another until new ideas become population-wide habits," (Zuboff, 2019, p. 431). The elaborate mapping of human behaviour, with the end result an overall game plan for society, "could well see the creation of a quantitative, predictive science of human organizations and human society. At the same time, these new tools have the potential to make George Orwell's vision of an all-controlling state into a reality" (Pentland, A., 2011, p. 11). All of which is, perhaps not too surprisingly, a 21st century version of Bernays' "engineering of consent." Pencil, paper and careful observation have been replaced by artificial intelligence, with the potential to make *everyone* a profit engine, drawing on everything from ideas and behaviours to fantasies and cravings and, ultimately, buying habits.

Among the tools of public relations that came out of the work of Bernays and others are *key messages*. These are statements crafted and delivered by organizations to audiences and stakeholders through traditional and social media and via public-facing announcements, and are found in news releases and any statement or speech issued by an organization, as well as in fact sheets, Q&A documents and website content (James, 2011). Created with specific audiences in mind, key messages deliver information designed to improve the image of an organization, change attitudes (think of Bernays's engineering of consent), and essentially "to nudge ... companies back into the good graces of their primary stakeholders, and to improve or maintain organizational reputation" (Pratt, 2004, p. 15).

Key messages form a core component of communication plans, which are designed to deliver those key messages in a carefully orchestrated way. There are as many different ways to design communication plans as there are public relations firms in the world, but basic formats will include:

- Situation analysis (a gathering of information relevant to our plan, especially answering the question "Why are we making an announcement?");
- Objectives (using the now-standard SMART formula [Doran, 1981]: Specific, Measurable, Achievable, Realistic and Time-focused goals);
- Audiences (whom do we want to reach? Think of media, the general public, specific stakeholders and interest groups);
- Media channels (how are we getting the message out? Through traditional media—television, radio, newspapers; or social media—Twitter, Facebook, websites, etc., or both);
- Timetable (when will we deliver our messages?);
- Evaluation (how will we evaluate our plan's success? Think of newspaper stories, website visits, newscasts and social media hits) (Dionova, Y., 2017, July 7).

ETHICAL GUIDELINES

Clearly, Bernays knew his audiences, and his skill as a communicator was a result of a combination of experience, intellect, creativity and sweat equity, in hands-on research grounded in the painstaking methods of asking myriad questions and carefully noting ideas down—and using these to form the nucleus of effective public relations planning. The public relations industry took shape over the course of many years, and organizations like the Canadian Public Relations Society (CPRS), created in 1948, and International Association of Business Communicators (IABC), founded in 1970, worked to create ethical guidelines for practitioners to use when plying their trade. The guidelines offer general rules for practice, including honesty, accuracy, and respect for the use of confidential client information. The Canadian Public Relations Society's Code of Professional Standards includes fair and honest dealings, and practitioners are expected to "conduct their professional lives in a manner that does not conflict with the public interest and the dignity of the individual, [and] with respect for the rights of the public as contained in the Constitution of Canada and the Charter of Rights and Freedoms" (Canadian Public Relations Society, 2020b).

Section 15 of the Charter is designed to ensure that:

> … every individual in Canada—regardless of race, religion, national or ethnic origin, colour, sex, age or physical or mental disability—is to be treated with the same respect, dignity and consideration.… [S]ection 15 also protects equality on the basis of other characteristics.… For example, this section has been held to prohibit discrimination on the grounds of sexual orientation, marital status or citizenship (Government of Canada, 2020).

The International Association of Business Communicators requires that its members demonstrate that they are "sensitive to others' cultural values and beliefs" and "IABC requires its members to embrace these ethical guidelines in their work" (International Association of Business Communicators, 2020).

MAKING THE LEAP ACROSS CULTURAL LINES

We live in a North American society that is increasingly stratified, and which, in Canada, is distinguished by increased immigration, heightened awareness of Indigenous rights, and the need to find the ways and means to get along with each other.

This challenge is not new, for Canada was created on the basis of transplanted Eurocentric values, a place dominated by English and French laws and customs; while we pat ourselves on the back for our seemingly open, receptive, culturally diverse approach to life, the rough dynamics at play are obvious to most if they grew up outside the dominant white culture, and clear enough to those within the dominant culture if they look hard enough and open themselves up to dialogue with others. As seen with respect to Indigenous rights and culture, Canada's historical practices of oppression against First Nations, Métis and Inuit served to underscore its role as a colonial government; in later chapters we will look at aspects of communications focusing on the treatment of Indigenous groups. Canada's dismally poor treatment of other oppressed groups, expressed through issues such police harassment and carding of young Black men in Toronto, discrimination against Canadians of Chinese descent, government-sanctioned persecution of immigrant Roma families, and the rise of Islamophobia, all serve to accentuate the significant social challenges facing the country.

Traditionally, Canada espouses equality in its communities and prides itself on dedication to balance and fairness. Unfortunately this isn't the case today. Systemic discrimination (bias that is built into a pattern of behaviours, but not expressed openly, for example favouring some people over others in job interviews) is a part of the everyday lives of many Canadians. In the past, both systemic and overt discrimination were the norm. Overt discrimination, often involving acts of violence, oppression, and the use of hateful language, is largely against the law today, though it still takes place. Consider also the use of government-approved discrimination—the permission by and for government to openly treat people in negative and hurtful ways, ways that touch on not just social status but economic status as well.

Consider, for instance, the plight of more than 20,000 Japanese Canadians in World War II, interned by their country as enemies of the state, their homes and businesses confiscated and whole families moved far away, kept in often rough-hewn, ramshackle housing for the duration of the war, subjugated and demeaned. "[P]erhaps more than any other event in recent history, the internment continues to haunt policy makers and historians, as well as serving as the fulcrum in the tension between historical memory and scholarship" (Grenon, 2001, p. 8). That overt discrimination in British Columbia was commonplace was well-known, and Japanese Canadians were barred from whites-only sections of movie theatres and tennis courts, prevented from serving on juries or running for office, and in the early years of the war, forced to obtain identity cards. White-run media perpetuated stereotypes and curried fear beginning in the 19th and continuing well into the 20th century.

So it was no surprise that during the war Ottawa's official position was that discrimination was acceptable, even necessary, and it was based on the racism of the times, on uncertainty, fear, and a perceived need to demonstrate strength to the populace. The temperament of wartime Prime Minister William Lyon Mackenzie King was such that "defending the status quo was of greater value politically than to be a social crusader for racial justice in twentieth-century Canada" (Grenon, 2001, pp. 10–11). Racial hatred of Japanese-Canadians wasn't limited to British Columbia, for it was widespread and largely supported. But B.C. was the crucible. "One of the most troubling aspects of internment is that it wasn't simply a top-down measure by out-of-touch bureaucrats or paranoid military commanders. It was a policy that came firmly from the political grassroots.... Petitions poured into Ottawa from B.C. communities demanding an immediate round-up of their Japanese-Canadians" (Hopper, T., 2016, December 14).

King's words in Parliament in February 1942 were measured and their tone serious:

The situation created by the presence in British Columbia of a population of nearly 24,000 men, women and children of Japanese race has for a number of reasons received the closest attention of the government over the past four years ... a special committee [investigated and reported] upon the problem of Japanese in British Columbia from the standpoint of national security.... The most important recommendation was that there should be a re-registration of the Japanese population of British Columbia and that a small standing committee should be set up to keep the government constantly informed as to the oriental situation in that province.... [R]e-registration was carried out by the Royal Canadian Mounted Police ... [and] included the photographing and finger-printing of all persons of Japanese origin....

Individuals, whatever their nationality [Germans and Italians were included], who there was reason for believing might act in a manner prejudicial to the public safety or the safety of the state, were promptly interned. Steps were also immediately taken to immobilize for the duration of the war all fishing boats operated by men of Japanese race.... Legitimate apprehensions in British Columbia were concerned with three things: the aid which might be given to enemy submarines and enemy raiders if they should be supplied with fuel or furnished with information; the possibility of acts of sabotage; and the possibility of anti-Japanese riots in which military force might have to be used to restore order....

Persons of Japanese race, who are Canadians either by birth or by naturalization, and Japanese nationals resident in Canada will be justly treated. Their persons and property will receive the full protection of the law. No action will be taken which would give any excuse for the ill-treatment of Canadians under the control of Japan.... As specific measures, all persons of Japanese race will be removed from fishing boats and other vessels for the duration of the war. For the same period the sale of gasoline and explosives to persons of Japanese race will be controlled by the Royal Canadian Mounted Police. Japanese nationals have been forbidden to possess or use short-wave receiving sets, radio transmitters and cameras. Their present surveillance by the Royal Canadian Mounted Police similar to that successfully exercised over German and Italian nationals will be continued. … Enemy aliens, whether nationals of Japan or of Germany or of Italy, will be required to leave the protected area on the coast of British Columbia. …

It will be recognized that Canadian citizens of Japanese race have been placed in a very difficult position. They are being asked to bear with patience inevitable hardships and losses. A situation of this kind can only be effectively met by an equal measure of tolerance and understanding on the part of the people of Canada generally. In the national interest it is of the utmost importance that the problem should be approached in this spirit (King, 1942, February 9).

To appreciate the impact of these words from our position in the 21st century is sobering. While purporting to project empathy, King was engaging in an act of oppression. This would not necessarily have come as a surprise to Bernays, for discrimination of the time was engrained in North American society and anti-Black bias was a constant. And as a Jew, Bernays would have been familiar with the anti-Semitism that was layered into both European and North American society (Wise, n.d.). King could be variously *clearly aware of* (or, for political expediency, vaguely oblivious to) the power differential between the white power structure and Japanese Canadians, underscoring the fact that "most humans are oppressors because they are members of groups that have relative privilege over those of other groups with even less power" (Allen, 2004, p. 123). King's language is steeped in denials; for instance, in his references to manners "prejudicial to the public safety" or "potentially providing aid to enemy submarines" or fears of "anti-Japanese riots" (as in, "We're locking you up for your own safety!"). The language is clear, demonstrating that "Whiteness is shrouded with denials that give White people yet another form of privilege: the ability to avoid discussion of how oppression continues to benefit White people" (Lund and Carr, 2010, pp. 230–231).

A few years after World War II ended, the Canadian government first considered the notion of compensation and proper redress, though it hit a dead end. It wasn't until the 1970s that human rights organizations' searches of declassified government files fully confirmed what people already knew, that "the government's wartime actions were motivated by anti-Asian fears and the racist feelings of that period. … [T]he war provided the government with an opportunity to respond to what was referred to as the 'Japanese problem.' The wrongs of the past … could no longer be denied" (The Critical Thinking Consortium, 2015). It was estimated that the financial losses to Japanese Canadians amounted to $443 million in 1986 dollars, or a little over a billion dollars in 2020. A redress campaign by the National Association of Japanese Canadians resulted in a 1988 apology from Prime Minister Brian Mulroney, who promised a "solemn commitment and undertaking to Canadians of every origin that such violations will never again in this country be countenanced or repeated," along with financial redress, including personal payments to the interned, a community fund, and recognition of Japanese Canadian citizenship (Roberts-Moore, 2002).

HOW DIVERSE IS CANADA?

According to Statistics Canada's *Diversity in Canada*:

- In 2018, 23.6 percent of Canada's population was born outside the country—highest of the G8 countries.
- From 2006 to 2020, Canada's largest source of immigrants was Asia.
- A 2017 Ontario Human Rights Commission survey found that 40 percent of racialized people surveyed reported experiencing discrimination over the previous five years because of race or colour.
- More than 6.2 million people identified as a member of a visible diversity group. The vast majority live in Canada's largest census metropolitan areas: Montreal, Toronto, and Vancouver.
- In 2016, Canada was home to 250 ethnic or cultural ancestries.

(Jessica, 2020, November 15)

DEFINING CULTURE AND RACE

It is generally understood that communicators have a responsibility to both represent the publics and stakeholders they serve, and ensure that the language they use is appropriate to their audiences. In a diverse world, "public relations as an organizational function will be shaped by organizational and national cultures—values, beliefs, and expectations. If the organization believes in a diverse workforce, then the public relations department will have greater permission to include practitioners from different backgrounds and standpoints. Similarly, each national culture will influence how organizations communicate with one another" (Toth, 2009).

Culture is seen as fluid and changing, an "amalgamation of human activity, production, thought, and belief systems. ...[W]e ascribe notions of culture to people who are a part of a nation-state, an ethnic group, or a religious group" (Ladson-Billings, G., 2014, p. 75). It is also defined as "a dynamic system of values, beliefs and behaviours that influence how people experience and respond to the world around them" (Guo and Jamal, 2007, p. 29). Culture is about responsiveness, synergies and sharing, and embodies "the tacit knowledge and overt practice of social roles, values and ways of being shared by a community" (Everett, 2017, p. 275).

The subject of race is often a more troubling, explosive and violent concept. It can be seen as a complicated mixture of genetic differences linked to experiences and social issues, and layered into historical events that can range from economics to scientific misinterpretation (Key, 1995). As geneticist Albert Jacquard wrote, race is based on false assertions, on the belief "that the human species is made up of very distinct groups with different biological characteristics—in other words, 'races'; and ... that these 'races' can be ranked in hierarchies according to a scale of 'values'" (Jacquard, 1996, p. 22). In fact, there is no basis for race, such that "the concept of race is not valid for human populations. ... [It] has so little content that the word becomes meaningless" (Jacquard, p. 24).

Yet, as a social construct, "race plays a huge role in determining how long a person can expect to live, the quality of that life, the educational possibilities that will or won't open up, and the manner in which that person ... will be viewed in a given society at a given point in time" (Tompkins, 2005, p. 534). "In America, the idea of race emerged as a means of reconciling chattel slavery—as well as the extermination of American Indians—with the ideals of freedom preached by whites in the new colonies" (Alexander, 2012, p. 23). Racism is a matter of power, and "a system of oppression based on race ... is perpetrated by white people against people of color. It involves an unequal distribution of systemic power for people with white-skin privilege in four main areas: 1. the power to make and enforce decisions; 2. access to resources, broadly defined; 3. the ability to set and determine standards for what is considered appropriate behavior; and 4. the ability to define reality" (Bivens, 1995). Canada was often distinguished from the U.S. by its wide-ranging denial of racism. According to

Aylward (1999), in the U.S., racism is generally acknowledged as a fact of life, but in Canada, "it is hard even to reach this issue because of pervasive denial of the very existence of racism in Canadian society" (p. 40).

So, how easily learned is racist behaviour? According to a study by researchers at Harvard, Princeton and the University of California (Berkeley), it can be transmitted like a virus (but one that can be cured):

> Consciously we may want, and try, to hold egalitarian beliefs. However, despite the fact that many of us consciously will ourselves to be egalitarian, the deeper recesses of our minds continue to be held hostage by the history of racism in our culture.... [D]aily exposures—even if the stereotypes are untrue—leave a consequential residue on our minds that can be measured scientifically. These residues, or, implicit biases, are pervasive and costly ... (and) can also be contagious (Willard et al., 2015, p. 96).

In other words, we can fall victim to patterns of behaviour that become engrained in our unconscious.

In the U.S., the protracted, difficult relationship between whites and Blacks was written about, examined, discussed, long before the advent of the modern civil rights era of the 1950s onwards. The African American writer James Baldwin established a reputation as someone who clearly saw through the thick and layered rhetoric that was baked into discussions of race. In his book *The Fire Is Upon Us*, an examination of the debates that took place between Baldwin and white, ultra-conservative firebrand William F. Buckley, Nicholas Buccola wrote of Baldwin's contention that white people are consumed by a guilt that allows them—perhaps encourages them—to pretend that the situation of racism as it exists *doesn't exist*, and "until white Americans are willing to confront the source of their guilt—the historical record that has produced the world in which we live—they will remain trapped in a web of delusions.... [T]o escape this trap, white people must develop the ability to listen..." (Buccola, 2019, p. 346).

How do we perceive the interconnectedness of relationships and communication around us, and especially the perceptions of one culture by another? I recall sitting in a packed movie theatre with my wife in the late 1990s, watching the Jack Nicholson movie *As Good As It Gets*, the story of an obsessive-compulsive writer (Nicholson) who falls in love with a single mom (played by Helen Hunt). Not only does Nicholson's character, Melvin, display various traits of OCD, he is also (in addition to being misanthropic) homophobic, racist and anti-Semitic. When I watch movies, I am interested in getting a "read" of the audience's reaction to what is happening onscreen, especially given the relative anonymity of being in a darkened theatre. In the case of this movie, three scenes said as much about this largely white audience as it did about the character Nicholson portrayed. In one scene, Melvin makes anti-Semitic comments to a couple in a restaurant. The movie theatre crowd groaned in a "this-is-wrong," shared gesture. In a later scene, Melvin insults Blacks; the crowd giggled nervously (as in "am I allowed to laugh at this? Is it okay for me to laugh?"). Finally, Melvin makes a homophobic comment and the crowd goes wild, guffawing out loud. Clearly, this community of disparate individuals in a suburban theatre grew up learning: A) it is wrong to be anti-Semitic; B) it is questionable to be critical of Black people; C) it is still okay to make jokes about gay men.

Or were people simply confused about seeking an outlet for pent-up social frustration? James Baldwin, in the interview with Studs Terkel, spoke of twice watching the movie *The Defiant Ones* (about two escaped convicts, chained together: one Black, one white), and cited the scene in which Sidney Poitier's character goes out of his way to help Tony Curtis in a crucial escape-via-train scene; in a theatre of white liberals, Baldwin spoke of the "sigh of relief and clapping" emanating from the audience at the nobility of Poitier helping the white man, and, in a theatre of Black patrons, the "tremendous roar of *fury* from the audience. ... They told Sidney, 'Get back on the train, you fool'" (Melville House, 1961: Baldwin, interviewed by Studs Terkel, p. 16).

Examples like those above are the linchpin of engagement; by getting ideas of race, culture, positionality (and the perception of these societal components) into the open we can engage in the "difficult conversations" that are necessary to bridge gaps between people; these conversations help to generate opportunities to understand the world around us and to embrace diversity (Miretzky and Stevens, 2013; Watt, 2007).

As we know, the history of the world often proceeds in a way that causes much muddling, much extrapolation of "facts" against "feelings" and the questioning of what *is real* and what isn't. Alex Carp, writing in the *New York Review of Books*, says that, over the last quarter of the 20th century and into the 21st:

... a generation of Americans [to which I would add Canadians, and frankly, everyone else, for we are *altogether the recipients* of this change] has had their imaginations narrowed, on one side by populist myths blind to the evidence of the past, and on the other by academic histories blind to the power of stories. Why, at a time when facts are more accessible than at any other point in human history, have they failed to provide us with a more broadly shared sense of objective truth? (Carp, 2018, October 19).

The fudging of the truth is happening in many places, under many circumstances. For example, consider the case of American Republican senator Dale Zorn of Michigan, who wore a face mask during the COVID-19 pandemic; the mask-wearing not unusual for the times, *except* that the mask was fashioned after the stars-and-bars flag of the American Confederacy. The Confederate flag is considered a symbol of racial hatred, given the southern states' support for slavery and, following the American Civil War, their creation of discriminatory laws as well as campaigns of violence against Black Americans. It stands to reason that wearing it makes a clear statement of one's positionality, yet Zorn first chose to defend his actions and dissemble about his behaviour—saying that the mask was a "flag of Tennessee" and then launching into a commentary on the necessity of "teaching American history"—before finally apologizing.

As defined by the Cambridge Dictionary, to "dissemble" is "to hide your real intentions and feelings of the facts" (Cambridge Dictionary, 2020). In an environment where racist feeling exists, people frequently dissemble in order to appear innocent of acting in a racist way. Zorn only admitted to doing something wrong when he was forced to admit his error, and he continued to dissemble on Twitter as he sought to provide an answer he presumably could live with, calling the racist symbol a "choice of pattern":

I'm sorry for my choice of pattern on the face mask I wore yesterday on the Senate floor. I did not intend to offend anyone; however, I realize that I did, and for that I am sorry. Those who know me best know that I do not support the things this pattern represents. ... My actions were an error in judgment for which there are no excuses and I will learn from this episode (Zorn, 2020).

To which one might ask, "Then why wear such a mask in the first place?"

A TIP FOR CROSS-CULTURAL COMMUNICATION

Listen: "Active listening is the single most useful way to overcome barriers to effective communication. We listen for meaning by checking back with the speaker to ensure that we have accurately heard and understood what was said. Communicating across cultures adds another layer to the 'noise' that is already present, which makes it critical to add that extra step of checking back" (Zofi, 2017, June 6).

WHY THE NEED FOR CROSS-CULTURAL COMMUNICATION?

As a country, Canada is among the top four nations (along with Australia, Switzerland and New Zealand) in population growth through immigration on a per capita basis, taking in an average of 300,000 migrants a year; currently 21 percent of its population is foreign-born, compared to 30 percent for top-ranked Australia (BBC News, 2017, October 17).

According to Statistics Canada, Canada's internationally born population ranks highest among the G8 countries (the others are France, Germany, Italy, Japan, Russia, the UK and the US) and the 2016 census revealed a population with more than 250 ethnic origins; close to 7 million people identified as members of a visible diversity group, representing just under 20 percent of the total population. Of those, almost a third were born in Canada and two-thirds outside the country; the three largest groups are South Asian, Chinese and Black, and they account for 62 percent of that total of 7 million; additionally, the Indigenous population (First Nations, Métis and Inuit) stood at 1.6 million in 2016 and accounted for 5 percent of the population. With respect to a "mother tongue" (and keeping in mind that respondents to Statistics Canada may report more than one), 58 percent reported English as a mother tongue, 21.5 percent French, 0.6 percent an Indigenous language, and 22 percent a language other than English or French, the top four being Mandarin, Cantonese, Punjabi and Tagalog (Statistics Canada, 2016).

With such a wealth of diversity, and a stated commitment by Canada to embrace it, it is difficult, though not surprising, to see pushback against the accommodation of differences. In looking at our culture, we need to consider cultural relativism and ethnocentrism.

Cultural relativism focuses on accepting and respecting another's worldview based on *their culture*, not your own, understanding that knowledge, meaning and values are "relative to a particular framework (e.g., the individual subject, a culture, an era, or a language)" and that no position "is uniquely privileged over all others" (EBSCO, 2009). Linguistics professor Daniel Everett found that in his research of the Pirahã tribe, deep in the Amazon rain forest, his world-view changed as he came to appreciate the culture of the people he studied; for instance, the building of (by western standards) what were flimsy houses made of branches and leaves was an instance where the application of cultural relativism was necessary: "Pirahã houses reveal important distinctions between their culture and ours. ... The Pirahãs don't need walls for defense, because the village is the defense—every member of the village will come to the aid of every other member. They don't need houses to display wealth, because all Pirahãs are equal in wealth. They don't need houses for privacy, because privacy is not a strong value" (Everett, 2008, pp. 71–72).

By contrast, *ethnocentrism* is the tendency of people to "divide the population into those who are considered as part of their group or their 'type' (what we will call the in-group) and the rest who are seen as outsiders (the out-group). Where such distinctions are made, there is often a propensity for more positive behavior toward the in-group than toward the out-group" (Hales and Edmonds, 2018). There is a belief that one's own culture is "the best." Examples include people sharing a common religion and, as a result, favouring each other's viewpoints over those "outside" that shared religion, or people who are committed to capitalist culture disliking those who tend toward socialist views. For the dominant "western" culture of North American, it can take the form of "us" versus "them," as in "this is our culture, this is who we are, why can't *they be more like us*?" In extreme cases, it takes the form of "Go back to where you came from!" which is unfortunately a frequent refrain, but not one that goes unchallenged. For instance, in 2016, the City of Toronto and the Ontario Council of Agencies Serving Immigrants sponsored anti-racism-focused bus shelter public service announcements, one of which had a white male facing a hijab-wearing female. "Go back to where you came from," the young man says. The young woman responds with "Where, North York?" (Freeman, 2016, June 16).

In the late 1990s I wrote a book about Ray Lewis, the first Canadian-born Black man to win an Olympic medal (a bronze in the 4 x 100-metre relay at the Los Angeles Games in 1932). Ray was born and raised in Hamilton, Ontario. At age 87, seated in an easy chair in his apartment overlooking downtown Hamilton, and relating the details of his long and sometimes not-so-easy life, the memories came back effortlessly for Ray. On one occasion he told me of travelling as a teenager with a friend to Orangeville, where a white man pushed him on the street, shoving him off the sidewalk, shouting "Go back to where you came from!" To which, without hesitation, Ray replied, "Where? Hamilton?" This was in the 1920s. Things haven't changed much over the years.

A lack of willingness to respect cultures can take the form of *homogeneity*, the cultural tendency toward a "sameness" of behaviours, attitudes and ideas; in a rapidly globalizing world, it is often perceived as a sign of intolerance and coercion. Consider Quebec's Bill 21. Enacted in 2019, it was seen widely as a means of enforcing cultural homogeneity, by banning the wearing religious symbols by people in government-related work, including teachers, police and members of the legislature. Called "An Act Respecting the Laicity of the State," it was passed by the Quebec government under Premier François Legault, leader of the Coalition Action Démocratique (CAQ) party. *Laicity* is the process of governance that excludes religious control or influence, and the ruling party stated that "as a stricter duty of restraint regarding religious matters [a law] should be established for persons exercising certain functions, resulting in their being prohibited from wearing religious symbols in the exercise of their functions" (National Assembly of Quebec, 2019). Religious symbols included headwear (such as hijabs or niqabs worn by Muslim women) or jewelry and clothing. Bill 21 was widely seen as "a device to keep female Muslim clerks, cops and teachers from wearing headscarves or veils at work" (Wells, 2019, November 8). Law professor Phil Lord suggests that

> Some opponents indeed believe that ... when faced with a choice between their religion and public service (or access to public services), Muslim women will choose their religion. They believe that Bill 21 will, therefore, simply prevent Muslim women, an already marginalized community, from obtaining (or keeping) employment in the public service and accessing basic and essential public services—further marginalizing them (Lord, 2020).

In response to the legislation, organizations like the Canadian Race Relations Foundation stated that it was discriminatory, in that "the legislation interferes with the ability of individuals to practice their faith and places members of some faith communities in the untenable position of having to choose between their faith and employment" (Canadian Race Relations Foundation, 2019, August 6).

MINDFULNESS AND CULTURAL AWARENESS

Being mindful of cultures other than your own takes effort. An example of a successful practitioner of cross-cultural communications is former New Zealand Prime Minister Jacinda Ardern, who acknowledged the importance of the Indigenous Maori language, calling it "a living, thriving language and 'part of who we are as a country'" and committing herself to making the language universally accessible, hoping that it will be "spoken more and more informally as it became integrated into the education system" (Cheng, 2019).

Awareness of culture—"the ability to understand, value, and respect our own culture and the differences between other cultures"—and being able to appreciate diversity can take patience and time. Communication practitioners need to ask questions, listen, immerse themselves in learning, open themselves to new experiences, and understand, through empathy, another person's reality (O'Donoghue, 2019). Clearly, "empathy orients people toward other people. It allows one to get absorbed in emotional experience and to resonate with others' experiences" (Zuboff, 2019, p. 301).

It is important to think of the contrast between intercultural empathy and intercultural awareness. *Intercultural awareness* focuses on the ability to see one's one culture contextualized against another. As an example, Honglin Zhu of Changzhou University cites the Chinese perception of an American as someone who will

> always work, wear casual clothes, eat fast food, drink Coca Cola and talk about business over lunch. ... In China, where relationships are highly valued, lunch, dinner or a gathering for tea has a social connotation: people get together to talk and relax, and more importantly, to build an intimate relationship. Misinterpretations occur primarily when we are not aware of our own behavioral rules and project them onto others (Zhu, 2011).

By contrast, *intercultural empathy* "means understanding others by entering their world, or "standing in somebody else's shoes" and being able to understand another's culture from their (not our own) viewpoint; empathy "leads us not only to experience the feelings of another but also to reflect on those feelings and compare them to our own" (Zhu, 2011). It is a movement from distanced respect to emotional immersion.

Effective communication across cultures is especially important on teams. As organizational behaviour professor Erin Meyer said, "Whether or not we realize it, small variations in communication patterns can have a tremendous impact on how we understand each other. These subtle differences—such as when to speak or stay quiet, or how to provide feedback—may seem minor, but if you don't understand them, it can lead to a frustrated workforce" (Anikst, 2016). Yet for all the attempts at connectivity between cultures, there are numerous stumbles. Consider these examples from an article on major brand blunders:

- A store in London, England offered a special "smoky bacon flavour" of Pringles potato chips during the Muslim holy month of Ramadan, with a sign on the display case of the circular tins stating "Ramadan Mubarak" ("Happy or Blessed Ramadan"). The store apologized and removed the display.
- Coffee chain Starbucks encouraged patrons to engage in dialogues about race relations, in a "Race Together" campaign. A feeling that the issue was too contentious led the company to drop the campaign after six days.
- Sportswear giant Nike created women's sports gear that had, as its source of inspiration, traditional "tatau" tattoos from the southwest Pacific. It was forced to apologize and remove the product when it was revealed that the leggings for women in fact looked like the Samoan *pe'a* tattoo, which is worn only by men (Fromowitz, M., 2017, February 10).

In my own household, my wife Maria, who is Portuguese, was incensed when an ad for the Hyundai Kona car came up on the television. I wondered why she declared "We will never buy that car." It turned out that the word "cona" (which sounds the same) is a derogatory term for female genitalia in Portuguese (and also in Galician). Why didn't the car company know? It's likely because the Hyundai marketing team was thinking only of the Kona region in Hawai'i (pleasant climate, excellent coffee, great deep-sea fishing) when it gave the car its name. The company soon enough found out how people felt after an outpouring of social media rage, and the company made the decision to change the name of the model *being sold in Portugal*—though models sold elsewhere kept the Kona name. It wasn't just the Portuguese who raised their eyebrows, but Poles and Norwegians too: in Polish "kona" means "dying," and in Norwegian it means "the wife" (and not necessarily in a nice way!) (Kroulek, A., 2018, May 25).

Over time and with practice, cultural competencies can be developed; these should focus on knowledge (such as personal understanding and cultural self-awareness and awareness of other cultural groups), personal attributes (adaptability and empathy) and skills (cross-cultural communication, teamwork and conflict resolution), all being used to develop stronger cross-cultural links (Toth, 2009). For example, during the COVID-19 pandemic, Ascend (a non-profit Pan-Asian organization for North American executives and business professionals) announced a collaborative action agenda among 100 corporations and partner organizations to promote inclusion, denounce bias against targeted groups like Pan-Asians, raise awareness of the effect of COVID-19 on vulnerable groups, donate to effective COVID-related programs and support communities, pledging to "combat stigma, biases associating Pan-Asians with the novel coronavirus, and all forms of discrimination based on age, color, disability, ethnicity, gender, gender identity, national origin, race, religion, sexual orientation and veteran status" (Ascend, 2020).

Microaggressions are common and sometimes not-so-subtle responses to anxiety over fears of "outsiders. They can range from verbal assaults and insults (for example suggesting that a person might be in the country illegally) to invalidating the existence of racism" (Boysen, 2012). Comments like (said with mock surprise) "Your English is very good!" (suggesting that a person who is not white is expected to speak English haltingly or with difficulty, regardless of their origins) or asking someone who is Asian to translate a language they do not know, for example asking someone who is Chinese to translate something written in Japanese. These examples are all too real, hurtful and shocking, and in general are delivered by people who aren't aware of their privilege (or who pretend that they aren't) (Suárez-Orozco et al., 2015). Countering microaggressions are "microaffirmations," which, according to the University of Oregon's Donalynn Pompper, can best be delivered within an organization by public relations practitioners as a means of promoting "insider activism" and to "inspire positive microresistance" (Pompper, 2019). Microaffirmations are positive, supportive messages that affirm excellence, encourage healthy workplace relationships and focus on active listening practices and team building. Because public relations practitioners have strong social capital within organizations, they are well-equipped to spread positive messages thanks to their "access to organizational leadership and relationship building know-how" (Pompper, 2019).

For professionals whose stock in trade is communication, whether in public relations, corporate communication, managing social media accounts, writing documentary scripts or crafting blogs, the challenge presented by a communications environment populated by the vagaries of melting facts and refashioned truths might have Bernays, were he alive today, scratching his head. But not likely for long—a pragmatist like Bernays could say, "No surprise. This is exactly how I expected the world to be." The question for communicators today might be: How will history assess the validity of what we are writing? In 25 or 50 years, how will we view our own current truths?

CASE STUDY
UNION CARBIDE AND THE BHOPAL DISASTER

It was a horrifying disaster that would become the world's worst industrial accident: in the period from December 2 to 3, 1984, a Union Carbide pesticide plant in the central Indian city of Bhopal leaked upwards of 40 tons of methyl isocyanate gas following a maintenance mishap. The accident killed more than 3,000 citizens immediately and poisoned tens of thousands more in the shanty town surrounding the plant; many victims died lingering, painful deaths (Broughton, E., 2005, May 10). Terror and uncertainty reigned: "The leak occurred shortly after midnight, and some victims died in their sleep. Others, blinded by tears and gasping for breath, tried to flee but collapsed in death" (Associated Press, 1989).

In a scenario that underscored an initially far-distanced lack of empathy as well as a desire to avoid moral accountability and reduce legal responsibility, Union Carbide would eventually settle, through mediation, with the Indian government, paying compensation of U.S. $470 million, which was considered a very small sum given the long-term health implications for the thousands of survivors (Associated Press, 1989).

Founded in 1917 and headquartered near Houston, Texas, the company has since 2001 been a subsidiary of the Dow Chemical Company. In fact, financial difficulties in the years following the Bhopal disaster eventually led to United Carbide's acquisition by another firm after it had been forced to raise funds by divesting itself of top brands like Glad garbage bags and Eveready batteries.

The Indian government had a 20 percent stake in the Bhopal plant and the facility had seen several operational issues crop up since opening in 1981 (Shrivastava, 1987). Following the accident, when Union Carbide's chair Warren Anderson was asked by reporters

whether he really cared about anything besides profit and loss, [he said], "During the last week, I haven't been able to give profits much thought"…
Mr. Anderson and his colleagues … have been trying to strike a diffi-

cult balance between the instincts of human compassion, the demands of public relations and the dictates of corporate survival (Lueck, 1984, December 14).

Ethnocentrism also played a role. According to Shrivastava (1987):

Cultural traits were blamed by some … roughly as follows: Indian workers at the plant were not acclimated to a culture of technology and hence did not realize the importance of following maintenance and safety procedures …This explanation of the Bhopal tragedy is simplistic and ethnocentric because it identifies culture as the cause for a series of interrelated failures in design, equipment, procedures, supplies, human errors, organizational policies and government policies (p. 253).

A trip to India by Union Carbide head Anderson, with a "symbolic" arrest-and-release of him on bail, set the stage for a series of news stories that, because of cultural differences and distance, focused more on adept public relations handling than compassion:

In his handling of the press, Mr. Browning [Jackson Browning, the company's director of safety and environment affairs] maintained a calm, measured and confident composure … When reporters raised their voices, the Carbide spokesman responded in warm tones, and when reporters asked questions out of turn, they have simply been ignored … Mr. Browning has been dealing with a presumption on the part of reporters that the company, if not negligent, must bear some guilt for the profound suffering in Bhopal that has been portrayed nightly on television" (p. 253).

Discourse—the communication and debate that springs from contentious issues such as this disaster—was important in this issue because

discourse involving social conflicts is distorted in several respects because of power differentials between parties in discourse. Dominant groups [in this case Union Carbide and the government of India] have better access to information and discourse forums. Their goals and interests are generally better known and accepted… (and) they often possess more legitimacy in society (Shrivastava, 1987, p. 248).

Emphasizing the cultural distance between the victims in Bhopal and the American industrial giant, commentators likened the power of Union Carbide to that of a head of state: "'At times like this symbolism becomes very important,' said John Jueck, a professor of management and former dean of the University of Chicago's Graduate School of Business. He compared Mr. Anderson's trip to those of governors and presidents visiting the scenes of disasters in this country [the United States]" (Lueck, 1984, December 14).

Activists in Bhopal mobilized thousands of protesters—victims, family members and supporters—in a "morcha" (demonstration march) in early January 1985 to draw attention to their plight (Shrivastava, 1987, p. 254).

According to Dutta et al. (2012), a focus on a grassroots, civil rights activist culture in Bhopal was a means of resisting the power of western public relations through "different resistive strategies by activists such as hunger strikes and protest marches ... [by doing so] dominant public relations messages are resisted, and alternative discursive articulations are put forth. This, for instance, is exemplified in how the public relations strategies of Union Carbide are deconstructed and resisted by activist publics who were affected by the Bhopal gas tragedy" (p. 10).

For Union Carbide workers, the disaster struck an emotional chord, and as they saw the news briefings on closed circuit television and read the news releases on the company bulletin boards, "the full scope of the tragedy became clear ... at noon on Dec. 6, in a gesture by Carbide's 10,000 workers worldwide, flags were flown at half-mast and a moment of silence observed ... the disaster in Bhopal has generated a painful emotional response" (Lueck, 1984, December 14).

In February 1989 the company was ordered to make the almost half-billion-dollar payout to the Indian government to settle all claims, though human rights groups protested that the settlement wasn't enough given the seriousness of the accident (Associated Press, 1989).

Case Study Questions

1. In a situation like the Union Carbide disaster, are there legal implications that might compel organizations to keep a "tight lid" on their messages? How does this affect communications?
2. How can communicators balance the need for legal responsibility with the need to demonstrate compassion?
3. How difficult is it for organizations to manage long-distance communications across cultural lines?

4. Given the prevalence of social media, what are some of the challenges that a company like Union Carbide would face if such a disaster happened today?
5. What are some ways that an organization can demonstrate empathy for others in crisis situations?

PROFILE
MARYJANE MARTIN:
TECHNOLOGY AS A CROSS-CULTURAL EQUALIZER

Maryjane Martin has spent many years working as a public relations practitioner, communications manager and teacher. A past president of the Canadian Public Relations Society's Toronto chapter and a graduate of Syracuse University (MS, Communications Management), Queen's University (Honours BA, Film Studies) and Humber College (Public Relations), Martin has put her planning and problem-solving skills to work as an instructor at Toronto Metropolitan University and the University of Victoria and for private sector clients, and also teaches in continuing education programs. Most of her work has focused on the use of emerging technologies in the communications field.

Why is technology important in cross-cultural communications?
I think technology has been a real equalizer, and I would say enterprise social media has accelerated cross-cultural communication, especially in providing access to broader communities. Teams use collaborative tools to build communities and share information. In my current work in the private sector, whether we're using Zoom, Webex, or Skype video conferencing, I see colleagues, I hear them, I connect with them. And their voices are heard. Technology—and the use of it—accelerates the cross-cultural environment. It gives us a chance to sit back and listen. Never before have we had such an opportunity to hear such diverse voices.

How attuned are corporate communications departments to cross-cultural communications?
Most corporate communications departments are well-versed in diversity and communicating across cultures and are trying to find ways to reinforce it and encourage it. Corporate communicators today are focused on continuous improvement, which requires a certain degree of flexibility and willingness to try different ways of doing things. They are focused on increasing awareness of

unconscious barriers or subconscious biases to help people become more open to adapting.

Workplaces are more diverse, remote teams are located across the country or around the world, and businesses that once sold products to a single demographic are now selling to a global market. All of these factors have converged to make cross-cultural communication a vital part of organizational success.

How effective is technology in the classroom?
I have found that the various technology options at hand are very useful. For instance, the use of online polling exercises on various issues helps students from different cultures have a voice. After voting, they have the option to discuss their own opinion or to talk about the "class response." This is essential in helping to bridge some of the perceived gaps between cultures and the anonymity that technology allows is an equalizer in so many different ways. Students are able to talk in general terms and cross these boundaries without having to explain where they are necessarily coming from. A lot of the group work that we do encourages discussion and engagement, and this is especially important in online classes.

How does cross-cultural dialogue help students prepare for the workplace?
Through technology, we are cultivating a dialogue and getting students to talk about their position in their own words. The tools that we're using are helping them cross the boundaries, and as a result they don't feel singled out. We can use these tools to help students so that when they are in the workplace they can use the tools they have to help guide discussion and contribute to the dialogue.

I think we're modeling good cross-cultural communication, and I think we're saying we want to hear from everyone. We seek out opinions and the exchange of ideas through thoughtful discussion. We're cultivating that dialogue and encouraging that discussion. At the same time, the communication tools are getting better and there are more platforms to use. In distance learning, for example, we can show videos, things can be translated, and there are so many ways to ensure that the message is clear. At the same time, it has helped me as an instructor to aim for greater clarity at times. When we have a situation where someone steps back and asks "what do you mean by that?" it helps me to find the ways to explain it so that everyone understands. And that has broadened to become not just a professional but a personal experience too, in learning how to be more receptive and ensuring that everyone understands the directions.

This helps me to work on the way I communicate—to be clear and direct and understandable. And it results in the creation of an effective partnership where we learn from each other.

LET'S CHECK IN!

In this self-assessment, you will be asked to think about your attitudes toward, and knowledge of, the subject matter discussed in this chapter. Looking at the chart, shade in (or put a check mark on) the square that most applies to you: Agree Strongly; Agree Somewhat; Neither Agree nor Disagree; Disagree; or Disagree Strongly. Try to avoid "sitting on the fence" (i.e. Neither Agree nor Disagree). Then compare what you have with your peers. Discuss your results, thinking in particular about why you made your decision.

	Agree Strongly	Agree Some-what	Neither Agree nor Disagree	Disagree	Disagree Strongly
Most public relations is propaganda					
Governments use public relations to mislead people					
It is essential for public relations practitioners to follow a code of ethical conduct					
Racism will always be with us					
Public relations practitioners have a responsibility to take the lead in encouraging cross-cultural dialogues					
Governments should be allowed to make and enforce rules that reflect the biases of the people they govern					

KEY TERMS

Cultural competencies: knowledge and understanding based on awareness, the development of personal attributes and effective cross-cultural communication.

Cultural relativism: accepting and respecting another's worldview based on their culture, not your own.

Culture: a fluid collection of activity, thought and belief systems and values

Discourse: discussion, debate, communication on an essential topic.

Dissemble: to hide your true intentions or your perception of the facts as they are presented.

Engineering of consent: action based on research and focused on influencing people to support new ideas and change their behaviour.

Ethnocentrism: the tendency of people to identify/divide/exclude populations based on similarity/dissimilarity to their own perceived group.

Key messages: communication messages designed to deliver information in order to improve the image of an organization and change attitudes.

Microaffirmations: positive, supportive messages affirming positive values and promoting healthy workplace relationships.

Microaggressions: behaviours based on racially- or culturally-motivated anxiety and fear, ranging from verbal assaults and insults to aggressive behaviours.

Overt discrimination: behaviour involving acts of violence, open oppression and the use of hateful language, based on biased attitudes.

Race: a complicated blend of genetic differences linked to economics, science, social structure and power.

Racism: a power-based system of oppression based on skin colour and perceived genetic differences.

Systemic discrimination: bias built into a pattern of behaviours, but not necessarily expressed openly.

QUESTIONS TO EXPLORE

1. What were Edward Bernays's major contributions to public relations? What influence did these contributions have on the way organizations communicate with their publics today?

2. Consider the way that the Canadian government treated Japanese Canadian citizens in World War II. Could this kind of treatment happen today? Are there jurisdictions in the world today where this might happen? What would be some of the reasons for this kind of behaviour on the part of a government?

3. If you were working in communications for a human rights organization, what would be your response to Quebec's Bill 21? Explain your position.

4. What are the differences between race and culture? How does this affect our work as communicators?

5. Find an example through research, or from your own experience, of either (a) cultural relativism or (b) ethnocentrism and explain why you chose it.

EXERCISE

You work in the communications department of a medi-um-sized, Canadian-based mining company that is open-ing up an operation in Ghana. You have been tasked with the job of creating a communication plan and key messages outlining your company's intention to:

- Develop strong cross-cultural ties with Ghana;
- Employ fair hiring practices on the ground; and
- Demonstrate responsibility for the environment.

As writer Benjamin Musampa has noted, "Canada's mining industry, with its skilled and diverse workforce and leadership in corporate social responsi-bility, could assist mineral-rich African nations with addressing their lack of skilled workforce in this competitive industry" (Musampa, 2019).

Basing your approach on the assumption that your company has worked through federal agencies like the Trade Commissioner Service to get estab-lished in Ghana, your job is to ensure that your company is getting off on the right foot in its new venture. Create a short communication plan and three or four key messages and explain the approach you intend to take with this initiative.

REFERENCES

Alexander, M. (2012). *The new Jim Crow*. New York: The New Press.

Allen, R. (2004). Whiteness and critical pedagogy. *Educational Philosophy and Theory: Incorporating ACCESS*, 36(2), 121–136. doi: 10.1111/j.1469-5812.2004.00056.x

Anikst, J. (2016, Spring). An expert in cross-cultural management describes the importance of subtle behavioural cues. *Rotman Management Magazine*, University of Toronto. https://www.rotman.utoronto.ca/Connect/Rotman-MAG/IdeaExchange/Erin-Meyer

Ascend (2020, April 30). 100+ Corporations & Partner Organizations Support COVID-19 Action Agenda. *Ascend*. https://www.prnewswire.com/news-releases/100-corporations--partner-organizations-support-covid-19-action-agenda-301049962.html

Associated Press (1989, February 14). Union Carbide to Pay India Gas Victims $470 Million: Activists Denounce Settlement. *Los Angeles Times*. https://www.latimes.com/archives/la-xpm-1989-02-14-mn-2325-story.html

Aylward (1999). Aylward, C. (1999). *Canadian critical race theory: Racism and the law*. Halifax, NS: Fernwood Publishing.

BBC News Reality Check Team. Is Canada taking more migrants than other Western nations? BBC News. https://www.bbc.com/news/50061529

Beck, M. (2018, July 6). Liberal celebrating 140 years of newspaper service to Richmond Hill. *York Region Media Group*. https://www.yorkregion.com/community-story/8726140-liberal-celebrating-140-years-of-newspaper-service-to-richmond-hill/

Bernays, E. (1947, March 1). The engineering of consent. *The Annals of the American Academy of Political and Social Science*. https://journals.sagepub.com/doi/10.1177/000271624725000116

Bivens, D. (1995). Internalized racism: A definition. Women's Theological Centre. https://www.racialequitytools.org/resourcefiles/bivens.pdf

Blakemore, E. (2015, February 4). "Birth of a Nation": 100 years later. JSTOR Daily. https://daily.jstor.org/the-birth-of-a-nation/

Boysen, G. (2012). Teacher and student perceptions of microaggressions in college classrooms. *College Teaching*, 60(3), 122–129. doi: 10.1080/87567555.2012.654831

Broughton, E. (2005, May 10). The Bhopal disaster and its aftermath: A review. *Environmental Health 2005*, 4 (6). https://www.ncbi.nlm.nih.gov/pmc/articles/PMC1142333/

Buccola, N. (2019). *The fire is upon us.* Princeton, NJ: Princeton University Press.

Cambridge Dictionary (2020). Definition of "dissemble." https://dictionary.cambridge.org/dictionary/english/dissemble

Canadian Public Relations Society (2020a). CPRS: Who We Are. https://www.cprs.ca/About.aspx

Canadian Public Relations Society (2020b). Code of Professional Standards. https://www.cprs.ca/About/Code-of-Professional-Standards

Canadian Race Relations Foundation (2019, August 6). Call for papers—Bill 21: An act respecting the laicity of the state. https://www.crrf-fcrr.ca/en/news-a-events/articles/item/27026-call-for-papers-bill-21-an-act-respecting-the-laicity-of-the-state

Carp (2018, October 19). History for a post-fact America. *The New York Review of Books*. https://www.nybooks.com/daily/2018/10/19/history-for-a-post-fact-america/?fbclid=IwAR1pUBbGnLGl6XaAY9bevZAD5MJQGzXuYUo3b7t8a4pLcrxBBM30KKdjleE

Chandler, G. (2016, September 7). Selling the prairie good life. *Canada's History*. https://www.canadashistory.ca/explore/settlement-immigration/selling-the-prairie-good-life

Cheng, D. (2019, September 9). Māori language a part of 'who we are': Jacinda Ardern. *New Zealand Herald*. https://www.nzherald.co.nz/nz/news/article.cfm?c_id=1&objectid=12266202

Cooper, J. (2020, April 27). Interview with Maryjane Martin.

Critical Thinking Consortium (2015). Background briefs: Response to Japanese internment. Critical Thinking Consortium. https://tc2.ca/uploads/backgroundbriefs/BBJapaneseIntResp.pdf

Dianova, Y., (2017, July 7). Six steps to creating an effective communication plan. Axia Public Relations. https://www.axiapr.com/blog/6-steps-to-creating-an-effective-communication-plan

Doran, G. (1981, November). There's a S.M.A.R.T. way to write management's goals and objectives. *Management Review.* https://community.mis.temple.edu/mis0855002fall2015/files/2015/10/S.M.A.R.T-Way-Management-Review.pdf

Dutta, M. J., Ban, Z. & Pal, M. (2012). Engaging worldviews, cultures, and structures through dialogue: The culture-centred approach to public relations. *PRism 9*(2). https://www.prismjournal.org/uploads/1/2/5/6/125661607/v9-no2-a2.pdf

EBSCO (2009). Cultural relativism. EBSCO Research Starters. https://www.ebscohost.com/uploads/imported/thisTopic-dbTopic-1247.pdf

Everett, D. (2017). *How language began.* New York: Liveright Publishing.

Everett, D. (2008). *Don't sleep, there are snakes.* New York: Vintage Books.

Freeman, J. (2016, June 16). Anti-Islamophobia ads stir online debate. CP24. https://www.cp24.com/news/anti-islamophobia-ads-stir-online-debate-1.2948604

Fromowitz, M. (2017, February 10). Hall of shame: More multicultural brand blunders. Campaign US. https://www.campaignlive.com/article/hall-shame-multicultural-brand-blunders/1423941

Goldman Communications (2017, August 17). The evolution of public relations. https://www.goldman-communications.com/single-post/2017/01/17/The-Evolution-of-Public-Relations

Government of Canada (2020). Guide to the Canadian Charter of Rights and Freedoms. https://www.canada.ca/en/canadian-heritage/services/how-rights-protected/guide-canadian-charter-rights-freedoms.html#a2f

Grenon, T. (2001). Offensive history and the good war: The internment of Japanese Canadians and Japanese Americans in World War II. Master's Thesis, Queen's University, Kingston, ON.

Guo, S., & Jamal, Z. (2007). Nurturing cultural diversity in higher education: A critical review of selected models. *Canadian Journal of Higher Education, 37*(3), 27–49.

Hales, D., & Edmonds, B. (2018, June 21). Intragenerational Cultural Evolution and Ethnocentrism. *Journal of Conflict Resolution.* https://journals.sagepub.com/doi/full/10.1177/0022002718780481

Hopper, T. (2016, December 14). Rare views of Japanese-Canadian internment: 19 images remembering one of Canada's darkest hours. *The National Post.* https://nationalpost.com/news/canada/rare-views-of-japanese-canadian-internment-19-images-remembering-one-of-canadas-darkest-hours

International Association of Business Communicators (2020). IABC Code of Ethics for Professional Communicators. https://www.iabc.com/about-us/purpose/code-of-ethics/

Jacquard, A. (1996, March). An Unscientific Notion. *UNESCO Courier: The Roots of Racism*, pp. 22–25. https://unesdoc.unesco.org/ark:/48223/pf0000102577

James, M. (2011). Ready, aim, fire: Key messages in public relations campaigns. *Prism, 8* (1). http://www.prismjournal.org/homepage.html

Jessica M. (2020, November 15). Diversity in Canada. *Diversity.Social.* https://diversity.social/canadian-diversity/

Key, S. (1995). The definition of race. *American Psychologist*, 50(1), 43–44

King, W. L. M. (1942, February 9). Remarks in Parliament. Lipad: Canadian Hansard. https://www.lipad.ca/full/1942/02/09/1/#1254820

Kroulek, A. (2018, May 25). The Hyundai KONA: A translation fail in 3 languages. The Language Blog. https://k-international.com/blog/hyundai-kona-translation-fail/

Ladson-Billings, G. (2014). Culturally relevant pedagogy 2.0: A.K.A. the remix. *Harvard Educational Review*, 84(1), 74–84.

Lord, P. (2020, March). What is the true purpose of Quebec's Bill 21? Canadian Race Relations Foundation. https://www.researchgate.net/publication/338558572_What_Is_the_True_Purpose_of_Quebec's_Bill_21

Lueck, T. (1984, December 14). Crisis management at Carbide. *The New York Times.* https://www.nytimes.com/1984/12/14/business/crisis-management-at-carbide.html

Lund, D., & Carr, P. (2010). Exposing privilege and racism in the Great White North: Tackling whiteness and identity issues in Canadian education. *Multicultural Perspectives*, 12(4), 229–234. doi: 10.1080/15210960.2010.527594

Lutz, T. (2020, April 25). Michigan senator apologizes for wearing Confederate flag face mask. *The Guardian.* https://www.theguardian.com/us-news/2020/apr/25/michigan-senator-mask-confederate-flag

Malherek, J. (2017, March 23). Creating circumstances: Edward Bernays, Psychoanalysis, and the Making of American Consumer Culture. *APA Today.* https://www.historians.org/publications-and-directories/perspectives-on-history/march-2017/creating-circumstances-edward-bernays-psychoanalysis-and-the-making-of-american-consumer-culture

Melville House (2014). *James Baldwin: The Last Interview.* Melville House: New York.

Miretzky, D., & Stevens, S. (2013). Difficult conversations. *About Campus*, 17(6), 22–29. doi: 100.1002/abc.21102

Musampa, B. (2019, November). Canada's mining industry in Africa and social responsibility. *Policy Options.* https://policyoptions.irpp.org/magazines/november-2019/canadas-mining-industry-in-africa-and-social-responsibility/

Museum of Public Relations (2020). Pioneer—Edward Bernays. https://www.prmuseum.org/pioneer-edward-bernays

National Assembly of Quebec (2019). Bill 21: An Act respecting the laicity of the State. File:///C:/Users/John/Downloads/19-021a%20(1).pdf

O'Donoghue, D. (2019, April 15). PR experts weigh in on why cultural awareness is crucial. *Learning Hub.* https://learn.g2.com/cultural-awareness

Pentland, A. (2011). Society's nervous system: Building effective government, energy, and public health systems. MIT Open Access Articles. https://dspace.mit.edu/bitstream/handle/1721.1/66256/Pentland_Society%27s%20Nervous.pdf?sequence=1&isAllowed=y

Pompper, D. (2019, December 3). Want to advocate for diversity? Start nurturing microaffirmations. Institute for Public Relations. https://instituteforpr.org/want-to-advocate-for-diversity-start-nurturing-microaffirmations/

Pratt, C. (2004, Fall). Crafting key messages and talking points—or grounding them in what research tells us. *Public Relations Quarterly*, 15–20. http://connection.ebscohost.com/c/articles/15783294/crafting-key-messages-talking-points-grounding-them-what-research-tells-us

Roberts-Moore, J. (2002). Establishing recognition of past injustices: Uses of archival records in documenting the experience of Japanese Canadians during the Second World War. *The Journal of the Association of Canadian Archivists*, 53. https://archivaria.ca/index.php/archivaria/article/view/12837/14056

Shrivastava, P. (1987, November). A cultural analysis of conflicts in industrial disaster. *International Journal of Mass Emergencies and Disasters, 5*(3), 243–264. http://www.ijmed.org/articles/147/download/

Statistics Canada Census Survey (2016). Statistics Canada. https://www12.statcan.gc.ca/census-recensement/2016/dp-pd/index-eng.cfm

Suárez-Orozco, C., Casanova, S., Martin, M., Katsiaficas, D., Cuellar, V., Smith, N., & Dias, S. (2015). Toxic rain in class: Classroom interpersonal microaggressions. *Educational Researcher, 44*(3), 151–160. doi: 10.3102/0013189X15580314

Tompkins, J. (2005). Race. In L. English (Ed.), *International Encyclopedia of Adult Education*, pp. 534–537. Palgrave-MacMillan: New York.

Toth, E. (2009). Diversity and Public Relations Practice. The Institute for Public Relations. https://instituteforpr.org/diversity-and-pr-practice/

Watt, S. (2007). Difficult dialogues, privilege and social justice: Uses of the privileged identity exploration (PIE) model in student affairs practice. *College Student Affairs Journal, 26*(2), 114–126

Wells, P. (2019, November 8). The battle against Quebec's Bill 21. *Maclean's*. https://www.macleans.ca/news/canada/the-teachers-taking-on-quebecs-bill-21/

Willard, G., Isaac, K-J., & Carney, D. (2015, May). Some evidence for the nonverbal contagion of racial bias. *Organizational Behavior and Human Decision Processes* (128), 96–107. http://faculty.haas.berkeley.edu/dana_carney/bias.contagion_finalpublished.OBHDP.pdf

Wise, Y. (nd). European Judaism, Freud, Bernays and the birth of Public Relations. *Academia*. https://www.academia.edu/27471760/European_Judaism_Freud_Bernays_and_the_birth_of_Public_Relations

Yarhi, E., & Walkom, T. (2017, October 24). Newspapers in Canada: 1800s–1900s. *The*

Canadian Encyclopedia. https://www.thecanadianencyclopedia.ca/en/article/newspapers-in-canada-1800s1900s

Zhu, H. (2011, March). From intercultural awareness to intercultural empathy. *English Language Teaching,* 4 (1). https://files.eric.ed.gov/fulltext/EJ1080436.pdf

Zofi, Y. (2017, June 6). 5 strategies for effective cross-cultural interactions. *International Association of Business Communicators.* https://www.iabc.com/5-strategies-for-engaging-in-effective-cross-cultural-interactions/

Zorn, D. (2020). Twitter. https://twitter.com/search?q=Dale%20zorn&src=typed_query

Zuboff, S. (2019). The age of surveillance capitalism. New York: PublicAffairs Publishing.

CHAPTER TWO

Reaching Out, Rants, and Dog Whistles: Making Mistakes and Making Things Right

OBJECTIVES OF THIS CHAPTER

This chapter is designed to assist in developing a better understanding of the issues of white privilege and diversity, inclusion and power, through:

- An examination of former hockey commentator Don Cherry's rant against immigrants;
- Examining repressive tolerance as a component of society;
- A discussion of white privilege as seen in the "Central Park Incident," a confrontation between a white woman and African American man;
- Considering the topic of white neutrality and colour blindness as seen in the treatment of professional hockey players of colour;
- Discussing the concept of image restoration by organizations;
- Understanding diversity, inclusion, and power, and their expression through "dog whistles" and micro- and macro-aggressions;
- Considering how environmental scans and SWOT analyses are used in contextualizing cross-cultural engagement;
- An examination of cross-cultural messaging as interpreted in a case study of the May 2020 killing of George Floyd in Minneapolis;
- An interview with crisis communications expert Dr. Timothy Coombs.

DON CHERRY'S RANT

When hockey commentator Don Cherry delivered a 2019 Remembrance Day–themed rant against newcomers to Canada, the responses that followed were perhaps somewhat surprising. Given the octogenarian's penchant for crusty, xenophobic tirades on his between-periods segment *Coach's Corner*, during National Hockey League (NHL) broadcasts, Cherry's bombast had in the past generally met with a shake-of-the-head dismissal of his "old-school" approach to the game. That is, until it was too much, first for fans, and then for Rogers Sportsnet, the broadcaster responsible for *Hockey Night in Canada* (and essentially Cherry's boss) and the National Hockey League.

On November 9, 2019, Cherry, a former player and coach and a cornerstone of *Hockey Night in Canada* broadcasts for almost 40 years, delivered remarks that infuriated Canadians. During an on-air tribute to war veterans, Cherry singled out Greater Toronto-area immigrants for what he believed was a refusal to wear a poppy, the symbol of Canadian national remembrance:

> "You people love … our way of life, you love our milk and honey, at least you could pay a couple of bucks for a poppy or something like that," Cherry said. "These guys [war veterans] pay for your way of life that you enjoy in Canada, these guys paid the biggest price" (Klinkenberg, 2019, November 11).

To put some context around this issue, consider that, according to Catalyst (2019, May 28), upwards of 20 percent of Canadians (almost 7.7 million) are people of colour (South Asian, Chinese, Black, Filipino, Latin American, Arab, Southeast Asian, West Asian, Korean, and Japanese); by 2036, fully one-third of Canadians will be people of colour. As well, the majority of immigrants to Canada are people of colour (acceptable terms to describe groups of people change over time; "people of colour" in recent years became an increasingly acceptable term to replace the outdated and condescending "minority group." Note, however, that over time other terminology may arise. As such, I use the term cautiously).

Hockey is a sport dominated by white players. The league broke its colour barrier in the 1940s with Larry Kwong, a Canadian of Chinese descent (Douglas, 2018), and at one time there was a Coloured Hockey League (founded 1895) in Canada's Maritimes, boasting players who were refused entry into the NHL. The first Black player was Willie O'Ree, who strapped on the blades for the Boston Bruins in 1958, and since then, Black hockey stars like Jarome Iginla, Evander Kane and P. K. Subban have become well-established in the league (Drake, 2014, March 18). Out of more than 700 players in the NHL, approximately 43 are players of colour, a little under 5 percent (Hooper, 2020, January 17). In terms of nationality, Canada has the highest number of players in the National Hockey League, at 45 percent, followed by the U.S. at 27.4 percent, Sweden at 10 percent and Russia and Finland at about 4 percent apiece (Quant Hockey, 2020). Cherry's comments—especially the ethnocentric "you people"—were a deal-breaker in his long and sometimes-contentious relationship with sports broadcasting, and, indeed, with "the other"—"othering" is the dominant cultural practice of placing together people of the same background, diminishing their significance and social power, a case of "us" versus "them" (Habermas, 1998). Cherry's position was a proverbial elephant in the room, the unspoken but implicit case of seeing Us (as in white people) as good, inclusive and helpful, and "Them as threatening, angry and untrustworthy.... In economic games people implicitly treat members of other races as less trustworthy or reciprocating" (Sapolsky, 2017, p. 398).

By extension, Cherry was in the position of being the spokesperson for a sport that "has been dominated by white people at professional and amateur levels in Canada. One of the major reasons this continues to be the case is racialized people have been faced with discrimination and racism when attempting to play or watch hockey" (Snelgrove and Kabetu, 2019). Given that most of the "you people" to whom Cherry was referring would be outside the dominant white culture based on their background, religion or colour, Cherry's comments could also be interpreted as a dog-whistling statement "in which race is not explicitly mentioned but instead is cued through coded language or accompanying visuals" (Wetts and Willer, 2019). If questioned, these silent-but-sensed-and-understood messages can be dismissed or dissembled by the deliverer or by their supporters, and we will talk more about dog-whistling later in the chapter.

Apologists may have pointed out that Cherry was well-known for embracing hockey players who were "different" (i.e., outside the white mainstream), such as former Toronto Maple Leaf Nazem Kadri, who is of Lebanese background and whose career highlights were lauded by Cherry over the years; Kadri even expressed some sadness at Cherry's exit and suggested that Cherry's comments were taken out of context (Wegman, 2019, November). But this was the exception rather than the rule. Even in a sports industry distinguished by homogeneity, Cherry's actions in denouncing immigrants stood out, and what was also challenging (for the broadcaster and the league) was the intractability of Cherry in not acknowledging his mistake. As well, his co-host Ron MacLean failed to admonish him during the broadcast. The next day, during a separate broadcast, MacLean expressed his grief over Cherry's remarks, apologizing on air:

> "During last night's broadcast, Don made comments that were hurtful and prejudiced and I wish I had handled myself differently. It was a divisive moment and I am truly upset with myself for allowing it," he said on Twitter. "I have worked with Don for 30 years, and we both love hockey. But last night, I know we failed you" (Jackson, November 10, 2019).

Not just "last night," for as Wilfrid Laurier University professor Tim Elcombe said in *The Conversation*,

> there have been countless examples of Cherry publicly expressing hyper-masculine, culturally insensitive and overtly xenophobic views about Indigenous Peoples, immigrants, women, the LGTBQ+ community, francophone Canadians, Europeans, Perrier-drinkers, non-Christians, environmentalists, academics, the media, left-leaning politicians, "pinkos," visor-wearing hockey players and, of course, bicycle riders. But it was Cherry's anti-immigrant poppy rant that finally led to his firing (Elcombe, 2019, November 17).

Days later, MacLean would repeat his concerns but also apologize for using Cherry's name *in his apology*, showing empathy for Cherry and stating that he didn't believe Cherry was racist, just misguided (Derworiz, 2019, November 19). It was a case of dissembling to avoid making the "racist" claim against someone. Such an approach suggests white fragility, a term coined by professor and whiteness studies researcher Robin DiAngelo:

> White people in North America live in a social environment that protects and insulates them from race-based stress. This insulated environment of racial protection builds white expectations for racial comfort while at the same time lowering the ability to tolerate racial stress, leading to what I refer to as White Fragility ... a state in which even a minimum

amount of racial stress becomes intolerable, triggering a range of defensive moves … (including) the outward display of emotions such as anger, fear, and guilt, and behaviors such as argumentation, silence, and leaving the stress-inducing situation … (which) function to reinstate white racial equilibrium (DiAngelo, 2011, p. 54).

White guilt was also front-and-centre in MacLean's response; it is a position of intense self-focus, implying a state of discomfort motivated by an implied need to "right wrongs" against people outside the dominant white culture; the challenge with white guilt is that it doesn't actually make things better, and may only make the person initiating this emotional state feel better (Iyer et al., 2003). Following the firing, official statements from the organizations involved in the matter ranged from an announcement by the broadcaster Sportsnet (owned and operated by Rogers Media) supporting the unifying aspect of sports while justifying the firing, to the National Hockey League's statement that Cherry's comments were divisive and in conflict with the league's values of inclusion and diversity (Klinkenberg, 2019, November 11).

"Hockey is at its best when it brings people together," said the NHL on its Twitter feed. "The comments made last night were offensive and contrary to the values we believe in" (NHL, 2019). "'Don's discriminatory comments are offensive and they do not represent our values and what we stand for as a network,' Sportsnet President Bart Yabsley said in a statement Sunday [November 10]. 'We have spoken with Don about the severity of this issue and we sincerely apologize for these divisive remarks'" (TSN, 2019).

The key phrases: "Don's comments do not represent our values" and "We sincerely apologize." The use of the word "divisive" is interesting, as it implies that Cherry's statements served to *drive people apart*, when in fact what Cherry said could more accurately be described as simply outdated and reflective of the status quo of a previous generation. The statement didn't in fact divide people, it unified them and was suggestive of the imposition of Cherry's dominant-culture opinion about a situation in a unilateral way; there was no "shared stage" for Cherry and others. It was a statement directed from someone holding social power to those who are marginalized in society, not dividing people but simply widening an already-existing gulf, and triggering unity and a coalescence of feeling against Cherry's opinion.

Sportsnet and the NHL were quick to avoid being caught in the blast of anger against Cherry. The NHL has a vested commercial and sports-focused interest in promoting diversity and the National Hockey League sponsors a variety of programs to promote inclusion, from Hockey is for Everyone (focused on reaching out across gender, sexuality and racial lines) and Learn to Play, an initiative designed to inner-city and lower income communities, to Ice Hockey in Harlem and Fort Dupont Ice Arena in Washington, D.C. (Thomas, 2018). According to the league, the traditional primary (white) target group of potential players (and their parents) in the U.S. is in decline. "Sometime after 2040, there will be no racial majority in the country" and the country will have "the first minority white generation in America, born in 2007 and later. Between 2010 and 2030, the primary labor force–age population—the primary hockey parent and customer—will experience a net loss of 15 million whites." During the same period, that same demographic will add "some 27 million members of racial minorities. Many of them will be Hispanics and Asians, who will roughly double in number between 2015 and 2060, while the multiracial population as a whole will triple. Hockey—a sport which tends to be generationally shared— will need a deliberate effort to introduce the value of the game to new parents who may not have played as children" (Frey and Davis, 2018).

The case of Don Cherry represents a confluence of factors that go beyond simply replacing "the old guard," as it impacts the culture of professional hockey and its challenge in reaching out and embracing new cultures in order to maintain its viability as a business and social entity. Hockey culture is (to use the words of economics and social history professor Eric Hobsbawm), among other iconic practices in society, an "invented tradition ... a set of practices, normally governed by overtly or tacitly accepted rules and of a ritual or symbolic nature, which seek to inculcate certain values and norms of behaviour by repetition" (Hobsbawm, 1983, p. 1). Indeed, the sport of ice hockey is claimed to have Canadian origins (Windsor, Nova Scotia) dating back to 1800 (Vaughan, 1999), yet it was an amalgam of previous sporting activities, versions of the sport being credited variously to the Dutch, English and Scottish, and to the Mi'kmaq (also the possible inventors of the modern hockey stick) (Meloney, 2019), suggesting an intriguing blend of ideas that were merged and homogenized into a single Canadian "brand." Canada's colonial-settler culture (almost exclusively white and European) took up the sport, named it as its own, developed hockey into a national institution, and then used it as the source of long-held "invented" traditions—*Hockey Night in Canada*, the Stanley Cup [if you want a sense of its iconic status, visit Toronto's Hockey Hall of Fame, as I did several years ago, and have a look at the awestruck faces of people viewing it under the spotlights], playoff beards, the singing of "O Canada" or "The Star Spangled Banner" before each game, fans cheering so loudly during the singing of the anthem that it drowns out the anthem singer, and so on (Kurtzberg, 2012).

Cherry's rant also underscored an ethnocentric, in-group whiteness. The breakdown of this ethnocentrism, and the fabricated culture of which it is a component, created a communications crisis-point in which racially- and culturally-charged attitudes were no longer tolerated, at the systemic grassroots level and within the purview of the institutions running the sport.

Researcher Maria de Fatima Oliveira interviewed 25 communication specialists regarding the influence of multiculturalism on crisis communications situations and found that "at different contexts, different aspects of individual cultural identities increase or decrease salience. As a consequence, broad cultural categorizations overlook cultural nuances, which are affected by and adjusted in response to social context. Therefore, a comprehensive framework for crisis communication should incorporate cultural diversity" (Oliveira, 2013, p. 271). The approach of communicators must be synchronized with the cultural expectations of audiences, and practitioners "can benefit from training initiatives promoting cultural competence ... (equipping them) with the necessary skills to understand their own cultural biases, to learn about diverse worldviews, and to adjust crisis responses to different cultural expectations" (p. 272). This ability to "adjust the message" underscored the official response of hockey's infrastructure to the Cherry crisis. Cherry's comments created a flashpoint, an "enough is enough" scenario that forced change and though the league had been working to make the sport cross-culturally appealing for years, when change happened, the messaging delivered by the NHL and Sportsnet was worded to indicate clear and unequivocal support for diversity.

This might not have been a surprise, given that following a general decline in youth activity in sports, sports industries became reliant on boosting interest in spectator sports (and this in turn was used to increase sometimes-flagging interest in youth sports activities); as spectatorship (rather than overall participation) grew for several decades beginning in the 1960s (Putnam, 2000), this made outreach to new audiences essential. New audiences are the proverbial bread-and-butter of sports. Thus the social capital that bonded white hockey enthusiasts together when Don Cherry was a player in the 1950s and 1960s, then a coach in the 1970s and a commentator from the 1980s on—social capital being defined as the "social networks and the norms of reciprocity and trustworthiness" (Putnam, 2000, p. 19)—was slowly eroded by changing attitudes and demographics. Recognizing the change, the NHL worked to engage those new audiences.

Finally, it's important to note that Cherry was neither the first—nor likely the last—sports commentator to be fired for making bigoted comments. Following a 1988 television interview, CBS Sports commentator Jimmy (The Greek) Snyder was fired for making comments about Black athletes, "in which he said many blacks were superior athletes because of breeding from the time of slavery and that the only area in sports left for whites was coaching" (Solomon, 1988, January 17).

MARCUSE AND REPRESSIVE TOLERANCE

Attitudes engrained in dominant cultural behaviours are not easy to change in the short term; they take time. The German-American philosopher and professor Herbert Marcuse said society is bound by domination of one group by another; the idea of a tolerant society, where repression and fear are reduced, is an aim, but not yet a reality (Marcuse, 2007). Tolerance, as defined by Freire (2005), is considered "the virtue that teaches us to live with the different. It teaches us to learn from and respect the different" (p. 76). Under Marcuse's approach, tolerance becomes a passive component of a society in which the status quo (the standard or current state of affairs in society)—driven by the mores, attitudes, and behaviours of the dominant culture—is protected. In an affluent society, difference is tolerated, but only to the degree in which it can be controlled, and "minorities which strive for change of the whole itself will under optimal conditions which rarely prevail be left free to deliberate and discuss, to speak and to assemble—and will be left harmless and helpless in the face of the overwhelming majority, which militates against qualitative social change" (Marcuse, 2007, p. 41).

Much has been said of Marcuse's theory, and at its core is the notion of an "unthinking acceptance of entrenched attitudes and ideas, even when these are obviously damaging to other people" as well as "the vocal endorsement of actions that are manifestly aggressive towards other people. ... Genuine tolerance, Marcuse argues, can only exist in a situation of intolerance for these limits on real freedom" (Oxford Reference, 2020).

In building on this theme, Marcuse cites inequality as a *rule in* (rather than an *exception to*) the operation of affluent societies, where capitalism, propaganda, militarism and a corporatized, entertainment-focused media, reign, and where citizens lose their ability to think as individuals (Marcuse, 2007). Writing long before our current age of surveillance capitalism, Marcuse foresaw clearly the use of technology to generate a system that would rob people of control over their own lives; Zuboff (2019) writes of the drive by technological giants like Google to create "social relations of surveillance based on asymmetries of knowledge and power" and to in effect rewire the way people behave (p. 81). As such, language draws on the tropes, colloquialisms and aphorisms used by the dominant culture to continue oppressing people (the "you people," and "why can't you be more like us?" language), and despite pleas for change, the attitudes of those in power are tolerated.

That situation changed in the Don Cherry incident; in the case of Don Cherry, the language delivered by the corporate players (the National Hockey League and Sportsnet) was carefully chosen to reflect support for a growing majority view ("bigotry is bad," and "Don Cherry said the wrong thing") but the issue only took that turn after an explosion of angry words and the organizations saw clearly the path they needed to take in order to maintain the trust of their audiences. This shift still allows an affluent society to operate; it absorbs the new language and attitudes of fairness and equity into its contextual whole, manipulates and controls them, and continues on. But for corporate entities, there is a need for them to be clearly seen as separating themselves from the issue at hand in order to be viewed as "fair and equitable," a means of image restoration elaborated on by Benoit (1995) and Coombs and Schmidt (2009) and which will be discussed in more detail later on.

Consider one example: the acceptance—and the language *around* that acceptance—of perceived disparities between Black and white citizens in the U.S. during the COVID-19 pandemic, in which non-partisan data demonstrated that African Americans "died from the disease at almost three times the rate of white people. ... Despite the glaring gulf, the Trump administration continues to be sluggish in responding to the crisis. ... Trump administration officials have blamed the disparities on the high incidence among black people of underlying health conditions such as diabetes, hypertension and obesity ... [yet] there is mounting evidence that black Americans are disadvantaged in terms of access to diagnostic testing and treatment for the disease" (Pilkington, 2020, May 20).

The Trump administration stereotyped African Americans, dog-whistling that Blacks were "prone" to health conditions as a result of genetics or lifestyle choice rather than the stressing economic and social conditions under which they live. As we know, an actual dog whistle is tuned to a frequency beyond the human range of hearing. In politics dog-whistling is "silent" to many but "heard" by those who are listening for it; it is the use of "a phrase that may sound innocuous to some people, but which also communicates something more insidious either to a subset of the audience or outside of the audience's conscious awareness—a covert appeal to some noxious set of views" (Olasov, 2016) and its direct-messaging to culturally engrained systemic biases is a standard approach used by some to appeal to white audiences. An example of dog-whistling is a statement by Karl Rove, a former adviser to George W. Bush, about a speech by former U.S. president Barack Obama to graduates at historically Black colleges, in which Obama delivered some discreet condemnations over U.S. President Donald Trump's lack of decisive action with respect to COVID-19. Rove compared Obama's comments to a "political drive-by shooting," thereby attaching to Obama the Black stereotypes of violence, crime and mayhem, a comment for which Rove was later widely condemned (Baragona, J., 2020, May 18).

Dog whistles are a component of racialized generalizations and stereotyping. Studies also show that people of African descent are treated differently than whites by the medical community because of race, and the stereotypes can run the gamut from a perceived unwillingness to take proper medications and being seen by doctors as "less intelligent," to supposedly being less prone to feeling pain than whites (Ro, 2019, July 27):

> One clinical research study showed that in almost all cases treating Black patients, but only with half of white patients, medical staff mentioned patients' race. And when staff mentioned Black patients in a negative light, they mentioned the Blackness of all these patients, but only mentioned the whiteness of half of white patients.

To use journalistic jargon, a lot of ink has been spilled in writing about the issue of Blacks having a higher rate of COVID-19 deaths. A Google search of the term "Blacks dying of COVID-19" resulted in 785 million results; the top stories were about a Black personal support worker dying of the virus after being sent home from hospital; an increase in COVID-19 deaths among persons of African descent due to air pollution; and stories about systemic discrimination against Blacks in the health care system.

In a Eurocentric, repressive society, social reality and culture blend together, such that

... traditional values ... (become) part of their (society's) mental equipment. If mass communications blend together harmoniously, and often unnoticeably, art, politics, religion, and philosophy with commercials [and today, social media], they bring those realms of culture to their common denominator—the commodity form ... Exchange value, not truth value, counts (Marcuse, 1964, p. 57).

It is a reason why we see the mass marketing of images of revolutionary Ernesto "Che" Guevara (a leader of the Cuban Revolution in the 1950s) on T-shirts and posters (the height of capitalistic commodification for the image of an avowed socialist!), the use of Bob Dylan protest songs to market the services of a major Canadian bank, and, in 2020, the uproar created by the controversial painting *Hanky Panky* by Fisher River Cree Nation artist Kent Monkman.

Hanky Panky is a thought-provoking example of how outrage fuels cross-cultural dialogue. The painting depicts a pants-less, anxious Canadian Prime Minister Justin Trudeau on all fours, held down by Indigenous women, and being prepared to be sexually penetrated by the artistic alter ego of Monkman. To one side is a huddle of former prime ministers, and a prostrate Mountie in the painting's foreground. It offended many, yet

there's more to *Hanky Panky* ... the setting of the ceremony room, full of Cree women in various forms of traditional and modern dress, all of them laughing, presumably at Trudeau's fate; there's the huddle of aghast, gray-faced men, several of them physically comforting a concerned John MacDonald [sic], Canada's first prime minister, who ignored treaties and intentionally starved the Indigenous population to make way for the national railroad (Martin, 2020, May 21).

Monkman would later offer an apology to those who were offended (Grabish, 2020, May 20). In our repressively tolerant society, the attitudes of the status quo (some critics said they were sickened by the image of sexual violence-as-restitution for crimes against Indigenous women and girls, while supporters urged critics to look deeper into the intersection of social issues at play) came up firmly against the presumed freedoms usually accorded artists to allow them to create works that disrupt the flow of common thought (traditional ideas of what is right and wrong) in society. Still, Monkman's work served its purpose: to generate discussion and the sometimes uncomfortable but necessary churn of diverse opinion, pushing against the perimeter of what is and isn't acceptable. Repressive tolerance at play in society means that this story, and those relating to COVID-related oppression, will have their "Warholesque 15 minutes" of fame, before media move on to other topics. Over the long term, change might take place to improve society: more freedom for artists (and a more enlightened view of the issues they are throwing light on); better treatment for COVID-19 victims; more effective identification of the key factors affecting African Americans in the health care system; subsequent changes in the way the system is structured. But change will be tolerated only if it becomes part of the system, if it becomes instrumental in altering the infrastructure. But the messaging (and the core of ideas that drive the messaging) needs to reach a point of critical mass—a point of self-sustaining repetition and use—in order to be given consideration for absorption by the status quo.

A TIP FOR CROSS-CULTURAL COMMUNICATION

Effectively communicate:
- Respond with appropriate words
- Deliver balanced feedback
- Build on an idea
- Give credit and positive reinforcement

(Zofi, 2017, June 6)

THE CENTRAL PARK INCIDENT

Let's look at how a repressive-tolerant society works, using a May 2020 incident in New York's Central Park as an example. A white woman (Amy Cooper) walking her dog off-leash in a dogs-must-be-leashed area of the park (called the Ramble) is asked by a bird-watching African American man (Christian Cooper, no relation to Amy, and neither one related to the author of this book) to please leash her dog. An argument ensues. The woman states that she is going to call the police and tell them she is being threatened by an African American man. The Black man invites her to call the police. She does so, and he uses his cell phone to record the encounter; the woman proceeds to become increasingly agitated as she calls 911. "In the video, he is largely silent while she frantically tells police he is threatening her and her dog" (Vera and Ly, 2020, May 26). Given the violent behaviour of police toward Black men, it was considered by media to be a situation where the woman was urging violence against the man based on his race. It was also seen as an example of white privilege, an attempt by Amy Cooper to *work around* the ideas of fairness and proper behaviour (i.e., leashing the dog in a public area); in doing so, she ties her privilege to feelings of being threatened and leverages the white social power at her disposal.

The "trigger" phrases are clear:

- "African American man is threatening me."
- "Please don't come close to me."
- "There's a man, African American.... He is recording me and threatening me and my dog."
- "I'm being threatened by a man in the Ramble.... Please send the cops immediately!" (Vera and Ly, 2020).

The outcome? Following the incident, Amy Cooper faced a barrage of social media outrage, including death threats, and was fired from her job. She later apologized, saying that she was scared and that there was "no excuse" for her behaviour (Vera and Ly, 2020). Christian Cooper, a member of the New York City Audubon Society, said he would accept the woman's apology, stating that it was questionable whether or not she was a racist, but said the act itself was "definitely racist." He also asked people to stop issuing death threats to Amy Cooper, denouncing the threats as abhorrent (Maxouris, 2020, May 27).

The Audubon Society, which oversees bird-watching programs, supported Christian Cooper. Audubon senior vice-president for state programs Rebeccah Sanders said, "Black Americans often face terrible daily dangers in outdoor spaces, where they are subjected to unwarranted suspicion, confrontation, and violence. ...The outdoors—and the joy of birds—should be safe and welcoming for all people" (Vera and Lyn, 2020, May 26).

Amy Cooper's former employer, investment company Franklin Templeton, stated its position on Twitter: "Following our internal review of the incident in Central Park yesterday, we have made the decision to terminate the employee involved, effective immediately. We do not tolerate racism of any kind at Franklin Templeton" (Franklin Templeton, 2020, May 26). The approaches of Franklin Templeton and the Audubon Society were supportive and clear; in the case of Franklin Templeton, its corporate message was in line with a desire to maintain the appearance of equity and fairness by dissociating itself from the "culprit" in the issue, especially given that these principles of equity are essential components in corporate culture today; for the Audubon Society, it was about upholding the egalitarian nature of a nature conservancy organization.

Corporate interests historically drive organizations (Benedict, 2017, p. 41). The communications technique known as *dissociation* (Hearit, 1995) was used by Franklin Templeton in order to distance itself from Amy Cooper. Dissociation is a way to "distance organizations from claims of wrongdoing or responsibility during a crisis. This is a valuable strategy for these crisis responses because this rhetorical practice of distancing the organization from blame during a crisis allows the organization to protect and rehabilitate its image" (Brand, 2012, p. 37).

Thus Franklin Templeton's messaging fell within the umbrella of a public relations component that is used to support the corporate intention of maintaining a focus on the interests of the organization ("how will the public see us?") and these positive-value corporate messages ("we are not a racist organization") intersect with the commitment to fairness and "doing the right thing" that they want to have embedded clearly in the public's mind.

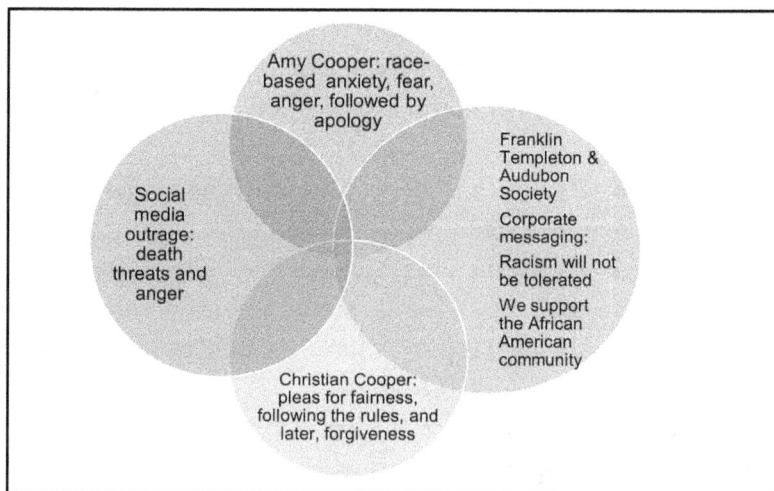

Venn diagram of the Central Park incident

AKIM ALIU

NHL player Akim Aliu was one of a handful of cultural outsiders seeking to make a name for himself in the National Hockey League (NHL) and, as a member of that under-five-percent group of players of colour (Aliu is a Black Nigerian) he was looking for employment as a regular player. As such, it was "normal" for players like Aliu to ignore racial taunts. The establishment of whiteness as a "neutral norm" is common in society; white privilege mutes the seriousness of racialized behaviour, and "neutrality is a problem because whites consider whiteness the norm; neutrality is perceived as equivalent to whiteness" (Bergerson, 2003, p. 53). Additionally, colour blindness—the practice of pretending that one doesn't see colour (as when someone says "I don't care if you're Black, white, green, or blue, everybody is the same to me!")—allows people to avoid acknowledging race issues, and colour blindness creates a "comfort zone" that negates engagement and dulls anxiety by allowing the denial of the existence of colour (Guo and Jamal, 2007; Lund, C., 2010).

So it was not a big surprise for those close to the issue of racism in hockey that Aliu, in 2019, talked openly about the racist treatment he had received, not only at the hands of a former coach, but from coaches and players throughout his career, from his early days to his long career as a professional, including several years in the NHL. It was more of a surprise for people in the dominant white culture, who registered shock at seeing the revelations of Aliu brought to light.

Controversy broke when Aliu reported, on Twitter, the racist behaviour of coach Bill Peters during a time when Aliu was playing for the American Hockey League's Rockford Ice Hogs, and "his then-coach Bill Peters directed the N-word at him repeatedly in 2009 over Aliu's taste in music" (Manza Young, 2020, May 20). It was just part of a pattern of abuse that started when Aliu was a junior player (and included a hazing incident that took place in 2005 that made headlines) and horrendous ill-treatment from another player Aliu called a racist sociopath, underscoring the "racism, misogyny, bullying and homophobia that permeates the culture of hockey. These issues have ramifications that most cannot—or will not—see" (Aliu, 2020, May 19). Those ramifications included a delayed entry into the NHL, for while he was "selected by Chicago in the second round (56th overall) of the 2007 NHL entry draft, Aliu couldn't shake his reputation as a troublemaker in a sport that values conformity.... He didn't play his first NHL game until 2012 with the Calgary Flames" (Hall, 2019, November 27). As such, Aliu was forced to pay a price for being a Black man in a league dominated by whites. In fact, white privilege, which was at play in ignoring the plight of Aliu and others, is enmeshed in denial and the dismissal of the importance of diversity in ways that allow people to deny oppression, refute marginalization and avoid discussion of racism (Vaccaro, 2010).

That there was a culture of denial in the NHL is clear. Denial runs through white culture, and the denial of oppression and the inability to shoulder responsibility for changing attitudes includes white people not acknowledging their own whiteness:

> although most Canadians do not condone blatant racist behavior, widespread systemic racism is part of our social reality....Whiteness is shrouded with denials that give White people yet another form of privilege: the ability to avoid discussion of how oppression continues to benefit White people (Lund and Carr, 2010, pp. 230–231).

According to an article in *The Athletic*, San José Sharks hockey player Evander Kane, an African Canadian,

> said conversations about race and racism are not often had in the NHL. He said teammates can be close with each other but that does not mean those discussions are necessarily going to take place. He said it goes back to the fact "nobody really wants to ruffle any feathers," and he said black players throughout the league discuss those issues among themselves (Clark, 2020, June 1).

Following Aliu's claim, Peters was forced to resign from his position in 2019 as coach of the Calgary Flames; when approached by the media, the mostly-white hockey playing fraternity, instead of speaking up about the subject (with the exception of several players of colour), was strangely silent, reluctant to talk about Aliu's situation and the culture of the sport (Cox, 2020, May 21), although following the death of African American George Floyd at the knee of a Minneapolis police officer in May 2020 (discussed later in this chapter), white, Latino and Black hockey players began to come forward with statements of support for an end to racism and systemic discrimination (Sportsnet, 2020, June 1). In Aliu's case, it took several days for the NHL to respond to his concerns, but Aliu later met with NHL commissioner Gary Bettman, an outcome with which Aliu was pleased, and Bettman and deputy commissioner Bill Daly subsequently issued a statement of support:

We are pleased to have met with Akim Aliu today and had a productive and candid conversation. Today's discussion is part of a broader, thorough review and process that the league is undertaking. We share a mutual objective: ensuring that hockey is an open and inclusive sport at all levels (Canadian Press, 2019, December 3).

Note the key words in the statement, stressing the positive: productive; candid; a "broader, thorough review"; sharing a mutual objective; openness and inclusivity.

Changes were planned, though they took time. "At the Board of Governors meeting last December [2019], Bettman reportedly unveiled new league policies and training programs, including mandatory counseling on racism and bullying for NHL personnel. He also said there would be an anonymous hotline to report such incidents" (Manza Young, 2020, May 20).

Image restoration, a theory developed by and elaborated on by William Benoit (1995) outlines the methods organizations use to restore their reputations; in racial and cultural contexts, it can be especially applicable where organizations are trying to achieve established goals in order to maintain a favourable public image. Coombs and Schmidt (2009) cite a 1996 incident where, through secret recordings, executives of the Texaco oil corporation were revealed to have made racist comments regarding a racial discrimination lawsuit launched against the company. Texaco rebuilt its corporate image through a five-point approach employing the concepts of: bolstering (reminding the public of the company's anti-discrimination policies; corrective action (investigating the issue); shifting blame (focusing on the "bad apples" at fault in the organization); mortification (admitting guilt and apologizing); and separation (a combination of bolstering, shifting blame, and corrective action)—essentially moving the organization away from the issue at hand, clearly delineating its position, and effectively restoring its public image (p. 166).

In the case of the NHL and *Hockey Night in Canada* (Sportsnet) in the Don Cherry incident, it was significant for the league and the broadcaster to be seen as open, receptive and welcoming to new Canadians; therefore it was necessary for both league and broadcaster to take a stand based on the dismissal of Cherry, and by doing so clearly establishing that they were not associated with his views, and promising corrective action in future. With the Akim Aliu incident, NHL head Gary Bettman had to ensure that the league was seen to be working to "make things better." In this way, the league acknowledged that wrongs had been done, and that, through dialogue and support (especially through the programs the league delivers), the future held potential for positive growth. In these ways, image restoration took place, the values inherent in the sport were salvaged, and there was suitable potential for the league's image to be improved over the long term.

DIVERSITY, INCLUSION, POWER

The issue of diversity revolves around inclusion, and the recognition of power. Efforts to deal effectively with prejudice "cannot be effective without understanding its up-side, white privilege. ... The study of power is not accurate unless it includes both disadvantage and privilege" (McIntosh, 2012, p. 195). This power differential, rooted in stereotyping, is grounded in the "oversimplifying of human perception so that judgments and decisions can be made quickly" (Toth, 2009). Too often, the oppressed (people of colour, women, persons with disabilities, the homeless, and members of the 2SLGBTQI+ community)—when seeking a means of survival in situations of close contact with members of the dominant culture—will mute their own sense of being different. "The oppressed, at a certain moment of their existential experience, adopt an attitude of 'adhesion' to the oppressor ... because of their identification with the oppressor, they have no consciousness of themselves as persons or as members of an oppressed class" (Freire, 2000, pp. 45–46).

This is problematic, and all members of society must recognize and act on it. Alexander (2012) notes that "the striking reluctance of whites ... to talk about or even acknowledge race has led many scholars and advocates to conclude that we would be better off not talking about race at all" (p. 238). Yet issues of race surround us, and establishments—private and public sector and non-profit—must respond. For communications organizations, diversity models are essential at the leadership level; organizations have to be seen to be committed to diversity. How they go about it can range from seeking job candidates from outside the dominant culture who bring requisite skills to the table, to an "integration and learning" approach, where perspectives within the workgroup are shared, and the knowledge gained from that sharing then applied to their work (Toth, 2009). Yet scholars warn of the dangers of affirmative action hiring programs, for "diversity-driven affirmative action programs seem to be the epitome of racial justice purchased on the cheap. They create the appearance of racial equity without the reality ... without fundamentally altering any of the structures that create racial inequality" (Alexander, 2012, p. 249).

According to Willard et al. (2015, April 30), in a study of the viral nature of bias when people see nonverbal cues:

> While many organizations are clearly intolerant of racial bias and dis-crimination, even the subtlest amount of racial bias is likely polluting the very organizational and society cultures that explicitly and proactively act to eradicate it … [on the other hand] individuals who possess and act with genuine egalitarianism … *can actually help to shape social structure to be more equal* (p. 104).

It is essential that the issue of race, though a social construct, is recognized for the role it plays in society. "Race is the most important embodiment of the ethical crosscurrents that swirl around the rocks of social capital in contempo-rary America" (Putnam, 2000, p. 361), and for the writer James Baldwin, it was clear that white people in the U.S. are

> still trapped in a history which they do not understand; and until they understand it, they cannot be released from it. They have had to believe for many years, and for innumerable reasons, that black men are inferior to white men. Many of them, indeed, know better, but … people find it very difficult to act on what they know (Baldwin, 1993, pp 8–9).

Historically, racial dynamics haven't changed a great deal since the Kerner Commission of 1967 (formed to investigate issues and provide recommenda-tions following race riots in major U.S. cities) and its report calling on the me-dia industry to hire more African American journalists and to provide more comprehensive reporting on race relations:

> "[By] failing to portray the Negro as a matter of routine and in the con-text of the total society [the Kerner report said] … the news media have, we believe, contributed to the black-white schism in this country." Now, half a century later, the problems outlined in this report persist. There is still a lack of journalists and editors of color … news coverage still fails to serve the information needs of our communities … [and] the news me-dia continues to contribute to the racial divisions in our country (Torres, J., 2018, March 7).

Microaggressions, discussed in Chapter 1, along with more structurally-focused macroaggressions (institutionalized racism and cultural attitudes that impose ethnocultural expectations and "rules" upon people and can include standards for physical appearance as well as language, religion, and art), are especially problematic, creating chronic "racial battle fatigue" for people of colour (Sue et al., 2019, p. 129).

Sue et al. (2019) use three categories for defining actors who are involved in addressing/confronting microaggressions: targets (marginalized or oppressed persons of colour or an "outside culture" who become the objects of threats or anger); white allies (members of the dominant social group) who work to end social disparities and who hold themselves accountable to promote the rights of the oppressed; and bystanders, who are witnesses to racist behaviour.

Bystanders may be from an oppressed group or from the dominant group, and "their naiveté about race and racism makes it very difficult for them to recognize bias or discrimination in others." As such, "when they witness a discriminatory incident ... they may have difficulty labeling it as a racist act or they may excuse or rationalize" the event (Sue et al., 2019, p. 133). It is essential that in all three categories:

- People "choose their battles" if confronting aggression, understanding the dynamics of all involved (i.e., don't put yourself in harm's way, and contextualize the relationships of people involved in the situation);
- People build confidence and knowledge, by seeking out "external sources (community centres, support groups) ... that allow targets, allies, and bystanders to express their emotions in ways that are safe, to connect with others who validate and affirm their being, and to offer advice and suggestions" (Sue et al., 2019, p. 139).

It is essential for communicators to appreciate their audiences, and to understand what their role might be in any environment in order to act effectively within it; this is especially true in a workplace environment or in responding to questions from the public, where awareness of knowledge, experience and behaviours will help the communicator better shape the message, from the initial idea stage through to execution and delivery. One of the ways in which communicators can begin the process of reaching out across cultures is by conducting an environmental scan, which is "a way professionals can gather information from [their] publics in an effort to better serve them, communicate with them, and represent them. ... Social media is a platform that PR practitioners can specifically use for environmental scanning ... [allowing] us to search and document important information related to our audiences" (Grunig, 2013).

The scan also creates the opportunity to employ a "two-way symmetrical model" of dialogue, which ensures mutually beneficial decision-making between organization and stakeholder by ensuring that organizations listen to their audiences rather than delivering one-way "asymmetrical" messaging: "The goal of Grunig's symmetrical communication model is one that embraces negotiation between the organization and its publics, and one that also fosters mutual understanding" (Grunig, 2013). It involves listening, responding, and being proactive in reaching out to audiences.

In Chapter 1, we talked about acting with empathy, and environmental scanning is a "big picture" exercise that allows us to tackle topics with a sense of how people feel about (not just about *what they are doing with respect to*) an organization. This brings organizations closer to their stakeholders. "Acting ethically also means thinking long term—sometimes even sacrificing short-term gains in order to help build long-term quality relationship outcomes. ... It requires thinking beyond the immediate business needs and legal parameters, and considering what your organization "should" do to help manage important relationships" (Arthur W. Page Center, 2020). The ubiquitous SWOT analysis (for **S**trengths, **W**eaknesses, **O**pportunities and **T**hreats, and created in the 1960s by management consultant Albert Humphrey) is often used as the framework for an environmental scan, where Strengths and Weaknesses are elements internal to an organization, and Strengths and Weaknesses are external. As an example, an environmental scan of the communications around the Don Cherry issue, conducted by the National Hockey League head office, might look like this:

Strengths	Weaknesses
• Large, centralized operation with links to all major league teams and cities • Guaranteed access to all media and social media commentators • Strong social media presence • Well-equipped public relations department • Connectedness of league to PR departments for all major league teams • Effective youth programs promoting cultural outreach: Learn to Play; Hockey is for Everyone	• Lack of control over actions of individual teams • No control over commentary by hockey game hosts/commentators • Messages from NHL head office may be diluted in team cities

Opportunities	Threats
• Strengthen social media channels (website, Twitter, Facebook) to deliver messages of inclusivity across cultures • Continued outreach to communities through programming • Refresh messaging with respect to inclusivity of the league • Ensure consistency of message shared by all league teams • Continued outreach to media outlets serving various communities • Promotion of human interest stories about diversity and inclusivity within the NHL	• Additional allegations of racial, cultural, homophobic commentary by members of the public or players (current or former) against NHL coaches or players • Possible incidents or acts of aggression toward different cultures by people associated with the NHL

CASE STUDY

THE DEATH OF GEORGE FLOYD: A MESSAGE ANALYSIS

The terms "I can't breathe" and "eight minutes" entered the social media lexicon in May 2020, after the police killing of an African American in the city of Minneapolis led to days of riots, police brutality, threats to send in the military by U.S. president Donald Trump—and promises of widespread social change.

According to media reports, George Floyd was a 46-year-old security guard who lost his job during the COVID-19 pandemic, and on the evening of May 25, he was accused of trying to pass a counterfeit $20 bill when paying for a pack of cigarettes at a local store. After he left the store, employees followed him outside, confronted him, and called police. During Floyd's arrest, white Minneapolis police officer Derek Chauvin put his knee to Floyd's neck, applying pressure for close to nine minutes. As onlookers pleaded with Chauvin to stop, the handcuffed Floyd, held down on the pavement by other police officers, cried out several times "I can't breathe" and "Please, man" and also called for his mother as he died from cardiopulmonary arrest resulting from the pressure on his neck (Forliti and Karnowski, 2020, June 1). Following the incident, Chauvin and the three other officers involved in the matter were fired, and Chauvin was charged with murder (later on, the other officers would be charged with being accessories to Floyd's murder); Minneapolis police chief Medaria Arradondo offered his opinion that "all four officers involved in the black man's killing bear the same responsibility" (Maxouris, 2020, June 1). Widespread protests erupted following the posting of a viral video clearly showing the act, especially Chauvin's nonchalant attitude while Floyd was dying, and the inaction of three other officers.

So graphic and incendiary was the murder and so widespread the coverage by social and traditional media, that riots almost immediately broke out in Minneapolis and other major cities across the U.S.

The event explicitly demonstrated the concept of repressive tolerance in action—two "status quo" ideas: the enlightened idea that racism and long-standing systemic discrimination are wrong, versus the "system" of discrimination. These two forces were pushing against each other—one to have its voice heard, the other to suppress that voice, in a power struggle that resulted in violence and death. To those who were hopeful that American citizens were living in a "post-racist" age ushered in by the election of its first Black president, Barack Obama, it was the proverbial slap in the face; as a student of mine said in class during a discussion of a potential "new" civil war brought about by far right-wing idealists clashing with liberal thinkers, "the Civil War never ended. It has been waged against Black people for generations."

The facts of George Floyd's death and its aftermath are well-known: within a week there were dozens of protests involving tens of thousands of protesters, five people were killed, and "the property destruction and looting during some of the protests … will cost insurers at least $25 million dollars—and that's in Minnesota alone" (Keshner, 2020, June 4). Jurisdictions imposed curfews, the National Guard was called out and more than 4,000 protesters were arrested (BBC News, 2020, June 1). That number rose to 9,000 by June 3 (Gottbrath et al., 2020, June 3).

The messaging started immediately: on social media, in traditional media, on corporate websites, on banners and placards and in the graffiti on the walls of structures in the protest zones. People watched, over and over, the video of the death of George Floyd, which was in itself a form of repressive tolerance, in that society "normalizes" violence against Black men, as University of Toronto professor Rinaldo Walcott pointed out:

I think it's important that we minimize the sharing of that kind of content, showing the degradation of Black peoples' bodies and images of Black people being indiscriminately killed. We live in a social-media culture, where there is a morbid fascination with showing images of Black people being killed. Sometimes, not always, those images can be used to make a political statement (Walcott cited in Miller, J., 2020, June 3).

In examining the response of organizations to the death of George Floyd and its aftermath, I looked at the major messages coming from officials as well as those of a sheriff involved in policing one of the protests—all individuals whose actions made an impact in the way responses were seen and felt.

On the morning of May 26 (the morning after Floyd's death), Minneapolis mayor Jacob Frey said during a news conference:

> Being Black in America should not be a death sentence.... When you hear someone calling for help, you're supposed to help.... What happened on Chicago and 38th [the intersection where the incident occurred] last night is awful. It was traumatic. It serves as a reminder of how far we have to go. For the better part of the night, I've been trying to find the words to describe what happened.... The man's life matters. He matters ... He was a human being and his life mattered ... To our Black community, to the family: I'm so sorry (Frey, Twitter feed, 2020).

Frey's statement spoke to unfairness and exclusion ("being Black ... should not be a death sentence), to outrage, to loss, and to shared responsibility ("you're supposed to help"); as well, in noting "how far we have to go," it acknowledges the division between the mainstream community (and its police services) and the Black community. He makes a human connection in talking about how George Floyd mattered and finally offered an apology to the Black community and Floyd's family, bringing his comments to a conclusion.

Melvin Carter, the mayor of Minneapolis' twin city, St. Paul, delivered an impassioned statement on the CBS News show *Face the Nation*:

> We're seeing an enormous amount of rage and frustration and anger on the ground. Much of that is totally understandable as the gruesome images of Mr. George Floyd's murder has created a—a groundswell in our community of anger and frustration. Our concern is that it seems very clear that while some of our folks are out there in the streets just crying out to be heard, that they believe that George Floyd should still be alive, that all four of those officers should be held accountable for their actions and we have deep soul searching work to do as a nation to stop this pattern from happening over and over and over again (Brennan, 2020, May 31).

On May 26, Minnesota governor Tim Walz said on Twitter: "The lack of humanity in this disturbing video is sickening. We will get answers and seek justice" (Walz, 2020, May 26). The following day Walz made several statements on Twitter, including "I'm pushing for a full, fair, and expeditious investigation that will bring us closer to justice. We must continue to examine and address the systemic inequities and discrimination that led to this incident and far too many that have come before," and "Our state watched George Floyd's humanity get erased. Our feelings of anger, anguish, and disillusionment are justified" (Walz, 2020, May 27).

The governor's comments were focused on these messages of "seeking justice," "addressing systemic inequities" and "feelings of anger, anguish and disillusionment" with pleas to reduce the violence that was taking place (looting, damage to property) in the rioting: "If you plan to turn your pain into action by joining a public demonstration, please do so peacefully and safely to protect your own health and the health of the people around you" (Walz, 2020, May 27). The governor would later condemn the looting: "George Floyd's death should lead to justice and systemic change, not more death and destruction" (Walz, 2020, May 28).

Frey, Carter and Walz would later draw public ire by suggesting that the violence caused during the riots came from people arriving in Minneapolis from "out of state," commentary which was later retracted; Carter in particular said that he "was given inaccurate information during a police briefing" (Klebniknov and Sandler, 2020, May 30).

U.S. President Donald Trump initially "called the death [of Floyd] 'a very sad event, a very, very sad, sad event,' when asked about it by reporters Wednesday [May 27] when he was in Cape Canaveral," then suggested that he was expediting an FBI investigation into the death (Goodin et al., 2020, May 27). Trump also called the video "a very shocking sight," which commentators said was unusual, for "Trump has been silent on a number of high-profile police-involved killings, including that of Stephon Clark, a black man shot by Sacramento police in 2018" (Colvin, J. and Long, C., 2020, May 28). There was a sense of waiting to see what Trump might do next, given the Republican Party's low approval ratings with African Americans and the fact that Trump was in an election year.

Within a week of the death, Trump's narrative shifted; he admonished the governors of states where demonstrations took place: "the president warned governors 'against being overridden' and argued that if they did not dominate protesters, 'you're wasting your time, they are gonna run over you, you're going to look like a bunch of jerks'" (Strauss et al., 2020, June 1). The president would also spend time in the White House emergency bunker during protests in front of the White House. He called himself "your law and order president," used police to disperse peaceful demonstrators through the use of rubber bullets and tear gas, and stated that "My first and highest duty as president is to defend our great country and the American people. I swore an oath to uphold the laws of our nation and that is exactly what I will do." He then threatened to invoke a presidential prerogative to deploy the military to restore order (Liptak and Westwood, 2020, June 2). Trump moved quickly away from a show of compassion for George Floyd and his family and instead began mercurially focusing on himself and on the gap between "uncontrolled" protests and his own view of law and order.

By contrast, empathy and the language of inclusion were the themes when Christopher Swanson, a sheriff in Genesee County, Michigan, during a march held to denounce police brutality, put down his baton and helmet and walked with protesters. In the *New York Times*, Swanson was quoted as saying,

> "We are walking with you because all you're asking for is a voice and dignity for all, no matter who you are. … I love you guys. The police love you." Sheriff Swanson was among several law enforcement officials who in the past few days have engaged with marchers and shown solidarity either by marching, kneeling or publicly denouncing the death of Mr. Floyd (Padilla, 2020, May 31).

In the same article, the *Times* reported that police had fatally shot more than 1,000 people in 2019, and Swanson's actions—and his language—ran counter to the approach generally taken by police services, which have used pepper spray, batons and rubber bullets to quell unrest.

Below, I have charted the messaging that the above-noted principals in the George Floyd issue delivered (bear in mind that since Floyd's death, there have been thousands of high-profile commentators making statements), and assigned a Red/Yellow/Green "communications response mark" based on my perception of the effectiveness of the messages that were delivered, with respect to building cross-cultural communication. The ratings range from red for "divisive, reactive, negative and harmful," to yellow for "messages that are moving toward a proactive approach but need reworking to reflect a stronger cross-cultural commitment," and green for "close alignment, committed, empathetic and positive." I have added commentary next to the rating in order to better elaborate on what was said, and how it might be perceived by stakeholders and the public, followed by potential action that could/should be taken to improve the relationship between the principal and stakeholders. In all cases, continued dialogue is necessary, as well as *action to demonstrate a vigorous commitment* to making positive change happen. Once a commitment is made, any public figure involved in offering support or empathy or espousing the values of caring must continue to engage in dialogue using Grunig's two-way symmetrical model of proactive communication by listening and responding to the concerns of the community.

Principal	Statement	Response	Comments	Continued Action
Jacob Frey, mayor of Minneapolis	"Being Black … should not be a death sentence" "You're supposed to help" "It serves as a reminder of how far we have to go" "The man's life matters. He matters" "To our Black community, to the family: I'm so sorry"	Green/Yellow	Expressed outrage and shock, the immediacy of feeling Statement has currency, as it came out the morning after the incident Frey was echoing the sentiments of community members	Frey needed to continue maintaining a dialogue with principals involved (family, civil rights representatives) but ultimately was shunted away from the public eye through the vast number of events and the involvement of politicians at state and federal levels. While the statement expressed shock and dismay, this also points to a need to really strengthen ties to the community
Melvin Carter, mayor of St. Paul	"Rage and frustration and anger" "Officers should be held accountable" "We have deep soul searching to do"	Yellow	Shared the emotions of the affected citizens Called for accountability Struck an emotional chord	Carter called for less violence but was caught in a situation where he and other officials suggested that out-of-towners were responsible for looting and damages. By focusing on the violence and seeming to cast blame, he pushed himself away from the message of inclusion and support, a message he sought to return to in the later that week

Principal	Statement	Response	Comments	Continued Action
Tim Walz, governor of Minnesota	"Seek justice" "Address systemic inequities" "Feelings of anger, anguish and disillusionment" "Justice and systemic change"	Green/Yellow	Demonstrated emotion and empathy; sought to connect with citizens	Showed concerns over safety of people and effectively continued to repeat key messages, though they changed largely from the "rights of citizens to protest" to "issues of public safety" due to dangers of rioting and damage to public buildings
Donald Trump, U.S. President	"A very, very sad event" "That's a very shocking sight" "You must dominate demonstrators" "I am your law and order president" "I will use the military to restore order"	Red	Demonstrated lack of understanding and empathy While his initial words focused on his shock at Floyd's death, the president soon moved toward messaging about power and control, (through state legislatures, police and military) over demonstrators	Trump veered sharply away from a sense of empathy and inclusion to threaten protesters and deliver threats of military use in order to restore order. Having clearly established his position of implied power and control, it would be difficult to create and deliver convincing messaging that would serve to promote inclusion
Sheriff Christopher Swanson	"Walking with you" "Asking for a voice and dignity" "I love you guys"	Green	Clearly demonstrated affinity for the protesters	Continue to build links to the community through engagement and support

Case Study Questions

1. In his 1967 speech *The Other America*, Martin Luther King, Jr., made the following statement: "Riots do not develop out of thin air. Certain conditions continue to exist in our society which must be condemned as vigorously as we condemn riots. But in the final analysis, a riot is the language of the unheard" (King, 1967). Violence, rioting, and destruction of property as a response to inequities or oppression are often met with anger and dismay. As a communicator, what is your job in understanding the root causes of such a response? What elements do you need to keep in mind? Discuss.

2. American Psychological Association president Sandra L. Shullman said in a news release that the events of violence against Black males was a "racism pandemic" contributing to "depression, anxiety and other serious, sometimes debilitating conditions, including post-traumatic stress disorder and substance use disorders. Moreover, the stress caused by racism can contribute to the development of cardiovascular and other physical diseases" (APA, 2020, May 29). Do you agree with this statement? What do you think needs to be done to make change happen? Also, outline briefly the organizations that need to contribute in order to change attitudes and behaviours. Finally, how would you communicate these actions to the public and stakeholders?

3. Have a look at the comments regarding the death of George Floyd. Now use the Internet to find statements made by organizations (including private sector organizations) and individuals outside the political ranks, about the incident. What are the key messages involved in their communications? Are they empathetic, sincere and direct? Do you question the validity/sincerity of what they are saying? Why or why not?

PROFILE

DR. W. TIMOTHY COOMBS, CRISIS COMMUNICATION RESEARCH, CONSULTANT, AND TRAINER

Timothy Coombs is a graduate of Purdue University with a Ph.D. in Public Affairs and Issues Management. An award-winning researcher, he has authored numerous books and papers on the impact of crisis communications on organizational reputation and is the developer of Situational Crisis Communication Theory (SCCT), which provides empirically tested advice for the selection of crisis response strategies.

In looking at the Central Park encounter, how well did Amy Cooper's company (investment firm Franklin Templeton) handle this situation?

The situation reflects the sensitivity of an organization being considered racist. This is one employee acting in a scenario that has nothing to do with work. Even the man involved in the incident felt that firing her was an overreaction. However, the media chose to name the employer, making them a part of the situation. It is a matter of guilt by association. The investigation and firing is an example of both distancing the organization from the situation (it is a paracrisis, not a crisis for the organization) and taking corrective action. [A paracrisis is defined by Coombs (2020) as an "organizational faux pas … an embarrassing or tactless act or remark in a social situation." As such it is not "genuine crisis" but an issue requiring corrective action, such as an apology.]

This relates to [Keith] Hearit's work on dissociation where an organization blames the employee or employees for the crisis, rather than saying the organization is responsible for the crisis. It works in this case because the situation is non-work related and the company removed an employee who had become problematic. I am not positive Franklin Templeton needed to do that because I am unsure if key stakeholders care about what one employee does on their own time. But the media attention creates a paracrisis and there was pressure to act. Franklin Templeton chose the action that would end the paracrisis immediately. Firing the employee effectively ends their [Franklin Templeton's] involvement in the story and connection to racism.

Following the death of George Floyd, the city of Minneapolis went through a major crisis. Given Martin Luther King, Jr.'s quote that "a riot is the language of the unheard," what will this mean for the city's administration and especially the police department? What do they need to do to build effective communication links to marginalized communities, and how well are they handling the situation, timewise and message-wise?

This is a scenario that has been repeated far too many times over the past four or five decades. Cities and police departments often have institutionalized racism. There is no easy fix or even clear way to handle the situation. The violence will make the situation worse before it can make it better. The route toward a solution is greater community engagement, especially involving the police and more hiring of minority police officers as part of the process. This is a case where crisis management plays little to no role. The institutional racism is a longer standing problem and the recent incident is just another marker of it. Until there is some meaningful engagement with the marginalized groups, nothing will change.

One of the tenets that you write about is the ethical responsibility of protecting stakeholders. How is this principle enhanced/harmed/affected in a cross-cultural communications scenario? What do communicators need to consider in this kind of scenario?

What is highlighted in crises with a racial dimension is a need to understand the emotions and reactions such crises are likely to evoke from victims and those who identify with the victims. The data shows race changes the emotions associated with a "racial crisis" and the sense of discrimination. The emotions and discrimination must be recognized in the crisis response to have any impact—it is still (focused on) the idea of protecting stakeholders but greater awareness is needed to help organizations understand the nature of the harm the crisis creates.

Reputation management is an essential element in effective communications practice and crisis management. What are some of the intersections between reputation management and cross-cultural dialogue and what considerations do communicators need to think about with respect to these elements?

When racism enters the situation, the threat to reputation intensifies as do the emotions and reactions to the crisis. Crisis managers need to be sensitive to how race and accusations of racism fundamentally change the nature of the situation (paracrisis or crisis) they are managing.

How effectively/ineffectively did organizations—in government and health care, for instance—communicate with respect to the racialized issues surrounding COVID-19 (higher incidences of the virus among marginalized and racialized populations)? Looking to the future, what must communicators do to build more effective cross-cultural dialogue?

The national and state levels have largely failed in addressing the racial aspect of COVID-19. These politicians are avoiding the topic because it makes them look bad and often is not their primary constituency. Local officials, especially mayors, have been much more active and effective at addressing the racial aspect of COVID-19. Like with so many concerns, the marginalized suffer disproportionally because of the lack of resources, including access to medical care and the financial resources necessary to survive the economic shutdown from the virus. [In the U.S.] many federal and state officials would like to ignore this information because it does not look good for them. Local officials have tried to not only provide resources but to correct misinformation. For instance, a dangerous myth circulating in the African American community has been that COVID-19 is a white disease and African Americans are unlikely to contract it.* The local officials better understand their communities and frequently have a much better understanding of commonly marginalized groups. In gen-

---

* There has been widespread coverage of this myth; Mock (2020, March 14) notes that "U.S. history evinces how unsubstantiated claims about race-based resilience to disease have led to devastating outcomes, particularly for African Americans."

eral, past disasters and now this pandemic reinforce the need to understand and to address the concerns of all segments of a community, not just those with power. The problem is the skepticism many marginalized groups have for the government. An example is the African American community's distrust of public health information that dates back to the Tuskegee syphilis abuse [a 40-year clinical study in Tuskegee, Alabama, of economically-challenged African American men suffering from untreated syphilis. Outrage over the ethics of the racially-charged study led to changes in the treatment of clinical study participants]. Public health crisis communication must partner with recognized leaders in marginalized communities to more effectively reach those communities. Marginalized communities must be engaged throughout the process not just [in] the response but also in the planning for public health crises. It is not so much dialogue as a willingness for the government to include marginalized groups in decision making (one form of engagement).

LET'S CHECK IN!

In this self-assessment, you will be asked to think about your attitudes toward, and knowledge of, the subject matter discussed in this chapter. List what you feel were the "greatest impacts" (include one example for each) of the chapter based on these topics:

1. How I felt after reading this chapter and why;
2. What needs to change in the way we approach crises;
3. Messaging that works;
4. How messages fail.

KEY TERMS

Colour blindness: the practice of pretending that one doesn't see colour in order to avoid the acknowledgment of race issues.

Dissociation: a way for corporations and other entities to clearly delineate themselves from situations of wrongdoing in a crisis situation.

Dog-whistling: statements that "cue" people into issues of race without being explicit but which instead use coded language and visuals.

Environmental scan: a method that is used to gather information about an organization's publics, in order to enhance the organization's communication with those publics.

Image restoration: methods used by organizations to rebuild their reputations.

Macroaggressions: the attitudes and behaviours that underpin a racist society, often imposing culturally-based expectations on people, ranging from art and religion to language and physical appearance.

People of colour: the increasingly acceptable term to replace the term "minority group." This includes people who are: South Asian, Chinese, Black, Filipino, Latin American, Arab, Southeast Asian, West Asian, Korean, and Japanese. Keep in mind that terminology changes, and what may be correct now may change in future.

Repressive tolerance: the acceptance of "status quo-entrenched" ideas in society, despite their potential damage to people, and the endorsement of aggressive and oppressive behaviours that result from such acceptance.

Social capital: networks of people based on trustworthiness, bonding and reciprocity.

SWOT: a tool for conducting an environmental scan, by examining Strengths, Weaknesses, Opportunities and Threats.

Symmetrical communication model: a two-way means of communicating between an organization and its publics that emphasizes listening, responding and negotiation, as opposed to the unidirectional *asymmetrical communication.*

Tolerance: the social virtue of living with, and learning from, those who are different.

White fragility: the expression of racial discomfort by white people due to social stress. It triggers defensive moves such as anger, denial and guilt.

White guilt: intense self-focus and discomfort; a need to "right wrongs" in order to make the initiator feel better about themselves and their position of whiteness.

White neutral norm: the state of whiteness in society that becomes the baseline or "neutral norm" by which behaviours and attitudes are measured. The result is that the severity of racist behaviour is not given serious consideration.

White privilege: the denial and dismissal of diversity's significance, allowing for the denial of oppression and avoidance of discussions about racism.

QUESTIONS TO EXPLORE

1. Take a look at the Venn diagram under the Central Park incident. Choose an intersection between any two of the participants in the issue, and write down your thoughts on how communication could be enhanced between them.

2. Think about the situations involving Don Cherry and Akim Aliu. What are your thoughts on the way behaviour has changed (or hasn't changed) in professional sports regarding issues of culture and race?

3. On a scale of 1 to 10 (1 being the least, 10 being the most) give a rating to the National Hockey League on the way it has managed communicating its commitment to facilitating change. Explain your answer.

4. Consider Marcuse's (2007, p. 41) statement that "minorities which strive for change of the whole ... will be left harmless and helpless in the face of the overwhelming majority, which militates against qualitative social change" (Marcuse, 2007, p. 41). How applicable is this to society today?

5. Think about the term "critical mass," the point at which something becomes self-sustaining, is used regularly in a society, and which requires little effort to sustain it. With respect to actions regarding protests against racism, have race relations reached the point of critical mass? Why or why not?

6. Consider this bit of history: in the decades following World War II, Germany eventually embraced a sense of responsibility for atrocities that took place under Nazi rule, such that today, German children "are taught at length in school about Nazi atrocities, and many of them are take on school outings to former KZs (concentration camps) that ... have been turned into exhibits" (Diamond, 2019, p. 230). Given the history of systemic and overt anti-Black racism in Canada and the U.S., how important is it for people to learn about it, beginning at a young age? How would this affect our communication across cultures?

7. Using a SWOT chart, do some research and develop an environmental scan for one of the Big Four tech companies (Amazon, Apple, Facebook, Google) with a focus on developing programs that demonstrate acknowledgement of, and respect for, members of BIPOC communities.

REFERENCES

Alexander, M. (2012). *The new Jim Crow*. New York: The New Press.

Aliu, A. (2020, May 19). Hockey is not for everyone. *The Players' Tribune*. https://www.theplayerstribune.com/en-us/articles/hockey-is-not-for-everyone-akim-aliu-nhl

American Psychological Association (2020, May 29). 'We are living in a racism pandemic,' says APA president. *APA*. https://www.apa.org/news/press/releases/2020/05/racism-pandemic

Arthur W. Page Center (2020). Environmental scanning and the ethical conscience. *Public Relations Ethics*. https://pagecentertraining.psu.edu/public-relations-ethics/media-framing-and-ethics/lesson-2-public-relations-media-scanning-role/environmental-scanning-the-ethical-conscience/

Baldwin, J. (1993). *The fire next time*. New York: Vintage International.

Baragona, J. (2020, May 18). Fox's Karl Rove: Obama's black college address was a 'drive-by shooting.' *The Daily Beast*. https://www.thedailybeast.com/foxs-karl-rove-says-obama-committed-political-drive-by-shooting-with-black-college-commencement-speech?source=TDB&via=FB_Page&fbclid=IwAR0Qw5R9nJPUao-E23LCdDks3N1rL9jWGB67oHCkF2axhYScJcOaVCOPPrg

BBC News (2020, June 1). George Floyd death: Violence erupts on sixth day of protests. BBC. https://www.bbc.com/news/world-us-canada-52872401

Bell, D. (2017, February 14). The NHL's first black player, Willie O'Ree, had a short but pathbreaking stint with the Boston Bruins. *The Undefeated*. https://theundefeated.com/features/nhl-first-black-player-willie-oree/

Benedict, B. (2017). Activism and Public Relations: Then and Now. Unpublished thesis. Halifax, NS: Mount St. Vincent University. http://dc.msvu.ca:8080/xmlui/bitstream/handle/10587/1841/BenBenedictMACThesis2017.pdf?sequence=1&isAllowed=y

Benoit, W. L. (1995). *Accounts, excuses, and apologies: A theory of image restoration*. Albany: State University of New York Press.

Bergerson, A. (2003). Critical race theory and white racism: Is there room for white scholars in fighting racism in education? *International Journal of Qualitative Studies in Education*, 16(1), 51–63. doi: 10.1080/0951839032000033527

Brand, J. (2012, March). Incidental crisis management: Strategies and tactics for success. In *15th International Public Relations Research Conference*, Z. Li and C. Spaulding (Eds.), Miami, FL: University of Miami, 34–43. https://www.instituteforpr.org/wp-content/uploads/15th-IPRRC-Proceedings1.pdf

Brennan, M. (2020, May 31). Transcript: St. Paul mayor Melvin Carter on "Face the Nation," May 31, 2020. *Face the Nation*, CBS News. https://www.cbsnews.com/news/transcript-st-paul-mayor-melvin-carter-on-face-the-nation-may-31-2020/

Canadian Press (2019, December 3). Akim Aliu believes change coming after meeting with NHL commissioner Gary Bettman. CBC. https://www.cbc.ca/sports/hockey/nhl/akim-aliu-nhl-investigation-racism-bill-peters-dec-3-1.5382904

Catalyst Research (2019, May 28). People of Colour in Canada: Quick take. Catalyst. https://www.catalyst.org/research/people-of-colour-in-canada/

Clark, R. (2020, June 1). Evander Kane on white NHLers addressing racism: We need 'strength in numbers.' *The Athletic*. https://theathletic.com/1847691/2020/06/01/evander-kane-on-white-nhlers-addressing-racism-we-need-strength-in-numbers/?sf123379501=1

Colvin, J. and Long, C. (2020, May 28). Trump tries a new response after George Floyd's death. Associated Press. https://apnews.com/89d86d28110b5f9a6d5a6df1b9f3be30

Coombs, T. (2018). Revolve's faux pas: Trying to do right goes so wrong. Crisis Communication Blog by Timothy Coombs. https://coombscrisiscommunication.wordpress.com/tag/paracrisis/

Coombs, T. and Schmidt, L. (2009). An empirical analysis of image restoration: Texaco's racism crisis. *Journal of Public Relations Research*, 12(2), 163–178.

Cooper, J. (2020, May 30). LinkedIn interview with Dr. Timothy Coombs.

Derworiz, C. (2019, November 19). Ron MacLean says he doesn't believe Don Cherry is racist. CBC Sports. https://www.cbc.ca/sports/hockey/nhl/ron-maclean-don-cherry-reaction-nov-19-1.5365690

Diamond, J. (2019). *Upheaval: Turning points for nations in crisis*. New York: Little, Brown.

DiAngelo, R. (2011). White Fragility. *International Journal of Critical Pedagogy*, 3 (3), 54–70. https://libjournal.uncg.edu/ijcp/article/viewFile/249/116

Douglas, W. (2018, March 21). Larry Kwong, the NHL's first player of color, passes away at 94. The Color of Hockey. https://colorofhockey.com/2018/03/21/larry-kwong-the-nhls-first-player-of-color-passes-away-at-94/

Drake, M. (2014, March 18). Being black in the NHL: From breaking the colour barrier to the Norris trophy. Montreal Canadiens Eyes on the Prize. https://www.habseyesontheprize.com/2014/3/28/5493088/the-history-of-black-players-in-the-nhl

Elcombe, T. (2019, November 17). Don Cherry's xenophobia forces Canada to grapple with tough questions. The Conversation. https://theconversation.com/don-cherrys-xenophobia-forces-canada-to-grapple-with-tough-questions-126914

Forliti, A., and Karnowski, S. (2020, June 1). Medical examiner: Floyd's heart stopped while restrained. *Toronto Star*. https://www.thestar.com/news/world/us/2020/06/01/george-floyd-family-to-release-results-of-own-autopsy.html

Franklin Templeton (2020, May 26). Twitter statement.

Freire, P. (2005). *Teachers as cultural workers*. Boulder, CO: Westview Press.

Freire, P. (2000). *Pedagogy of the oppressed*. New York: Bloomsbury Academic.

Frey, J. (2020, May 26). Statement regarding death of George Floyd. Twitter.

Frey, W. & Davis, K. (2018, October). Policy brief: Shifting demographics and hockey's future. NHL: SGL Lecture Series. https://nhl.bamcontent.com/images/assets/binary/300993502/binary-file/file.pdf

Goodin, E., Tanno, S., Sharp, R. and Ruiz, K. (2020, May 27). Donald Trump says he has ordered FBI and DOJ to 'expedite' probe into death of George Floyd and says 'justice will be served.' *Daily Mail.* https://www.dailymail.co.uk/news/article-8363287/Donald-Trump-calls-death-George-Floyd-sad-event-briefed-Thursday.html

Gottbrath, L., Abdalla, J. and Siddiqui, U. (2020, June 3). Over 9,000 arrested as Floyd protests continue: Live Updates. Al Jazeera. https://www.aljazeera.com/news/2020/06/outrage-peaceful-rally-tear-gassed-trump-photo-op-live-200602143946991.html

Grabish, A. (2020, May 20). Artist Kent Monkman's painting of partially nude Trudeau with laughing women creates uproar online. CBC. https://www.cbc.ca/news/canada/manitoba/kent-monkman-backlash-trudeau-painting-1.5577452

Grunig, J. (2013, May 27). Environmental scanning. James Grunig: Excellence Theory. https://excellencetheory.wordpress.com/tag/environmental-scanning/

Grunig, J. (2013, May 27). The two-way symmetrical model of communication. James Grunig: Excellence Theory. https://excellencetheory.wordpress.com/2013/09/27/the-two-way-symmetrical-model-of-communication/

Guo, S., & Jamal, Z. (2007). Nurturing cultural diversity in higher education: A critical review of selected models. *Canadian Journal of Higher Education*, 37(3), 27–49.

Habermas, J. (1998). *Inclusion of the other: Studies in political theory.* Cambridge, MA: MIT Press.

Hall, V. (2019, November 27). If hockey is for everyone, those in power need to listen—even if the message is difficult to hear. CBC Sports. https://www.cbc.ca/sports/hockey/nhl/calgary-flames-bill-peters-hall-analysis-1.5374929

Hearit, K. M. (1995). From "We Didn't Do it" to "It's Not Our Fault": The Use of Apologia in Public Relations Crisis. In W. N. Elwood (Ed.)., *Public Relations Inquiry as Rhetorical Criticism*, 117–131. Westport, CT: Praeger.

Hobsbawn, E. (1983). Introduction: Inventing traditions. In *The Invention of Tradition*, E. Hobsbawn & T. Ranger (Eds.). Cambridge, UK: Cambridge University Press.

Hooper, R. (2020, January 17). There Are Only 43 Players of Color in the NHL. Three of Them Play for the Red Wings—A Historic First. WDET Radio. https://wdet.org/posts/2020/01/17/89118-there-are-only-43-players-of-color-in-the-nhl-three-of-them-play-for-the-red-wings-a-historic-first/

Iyer, A., Leach, C., & Crosby, F. (2003). White guilt and racial compensation: The benefits and limits of self-focus. *Personality and Social Psychology Bulletin*, 29(1), 117–129. doi: 10.1177/0146167202238377

Jackson, H. (November 10, 2019). Ron MacLean apologizes for not challenging Don Cherry's 'hurtful and prejudiced' comments. Global News. https://globalnews.ca/news/6151647/don-cherry-immigrants-poppies/

Keshner, A. (2020, June 4). The insurance bill for damage and looting during protests over George Floyd's death will be at least $25 million—and that's just in Minnesota. MarketWatch. https://www.marketwatch.com/story/the-insurance-bill-for-damage-and-looting-during-protests-over-george-floyds-death-will-be-at-least-25-million-and-thats-just-in-minnesota-2020-06-04

King, M. (1967). The other America. Veterans of the civil rights movement. https://www.crmvet.org/docs/otheram.htm

Kelbniknov, S., and Sandler, R. (2020, May 30). Mayor walks back statement saying every person arrested in Minneapolis protests was from out of state. *Forbes.* https://www.forbes.com/sites/sergeiklebnikov/2020/05/30/mayor-says-he-was-incorrect-in-saying-every-person-arrested-in-minneapolis-protests-was-from-out-of-state/#61369b76233c

Klinkenberg, M. (2019, November 11). Sportsnet fires Don Cherry over remarks on immigrants, Remembrance Day poppies. https://www.theglobeandmail.com/sports/hockey/article-sportsnet-fires-don-cherry-over-remarks-on-immigrants-remembrance-day/

Kurtzberg, B. (2012, December 20). The 25 best traditions in hockey. Bleacher Report. https://bleacherreport.com/articles/1448849-the-25-best-traditions-in-hockey

Liptak, K., and Westwood, S. (2020, June 2). Trump threatens military force if violence in states isn't stopped. CNN. https://www.cnn.com/2020/06/01/politics/donald-trump-national-address-race/index.html

Lund, C. (2010). The nature of white privilege in the teaching and training of adults. In C. Lund & S. Colin (Eds.), *New directions for adult and continuing education, 125,* 15–25. doi: 10.1002/ace.359

Lund, D., & Carr, P. (2010). Exposing privilege and racism in the Great White North: Tackling whiteness and identity issues in Canadian education. *Multicultural Perspectives*, 12(4), 229–234. doi: 10.1080/15210960.2010.527594

Manza Young, S. (2020, May 20). Hockey has a racism problem, but its biggest stars remain silent. Yahoo News. https://ca.news.yahoo.com/nhl-akim-aliu-racism-hockey-212831790.html

Marcuse, H. (2007). Repressive tolerance (1965). In Feenberg, A. and Leiss, W. (Eds.), *The Essential Marcuse*, 32–62. Boston: Beacon Press.

Marcuse, H. (1964). *One-Dimensional Man*. Boston: Beacon Press.

Martin, N. (2020, May 21). The provocations of Kent Monkman. *The New Republic.* https://newrepublic.com/article/157742/provocations-kent-monkman

Maxouris, C. (2020, June 1). Minneapolis police chief says all four officers involved in George

Floyd's death bear responsibility. CNN. https://www.cnn.com/2020/06/01/us/minneapolis-police-chief-floyd-response/index.html

Maxouris, C. (2020, May 27). Christian Cooper is asking people to stop making death threats against the woman who called the cops on him. CNN. https://www.cnn.com/2020/05/27/us/amy-cooper-central-park-call-police-trnd/index.html

McIntosh, P. (2012). Reflections and future directions for privilege studies. *Journal of Social Issues, 68*(1), 194–206.

Meloney, N. (2019, February 3). New documentary investigates the possible Mi'kmaq origins of hockey. CBC News. https://www.cbc.ca/news/indigenous/mi-kmaq-hockey-history-nova-scotia-1.4998889

Miller, J. (2020, June 3). To be an "ally," you must do the work. *Toronto Star*, A12.

Mock, B. (2020, March 14). Why you should stop joking that Black people are immune to coronavirus. CityLab. https://www.citylab.com/equity/2020/03/coronavirus-immunity-racism-history-disease-yellow-fever/607891/

National Hockey League Public Relations (2019, November 10). Statement regarding Don Cherry's comments. NHL Twitter feed.

Olasov, I. (2016, November 7). Offensive political dog whistles: You know them when you hear them. Or do you? *Vox*. https://www.vox.com/the-big-idea/2016/11/7/13549154/dog-whistles-campaign-racism

Oliveira, M. (2013). Multicultural environments and their challenges to crisis communication. *Journal of Business Communication, 50*(3), 253–277. DOI: 10.1177/0021943613487070

Oxford Reference (2020). Repressive Tolerance definition. Oxford University Press. https://www.oxfordreference.com/view/10.1093/oi/authority.20110803100414515

Padilla, M. (2020, May 31). Michigan sheriff took off his helmet and marched with protesters. *The New York Times*. https://www.nytimes.com/2020/05/31/us/flint-sheriff-protestors-camden-police-ferguson.html

Putnam, R. (2000) *Bowling alone*. New York: Simon & Schuster.

Pilkington, E. (2020, May 20). Black Americans dying of Covid-19 at three times the rate of white people. *The Guardian*. https://www.theguardian.com/world/2020/may/20/black-americans-death-rate-covid-19-coronavirus

Quant Hockey (2020, March 13). Percentage of NHL players by nationality. *Quant Hockey*. https://www.quanthockey.com/nhl/nationality-totals/nhl-players-2017-18-stats.html

Ro, C. (2019, July 27). Racial stereotypes are making Americans sicker. *Forbes*. https://www.forbes.com/sites/christinero/2019/07/27/racial-stereotypes-are-making-americans-sicker/#69e0df4c207b

Sapolsky, R. (2017). *Behave: The biology of humans at our best and worst*. New York: Penguin Books.

Snelgrove, R., and Kabetu, V. (2019, November 16). Don Cherry debacle highlights the whiteness of hockey. *Canadian Immigrant*. https://canadianimmigrant.ca/news/don-cherry-debacle-highlights-the-whiteness-of-hockey

Solomon, G. (1988, January 17). "Jimmy the Greek" fired by CBS for his remarks. *Washington Post*. https://www.washingtonpost.com/archive/politics/1988/01/17/jimmy-the-greek-fired-by-cbs-for-his-remarks/27536e46-3031-40c2-bb2b-f912ec518f80/

Sportsnet Staff (2020, June 1). NHL teams, players condemn racial injustice following death of George Floyd. Sportsnet. https://www.sportsnet.ca/hockey/nhl/nhl-teams-players-condemn-racial-injustice-following-death-george-floyd/

Strauss, D., Smith, D., Borger, J., Gambino, L. and McGreal, C. (2020, June 1). Angry Donald Trump calls on governors to 'dominate' George Floyd protests. *The Guardian*. https://www.theguardian.com/us-news/2020/jun/01/donald-trump-protests-george-floyd-dominate

Sue, D., Alsaidi, S., Awad, M., Glaeser, E., Calle, C., and Mendez, N. (2019). Disarming racial microaggressions: Microintervention strategies for targets, white allies, and bystanders. *American Psychologist*, 74(1), 128–142. http://dx.doi.org/10.1037/amp0000296

Thomas, I. (2018, October 1). NHL looks to broaden diversity endeavors. *Sports Business Journal*. https://www.sportsbusinessdaily.com/Journal/Issues/2018/10/01/In-Depth/Diversity.aspx

Toth, E. (2009). Diversity and public relations practice. *The Institute for Public Relations*. https://instituteforpr.org/diversity-and-pr-practice/

Torres, J. (2018, March 7). Racism in the media persists 50 years after Kerner Report. *Free Press*. https://www.freepress.net/our-response/expert-analysis/insights-opinions/racism-media-persists-50-years-after-kerner-report

TSN (2019, November 10). NHL issues statement on Cherry's comments. TSN. https://www.tsn.ca/nhl-issues-statement-about-don-cherry-s-comments-1.1395657

Vaccaro, A. (2010). What lies beneath seemingly positive campus climate results: Institutional sexism, racism, and male hostility toward equity initiatives and liberal bias. *Equity & Excellence in Education*, 43(2), 202–215. doi: 10.1080/10665680903520231

Vaughan, G. (1999). Quotes prove ice hockey's origin. Birthplace of Hockey. https://www.birthplaceofhockey.com/origin/overview/

Vera, A., and Ly, L. (2020, May 26). White woman who called police on a black man bird-watching in Central Park has been fired. CNN. https://www.cnn.com/2020/05/26/us/central-park-video-dog-video-african-american-trnd/index.html

Walz, T. (2020, May 26-28). Twitter comments on death of George Floyd. https://twitter.com/GovTimWalz

Wegman, J. (2019, November). Kadri defends Cherry: 'People maybe took it out of context a little bit.' *The Score*. https://www.thescore.com/nhl/news/1878368

Wetts, R., and Willer, R. Who is called by the dog whistle? Experimental evidence that racial resentment and political ideology condition responses to racially encoded messages. *Socius: Sociological Research for a Dynamic World*. https://doi.org/10.1177/2378023119866268

Willard, G., Isaac, K-J., and Carney, D. (2015, April 30). Some evidence for the nonverbal contagion of racial bias. *Organizational Behavior and Human Decision Processes*, 128, 96–107. https://doi.org/10.1016/j.obhdp.2015.04.002

Zofi, Y. (2017, June 6). 5 strategies for effective cross-cultural interactions. *International Association of Business Communicators*. https://www.iabc.com/5-strategies-for-engaging-in-effective-cross-cultural-interactions/

Zuboff, S. (2019). *The age of surveillance capitalism*. New York: PublicAffairs Publishing.

CHAPTER THREE

Indigenous Communities and the Mainstream

OBJECTIVES OF THIS CHAPTER

This chapter is designed to assist in developing a better understanding of the issues underlying relationships between the dominant culture, Canada's government, and Indigenous communities, through:

- Developing an appreciation of provincial and federal government relationships with Indigenous Peoples;
- Evaluating the contentious history between the dominant culture and Indigenous Peoples;
- Reviewing specific terms, events, and historical issues relating to Indigenous communities;
- Recognizing the importance of land acknowledgements;
- Reading and responding to a case study on an issue that took place in Alberta;
- Using an exercise to explore ways to develop effective communications materials based on a specific issue.

MIKE HARRIS AND IPPERWASH

It was an occupation, a protest, a statement—one of many that had taken place over the course of decades, in different places across Canada. Its purpose: reclaiming sovereignty over hallowed land. In 1993 the Chippewas of Kettle and Stony Point First Nation began occupying land in Ipperwash Provincial Park, on the shores of Lake Huron—land that had been taken by the Canadian military during World War II for a military camp, expropriated by the government under the War Measures Act due to the First Nation being unwilling to part with the land due to its cultural and historical importance as a burial ground (Salomons, 2009).

The First Nations community was paid $15 an acre at the time and was given a promise that government would return the land within a few years; four decades later, when that promise went unfulfilled, the Stony Point First Nation made the decision to occupy the land, now known as Ipperwash Provincial Park and under the aegis of the province of Ontario. A larger group of 30 band members began a peaceful occupation on September 4, 1995. Their purpose was to make their message clear: give us back our land. Ontario Premier Mike Harris, angered at this, ordered the Ontario Provincial Police (OPP) to clear the occupiers out of the park.

Two days later, the OPP staged a nighttime raid, and unarmed band member Dudley George was shot to death. A 2003–06 inquiry found evidence of racist remarks being made by OPP officers prior to the raid, and Charles Harnick, a former attorney general, testified that during a cabinet meeting, Harris said "'I want the fucking Indians out of the park' ... Mr. Harnick's testimony lends credibility to the evidence of [OPP] Superintendent Ron Fox and his assistant, Inspector Scott Patrick, who were summoned to the meeting and both described Mr. Harris as upset by the OPP's failure to end the Ipperwash standoff" (Harries, 2005, November 29).

Harris's comment was angry, spontaneous, toxic, and it spoke to the traditional relationship between the oppressor and the oppressed, the idea that conquest brings to the conqueror *everything*, and whatever is acquired and passed from generation to generation in a colonial culture automatically belongs to the colonizers. Born in Toronto and raised in North Bay, Ontario, where his father ran a fishing camp, Harris was variously a ski instructor, a teacher for a short time, and golf club manager before entering politics (Canadian Encyclopedia, 2020), and was deeply embedded in that dominant culture. This was underscored by his policies relating to the reduction in spending on social programs and initiatives designed to help the poor.

The inquiry (note that it did not conclude until more than a decade after the incident, and four years after Harris left politics) found that the OPP and both provincial and federal governments shared responsibility for the death. Out of the inquiry came recommendations regarding land claims, including public education, the creation of an arm's-length body to oversee them, and a formalized process for consultation; the following year the province created a ministry of Aboriginal Affairs (Salomons, n.d.). The inquiry also recommended the repatriation of the land to the Chippewas of Kettle and Stony Point First Nation; in April 2016, the federal government confirmed a $95 million settlement with the community and transferred the land back to the band (Mehta, 2016, April 18). Then, in January 2021, as if the powers-that-be sought to take an eraser to the painful history of Ipperwash, Mike Harris was appointed to the Order of Ontario, an honour reserved for those who have "shown outstanding qualities of individual excellence and achievement in any field" (Order of Ontario, 2020). That announcement unleashed anger and dismay, not only in Indigenous communities but from teachers' organizations, civil servants, and nurses' unions (Harris was instrumental in making each of these sectors a target of cutbacks and criticism during his tenure). But for the Chiefs of Ontario, a representative body for Ontario's First Nations, Harris's Order of Ontario honour was especially troubling, given his role in the death of Dudley George and lack of respect for First Nations' rights (Edwards, 2021, January 9).

It might be said that the appointment of Mike Harris to the Order of Ontario underscored a general lack of understanding of the seriousness of Indigenous issues. It's a situation typified by a deficit of empathy for Indigenous communities on the part of the non-Indigenous Canadian public, and politically, inaction, or slowness to act, on Indigenous issues. According to Neylan (2018, June):

On one hand, public awareness of the problematic nature of the relations between the Indigenous peoples and settlers from other continents is likely greater than it has ever been. … On the other hand, uncomplicated and idealized visions of Canada's past abound at the popular, public level. Many assume that the Canadian motto "Peace, Order, and Good Government" informed the practice of Canadian "Indian" policy. Instead, violence, disorder and mismanagement, and a colonizing government have characterized Indigenous peoples' experiences with the state.

This is despite resistance efforts as well as attempts to develop comprehensive databanks of lived narratives and recommendations for action that have drawn considerable attention from the public, including the Idle No More movement (November 2012 onwards), the Truth and Reconciliation Commission, which ran from 2008 to 2015, and the 2016–19 National Inquiry into Missing and Murdered Indigenous Women and Girls. Initiated by the efforts of Indigenous activists and thinkers, these and other initiatives are components of a larger effort to work through four centuries of colonial violence and oppression, and to reclaim cultures; as Leanne Betasamosake Simpson notes:

> Part of being Indigenous in the 21st century is that regardless of where or how we have grown up, we've all been bathed in a vat of cognitive imperialism, perpetuating the idea that Indigenous Peoples were not, and are not, thinking peoples—an insidious mechanism to promote neo-assimilation and obfuscate the historic atrocities of colonialism (Betasamosake Simpson, 2011, p. 32).

It might be tempting to say that some "good" came, in a roundabout way, of Mike Harris's comments and actions back in the 1990s, leading as they did to an inquiry and changes in government structure. Yet a man died, and the history of colonial oppression against Indigenous peoples continues, and a reason for this is the unwillingness on the part of the dominant culture to understand that the oppressed are not "marginals," are not people living "outside" society. They have always been "inside"—inside the structure which made them "beings for others." The solution is not to "integrate" them into the structure of oppression, but to transform that structure so that they can become "beings for themselves" (Freire, 2000, p. 74).

As we discussed in the first two chapters, we exist in a culture that has too often been blithely unconcerned about the racism it practices, and Harris found himself embedded in it; it is a culture where, according to Delgado and Stefancic (2012), the "dominant racial group cannot easily grasp what it is like to be nonwhite."

Delgado and Stefancic point to a state of being described by W. E. B. Du Bois as "double consciousness." Double consciousness is the way in which "alienation and disenfranchisement blended one identity that seemed inescapable with another that appeared unattainable" (Lyubanksy and Eidelman, 2004, p. 2). It is the carrot-and-stick feeling of being held back, marginalized in a society that continues to promise out-of-reach social power and prestige. It's the recognition that despite one's best efforts in life, equity is a mirage. History books, Sunday sermons, and even case law contribute to a cultural hegemony that makes it difficult for reformers to make race an issue (pp. 45–46).

A HISTORY OF CONTENTION

If we were to think that the ill-treatment of Indigenous Peoples happened in a historical "yesterday," or that it is somewhat separated from the course of life in society, or the actions of a few "bad apples," we would be wrong. It is happening now, and it is systemic, not just in North America, but on every major continent save Antarctica.

Consider, for instance, the actions of the government of Brazil against its Indigenous Peoples. In 2018, Brazilian president Jair Bolsonaro made a campaign promise to open up the rainforest to development; on taking office in January 2019 he implemented polices dismantling the country's 1988 constitutional rainforest protections. With that loss went security for tribes living there, including several tribes that have remained out of contact with the outside world.

The language used by Bolsonaro is that of the oppressor; he vowed "not to designate "one centimeter" more as protected lands. "'The Indigenous person can't remain in his land as if he were some prehistoric creature,' he said in February [2020]. ... [Bolsonaro] presented a bill to Congress that could legalize mining ventures that have polluted rivers and authorize oil and gas exploration and hydropower plants on Indigenous land" (Londoño and Casado, 2020, May 2, p. 3). This would have the effect of destroying, in 567 Brazilian territories, the constitutional rights of Indigenous communities to practice their languages and traditions (p. 3).

Countries whose economic and social infrastructures are underpinned by Eurocentric capitalism share commonalities in the way they have treated Indigenous people. Canada's Indigenous populace of approximately 1.7 million is comprised of three groups that collectively form about 5 percent of Canada's population: First Nations (called in the past by the outdated term "Indians," still used in some government-related capacities, or variously "Native," or "Aboriginal"), Métis (those of mixed Indigenous and European ancestry), and Inuit (formerly referred to as "Eskimos," a pejorative and outdated term); First Nations number close to one million, Métis just under 600,000, and Inuit 65,000 (Statistics Canada, 2017).

The challenges inherent in the relationship between public relations and Indigenous culture stem from the treatment of the culture as *outside the norm,* even *exotic*, and being considered somehow "new and different" to the considerations of the mainstream culture, such that "the history of White supremacy, and the way that language and structures of feeling frame Whiteness as the natural, inevitable conceptual center, means that the newly included voices, sensibilities and traditions are always positioned as the exotic other" (Brookfield, 2007, p. 560).

Let's consider public relations. If you search on the web for the terms "public relations" and "Indigenous People" you will find numerous public relations firms offering assistance to companies seeking to negotiate business transactions with Indigenous communities, and given our capitalist society, most generally have the economic opportunities of mainstream/Indigenous collaborations in mind: "It's perplexing to see the potential of indigenous peoples as valuable economic partners not fully recognized by corporate Canada … the private sector seems largely unaware of the dynamic opportunity before them. It's essentially an emerging market at their doorstep. … Today, most private companies in Canada see indigenous constituents and entities as fraught with risk and challenges rather than opportunities" (Vekil, M., 2017, March 29).

Today, collaboration between mainstream and Indigenous organizations is not necessarily a bad thing, but both sides must profit equally, and it requires careful consultation beforehand. Joseph and Joseph (2019) cite as an example a mining company seeking to engage with an Indigenous community, where "consultation is a complex process that must take into account the tangible impact on economic, employment, and education opportunities … consultation also requires considering the social and spiritual impacts on affected communities" (p. 42). Otherwise, engagement may run the risk of becoming a source of discourse colonization, defined as the meaning of discourse within one domain (the colonized domain) being changed by the application of another domain's (the dominant culture) discourse:

> For example, the discursive practices of the dominant economic sphere have been strategically deployed in other discursive spheres and have colonized them. Thus the language of market philosophy has been used to rename things and people as new kinds of discursive constructs. Education has become a service, pupils have become products, human beings and the environment have become resources to be conserved or exploited (Motion and Leitch, 1996, p. 299).

As such, dominant cultural ideals change how Indigenous cultures are viewed, and run the risk of turning Indigenous culture into a potential "money-maker," creating an issue of economic cultural appropriation. This "happens when a dominant culture takes things from another culture that is experiencing oppression. . . . When different cultures come together on an equal footing, exchange happens. But when dominant groups take from an oppressed group, we're dealing with appropriation" (Reach Out.com, 2020). In my classes, I occasionally offer an anecdote about a situation when, in the early 2000s, I took a group of students on a field trip to the social service agency Anishnawbe Health Toronto. We had a tour of the facility, and our guide took us into a meeting room for a general overview and discussion. When our guide talked about Indigenous culture reclamation as one of the agency's tenets, one of my students asked, "Why don't you just make crafts, like dreamcatchers, and sell them? You can make money." Her comment underscored the fact that we live in a culture where we become embedded in corporatized profit motives, consciously and subconsciously.

This approach—cultural appropriation and economic domination (and adding to it, cultural *obliteration*)—underscores the history of the relationship between Canada and Indigenous peoples, and it speaks to a sense of exploitation and oppression. This land was always the focus of exploitation for profit: first the fur trade, then logging to obtain the timber needed for ships, then colonization, an influx of European settlers, then a concerted effort to move Indigenous Peoples from their lands, and then a cultural genocide (the destruction of the way of life and the culture of a people). One of the findings of the Truth and Reconciliation Commission was that "Canada is guilty of committing cultural genocide against Indigenous people. . . . The TRC builds a case that leads it to conclude Canada committed cultural genocide against Indigenous peoples and used Indian residential schools used as its main weapon" (APTN, 2015, June 2).

The oppressive relationship between the federal government and Indigenous communities is apparent if you consider the federal government's position in 1911, and the annual report from the Department of Indian Affairs. As Frank Oliver, Superintendent General of the department, noted:

> From their peculiar and separate position in society, Indians are open to ignorant censure from a class of the community that stands aloof from all efforts to improve their condition; but, considering their proneness to be sought out and influenced by the less desirable members of the white communities, who tempt them with their own vices, the Indians stand well as moral and law-abiding citizens. Their native code of morals is not, clause by clause, the same as that of the white race, but they are capable of practising Christian morals, and do so after education and experience. The great bar to moral progress from our point of view is the craving

for intoxicants, which brings many other evils in its train and a certain license in the relation of the sexes which varies in objectionable features in different sections of the country (Department of Indian Affairs, 1911).

As such, Indigenous peoples were seen as "child-like" but capable of "improvement" that would "raise" them to a standard close, but not equal, to white people; this is a reinforcement of the "white neutral norm" that we discussed in the last chapter. At its core is racism. According to Indigenous authors Arthur Manuel and Grand Chief Ronald Derrickson (2017), racism is "the silent and often hidden weapon that Canada uses against us, and exposing it is the only way to combat it ... it is the force behind the murder and disappearance of hundreds of our women and behind the police refusal to properly investigate what has and still is happening to them" (p. 77).

From its position of power, the federal government's desire to "take care" of the seemingly burdensome moral, economic, and physical load represented by the Indigenous community was reinforced by an official policy that sought to erase the culture altogether. As Duncan Campbell Scott, who directed the Department of Indian Affairs from 1913 to 1932 and who was behind an amendment making residential school attendance compulsory for First Nations children under age 15, said a century ago: "I want to get rid of the Indian problem. I do not think as a matter of fact, that the country ought to continuously protect a class of people who are able to stand alone. ... Our objective is to continue until there is not a single Indian in Canada that has not been absorbed into the body politic and there is no Indian question, and no Indian Department, that is the whole object of this Bill" (*Stolen Lives*, 2020).

Erasure was planned to take place through assimilation, an assimilation that the Canadian government had started in the 1880s and which would continue until close to the end of the 20th century. The process was harsh, measured in dollars and cents, and designed to wring every last dram of sweat equity from Indigenous youth—as part of residential school work programs—under the guise of "improvement."

It was a cold and calculated attempt at "bettering" a people. Paulo Freire, in *Pedagogy of the Oppressed*, speaks to that kind of process as *changing the consciousness* of the oppressed, such that the oppressed take on the consciousness and ideals of the oppressor, a state in which they accept the oppressor's terms and conditions as a way of life. Their own lives do not get better. "The oppressed suffer from the duality which has established itself in their innermost being. They discover that without freedom they cannot exist authentically. Yet, although they desire authentic existence, they fear it. They are at one and the same time themselves and the oppressor whose consciousness they have internalized" (Friere, 2000, p. 48). As Nicholas Flood Davin reported (in a study to measure the potential for establishing a Canadian residential school system by examining a U.S.-based operation) to the federal minister of the interior in *Report on Industrial Schools for Indians and Half-Breeds* (1879):

I have the honour to submit the following report on the working Industrial Schools for the education of Indians and mixed-bloods in the United States, and on the advisability of establishing similar institutions in the North-West Territories of the Dominion. ... The industrial school is the principal feature of the policy known as that of "aggressive civilization." This policy was inaugurated by President [Ulysses S.] Grant in 1869. But, as will be seen, the utility of industrial schools had long ere that time been amply tested. ... [The U.S.] Peace Commission recommended that the Indians should, as far as practicable, be consolidated on few reservations, and provided with "permanent individual homes"; that the tribal relation should be abolished; that lands should be allotted in severalty [separate sections of land] and not in common; that the Indian should speedily become a citizen of the United States" (Davin, N., 1879).

Such a policy of hostile assimilation, undertaken with a focus on cementing in place a permanent underclass of Indigenous citizens, was open, vigorous and unrepentant. Residential schools "brought immeasurable human suffering to the First Nations, Inuit, and Métis Peoples, the effects ... continue to reverberate through generations of families and many communities. Other policies were harsh [banned cultural ceremonies or forced movement to small reserves] ... but when the government took the children from their families, it was unbearable." More than 6,000 of the 150,000 children attending residential schools would die or disappear over the course of 110 years of residential school operations (Joseph, 2018, p. 53).

INDIGENOUS PEOPLES, LAND ACKNOWLEDGEMENTS AND THE FEDERAL GOVERNMENT

Officialdom hasn't changed a great deal over the 400 years since Europeans began colonizing North America, but attitudes are slowly changing, though practices—of overrepresentation of Indigenous people in prisons, of abusive treatment of Indigenous people by RCMP and other police forces, of a severe lack of infrastructure and medical and social services to Indigenous communities—continue to evolve at a glacial pace, and in some cases attitudes have been typified by governments spilling out nice language, magnanimous phrases and warm promises of respect and support while turning a proverbial blind eye to Indigenous concerns. Talaga (2018) wrote of the denial of federal support for mental health services to Nishnawbe Aski Nation (NAN), which covers two-thirds of northern Ontario, despite the pressing need for help: "From 1986 through December 2017, there were more than 558 suicides across NAN territory, a community comprising only 49,000 people. … Since 1986, an almost incomprehensible eighty-eight children between the ages of ten and fourteen have killed themselves" (p. 11). In addressing issues, pity, platitudes, and false empathy from the mainstream are not only ineffective but insulting. Reaching across a culture requires understanding and humility, along with respect and acknowledgement of the land on which you are situated. As Freire (2005) notes,

> humility requires courage, self-confidence, self-respect and respect for others. Humility helps us to understand this obvious truth: No one knows it all; no one is ignorant of everything. … How can I listen to the other, how can I hold a dialogue, if I can only listen to myself, if I can only see myself, if nothing or no one other than myself can touch me or move me? (p. 72).

Today, there is often a general acknowledgement (with resistance still in some places) of the fact that we in Canada are on treaty land, and that we are part of a long-standing settler-colonial society. According to Joseph and Joseph (2019), "a land acknowledgement is a sign of respect and recognition. … You are acknowledging the ties that Indigenous Peoples have to the land—its importance to their culture, ceremonies, and traditions" (p. 104). For instance, before the classes I teach, I will acknowledge the lands on which I am delivering my classes; in the case of writing this textbook, I acknowledge the fact that I am living and working on the lands of the people of the Mississaugas of Scugog Island First Nations, within the traditional territory of the Mississauga and in the territory covered by the Williams Treaties of 1923. According to Shahzad (2017, July 15), "A territorial or land acknowledgement is an act of reconciliation that involves making a statement recognizing the traditional territory of the Indigenous people who called the land home before the arrival of settlers, and in many cases still do call it home." These kinds of acknowledge-ments are generally met with approval, and according to Isador (2019, August 9), "the better Land Acknowledgments I've witnessed have served as a jump-ing off point for learning about both the brutal ways Canada has treated its Indigenous people, and the vibrant cultures that have persevered despite that brutality," although the perception of land acknowledgements can also range from them sounding "like condescending bullshit," "like a eulogy," or "like reading names off a piece of paper," in other words, patronizing, empty, and meaningless. Acknowledgements must be done with sincerity, honesty, and a truthfulness that welcomes difficult conversations. But there is a long way to go. According to Joseph and Joseph (2019), today's approach must be focused on "Recognition, Respect, and Reconciliation.... [R]ecognize constitutionally protected Aboriginal Rights.... Respect means to address the uniqueness of individual Indigenous Peoples.... Reconciliation means to restore harmony between Indigenous and non-Indigenous people" (pp. 71–72).

Let's look at the language used by two academic institutions and one private sector firm in accepting their responsibility to work toward reconciliation:

Centennial College

Centennial College is proud to be a part of a rich history of education in this province and in this city. We acknowledge that we are on the treaty lands and territory of the Mississaugas of the Credit First Nation and pay tribute to their legacy and the legacy of all First Peoples of Canada, as we strengthen ties with the communities we serve and build the fu-ture through learning and through our graduates. Today the traditional meeting place of Toronto is still home to many Indigenous People from across Turtle Island and we are grateful to have the opportunity to work in the communities that have grown in the treaty lands of the Mississau-gas. We acknowledge that we are all treaty people and accept our respon-sibility to honour all our relations (Centennial College, 2020).

(The key words and phrases: the acknowledgement of existence on treaty lands; paying tribute to the legacy of the Mississaugas of the Credit First Na-tion, and broadening it to include all First Peoples; strengthening ties between communities; gratefulness for being able to work on the treaty lands; accepting responsibility to honour the relationships.)

Durham College

Durham College (DC) is situated on the Traditional Territory of the Mississaugas and the territory that is covered by the Williams Treaty, and we are thankful for the opportunity to teach and learn on the lands of the Peoples of Mississaugas of Scugog Island First Nation. We celebrate this history in a number of ways on campus including rich programming through our First Peoples Indigenous Centre. In this space students can learn through tradition teachings and cultural activities and have access to an elder. In response to the Truth & Reconciliation Calls to Action, DC established the Indigenization Council comprised of key members of the college to provide guidance and oversight to the institution in meeting commitments outlined in the Indigenous Education Protocol. One way of showing our RESPECT for the Land that we are on is to take time to acknowledge the land we are on. This can be done with a Land Acknowledgement at the beginning of college events, activities and classes (Durham College, 2020).

(The key words and phrases: thankfulness for the opportunity to teach on treaty lands; celebration of this reality through programming; ensuring access to traditional teachings; a commitment to the school's Indigenous Education Protocol; discussion of respect through a land acknowledgement.)

Imperial Oil

Mutually beneficial relationships with Canada's Indigenous Peoples are critical to the success of Imperial and Canada's energy industry. What does mutually beneficial mean to us? It means that in the areas where we operate, Indigenous communities are engaged through consultation, employment and business development, and where economic opportunities in the communities are enhanced through educational and program investments. … We conduct business in a manner that respects the land, environment, rights and cultures of Indigenous communities. And we seek to understand Indigenous perspectives on issues of mutual interest and to deal constructively with differing views. ∴.. Reconciliation is the responsibility of all Canadians, including businesses. We continue to respond to the calls to action for business through enhanced consultation, workforce and business opportunities. Additionally, Imperial provides education for management and staff on the history of Indigenous peoples in Canada, including the legacy and impacts of residential schools (Imperial Oil, 2020).

(Though this acknowledgement is wide-ranging and business-focused, note the key words and phrases: mutually beneficial relationships are critical to success; consultation, educational and program investments; respect for Indigenous communities [land, environment, rights, culture]; seeking to understand Indigenous perspectives; a commitment to reconciliation through consultation and education.)

A process of reconciliation takes time, and the activities of politicians often hindered progress. For instance, in 1969, then prime minister Pierre Trudeau introduced a piece of legislation, called a White Paper, designed to promote the assimilation of First Nations into Canadian society by eliminating the 1876 Indian Act, which had sought to treat Indigenous people as wards of the state and "potential citizens-in-waiting," and engaging in a full-blown "paternalistic attitude [that] gave way to increasingly punitive rules, prohibitions, and regulations that dehumanized Indians." In attempting to eliminate the Indian Act by eradicating the legal status of the term "Indian," and voiding "all treaties between Indigenous Peoples and Canada, and dismantl[ing] the Department of Indian Affairs … [Trudeau's] White Paper elicited an unanticipated wrath of opposition from Indigenous Peoples. They felt that its terms were unacceptable and they found its tone both paternalistic and accusatory" (Joseph, 2018, p. 8). As King (2012) put it:

> In 1969, the Canadian government tried to pull a homegrown Termination Act—the 1969 White Paper—out of its Parliamentary canal. … Trudeau blithely intimated that there was no such thing as Indian entitlement to land or native rights and suggested that it was in the best interests of First Nations people to give up their reserves and assimilate into Canadian society. The reaction was immediate and fierce. … Native people were sure that giving up their land and their treaty rights was not the answer (p. 73).

To say that Pierre Trudeau didn't "get it" is an understatement—he was trying to take away sacred ties between Indigenous communities and the land in a unilateral way, seeing Canada from the perspective of the dominant culture. In a piece of legal/political sleight of hand, he sought to turn them into "Canadians," eliminating the historical, land-rights and cultural significance they held. First Nations communities would turn away from Trudeau, and the White Paper was withdrawn the following year. According to Trudeau biographer John

English: "Since the failure of the White Paper … Trudeau had largely ignored the Aboriginal question, not so much from lack of interest as because other items took priority" (English, 2009, p. 513). The subtext here might also be that he didn't like to lose, or back down, or be seen as nefarious in his dealings, and though an astute politician, Trudeau didn't understand the depth of the issues with which he was dealing. Or, if we prefer to see a more disreputable side, success of the White Paper would perhaps just make it easier for business and industry to acquire lands that were suddenly "up for grabs," and effectively erase a colonial power's historical embarrassment.

Fast forward a few decades and the prime ministerial successors to Trudeau didn't fare much better either in understanding the issues or in making positive change happen. Even when doing "the right thing," prime ministers have somehow managed to either misread their audience or misuse the message. In 2008, then prime minister Stephen Harper "stood up in the House of Commons and said that "assimilation was wrong, has caused great harm and has no place in our country. … We are sorry" (King, 2012, p. 122). The problem was that the apology was "a stingy thing, limited only to the abuse that Native people had endured in the residential school system. There was nothing in the apology about treaty violations. Nothing about the theft of land and resources. Nothing about government incompetence, indifference, and chicanery" (pp. 122–123). But the trust that people were ready to place in what seemed a piece of honesty from the government began to evaporate "following a well-scrutinized address by Harper at a gathering of the G20 [leading industrialized nations] in Pittsburgh, Pennsylvania, on September 23, 2009. It was there that Harper made the somewhat astonishing (but typically arrogant and self-congratulatory) claim that Canadians had 'no history of colonialism,'" with Indigenous leaders reacting strongly and swiftly, calling for a greater commitment to truth and respect. In fact, Harper's "sorry" marked another milestone in the history of "a global industry [that] has emerged promoting the issuing of official apologies advocating "forgiveness" and "reconciliation" as an important precondition for resolving the deleterious social impacts of intrastate violence, mass atrocity, and historical injustice" (Coulthard, 2014, p. 106).

Then there was Pierre's son Justin Trudeau, who took office in 2015, and who has on occasion delivered what appeared to be positive messages of support and conciliation to Indigenous Peoples; for instance, his June 21, 2020, statement recognizing National Indigenous Peoples Day:

On this day, we recognize the contributions of Indigenous peoples to our past, and the important role they will continue to play in building our future … as we look to the future, we know that we can only move forward together, with a relationship based on respect, partnership, and affirmation of rights. By doing so, we create stronger communities. We have been working with Indigenous leaders and communities, and we know there is much more to do. Together, we must continue to address the systemic inequalities and discrimination that Indigenous peoples experience in Canada—issues that have been amplified by the social, health, and economic impacts of COVID-19. The latest tragic events and protests have also underscored how far we still have to go as a country, and the work we need to do to eliminate systemic racism from our society. … As we move forward on the path of reconciliation, and work to implement the Calls to Action from the Truth and Reconciliation Commission and the Calls for Justice from the National Inquiry into Missing and Murdered Indigenous Women and Girls, we must continue to listen to Indigenous peoples, partners, and communities"(Trudeau, 2020, June 21).

Trudeau went on to mention the implementation of Indigenous rights, addressing Indigenous child family services legislation and the protection of Indigenous languages.

(Note the key phrases, similar to others we have seen in public relations material: respect; partnerships; communities; addressing inequities; eliminating systemic racism, moving forward on reconciliation.)

The challenge with Justin Trudeau? His support was fleeting, lacking substance and commitment. Away from the discussion table with Indigenous groups, his message changed. For example, his policies supported clean energy, but away from the podium he promoted non-renewable initiatives like the oil sands of northern Alberta; in 2016 he approved the Pacific NorthWest Liquified Natural Gas pipeline, a multi-billion-dollar project (ultimately cancelled) that threatened the environment and "had been fiercely opposed by environmentalists and Indigenous land protectors" (Manuel and Derrickson, 2017, p. 236). The Kinder Morgan (Trans Mountain) pipeline, another project supported by Trudeau and slated to pass through hundreds of square kilometres of the traditional territory of the Secwepemc First Nation, with potential damage to environmentally-sensitive land and salmon rivers, was a point of contention as well, and its approval was "the second gravest criminal act Justin has committed—after the abandonment of the international declaration of our rights in UNDRIP" (Manuel and Derrickson, 2017, p. 241). According to Manuel and Derrickson, "Trudeau is committing intergenerational warfare against my children and grandchildren, as he is with his own. ... Trudeau and his tricksters never miss a chance to speak glowingly of clean energy while at the same time devoting all of their energies and energy policies to ensuring the continued domination of dirty energy" (2017, p. 243).

It's essential to contextualize the government's behaviour in the framework of world recognition of Indigenous rights; in 2007, the United Nations created the United Nations Declaration on the Rights of Indigenous Peoples (UNDRIP), which Canada "had fiercely lobbied against before it was enacted by the UN General Assembly on September 13, 2007" (Manuel and Derrickson, 2017, p. 53). UNDRIP provides "guarantees for our right to our own nationality ... [it] calls for the cessation of violence against us [including forced removal of children] ... [it] demands our protection from 'any action which has the aim or effect of dispossessing us of our lands, territories or resources'" and requires the provision of restitution for the taking of property—cultural, intellectual or spiritual—and establishes the Indigenous right to self-determination of education in their own languages (Manuel and Derrickson, 2017, p. 53). The challenge was that, though Canada tacitly agreed to UNDRIP, the federal Liberal government refused to adopt it into law; instead, it opted for a "Canadian version" to be developed behind closed doors. For Manuel and Derrickson, "when politicians like Justin Trudeau speak about Indigenous peoples they invariably use relationship language, like they are discussing a failed marriage. They offer mea culpas for Canada's past behaviour and call for reconciliation, as if all we needed was a bit of counselling ... the issue is not merely behaviours, but fundamental rights—our land rights and the inalienable right to self-determination" (Manuel and Derrickson, 2017, p. 57).

A TIP FOR CROSS-CULTURAL COMMUNICATION

Avoid ambiguity: "Avoiding or tolerating ambiguity doesn't necessarily mean that you deliberately avoid ambiguous situations. The goal is to avoid the uneasiness that could lead to frustration, which hinders your ability to effectively communicate.... The greater your knowledge about another culture the less ambiguous it becomes" (Zofi, 2017, June 6).

THE CHALLENGE TODAY, AND MOVING FORWARD

The challenge today is that communicators and the organizations for which they work are in a position where it is necessary to acknowledge the history of the treatment of Indigenous people in Canada, and around the world. There is a long way to go; a poll surveying 1,000 Canadians, commissioned by Historica Canada in 2020 and seeking to find out just how much Canadians knew about the historical and cultural benchmarks established by Indigenous and other racialized people in Canada, discovered that

> most Canadians have a lot to learn.… Only 16 per cent of respondents were able to pass the quiz, which featured facts about the contributions of prominent Canadians ranging from Olympic athletes to scientists. The poll found survey participants generally knew the least about figures from Indigenous or other racialized backgrounds, with the exception of civil rights crusader Viola Desmond. Less than six per cent of respondents recognized figures such as Indigenous filmmakers and human rights activists, or the first RCMP officer to wear a turban. (McQuigge, 2020, June 26).

The government of Canada's relationship with Indigenous Peoples is enshrined in several documents, including the Constitution Act of 1982. According to the federal government website, there is a commitment

> to achieving reconciliation with Indigenous peoples through a renewed, nation-to-nation, government-to-government, and Inuit-Crown relationship based on recognition of rights, respect, co-operation, and partnership as the foundation for transformative change. Indigenous peoples have a special constitutional relationship with the Crown. This relationship, including existing Aboriginal and treaty rights, is recognized and affirmed in section 35 of the Constitution Act, 1982. Section 35 contains a full box of rights, and holds the promise that Indigenous nations will become partners in Confederation on the basis of a fair and just reconciliation between Indigenous peoples and the Crown (Government of Canada, Department of Justice, 2018).

That commitment focuses on recognizing self-determination, respecting treaties and rights, and a commitment to reconciliation. But getting to that government-sanctioned idealized version of a relationship is challenging. As

Coulthard (2014) notes, a massive decolonization and reforming of political thinking is required, and unless that reformation happens, "any efforts to rebuild our nations will remain parasitic on capitalism, and thus on the perpetual exploitation of our lands and labor" (p. 171).

Is there a backlash against efforts towards decolonization and reconciliation? Emory University professor and historian Carole Anderson investigated the topic of white rage in her book of the same name; it is based on "Anderson's thesis … that every advance made by African Americans since the end of slavery has been followed by white pushback aimed at regaining control" (Schenck, 2020), and "whenever African Americans made significant advances toward gaining equal rights, 'white reaction' fueled a rollback of these achievements" (Merchant, 2018, January 8).

Given the responses of some Canadians to issues involving Indigenous rights, the same could be said of this country. For example, the CBC reported that then Alberta premier Jason Kenney's speechwriter, Paul Bunner (who was also a speechwriter for former prime minister Stephen Harper), wrote a 2013 online article "dismissing the 'bogus genocide story' of Canada's residential school system and [saying] Indigenous youth could be 'ripe recruits' for violent insurgencies." While the premier's office attempted to dissemble in the face of the story, critics argued that Bunner's actions served to drive a wedge between a government that had claimed to be working to advance partnerships between Alberta and its Indigenous communities (von Scheel, 2020, June 25).

Social and traditional media continue to provide a platform to discuss the hot button issues that speak alternately of increased anger, outrage, and anxiety (note the protests that emerged from the 2023 Israel-Hamas War) or greater enlightenment (for instance, the Ontario government's 2023 decision to ban caste discrimination). Consider these other items:

- Staff of a British Columbia hospital involved in a cruel and dehumanizing game of "guessing" the blood alcohol content of Indigenous patients, an activity condemned by British Columbia premier John Horgan, with a promise of an investigation in conjunction with the First Nations Health Council and the First Nations Health Authority (Bains, 2020, June 19).
- A "Take Back Canada" slogan used by Conservative Party leadership candidate Erin O'Toole prompted the statement that "one does not simply say 'take Canada back' in a country built on colonization and forcibly seizing land from Indigenous people without raising a few eyebrows" (Woods, 2020, June 11).

- A controversial "Bill 1" (the Critical Infrastructure Defence Act) that the Alberta government was looking to pass, which would outlaw protests "and other disruptions to 'critical infrastructure,'" a piece of legislation to prevent demonstrations against, for example, any built structures, from pipelines to highways, avenues, and processing plants. It was heavily criticized by First Nations in Alberta: "Arthur Noskey, Grand Chief of the Treaty 8 First Nations of Alberta, said the … Act violates Indigenous and treaty rights, calling it a "racialized bill," and one that will aggravate tensions between police and Indigenous people" (Morin, 2020, June 11).
- A Canadian Senate ethics committee recommendation to reinstate Senator Lynn Beyak, who was suspended in May 2019 "for posting derogatory letters about Indigenous Peoples on her website. … The offending letters were posted in response to a 2017 speech in which Beyak argued that residential schools did a lot of good for Indigenous children, although many suffered physical and sexual abuse and thousands died of disease and malnutrition. The committee decided that, after taking a four-day anti-racism training program and delivering an apology, she should be reinstated, and that "Beyak said she now understands how hurtful her conduct was and expressed her gratitude to the education program" (Bryden, 2020, June 22). However, an alliance comprised of residential school survivors and First Nations Chiefs rejected the endorsement to remove the suspension and allow Beyak back into the Senate, saying that, among other issues, the lack of communication between Beyak and residential school survivors was "an insult," according to Nishnawbe Aski Nation Grand Chief Alvin Fiddler (Canadian Press, 2020, July 2).
- The decision by Land O' Lakes to remove the image of an Indigenous woman on its consumer packaging, the company stating that it would focus on the farmer-producers of butter and cheese and choosing to avoid discussions of racism (Stone, 2020, April 17).
- Choices by PepsiCo and Mars Food to replace their food "mascots" for (respectively) "Aunt Jemima" syrup and "Uncle Ben's" rice (Olito, 2020, June 17), and a decision by B&G Foods to retire its "Cream of Wheat" logo (Bradley, 2020, June 18). Aunt Jemima, Uncle Ben's and Cream of Wheat all displayed racist stereotypes of Black people.
- A move by the Crown Corporation Newfoundland and Labrador Liquor Corp., producer of a brand of rum known as "Old Sam," to replace the image of a laughing Black man on its product label. The company said it

was uncertain as to whether the image "was rooted in racist stereotypes … in a statement announcing the character's removal, the agency reported it is impossible to reach a definitive conclusion about the logo's origins" (McKenzie-Sutter, 2020, June 30).

- A resolution from Dreyer's Grand Ice Cream to rebrand its "Eskimo Pie" ice cream treat, given that "the word 'Eskimo' has long been a polarizing term, with critics calling it a racist nomenclature first used by colonizers to Arctic regions to refer to Inuit and Yupik people" (Newman, 2020, June 19).

- A movement by federal Conservative Members of Parliament to put the face of Indigenous Second World War hero Sergeant Tommy Prince on Canada's $5 bill. "Prince earned 11 medals in the Second World War and the Korean War, and was one of three Canadians to receive both the American Silver Star and the Military Medal, presented by King George VI at Buckingham Palace in 1945. However, when Prince returned to his home province of Manitoba, he endured discrimination, poverty and illness and died while living in a Winnipeg shelter at the age of 62." Despite Canada's excessively poor treatment of the war hero, the MPs said that honouring Prince on the bill would be a great statement of reconciliation (Beattie, 2020, June 30).

- Plans for the federal government's Fisheries and Oceans ministry to work with an Indigenous group, the Assembly of Nova Scotia Mi'kmaw Chiefs, to rename the Coast Guard icebreaker *Edward Cornwallis*. Cornwallis founded Halifax in 1749, and was acknowledged as a murderer whose efforts "to establish a garrison town [Halifax] included eliminating Indigenous resistance and … approving a scalping proclamation to 'take or destroy the savages.'" Assembly co-chair Terry Paul "said the government's decision to recognize the dark legacy of early settlers was an example of 'reconciliation in action'" (MacDonald, 2020, June 30).

Clearly, large organizations, like Land O' Lakes, PepsiCo, Mars, B&G Foods, the Newfoundland and Labrador Liquor Corp. and Dreyer's, were sensitized (to varying degrees) to their audiences. For the Conservative politicians in Ottawa, their promotion of Sergeant Prince has broad hints of politicking (a reasonable question might be: "Wouldn't it simply be better to address the issues that Indigenous Peoples are facing, here and now, rather than grandstanding by putting an Indigenous face on Canadian money?"). For the federal Fisheries and Oceans ministry, the decision to work in concert with the Assembly of Nova Scotia Mi'kmaw Chiefs seemed like a positive step forward. Altogether,

FURTHER DISCUSSION: LAND O'LAKES

The removal of the Indigenous woman (named "Mia") from its butter containers by Land O'Lakes was met with both accolades and criticism; Indigenous rights supporters hailed it as a major (and long-overdue) step forward; from long-time fans of the Mia-logoed butter brand, there came harsh disapproval and the threat of boycotts. The company, in making what could only be a conscious (especially given the high profile of racist imagery related to advertising and sports teams), tone-deaf and colour-blind decision to avoid talking directly about Mia's removal from the packaging, and instead choosing to talk about the Mia-free, farmer-focused landscapes and trees of its reworked packaging, was criticized for missing "a chance to highlight a crucial discussion on indigenous representation in popular culture." A Smithsonian Institution curator lamented the fact that Mia was suddenly airbrushed out of existence, leaving lake, trees and skies on the package, and leaving no room for a company-led discussion of the impact of stereotyping in the presentation of images of Native Americans (Wu, 2020, April 28).

these organizations demonstrated an awareness of their audiences, and they knew what would strike a receptive chord.

For public relations practitioners, getting to know your audience or potential business partner is essential, as is working to develop strong connectivity. That starts with listening, and moving into a dialogue where viewpoints can be shared, because talking with diverse publics and asking tough questions can help ensure that they, in fact, accurately and ethically reflect the diversity of the communities they serve. The lack of honest, open dialog in the early stages of planning often can hinder an organization's ultimate success. "Paying attention" might prove ineffective, however, unless an organization takes formal steps to embed a focus on diversity across the organizational structure. Doing so begins with leadership (Mundy, 2015).

SOLUTIONS AND APPROACHES

In 2015, the Truth and Reconciliation Commission (formed to examine, analyze and understand the historical experiences of First Nations members in Canada's residential schools) delivered 94 Calls to Action, ranging from issues of Child Welfare through to Language and Culture, Health, and Reconciliation. For schools of communication and media, the Truth and Reconciliation Commission called for "education for all students on the history of Aboriginal peoples, including the history and legacy of residential schools, the United Nations Declaration on the Rights of Indigenous Peoples, Treaties and Aboriginal rights, Indigenous law, and Aboriginal-Crown relations" (Truth and Reconciliation Commission, 2015). For media, there is a need to find more effective representations of Indigenous communities, because, as Alexander Kim noted in *Possible Canadas*:

> Canadian journalism has a long history of repeating a particular kind of story about Indigenous people. This story legitimizes Canada as a nation that, unlike the United States, was established with fair treaties, not bloody conquest. This story teaches that Aboriginals willingly gave up their lands, eager to be civilized by white colonizers. This story tells us Indigenous peoples are innately inferior, they are stubbornly resistant to progress and their cultural extinction is a just cause (Kim, 2015, November 13).

Many post-secondary institutions across Canada have worked to Indigenize their curricula, and this has included hiring more Indigenous faculty, creating programs that centre the learning experience around discussion of Indigenous knowledge, and in some cases generating elective or mandatory programs focusing on the history of First Nations, Inuit and Métis, with a notion to counter the "damaging historical fictions and obfuscations [that] have cycled through generations of students in this country" (MacDonald, 2016).

There is a strong component of deontic justice in the Commission's calls to action, the application of deontic justice being the ability to take a moral stand on issues and to appreciate moral standards not from a position of self-interest but for the fact that moral justice stands alone and unhindered by external influences. Tindall (2005) says there is a need for public relations practitioners to engage in deontic justice, it is all the more essential in public relations

> because there is a need for honesty and fairness in organizational transactions and a need for individuals to take an active role in addressing the inequalities seen in society. For those of us who work in public relations, the focus of public relations should center on our organization's actions to the publics with whom we communicate. As the members of our organization charged with being the social conscience, the public relations

practitioner must ponder over the obligations toward the publics known and unknown to the organization and consider what is fair and equitable treatment for publics who may not have access, privilege, money, voice, or rights (Tindall, 2005, p. 515).

In an interview conducted by Dana Oancea, public relations professor James Grunig speaks to the need for the application of both deontic justice and teleology, or "ethics based on the consequences of actions. ... Teleological theories, in other words, judge rightness or wrongness by the ends to which decisions lead—their consequences." With teleology, "ethical public relations professionals ask what consequences potential organizational decisions have on publics. They also ask what beneficial consequences (or solutions to their problems) that publics ask from an organization" (Grunig, in Oancea, 2020, June 15).

Many organizations and institutions—especially post-secondary schools—are keeping these moral components of deontic justice and teleology in the forefront as they work to decolonize and Indigenize their work processes and corporate worldviews; according to Indigenous Corporate Training (2017, March 29):

Decolonization is about shifting the way Indigenous Peoples view themselves and the way non-Indigenous people view Indigenous Peoples. ... Decolonization requires non-Indigenous Canadians to recognize and accept the reality of Canada's colonial history, accept how that history paralyzed Indigenous Peoples, and how it continues to subjugate Indigenous Peoples. Decolonization requires non-Indigenous individuals, governments, institutions and organizations to create the space and support for Indigenous Peoples to reclaim all that was taken from them.

Indigenization has particular applications for (but is not restricted to) post-secondary learning environments, and is a process that seeks to engage people within mainly academic settings in an effort to promote an inclusive atmosphere that accepts, promotes and celebrates the contributions of Indigenous knowledge in a proactive way:

Power, dominance and control are rebalanced and returned to Indigenous peoples, and Indigenous ways of knowing and doing are perceived, presented, and practiced as equal to Western ways of knowing and doing. Examples of Indigenization in education could include the inclusion of Indigenous readings (and) adoption of Indigenous learning approaches in the classroom. For non-Indigenous people, there can be a fine line between Indigenization and cultural appropriation and it is important to seek appropriate guidance while recognizing that guidance can come from many sources (Queen's University, 2020).

According to Rodrigues and Raby (2019), "Professors should acknowledge the special insight and perspective of their Indigenous leaders on campus and let them guide and advise on all matters related to Indigenizing curricula." In my own teaching at Durham College, the place I start is the campus's First Peoples Indigenous Centre, where I have met extensively with Indigenous coaches Peggy Forbes and Julie Pigeon. In the business world, as Joseph (2018) notes, Friendship Centres are a good place to go for information on local Indigenous communities and treaty land. It is essential to approach Indigenous topics in a humble way, emphasizing and underscoring a desire to learn; for instance, every semester I take public relations students to the Indigenous Centre, and I ask the coaches to guide us in understanding elements of Indigenous life, in a sharing atmosphere, where we all continue to learn as we go; the questions that come up are often wide-ranging and lead to even more questions (which is good!) and the approach is one of openness, a sense of community, and building a receptive connectedness to others.

In approaching the topic of Indigenization, it is essential to use proper terminology. Indigenous trainer Bob Joseph, in tackling the sometimes complicated issue of using proper names, acknowledges that sometimes "Indian" is still used, for instance when referring to the Indian Act, as in a "status Indian" (someone registered under the Indian Act) or to historical writing, where the term "Indian" is applied, though it needs to be clearly delineated in quotations. Today, the generally accepted term is "Indigenous" when referring to the original inhabitants of North America: the First Nations (First Peoples may also be used), Inuit (Inuk is the singular form, Inuuk for two people, Inuit for three or more), and Métis; it is also essential to capitalize these nouns (Joseph, 2020).

On a cautionary note, it is also important that consultation be done *in concert with*—not separate from—Indigenous communities, or else there is risk of doing more harm than good. Sometimes the most well-intentioned efforts are marred by white saviourism or the white saviour complex: the apparent need for white people to use their social power to help People of Colour; it is a form of white privilege that suggests that *only those from the mainstream have the answers to problems.* As Métis lawyer and teacher Chelsea Vowel said in an interview for the University of Alberta Faculty of Law blog, "even attempts at reconciliation can be so informed by white saviourism—there's this belief that maybe Indigenous peoples should be consulted but that we don't understand how things work in the real world. It's always, 'that's a great idea, but...' so Indigenous people are saying what they need but then the restraints come in and chip away the original vision so much that we no longer recognize what's been created! ...I also think that our vision gets filtered through a non-Indigenous understanding that ultimately takes what we're saying and changes it into something completely different" (Vowel, 2018, March 19).

While the media and the public often focus on the realities of a violent and difficult past and present in the relationships between Indigenous Peoples and the mainstream, success stories, stories of hope and inspiration, abound, and we need to pay attention to them. For example, Indigenous Guardian programs speak to protecting the land and water, at the same time engendering and nurturing values that make Indigenous communities whole and self-determining:

> Indigenous guardians have been on the front lines of the response to the COVID-19 pandemic in their communities: they've been monitoring who is entering their communities, delivering groceries and firewood to Elders and carrying on field research when outside scientists couldn't travel.... Steve Ellis, northern Canada program lead for MakeWay (formerly Tides Canada) takes that a step further. He believes guardians should be considered as just one element of a broader move towards First Nations stewarding their own lands, not simply acting as stand-ins for public government (Thomson, 2020, June 26).

And in Standing Rock (Sacred Stone Camp), North Dakota, the "first annual Sovereign Sisters Gathering brought together women and their allies to talk about how to oppose the current industrialized economy and establish a new model, one in which Indigenous women reclaim and reassert their sovereignty over themselves, their food systems, and their economies" (Barnett, 2019, August 24).

As the promise of a future where sharing is emphasized unfolds, organizations working to build economic ties to Indigenous communities—and individuals from the mainstream whose job it is to build links, work with and develop an understanding of Indigenous communities—must also be keenly aware that they are building social ties, and they have a responsibility to show that they care enough about a project to learn more than just a little something about the community beforehand. For example, in the 1990s, when I was writing and editing a business magazine for the Ontario government, I had an assignment to visit and write stories on three businesses being run by the Rainy River First Nation, in Emo, west of Fort Frances, Ontario. The businesses were operated in conjunction with mainstream business people from Emo and Fort Frances. I was just becoming aware of the issues surrounding relationships between First Nations and governments, and about local history and culture, and while I strived to learn more, I lacked knowledge as I came into the community. Thank goodness my hosts were accommodating! They answered my questions with patience and kindness, took me for tours of their operations, showed me their cultural centre, and accommodated me as I gathered the raw data and information I needed to put together what I thought was a decent story. The humbling lesson I learned was that I needed to dig around and do my homework *at the front end*. Doing your preparatory work is essential!

The same is true for any business venture. For instance, the Canadian Wind Energy Association says that as you look at the political landscape before a project, in addition to the three levels of government, you must develop an understanding of the local First Nations with whom you will work. For instance, ask:

> Who are the elected Chief and Council? Who are the Hereditary Chiefs? What is the First Nation's governance structure and decision-making process? How do they make laws? Are they treaty nations? What agreements do they have in place with the federal or provincial government that may be relevant to your project (for example, consultation agreements and resource management agreements)? What are the positions on wind energy development? (Canadian Wind Energy Association, 2017, p. 8).

Rigorous planning is essential, and the community engagement strategies you create must consider "both individual and organizational approaches to the community's cultural and political issues, planning your verbal and nonverbal communications with care" (Joseph and Joseph, 2019, p. 84). As well, proper training is essential, especially ensuring that "Indigenous awareness training is provided to all staff/managers ... (and) consider enrolling your organization in the Progressive Aboriginal Relations (PAR) program of the Canadian Council for Aboriginal Business" (pp. 84–85).

It also helps to be connected to Indigenous public relations sites, in order to develop a better understanding not just of the issues, but to *see these issues* from the perspective of those most seriously affected by them. For example, the Assembly of First Nations' (AFN) communications website publishes the views and commentary of the AFN. In June 2020, following the death of George Floyd (which we discussed in an earlier chapter, and an event that resonated deeply with many Indigenous commentators) and the continued police violence against First Nations Peoples in Canada, AFN published a commentary from its National Chief Perry Bellegarde, in which Chief Bellegarde noted that

> Canadians cannot ignore the dangerous parallels that exist in how Canadian police officers interact with people of different ethnicities and how a distressingly high percentage of First Nations men and women end up either injured or dead at the hands of the people we expect to help and protect us… Let's spare ourselves another futile debate over whether systemic racism exists in Canada. There have been countless reports over the past 50 years, and the conclusion is always the same: First Nations face systemic racism in every aspect of life and from every institution of Canadian society. This is a fact (Bellegarde, 2020, June 15).

CASE STUDY
THE TIM HORTONS "TEENAGE PRANK" THAT SPARKED OUTRAGE

Clearly, the continuing history of systemic discrimination doesn't help move the cause of reconciliation forward. In 2007, a non-Indigenous teenage worker at a Tim Hortons donut shop in Lethbridge, Alberta, decided to put a sign in the window saying "No Drunken Indians Allowed." What the shop first likened to a "teenage prank" led to calls for a boycott of the franchise, then an apology from the teenager, her suspension from Tim Hortons and re-education about the company's harassment policies, an apology from the teen to two First Nations staffers at the franchise, and finally a corporate letter of regret to the Lethbridge area Blood Tribe (Walton, 2007, May 30).

According to King (2012), "for as many people who called in to radio shows or wrote letters to the Lethbridge Herald to voice their outrage … there were almost as many who expressed their support for the sentiment [on the sign in the window]. … I lived in Lethbridge for ten years, and I can tell you with as much neutrality as I can muster that there were many more White drunks stumbling out of the bars … than there were Native drunks" (p. 187). Thompson (2009, January 1) said in an article outlining the work of the Alberta Human Rights Commission that

> people seemed to have felt no reluctance to freely sound off about the sign at Tim Horton's [the brand name was spelled with an apostrophe at the time]. The public expressed a wide range of opinions on radio call-in shows and in letters to the editor. Nearly 200 messages were posted at the online news forum topix.com. Online … the responses were blatantly hateful. A sampling: "How much longer are you going to sit in limbo living on handouts and pouting because you got your asses kicked 100 years ago?" "I think we have given enough to their cause. It's bad enough that they take our hard earned dollars now they are asking for the change in our pockets.… You want your traditional lands then go back to the traditional way of living. Get rid of your cars and housing. Live in tee-pees and follow the wildlife around like you used to do." "The problem isn't racism, it's the drunk natives." "They blew their chance a long time ago … sympathy has run out … tired of seeing them walking around the streets all drunk looking like victims etc." (Thompson, 2009, January 1).

In 2014, Tim Hortons announced the Horizons initiative. According to a news release, Horizons was a plan to "develop relationships with Aboriginal communities, and to create awareness of the diverse Aboriginal people within Canada" (Tim Hortons, 2014, April 22). Plans included sustainable, community-based programs and "Tim Hortons has worked with Millbrook First Nation to develop education for the Tim Hortons Family regarding 'issues and opportunities facing the Aboriginal community.'… Online training is available for Restaurant Team Members and Corporate Employees." The company stated that in 2012, 42,000 staffers (referred to as "team members") completed "Aboriginal awareness training and since 2009, over 200,000 Restaurant Team Members have completed this training." While a visit to the Horizons site in 2020 found no mention of any community-based programs in conjunction with local Indigenous communities, Tim Hortons continued to promote initiatives supporting Indigenous communities. In October 2023 it stated in a news release that its third annual Orange Sprinkle donut campaign raised $1 million for Indigenous organizations and "[o]ver the past three years, Tim Hortons and its guests have raised over $3.6 million for the Orange Shirt Society, the Indian Residential School Survivors Society, and New Pathways Foundation in Quebec" (Tim Hortons, 2023, https://www.newswire.ca/news-releases/more-than-1-million-raised-for-indigenous-organizations-during-tim-hortons-third-annual-orange-sprinkle-donut-campaign-845429743.html).

Case Study Questions

1. If you were working for Tim Hortons in a communications capacity, what recommendations (in addition to the actions already taken) would you make to the company with respect to improving its standing with the Indigenous community? Outline the proactive steps that could be taken to build a stronger sense of community.
2. As a communicator, your feelings are important. In reading the case study, how do the details of what happened make you feel? How will this influence the way you approach communications in future?
3. What do you think the Tim Hortons owner said in the statement of apology to the Blood Tribe?
4. In adopting a stance of deontic justice (as discussed by Tindall, 2005), outline the steps you would take if you were working for:
   a. The City of Lethbridge
   b. The Alberta government

To that end, create a 250-word statement for a representative of each of these jurisdictions, focusing on the general premise of working with Tim Hortons and the Indigenous community and their support for building a positive future together with the Indigenous community.

PROFILE

BOB JOSEPH, FOUNDER AND PRESIDENT, INDIGENOUS CORPORATE TRAINING INC.
Since 1994, Bob Joseph has provided training on Indigenous relations and has assisted both individuals and organizations, in Canada and internationally, with a focus on building strong relationships with Indigenous communities. His clients include governments, financial institutions, small and medium-sized enterprises, and Indigenous Peoples.

The author of the best-selling *21 Things You May Not Know about the Indian Act* and *Indigenous Relations: Insights, Tips and Suggestions to Make Reconcilia-*

tion a Reality, Joseph has worked as an associate professor at Royal Roads University and has guest lectured at other academic institutions. His educational background is in Business Administration and International Trade and he is a certified Master Trainer. An Indigenous person and status Indian (registered with the federal government under the Indian Act), he is an initiated member of the Hamatsa Society; he also inherited a chief's seat in the Gayaxala (Thunderbird) clan, the first clan of the Gwawa'enuxw, one of 18 tribes that make up the Kwakwaka'wakw.

Getting Started

Bob Joseph first got a hint of his future as an Indigenous relations consultant and trainer while working as a fishing guide on British Columbia's Campbell River in the early 1990s. He was guiding a corporate human resources manager from BC Hydro, the province's major electricity distributor, on a three-day fishing trip, and "an hour into the first day, he said to me, 'this is fun, but what do you do when you're not doing this?' I said that my wife had just graduated from law school, and if I wanted to stay married I would have to move to Vancouver and find a job." Discussion about Bob's business administration background led to many questions from the manager, and the trip itself turned into what would become a long but pleasurable job interview.

"At the end of the trip he said 'Hey, if you're looking for a big company to work for, and if you're done with fishing, give me a call.'" Later in the year Joseph did just that, and the phone call led to a job where he gained experience in a variety of departments at BC Hydro. During his tenure he was brought into his manager's office and asked, "'how would you like to do presentations?' It turned out that I would be taking responsibility for a cross-cultural communications course. That was the beginning, and I started out training BC Hydro employees."

Later on, Joseph was contacted by a railway company executive and asked if he would train their personnel. "They ended up being our first customer when we went out on our own," he says.

Bridging the "Miscommunication" Gap

Joseph recognized early on that a lot of miscommunication between the mainstream culture and Indigenous communities is based on a lack of awareness of history. For instance, "Canadians, when I started doing the awareness training, were largely unaware of residential schools. I remember at a session early on, we were talking about residential schools and at the break a woman came up to me and said, 'I can't believe what you're telling me. I can't believe my church would be involved in something like that. I can't believe the RCMP were taking the kids away.' I told her I could provide information to back up what we were saying. I said, 'We're not making up history here!' " The woman's refusal to accept Canada's history gave Joseph some impetus to think about ways to reach people in the mainstream.

Joseph says that one of the exercises he is uses is to "challenge people to come up with a short sentence that tells the history of Canada … and we get references to Columbus, and Jacques Cartier," and later on, events like Confederation, the Oka Crisis and Ipperwash, and "we see a colonial picture that is taking shape. The problem is that when cultures come together they don't have the same history. If I have a group of 30 Indigenous people I get different answers [than from white participants], and I realize that between 1867 (Confederation) and 1982 (the Canadian Constitution) the picture is completely different to different people."

If you change a word you can change the way people see their history, Joseph notes. As he developed his coursework, he looked around at events in Canada where there was discord between Indigenous groups and government. For instance, at the time, Indigenous Peoples in the U.S. were protesting Columbus Day, but a review of Canadian events yielded little that was similar in tone and urgency. Events like the Calgary Stampede or Olympic events were generally accepted by Indigenous Peoples, and Joseph found that "they're not upset about celebrations. They will share their cultures." So he looked at perceptions of history, and focused on the Christopher Columbus story of "discovering the 'new world.'" It was known that "the western hemisphere could support 80 to 120 million before Columbus arrived, and so a reasonable estimate was that 100 million people lived on the continent when Columbus arrived—it is really hard to understand how you could 'discover' a place when somebody is already there."

The question that Joseph will put to cross-cultural training participants is " 'what would you change the phrase to, if it is agreed that Columbus never actually 'discovered' America?' The word that usually comes up is 'Columbus arrived,' and so it's really about picking words" and having an understanding of cross-cultural perspective, and Joseph works to move dominant white cultural worldviews gently away from a set of culturally embedded perceptions by talking about language, and asking participants to take a look at their own culture while considering the insights of Indigenous cultures.

The Safe Space

The creation of a safe space, where people are respected and can feel free to talk openly about difficult or sensitive subjects, is essential. "In a safe space you can ask questions," Joseph says. "It is about creating a safe space and tackling the elephant in the room and understanding how different people see the same thing in different ways." He will take on big questions like the stereotypes associated with Indigenous Peoples, for example the idea that they were "living short, brutish lives, or did not want to work, or were not paying taxes. I give people the wiggle room to confront and understand the issues."

The topic of consultation with Indigenous groups is a favourite one, and Joseph emphasizes that mainstream businesses must understand that no matter what their focus is on—and he provides a hypothetical example of a $400 million bridge upgrade—if the business is active in an area that is also home to an Indigenous community, all the critical paths and Gantt charts in the world will not move the project forward if an Indigenous community has any objections, and delays will add to the costs.

Mainstream businesses that fail to recognize or research the legal power held by Indigenous groups could find themselves in a deep financial hole; a $400 million project over time could balloon to twice that amount, if for instance the local Indigenous community calls for a judicial review over not being consulted on the project—and that could tie things up for anywhere from three to five years. Better, says Joseph, "to spend 50 to 70 million dollars on procurement and employment, in keeping with the Indigenous relations mandate, and make sure you're not killing their fish, or hurting their caribou or the environment, or whatever they are concerned about, and you will end up making the right decisions at the front end. Everybody will like you in that context. Otherwise they will call you a champion of the colonial government, they will call the media and create blockades," and the outrage felt over the refusal to recognize Indigenous rights will resonate within communities and with the greater general public.

Clarifying the History

Today, the federal government and Indigenous communities have a "nation-to-nation relationship. It is a recognition that they are different, and recognizes that we are all treaty people." Joseph says it is good to remember three dates in Canadian history: 1763, 1867 and 1982. He cites the Royal Proclamation of 1763 (issued by King George III) and its description of an equal partnership, a nation-to-nation relationship between the British Crown and First Nations. But over the next hundred years that relationship changed, and by Confederation, Canada assumed the role of "caretaker" of all matters relating to Indigenous Peoples. By 1982 and the signing of the Canadian Constitution, it was a "nation-to-nation relationship again," says Joseph. "Section 35 of the Canadian Constitution guarantees Indigenous rights, and it has a lot of political power."

The 1982 patriation of the Canadian Constitution by the Canadian government entrenched existing Aboriginal and treaty rights. As Joseph notes in Indigenous Relations: "Aboriginal Rights should never be referred to as special rights. There is no alternative phrase for Aboriginal Rights. Indigenous Peoples differentiate themselves from others in the body politic in that they did not come here from anywhere.... Aboriginal Rights—or Section 35 rights, as they are sometimes called by Indigenous Peoples—are human rights" (Joseph and Joseph, 2019, p. 122).

The point of Joseph's teaching, he says, is to try to "get Canadians to understand three distinct periods of history, first with the nation-to-nation relationship, and then we totally flip-flopped, and now we're back to nation-to-nation. Once [people] realize that, they can see there's a tremendous amount of political and economic power at play." He takes a moment to emphasize that most Indigenous communities are not against development. "They've never been against development, but it must be development that is not at the expense of for instance the caribou or the water or land. And that benefits not only Indigenous Peoples, but everybody."

The Future: Reconciliation

Reconciliation "is the future for this country," adds Joseph. "We're trying to create a space for people to hang onto their identity, a very broad human rights space. I'm bullish on reconciliation. When it comes to reconciliation—how do we address this notion? It takes a long time. With reconciliation we could be looking at it taking a thousand years."

There are no short-term solutions. But three major points of focus for Indigenous Peoples are self-determination, self-reliance and self-government. As Joseph says in Indigenous Relations, "self-determination is the right to decide who your people are. A major objective of Indigenous Peoples, country-wide, is to gain control over who belongs to their nation.... [Self-reliance is] the ability to participate in the political and, more importantly, the economic mainstream, without having to rely on federal funding. ... [Self-government involves a] change "to a system in which the governing leaders are elected and accountable to their people, instead of to the Crown" (Joseph and Joseph, 2019, pp. 49–50).

Language issues figure highly and are part of an urgent effort to regain cultural autonomy and rebuild cultures and this will be achieved through enhancements to learning systems for Indigenous Peoples, such as improved access to language education, says Joseph. For instance, 48 percent of Cree People will speak Cree on a daily basis and "the worst cases ... are where it's 6 percent to 7 percent of people speaking the language. At less than 50 percent linguists will tell you that you will lose your culture—that is what I mean by the urgency of finding negotiated solutions."

A very positive sign is that "colleges and universities are decolonizing and Indigenizing," he says. "It doesn't have to be a complicated process. To decolonize, we change discovery to arrival and it opens up the door to discussion of issues like Manifest Destiny and *terra nullius* [or "nobody's land," which along with the Doctrine of Discovery, was used to justify colonization and the subjugation of Indigenous Peoples worldwide]. In Canada in 50 years, if most of the educational institutions are doing reconciliation education, we will be in a much better position to deal with our relationships. It all boils down to respect."

LET'S CHECK IN!

In this self-assessment, you will be asked to think about your attitudes toward, and knowledge of, the subject matter discussed in this chapter. On a scale of 1 to 10 (1 being low/disagree/doesn't apply, 10 being high/fully agree/fully applies) rate your knowledge and comfort level. These statements may also be used as dialogue starters in group discussion.

Statement	Your Score
I already knew a great deal about this topic before this chapter.	
I would be very comfortable discussing this topic in a group.	
I will look for future opportunities to expand my knowledge on this subject.	
This information is unlike what I have learned in the past.	
This subject matter is essential to my development as a public relations professional.	
This subject struck an emotional chord with me.	

KEY TERMS

Cultural appropriation: the term for a situation when a dominant culture obtains goods or other items from another culture that is experiencing oppression.

Cultural genocide: the destruction of the way of life and the culture of a people.

Decolonization: the act of recognizing and accepting the reality of Canada's colonial history; supporting and creating space for Indigenous Peoples to reclaim what was taken from them.

Deontic justice: the ability to take a moral stand on issues on the basis of moral justice being independent from self-interest and unhampered by external influences.

Discourse colonization: the effect of discourse within one domain (the colonized domain) being changed by the application of another domain's (the dominant culture) discourse.

Double consciousness: the state of feeling marginalized in a society that continually benefits only certain members and promises benefits that can never be achieved by the oppressed.

Exoticism: the trend to treat people who are "different" as singularly unique and outside the margins of the mainstream, and emphasizing their "otherness."

Indigenization: a process that engages people in promoting an atmosphere of inclusivity that celebrates and promotes Indigenous knowledge.

Land acknowledgement: a sign of respect and recognition, usually made at the beginning of a meeting, in which people acknowledge the land that they are on, and the ties that Indigenous Peoples have to that land.

Reconciliation: the restoration of harmony between Indigenous and non-Indigenous people.

Residential schools: a form of cultural genocide that lasted 110 years, during which 150,000 Indigenous children were taken from their families; 6,000 disappeared or died while in residential school custody.

Teleology: the judgement of rightness or wrongness based on the end results of moral decisions.

Truth and Reconciliation Commission: a commission created to examine, analyze and understand the historical experiences of members of First Nations in Canada's residential schools. When it completed its mandate in 2015, it delivered 94 Calls to Action.

United Nations Declaration on the Rights of Indigenous Peoples (UNDRIP): a 2007 declaration of guarantees for Indigenous Peoples, including nationality, cessation of violence, protection from the dispossession of Indigenous lands, restitution for property taken, and self-determination.

White rage: the "pushback" from white people, focused on getting back social control, every time People of Colour make significant advances towards equal rights.

White saviour complex: the implied need for white people to "help" People of Colour; a form of white privilege suggesting that only white people have answers to problems, and that People of Colour need "saving." A popular trope in movies, such as *The Blind Side, Freedom Writers, The Help,* and *To Kill A Mockingbird* (movie and book).

QUESTIONS TO EXPLORE

1. Think about the issue discussed earlier about racist brand packaging. Look around and find:

   a. A consumer product that fails the awareness test.

   b. A sports team that also fails the test.

2. Analyze the respective organizations' positions with respect to branding. Are there news articles or website news releases that try to explain the reasons for continuing to use the current logo? Why do you think organizations will continue to use racist iconography to sell their products? Suggest ways that the organizations in question can improve their images.

3. What do you think the major responsibilities are for non-governmental organizations with respect to Indigenous communities? Briefly list them, with an explanation as to what aspects drew you to make your decision.

4. Look back at the examples of federal government attempts to recognize Indigenous achievements (i.e., putting war hero Sergeant Prince on the five-dollar bill, or the renaming of the icebreaker *Cornwallis* with the assistance of Nova Scotia Mi'kmak Chiefs). What are your thoughts on these initiatives? Are they sincere? If not, what can be done to improve the relationship between the federal government and Indigenous communities?

EXERCISE

CREATE A BRIEFING NOTE AND A LAND ACKNOWLEDGEMENT

A briefing note is a useful tool for communicators to use when presenting information to decision-makers. Briefing notes are often used in corporate communications environments and allow senior staff to gain an effective snapshot of an issue. They are used mainly in government, but may also be used in academic institutions and the private sector. According to Queen's University's Andrew Graham, the briefing note gets to the point: it must be reader-focused and should use simple, straightforward language, and active words (subject-verb-object sentence construction); it is designed to help its readers do one or more of the following: prepare for a meeting; make a decision; generate a response; obtain an update or information on an initiative (Graham, n.d.). Briefing notes are usually about 300 words in length. Briefing notes have headings:

Subject: the briefing note's title.

Purpose: the "why" of the briefing note.

Summary: the facts of the matter at hand, and explanations that support the briefing note's purpose.

Recommendations: the briefing note will provide a recommended course of action.

Conclusion: a summary of what has been said; it is short and is focused on providing an accurate synopsis of the points that have been covered.

The task: You are manager of communications for the soon-to-be-opened (and fictional) South Prairie Community College in Medicine Hat, Alberta. The college, which will offer a variety of work-ready education and training programs, in the arts, sciences, skilled trades and technology, is set to have an official opening in four months, with an initial intake of 2,000 students, and with plans to grow the college to 10,000 students and 2,000 full- and part-time staff and faculty over the next 10 years. The campus is set on 12 hectares (30 acres) of land, and is partially supported by grants from the federal and provincial governments as well as funding from several private sector industry supporters. There is a pre-existing plan in place for the college to work closely with Indigenous business and community groups on shared skilled trades training initiatives as well as cultural activities, and there are plans for a $2 million Indigenous Culture

Centre planned for the site. Plans are for Indigenous students to comprise up to 20 per cent of the student body within the first five years.

You are tasked with the responsibility for connecting with the local First Nations community, and setting up an event for college officials and First Nations. Do the following:

- Create a 300- to 400-word briefing note outlining a plan for the event, with a theme of reconciliation, cooperation and community. Think about the key contacts in the First Nations community you need to connect with, as well as those in the municipal and provincial governments.
- Create a land acknowledgement that expresses the college's recognition of the local First Nations and their connection to the land.

Information on First Nations may be obtained through the Government of Canada (https://www.rcaanc-cirnac.gc.ca/eng/1307460755710/1536862806 124) or through the National Association of Friendship Centres (https://www. nafc.ca/en/).

REFERENCES

Aboriginal Legal Aid in BC (2020). Gladue Rights. https://aboriginal.legalaid.bc.ca/courts-criminal-cases/gladue-rights

APTN (2015, June 2). Canada guilty of cultural genocide against Indigenous peoples: TRC. *APTN National News.* https://www.aptnnews.ca/national-news/canada-guilty-cultural-genocide-indigenous-peoples-trc-2/

Bains, C. (2020, June 19). B.C. emergency room staff allegedly guessed Indigenous patients' alcohol levels. *HuffPost.* https://www.huffingtonpost.ca/entry/hospital-racism-alcohol-levels-indigenous-bc_ca_5eed330ec5b6d30db989a105?ncid=fcbklnkcahpmg00000001&fbclid=IwAR2wEMk9XxXYvRKvCVP8oODcJyCWZqz9kGEAj1_0y6vy2ADjPtuRB_pUQUo

Barnett, T. (2019, August 24). How the women of Standing Rock are building sovereign economies. *Yes!* https://www.yesmagazine.org/environment/2019/08/24/standing-rock-women-indigenous-independence-economy

Beattie, S. (2020, June 30). Sergeant Tommy Prince, Indigenous War Hero, Deserves To Be New Face Of Canada's $5 Bill: MPs. *HuffPost.* https://www.huffingtonpost.ca/entry/sergeant-tommy-prince-indigenous-war-hero-deserves-to-be-new-face-of-canadas-5-bill-mps_ca_5efb4e84c5b6acab2847629f?ncid=fcbklnkcahpmg00000001&fbclid=IwAR2rFkT5nP1UmomEVM0Ebz7_NSG9eCXq2z6bjKw_L_VIcqK7c0M7qt6Rr2A

Bellegard, P. (2020, June 15). Let's just admit it: Canada has a racism problem. Assembly of First Nations. https://www.afn.ca/news-media/

Betasamosake Simpson, L. (2011). *Dancing On Our Turtle's Back*. Winnipeg: Arp Books.

Bradley, D. (2020, June 18). Breakfast briefing: 5 things for PR pros to know on Thursday morning. *PR Week*. https://www.prweek.com/article/1686965/breakfast-briefing-5-things-pr-pros-know-thursday-morning

Bryden, J. (2020, June 22). Senate committee says Beyak has learned, recommends suspension be rescinded. *Toronto Star*. https://www.thestar.com/politics/federal/2020/06/22/senate-committee-says-beyak-has-learned-recommends-suspension-be-rescinded.html

Canadian Encyclopedia (2020). Mike Harris. *Historica Canada*. https://www.thecanadianencyclopedia.ca/en/article/michael-deane-harris

Canadian Press (2020, July 2). First Nations coalition rejects recommendation to lift Sen. Beyak's suspension. *Kamloops This Week*. https://www.kamloopsthisweek.com/first-nations-coalition-rejects-recommendation-to-lift-sen-beyak-s-suspension-1.24163939

Canadian Press (2018, May 13). Five things to know about the Gladue decision. *National Post*. https://nationalpost.com/pmn/news-pmn/canada-news-pmn/five-things-to-know-about-the-gladue-decision

Canadian Press (2014, September 23). Sask. dangerous offender's appeal dismissed. *CTV News*. https://regina.ctvnews.ca/sask-dangerous-offender-s-appeal-dismissed-1.2020284

Canadian Wind Energy Association (2017). Wind Energy Development: Best Practices for Indigenous and Public Engagement. Canadian Wind Energy Association. https://canwea.ca/wp-content/uploads/2017/11/canwea-bestpractices-engagement-web.pdf

Centennial College (2020). Indigenous Acknowledgement. Centennial College. https://www.centennialcollege.ca/indigenous-education/indigenous-acknowledgement/

Cooper, J. (2020, August 21 and August 14). Interviews with Andy Peekeekoot and Matthew Behrens.

Cooper, J. (2020, July 17). Interview with Bob Joseph.

Coulthard, G. (2014). *Red Skin, White Masks*. Minneapolis, MN: University of Minnesota Press.

Davin, N. (1879, March 14). *Report on Industrial Schools for Indians and Half-Breeds*. http://www.canadianshakespeares.ca/multimedia/pdf/davin_report.pdf

Delgado, R. & Stefancic, J. (2012). *Critical Race Theory*. New York: New York University Press.

Department of Indian Affairs (1911). Annual Report, 1911. http://central.bac-lac.gc.ca/.item/?id=1911-IAAR-RAAI&op=pdf&app=indianaffairs

Durham College (2020). Respect the Land (Indigenous Land Acknowledgement). Durham College. https://durhamcollege.ca/student-life/student-services/diversity/diversity-and-inclusion-2/respect/respect-the-land

Edwards, P. (2021, January 9). First Nations chiefs say Harris honour opens "unhealed wound."

Toronto Star, p. A16.

English, J. (2009). *Just Watch Me: The Life of Pierre Elliott Trudeau, 1968-2000*. Toronto: Alfred A. Knopf Canada.

Freire, P. (2005). *Teachers as Cultural Workers*. Cambridge, MA: Westview Press.

Freire, P. (2000). *Pedagogy of the Oppressed*. New York: Bloomsbury Academic.

Government of Canada (2020, August 6). Criminal Code of Canada: Dangerous offender definition. Justice Laws Website. https://laws-lois.justice.gc.ca/eng/acts/C-46/section-753.html

Government of Canada Department of Justice. (2018, February 14). Principles respecting the Government of Canada's relationship with Indigenous peoples. https://www.justice.gc.ca/eng/csj-sjc/principles-principes.html

Government of Canada (2017, June 6). Questions and Answers—Cleaning up the Criminal Code, Clarifying and Strengthening Sexual Assault Law, and Respecting the Charter. Department of Justice. https://www.justice.gc.ca/eng/csj-sjc/pl/cuol-mgnl/qa2-qr2.html

Graham, A. (n.d.) GOV talk: Get to the point. *Queen's University, School of Policy Studies*. https://www.queensu.ca/sps/sites/webpublish.queensu.ca.spswww/files/files/Resources/Gov-Talk/1_1Style%20Guide%20.pdf

Harries, K. (2005, November 29). Harris uttered slur, Ipperwash inquiry told. *The Globe and Mail*. https://www.theglobeandmail.com/news/national/harris-uttered-slur-ipperwash-inquiry-told/article985817/

Imperial Oil Canada (2020). Indigenous Engagement. Imperial Oil. https://www.imperialoil.ca/en-CA/Sustainability/Working-with-communities/Indigenous-engagement#Corporate-commitment

Indigenous Corporate Training Inc. (2017, March 29). A Brief Definition of Decolonization and Indigenization. Indigenous Corporate Training Inc. https://www.ictinc.ca/blog/a-brief-definition-of-decolonization-and-indigenization

Isador, G. (2019, August 9). Indigenous artists tell us what they think about land acknowledgements. *Vice*. https://www.vice.com/en_ca/article/j5yxbd/indigenous-artists-tell-us-what-they-think-about-land-acknowledgements

Joseph, B. (2020). *Indigenous Peoples: A Guide to Terminology* (e-book). Indigenous Corporate Training Inc. https://www.ictinc.ca/hubfs/ebooks/eBooks%202020/Guide%20to%20Terminology-1.pdf

Joseph, B. & Joseph, C. (2019). *Indigenous Relations*. Port Coquitlam, BC: Indigenous Relations Press.

Joseph, B. (2018). *21 Things You May Not Know About the Indian Act*. Port Coquitlam, BC: Indigenous Relations Press.

King, T. (2012). *The Inconvenient Indian*. Toronto: Anchor Canada.

Londoño, E. & Casado, L. (2020, May 2). Brazil's Indigenous Tribes Fear Ethnocide. New York *New York Times International Edition* (included in Toronto Star), p. 3.

Lyubansky, M., & Eidelson, R. (2004). Revisiting Du Bois: The relationship between African American double consciousness and beliefs about racial and national group experiences. *Journal of Black Psychology*, 2: 1–23. doi: 10.1177/0095798404268289

MacDonald, M. (2020, June 30). Federal government working with Indigenous group to rename icebreaker CCGS Edward Cornwallis. *The Globe and Mail.* https://www.theglobeandmail.com/canada/article-ottawa-working-with-indigenous-group-to-rename-icebreaker-ccgs-edward/

MacDonald, M. (2016, April 6). Indigenizing the academy. *University Affairs.* https://www.universityaffairs.ca/features/feature-article/indigenizing-the-academy/

Macdonald, N. (2016, February 18). Canada's prisons are the 'new residential schools.' *Maclean's.* https://www.macleans.ca/news/canada/canadas-prisons-are-the-new-residential-schools/

Manuel, A. & Derrickson, R. (2017). *The Reconciliation Manifesto.* Toronto: James Lorimer & Co. Ltd.

McKenzie-Sutter, H. (2020, June 30). 'Old Sam' logo to get makeover due to concerns about racist branding. *Toronto Star,* p. A8.

McQuigge, M. (2020, June 26). Only 16 per cent of participants pass quiz on prominent racialized, Indigenous Canadians. *CTV News.* https://www.ctvnews.ca/canada/only-16-per-cent-of-participants-pass-quiz-on-prominent-racialized-indigenous-canadians-1.5001140

Mehta, D. (2016, April 18). Federal gov't, Ontario First Nation formally sign settlement over Camp Ipperwash. *CBC.* https://www.cbc.ca/news/indigenous/first-nation-final-agreement-ipperwash-1.3541003

Merchant, S. (2018, January 8). Emory professor to explore concept of white rage. *University of Michigan Recmorinord.* Ann Arbor, MI: University of Michigan. https://record.umich.edu/articles/emory-professor-explore-concept-white-rage/

Morin, B. (2020, June 11). Alberta's Bill 1 is 'racially targeted': First Nations leaders. *HuffPost.* https://www.huffingtonpost.ca/entry/alberta-bill1-indigenous-first-nations-protests_ca_5ed9a4e9c5b6d90c9a5bb3b4?ncid=fcbklnkcahpmg00000001&fbclid=IwAR3acRptZ-pGGmixZT8Jvu-I0oqNtD961vUCAsZXmZhC-48mglfw7KL0WN4

Motion, J. & Lietch, S. (1996). A discursive perspective from New Zealand: Another world view. *Public Relations Review*, 22(3): 297–309. http://www.ask-force.org/web/Discourse/Motion-Discursive-Perspective-1996.pdf

Mundy, D. (2015, October). Diversity 2.0: How the public relations function can take the lead in a new generation of diversity and inclusion (D&I) initiatives. *Research Journal of the Institute for Public Relations*, 2(2). https://www.instituteforpr.org/wp-content/uploads/2nd-gen-diversity-2.pdf

Neylan, S. (2018, June). Canada's dark side: Indigenous Peoples and Canada's 150th celebration. *Origins.* https://origins.osu.edu/article/canada-s-dark-side-indigenous-peoples-and-canada-s-150th-celebration

Newman, J. (2020, June 19). 'Eskimo Pie' owner calls brand 'derogatory', vows to change name. *Rolling Stone.* https://www.rollingstone.com/culture/culture-news/eskimo-pie-owner-change-name-1017968/?fbclid=IwAR0QlHoHk7GjVPdKtuzqERm72rymyrVJHnZU3top2XthLsmz4IiEuJgKA8c

Oancea, D. (2020, June 15). Prof. James E. Grunig: Moral behavior does not occur without study, research and reflection. *PR Romania.* https://www.pr-romania.ro/articole/etica-in-pr/2321-prof-james-e-grunig-moral-behavior-does-not-occur-without-study-research-and-reflection.html

Olito, F. (2020, June 17). 7 food logos and mascots that didn't age well. *Insider.* https://www.insider.com/outdated-food-logos-mascots-2019-3

Order of Ontario (2020). Order of Ontario details. *Government of Ontario.* https://www.ontario.ca/page/order-ontario

Queen's University (2020). What is decolonization? What is Indigenization? Queen's University Centre for Teaching and Learning. https://www.queensu.ca/ctl/teaching-support/decolonizing-and-indigenizing/what-decolonizationindigenization

Reach Out.com (2020). Why cultural appropriation isn't cool. *Reach Out Australia.* https://au.reachout.com/articles/why-cultural-appropriation-isnt-cool

Rodrigues, A. and Raby, P. (2019). Lessons learned from Indigenizing a media program at an Ontario community college. *College Quarterly, 22* (1). http://collegequarterly.ca/2019-vol22-num01-winter/indigenizing-a-media-program.html

Salomons, T. (2009). Ipperwash Crisis. *Indigenous Foundations, UBC.* https://indigenousfoundations.arts.ubc.ca/ipperwash_crisis/

Schenck, P. (2020). White rage: The unspoken truth of our racial divide. *Friends Journal.* https://www.friendsjournal.org/book/white-rage-unspoken-truth-racial-divide/

Shahzad, R. (2017, July 15). What is the significance of acknowledging the Indigenous land we stand on? CBC. https://www.cbc.ca/news/canada/toronto/territorial-acknowledgements-indigenous-1.4175136

Statistics Canada (2017, October 25). Aboriginal peoples in Canada: Key results from the 2016 Census. Statistics Canada. https://www150.statcan.gc.ca/n1/daily-quotidien/171025/dq171025a-eng.htm

Stolen Lives: The Indigenous Peoples of Canada and the Indian Residential Schools/Historical Background (2020). "Until There Is Not a Single Indian in Canada." Facing History and Ourselves. https://www.facinghistory.org/stolen-lives-indigenous-peoples-canada-and-indian-residential-schools/historical-background/until-there-not-single-indian-canada

Talaga, T. (2018). *All Our Relations*. Toronto: House of Anansi Press.

Thomson, J. (2020, June 26). Australia just committed $650 million to Indigenous rangers programs. Should Canada do the same? *The Narwhal*. https://thenarwhal.ca/canada-indigenous-guardians-investment-covid/

Thompson, S. (2009, January 1). Our Human Rights Commission: A threat to free speech, or a safeguard of human dignity? *Alberta Views*. https://albertaviews.ca/human-rights-commission/

Tim Hortons (2014, April 22).Tim Hortons: Aboriginal Relations. *Transforming Relations: A Collaborative Collection*. https://www.timhortons.ca/important-information-about-the-current-public-health-environment

Tindall, N. (2005). The role of justice in public relations ethics: A personal philosophy of public relations. In Watson, M. (Ed.), *8th International Public Relations Research Conference Proceedings*, 513–522. Miami: University of Miami. file:///C:/Users/John/Downloads/The_Role_of_Justice_In_Public_Relations%20(1).pdf

Trudeau, J. (2020, June 21). Statement by the Prime Minister on National Indigenous Peoples Day. Office of the Prime Minister of Canada. https://pm.gc.ca/en/news/statements/2020/06/21/statement-prime-minister-national-indigenous-peoples-day

Truth and Reconciliation Commission of Canada (2015). *Calls to Action*. Winnipeg: Truth and Reconciliation Commission of Canada. http://www.trc.ca/websites/trcinstitution/File/2015/Findings/Calls_to_Action_English2.pdf

Vekil, M. (2017, March 29). The Indigenous: An overlooked emerging market in Canada's backyard. *Apex*. https://www.apexpr.com/indigenous-overlooked-emerging-market-canadas-backyard/

Von Scheel, E. (2020, June 25). Kenney speechwriter called residential schools a 'bogus genocide story.' *CBC*. https://www.cbc.ca/news/canada/calgary/paul-bunner-residential-school-bogus-genocide-1.5625537

Vowel, C. (2018, March 19). An interview with Chelsea Vowel. *University of Alberta Faculty of Law Blog*. https://ualbertalaw.typepad.com/faculty/2018/03/an-interview-with-chelsea-vowel.html

Walton, D. (2007, May 30). Tim Hortons serves up some controversy. *The Globe and Mail*. https://www.theglobeandmail.com/news/national/tim-hortons-serves-up-some-controversy/article17996444/

Woods, M. (2020, June 11). Erin O'Toole's 'Take Back Canada' slogan prompts plenty of questions. *HuffPost*. https://www.huffingtonpost.ca/entry/erin-otoole-take-back-canada_ca_5ee2af10c5b67f9eb84b61c9?ncid=fcbklnkcahpmg00000001&fbclid=IwAR0mDFskQDiyFj9PemAfoSzlfsItn73XXUfWGLfaL2xnMircOU-l1lfcxwA

Wu (2020, April 28). Land O'Lakes drops the iconic logo of an Indigenous woman from its branding. *Smithsonian Magazine*. https://www.smithsonianmag.com/smart-news/mia-land-olakes-iconic-indigenous-woman-departs-packaging-mixed-reactions-180974760/

Zofi, Y. (2017, June 6). 5 strategies for effective cross-cultural interactions. *International Association of Business Communicators*. https://www.iabc.com/5-strategies-for-engaging-in-effective-cross-cultural-interactions/

CHAPTER FOUR

The Thin Blue Line:
The Police, the Law, Race and Dialogue

OBJECTIVES OF THIS CHAPTER

This chapter is designed to help develop an understanding of diversity issues in policing through:

- Discussing the history of police oppression and systemic discrimination within police forces;
- Considering the "idealized" versus "reality-based" nature of policing;
- Examining the culture of police communication and the changing face of police/community interaction;
- Looking at the relationship of police forces with Indigenous communities;
- Reading a case study examining police brutality against a First Nations Chief and its outcomes;
- Reading a Q&A with Dr. James Walsh, Professor, Criminology and Justice, Ontario Tech University;
- Completing exercises to create communication products based on policing-related issues.

THE DRIVE AND DAFONTE MILLER

On a semi-regular basis for the last few years, I have awakened at 1 a.m., gotten dressed, made a Thermos of coffee and left the house by 1:30 to go to a 2 a.m.-to-6 a.m. volunteer shift at a local distress centre. I drive along mostly deserted streets, and on just about every drive I will pass a police car going in the opposite direction, or I will come up next to one at a set of lights. Nothing

120

happens. The police glance over at me; the light changes; they go their way, I go mine. That is my privilege of being a white male, a privilege that I, as a white person, can be blithely unaware of, unless and until I think of it. Understanding it is part of the process of coming to terms with the fact that my existence is often not defined by what happens to me, but by what *doesn't happen*. That is the nature of white privilege. Peggy McIntosh wrote of this in her research into the "invisible backpack" that white people carry around with them, and that backpack includes privileged treatment in stores, schools, and workplaces, along with assumptions of biological superiority; "scholars of white privilege write that white people benefit from a system of favours, exchanges, and courtesies from which outsiders of color are frequently excluded" (Delgado and Stefancic, 2012, p. 88). As McIntosh, who is white, says, "I have come to see white privilege as an invisible package of unearned assets that I can count on cashing in each day, but about which I was 'meant' to remain oblivious. White privilege is like an invisible weightless knapsack of special provisions, maps, passports, codebooks, visas, clothes, tools and blank checks" (McIntosh, 1989).

I have had Black male students and acquaintances who spoke openly, without hesitation, of their experiences with the police: the random pull-overs (one student was stopped 15 times in one year alone), the request/demand for identification, questions about where they are going and why—the constant need to be accountable for one's own *being*. And so it made me think of, among other situations, the case of Dafonte Miller. Early on December 28, 2016, Toronto police officer Michael Theriault and his brother Christian were in the garage of their parents' home in Whitby, Ontario. They heard a noise they took to be people breaking into their father's truck. They came out of the garage, saw two people flee, and took off after one of them, 19-year-old Dafonte Miller. Eight months later, the two brothers were jointly charged with aggravated assault, and each was separately charged with obstruction of justice. At their trial, the court heard that the brothers, who are white, had tackled Miller, who is Black, and Miller was beaten with a metre-long length of pipe. Miller tried to get help from a nearby home, and the homeowner, a high-ranking fire services official, called 911, thinking the fracas was a gang beating. The trial revolved around who had the pipe (Michael Theriault claiming he took it from Miller). Miller was so badly beaten he lost an eye. Neither Theriault brother sustained a serious injury; the brothers claimed in court that they acted in self-defence (Bascaramurty, 2020, June 25).

In June 2020, Christian Theriault was acquitted on both charges. Michael Theriault was found guilty of assault, which was "included" in the aggravated assault charge, and not guilty of aggravated assault and obstruction of justice (relating to alleged inconsistencies in how the brothers' story was told to police). The Criminal Code defines aggravated assault as assault that "wounds, maims, disfigures or endangers the life of the complainant" (though in this case the Crown brought the charge only on the first three grounds). It carries a sentence of no more than 14 years. Obstruction of justice involves acting "to obstruct, pervert or defeat the course of justice in a judicial proceeding" (Government of Canada, Justice Laws Website, 2020a, 2020b). Michael Theriault was subsequently sentenced to nine months in jail, followed by a year of probation, and a five-year weapons prohibition (The Canadian Press, 2020, November 5). In his decision, the trial judge wrote that he was "mindful of the need to carefully consider the racialized context within which this case arises." But, he added, his task was to "decide whether the Crown has proven the offences charged beyond a reasonable doubt." He concluded that reasonable doubt remained about when exactly the aggravated assault that cost Miller his eye occurred, and whether that was when the defendants could still claim to be acting in self-defence, however "razor thin" that justification might be. But in the next stage of the assault, "[t]he already razor thin self-defence justification evaporates," hence Michael Theriault's conviction on the assault charge (Christian Theriault had stepped away from his brother and Miller by then, and thus was not a party to Michael Theriault's assault on Miller) (*R. v. Theriault, 2020 ONSC 3317*).

Michael Theriault appealed his conviction, but it was upheld by the Ontario Court of Appeal (*R. v. Theriault, 2021 ONCA 517*). As well, four Durham Region police officers who investigated the incident faced disciplinary action: one pled guilty to neglect of duty, and a disciplinary tribunal found that three others committed professional misconduct for showing "pro-police bias."

Miller's beating happened not far from my home, and I didn't have to wonder as to how the community at large would respond. There were protests outside the court building in Oshawa as people awaited the verdict, there was commentary in the media and people were asking why this was happening. And some people were saying that things hadn't changed at all, that the verdict was shocking but not unexpected, given society's systemic racism.

In *The Fire Is Upon Us* (an account of the debates on race between African-American writer James Baldwin and white conservative William F. Buckley), Nicholas Buccola writes of James Baldwin's contention that people of colour are ghettoized, and that the police are charged with the responsibility of managing them; thus the police commit a great moral crime, being both the purveyors of oppression and a threat to the personal safety of Black Americans (Buccola, p. 332). Just as citizens have demanded inquiries into the treatment of Canada's Indigenous population, demands are there too for greater oversight of police departments, for defunding the police, for eliminating some police services (the ones with guns) in favour of a community approach. In the relationship between police services and African-Americans, James Baldwin called for the empowerment of civilians, through review boards, that would keep police services accountable (Buccola, 2019, p. 332). Baldwin's recommendations came *as early as the 1960s*. The demand for inquiries into police wrongdoing has continued in the U.S., Canada, and other jurisdictions for decades.

In the aftermath of the Theriault trial, the Toronto Police Services Board (TPSB) issued a news release, which said, in part:

This case has highlighted significant issues regarding public trust, accountability and transparency in policing, even more so during a time where, here in Toronto and in places around the world, these issues are at the forefront of public discussion and dialogue. In this case and others, the Board is committed to ensuring that where we can learn from what occurred, and make improvements to our training, procedures, systems and culture, we will do so. Our priority must always remain serving and protecting the public in an effective and equitable manner, incorporating community expectations and experiences into the work that we do. We must continue to focus on this priority, informed by cases like this one, as well as by a genuine and sustained desire to move forward, in partnership with the community (Toronto Police Services Board, 2020, June).

Note the key phrases in the above item: issues of public trust and accountability during a time of extensive public discussion; a commitment to learn and to make improvements; a priority of serving and protecting the public; incorporating community expectations into the work; focusing on serving and protecting the public; partnerships with the community.

Alvin Fiddler, Grand Chief of Nishnawbe Aski Nation, said "the Canada I live in is reflective of a long-standing broken relationship between racialized and Indigenous peoples and the policing and justice system ... the Canada that Dafonte Miller lives in is one where a teenage Black man is so viciously beaten by an off-duty police officer ... that he loses an eye.... Three years later [when the case came to trial], Dafonte was essentially put on trial ... revictimized by a justice system determined to criminalize racialized people" (Fiddler, 2020, July 1). And as columnist Royson James said in reference to the verdict: "If we want citizens to respect the law we must abide by the social contract: all of us—ALL—are equal before the law and protected by the law. What is the point of acknowledging the anti-Black racism convulsions engulfing North America and the world, and then ignore its effect in the courtroom?" (James, 2020, July 2).

In the wake of the verdict, one might well feel that Dafonte Miller's accountability (why was he walking the streets in the early morning hours?), culpability (was he stealing from cars?), and existence as a teenage Black man were as much on trial as Michael Theriault. Some in the justice system, like lawyer Annamaria Enenajor, saw the trial as only the beginning for policy change, but not the place for change itself to happen, understanding that "the trial judge was limited by the evidence that came before him … [yet] as a Black criminal defence lawyer, I'm particularly sensitive to police brutality. I remain haunted by the image of Dafonte calling for help, his left eye burst and oozing. … What we need is a federal commission of inquiry into police use of force against racialized and Indigenous people in this country" (Enenajor, 2020, July 2).

The existence of police violence against citizens, whether they be protesters, suspects or people in the proverbial wrong place at the wrong time, is not questioned any more, for evidence continues to pile up through social media on a regular basis; in July 2020, the non-profit newsroom ProPublica reviewed 400 protest videos with human rights and police foundations experts "and found troubling conduct by officers in at least 184 of them. In 59 videos, pepper spray and tear gas were used improperly; in a dozen others, officers used batons to strike noncombative demonstrators; and in 87 videos, officers punched, pushed and kicked retreating protesters, including a few instances in which they used an arm or knee to exert pressure on a protester's neck" (Buford et al., 2020, July 16).

In the aftermath of the Theriault case, an investigation conducted by Ontario's police complaints watchdog, the Office of the Independent Police Review Director, found that then–Toronto police chief Mark Saunders (who retired on July 31, 2020) failed to fulfill his duty as police chief by not contacting the Special Investigations Unit, yet he would avoid any charges of professional misconduct because he was not informed of the situation for several months after the incident (Gillis, 2020, August 8). In early August 2020, interim Toronto Police Chief James Ramer, in his first public news conference, issued a public apology to Dafonte Miller, acknowledging the broken trust "between the police, Dafonte Miller, and the broader community" and outlined his new duties as "addressing better ways to deal with mental health-related calls, implementing body-worn cameras and identifying and eliminating systemic anti-Black racism within the service" with a focus on transparency and accountability (Goodfield, 2020, August 6).

Apologies can be problematic for organizations. Legal concerns, the fact that an organization is apologizing for something that was caused by one or only a handful of people within it, or the perception of a loss of power associated with the apology (the apology may turn the table on the power structure) often cause organizations to hesitate in apologizing. What is essential is that organizations apologize as soon as possible after the event in question, make sure the organization is sincere, and, if change is promised, state that it will be delivered on, and then follow through. "While a good apology can restore balance or even improve relationships, a bad apology can make things much worse" (Schweitzer et al., 2015, September).

Noting that the interim police chief acknowledged that trust was broken and promised proactive initiatives as part of his job, along with accountability and transparency (all strong public relations statements, and we will see similar themes presented throughout this chapter), the apology was not accepted by Dafonte Miller, who, through his lawyer, Julian Falconer, called the move a "public relations exercise" (Farooqui, 2020, August 7). Following this, the police service responded with a second statement via the media, essentially sticking to its core messages of transparency, accountability and community engagement: "The Toronto Police Service stands by the comments yesterday by Chief Ramer and regrets the impression left with Mr. Miller; that was not our intention. We continue to take accountability for our actions and acknowledge mistakes when they are made. Our focus will be on working with the community to improve our relationship and seek legitimate ways of rebuilding trust and transparency" (CTV News, 2020, August 8).

That inquiries into the brutal treatment of People of Colour by police are necessary is not out of the question either—the challenge is what will be done with the results of such inquiries? Will they be used to make substantive change or just collect dust? In a society where Black men have to fear for their lives at the hands of the police, clearly the status quo has failed—or *succeeded*, if the point of a society is to oppress a significant number of its members. Perhaps a news conference, soft-edged words, the drawing together of a commission, the interviews, and a subsequent report, are all the status quo needs in order to say "our job is done. We have done some good." Yet there will always be the hard experiential data that counter the ideals. In 2015, activist and writer Desmond Cole wrote of his experiences as a Black man in a *Toronto Life* article, of being stopped more than 50 times by police for nothing other than his race, and the pressure and angst it created: "As my encounters with police became more frequent, I began to see every uniformed officer as a threat. The cops stopped me anywhere they saw me, particularly at night" (Cole, 2015, April 21). Cole's experiences were not out of the ordinary but the norm. It is hard to rationalize the notion of a "few bad apples"—the common phrase for the violent actions of police officers—when you think about the social infrastructure of society itself. As Ta-Nehisi Coates says in *Between the World and Me*, a book written to his son: "It is truly horrible to understand yourself as the essential below [relegated to the bottom rung] of your country. It breaks too much of what we would like to think about ourselves.... You have been cast into a race in which the wind is always at your face and the hounds are always at your heels" (2015, pp. 106–107).

POLICING AND THE COMMUNITY: THE IDEALIZED STATE OF BEING

The hackneyed phrase "actions speak louder than words" is appropriate when talking about police services. On websites, on paper and in news releases, police services serve an idealized function ("This is how we want to be seen by our publics") and their mottos reflect that—**To Serve and Protect** (Toronto Police Service; Thunder Bay Police Service); **Leaders in Community Safety** (Durham Regional Police Service); **A Safer Community Together** (Peel Regional Police Service); **Beyond The Call** (Vancouver Police Department); **Leading and Partnering in our Community to Serve and Protect** (Halifax Regional Police). In following the news about police shootings, tasering, and general abuse (to be fair, keeping in mind that there is always "good news" as well, where the police have certainly fulfilled their mandates in accordance with the mottos outlined above), I am reminded daily that we increasingly live in a society where too often our lack of empathy for others is on display; it calls to mind University of California public policy professor Robert Reich's position about the loss in recent years of the sentiment of the "common good," which is a sense of camaraderie and commonality that helps people to feel a sense of community: "Most people are hardwired for some degree of cooperation with and compassion toward others. Human beings would not have survived on earth to this point were we entirely selfish. Some people are downright heroic.... Yet the common good is no longer a fashionable idea. The phrase is rarely uttered today.... It feels slightly corny and antiquated if not irrelevant" (Reich, 2018, pp. 13–14).

And here we are in a society where selfishness reigns, where the myth of the rugged individual reigns supreme, where chasing our own ends at the expense of others is spun out to the nth degree, and where we may tacitly, unthinkingly accept our role in the subjugation of others in the pursuit of those goals.

But "a society characterized by generalized reciprocity is more efficient than a distrustful society, for the same reason that money is more efficient than barter" (Putnam, 2000, p. 21), and what may be lost today is the sense of community (regained, perhaps, through visits to social media sites, or farmers' markets, book clubs, discussion groups, or, increasingly, to public protests, where people can gather with others who have like-minded goals).

How important is trust? Zuboff (2019), notes that social trust as a whole is on the decline and this has been exacerbated by the rise of social media; she cites a U.S. General Social Survey study of attitudes demonstrating that while Americans' feelings of others' trustworthiness was steady in the 1970s (at 46 percent) and 1980s (50 percent), "that percentage steadily declined to 34 percent in 1995.... The late 1990s through 2014 saw another period of steady and decisive decline to only 30 percent. Societies that display low levels of interpersonal trust also tend to display low levels of trust toward legitimate authority" (Zuboff, 2019, p. 384). This may explain society's fractured sense of community. The 18th-century Genevan political theorist Jean-Jacques Rousseau said that the "common good" among citizens was achieved through a "mutual concern that is focused on (among other things) their common interests in physical security and property. This form of mutual concern requires each citizen to respond to an attack on the body or property of a fellow citizen as if this were an attack on her own body and property" (Hussain, 2018, February 26). According to Broom (2019),

> Community is understood in Rousseau's sense of a social contract: Each of us gives up some of our autonomy in order to receive advantages and help from others in a society. Community is a conceptual public "commons" in which each of us is given the advantages that come from living in a society (such as law, governance, order, protection from violence, security, specialization, and diverse services) in exchange for giving up some of our autonomy in the public space. That is, individuals are bounded in the public space (p. 80).

New Zealand criminology professor Philip C. Stenning refers in a 2004 report to the waves of migration that created a "Canadian kaleidoscope" of diverse groups, and this change "generated significant challenges for police. These include different attitudes towards government, law, justice, appropriate social order, interpersonal relations and child rearing, as well as a host of hitherto unfamiliar (and in some cases illegal) cultural and religious practices. The linguistic diversity of many of the new immigrants has presented additional challenges for police. Resistance to integration of immigrants has led to community tensions and the rise of openly racist groups, to which the police have been called upon to respond" (Stenning, 2004).

As such, police services exist in three parallel states: first, there is the state of the day-to-day, where police serve the public, often doing good work that gets little notice, but which is the reason why many police officers joined the force; secondly, there are the harsh speed bumps to understanding and equity that are a product of systemic racism in the system—arguably a plank in the infrastructure of western society: the violence, the racism (carding, random stops, demands for accountability), and the use of force that underscores the police force's role as a paramilitary unit of control; and finally there is the idealized version of policing that you see in news releases, on websites, in news conferences, and in the scripted quotes on the nightly news, and this version speaks to how police services *wish themselves to be seen*. Police use of social media creates both the potential for transparency and, in opposition, the use of social media by groups to scrutinize police actions. According to Walsh and O'Connor (2019):

> While social media augments the police's control over relations of visibility whether in regards to surveillance or information control it also unleashes countervailing forces and, in allowing new actors to enter the fold, unsettles these arrangements. Mapping this double movement accentuates key trends in policing, including the intensification of surveillance; growing investment in image work; community based participation and engagement; and the rise of countersurveillance, networked publics, and digital protest. Accounting for such dynamics not only illuminates the shifting social and technical environment in which policing occurs but also advances conversations regarding the capacity of digital tools to effectuate social and institutional change (p. 8).

That the police want to be seen in an empathetic light, and as a cornerstone of the community, is understandable, but tackling the realities takes some effort, and there has been an unwillingness to address some of the issues related to intercultural relations that have been deemed intangible or unreachable in the past. For instance, in 2018, the Ontario Human Rights Commission (OHRC) released the results of an inquiry into racial profiling and racial discrimination against Blacks by the Toronto Police Service:

> Between 2013 and 2017, a Black person in Toronto was nearly 20 times more likely than a White person to be involved in a fatal shooting by the Toronto Police Service (TPS). Despite making up only 8.8 percent of Toronto's population, data obtained by the Ontario Human Rights Commission (OHRC) from the Special Investigations Unit (SIU) shows that Black people were over-represented in use of force cases (28.8 percent), shootings (36 percent), deadly encounters (61.5 percent) and fatal shootings (70 percent). Black men make up 4.1 percent of Toronto's population, yet were complainants in a quarter of SIU (Special Investigations Unit) cases alleging sexual assault by TPS officers. (OHRC, 2018).

Racial profiling is defined as "any action undertaken for reasons of safety, security or public protection, that relies on stereotypes about race, colour, ethnicity, ancestry, religion, or place of origin, or a combination of these, rather than on a reasonable suspicion, to single out an individual for greater scrutiny or different treatment" (OHRC, 2020). The OHRC inquiry found serious "use of force infractions" and the report spoke to some attempts by previous police administrations to deal with the systemic issue of profiling and racism, and also called for an acknowledgement of the experiences of Blacks in Toronto, the public reporting of race-based statistics and the implementation of measures outlined in a report and action plan (OHRC, 2018).

The response to the findings, by former Toronto Police Chief Mark Saunders, himself a Black man, was measured, careful and non-committal. During an interview with the Canadian Broadcasting Corporation (CBC), Saunders acknowledged that racial profiling exists, but failed to answer questions focusing on the overrepresentation of Blacks in the sometimes violent encounters with police; he said that the force would review the OHRC's processes in putting together the report. He also said that he would have "no problems with the collection of race-based statistics," but added that "certain legal aspects of that process have to be explored first" and moved into the issue of the Black community not having trust in the police and emphasizing that improving the relationship was significant (CBC, 2018, December 11). (Note the use of the terms "certain legal aspects" and "explored." Saunders confronted the question, then blunted the impact of it, made his answer to it vague, and then moved on to softer messaging such as, and I am paraphrasing here, "overcoming the lack of trust" and "improving relationships").

A subsequent OHRC report in August 2020 said that "although Black people make up only 8.8 per cent of Toronto's population, they represent almost 32 per cent of people charged, while white people and other racialized groups were underrepresented. The report also found that only a fifth of all charges laid in that time frame resulted in a conviction, but charges against Black people were more likely to be withdrawn and less likely to result in a conviction, which the commission says "raises systemic concerns about charging practices." Police service change strategies for combatting anti-Black racism recommended by the OHRC included "the creation of an equity, inclusion and human rights unit, as well as anti-Black racism training and the implementation of a race-based data collection strategy" (Carter, 2020, August 10). A shift towards more equitable hiring would also appear to be a necessary move in the right direction, given that a Statistics Canada report released in December 2020 found that "police services around the country are overwhelmingly white and male. They still have low numbers when it comes to officers identifying as women, visible minorities and Indigenous" (Francis, 2020, December 9).

VISION, MISSION AND VALUES

Every police service has a service statement, or a vision/mission/values statement. For example, the Durham Regional Police Service, based in Whitby, Ontario, has this one:

Our Vision: To have the safest community for people to live, work and play.

Our Mission: As Leaders in Community Safety, we work proudly with all members of our community while holding ourselves accountable to improved effectiveness in everything we do. We proactively address future challenges while upholding our values.

Our Philosophy: We are a problem-solving organization that, in partnership with our community, addresses the root causes of crime, fear of crime and anti-social behaviour.

Our Values: Every member of the Durham Regional Police Service is committed to providing quality service in partnership with our community. While learning from each other, we will achieve excellence through pride, respect, understanding and ethical behaviour (Durham Regional Police Service, 2020a).

That community policing has been touted as a more receptive and ameliorative approach to policing is not new. Funk (2014), in *Community Police in Durham Region: Implications for Diverse Ethnic Groups*, sees community policing as "a law enforcement approach that has been used to connect police services with their respective communities. It has allowed police to be participative, accountable, and integrative in a localized context" that moves policing away from an aggressive or reactive posture (p. 1). Community policing is about dialogue, and the application of Grunig's two-way symmetrical model of communication (Grunig, 2013), where the flow of communication is a granular back-and-forth between parties, in this case the police service and citizens. Of course, we need to keep in mind the fluidity with which the term "community" is used; while he was U.S. president, Barack Obama revived a 1990s-era program called COPS (Community Oriented Policing Services) along with a war-on-drugs grant funding program (the Byrne program) and "these programs, despite their benign names, are responsible for the militarization of policing, SWAT teams, Pipeline drug task forces, and ... [a] laundry list of drug war horrors" (Alexander, 2012, p. 253).

From a historical perspective, Stenning (2004) says that "from the 1980's onwards, almost all of Canada's major police services introduced programs designed to bring police together with representatives of racial, ethnic, cultural and religious minority groups in the hope that police would understand the traditions and customs of such groups better, and that members of such groups would develop a more sympathetic understanding of police and the difficult jobs they are expected to do." The forms of these initiatives were generally twofold: cultural sensitivity training (often delivered by BIPOC representatives) and "minority community advisory or liaison groups with a mandate to advise police management as to the best ways to manage their relationships with such groups in the community." Yet the "add-on" nature of such programs (not sufficiently or consistently integrated into police training) meant that they were not often received with enthusiasm, and so their overall success was less than certain.

That has changed over the past decade through more focused efforts to train police in cross-cultural communication skills, and those skills are seen as key to the successful flow of dialogue between people; as Flavin (2018), notes, "law enforcement professionals need communication skills for a far greater number of populations and occasions than your average citizen. … If you've spent most of your time in one culture, it's hard to recognize the many different ways people communicate in body language and subtle conversational cues. If you were to suddenly step into a foreign culture, you'd realize in a hurry that people don't exactly say what they mean. There's a lot going on under the surface."

COMMUNITY POLICING

Building those communication links means being able to "establish trust and support from diverse ethnic groups, and not let the issue [at hand] exacerbate existing tensions. The community policing definition directly states that there needs to be proactive community initiatives to foster a positive working relationship" (Funk, 2014, p. 20).

For our purposes, community policing is the idealizing of the means and ways of helping people get along, all a good thing when it comes to policing. And necessary; Funk (2014) cited a study of Chinese Torontonians whose relationships with the police were strained due to a lack of police knowledge of their cultural backgrounds, underscored by an absence of understanding of both language and communication. This absence of connection leads to an erosion of trust, and "trust can be a very hard thing to earn in law enforcement—especially since officers tend to appear in a citizen's life when something has gone wrong. Law enforcement professionals need to be able to nurture trust and encourage everyone they work with to be as cooperative as possible. Think of situations where officers are interviewing people connected to a case—the information they gather can make all the difference in the world" (Flavin, 2018).

That trust can be improved upon by nurturing better communication across cultures. The Durham Regional Police Service in its 2020–2022 Equity and Inclusion Strategic Plan, states that it "is committed to communicating and fostering better relationships with communities across Durham Region, in a spirit of collaboration and trust-building" (Durham Regional Police Service, 2020b). The plan outlines five strategic commitments:

1. Total Engaged Community (equal engagement of all community members across all demographic categories)
2. Workforce Reflects the Region Demographically (attracting a skilled

workforce that reflects the community)

3. Leadership Reflects the Region Demographically (building a leadership team that reflects the community)
4. Diversity Competent Members (ensuring that the force's members develop the skills to better interact with the community through appropriate training and to apply those skills in an effective way)
5. Secure and Supportive Workplace (a commitment to develop and maintain a supportive, secure workplace) (Durham Regional Police Service, 2020b).

These commitments are significant to building relationships in a community where, according to Funk (2014), a deficiency of discourse between the community and the police "raises the question as to whether the DRPS has established contacts with the right groups, and whether these relationships encourage civilian participation. ... With respect to the DRPS, they had many partnerships within the community, but they did not offer an outlet for civilians to relay concerns about policing and crime" (p. 30). According to the Regional Municipality of Durham (2018), "in 2016, visible minorities comprised 27.1 percent of Durham's population, which represents an increase from 2011 (20.7 percent), 2006 (16.8 percent) and 2001 (12.4 percent). Respondents who reported being South Asian (8.6 percent), Black (8 percent), Filipino (2.3 percent) and Chinese (1.9 percent) comprise the largest groups of visible minorities" (p. 2).

The pamphlet-sized *DRPS Equity and Inclusion Plan* for 2020 to 2022 is a crisply written and clearly illustrated piece of upbeat, positive communications, from its image of an Indigenous police constable in traditional dress to its highlights of the previous plan (2017–2019). It contains commentary on support for the LGBTQ community, information on a past diversity recruiting symposium and previous hiring events at cultural festivals, an intergenerational dinner, a tribute during National Indigenous Peoples Day, and participation in Black History Month festivities (Durham Regional Police Service, 2020c).

Getting to this point—of reaching out and celebrating communities and diversity—is a long and detailed process; past reports from various police services speak to the necessity of a community approach to policing, and jurisdictions in and outside of Canada have spent decades working to figure out the nuances of effective police-community interaction. The U.S. Department of Justice, in 1994, issued a report entitled "Understanding Community Policing:

A Framework for Action," emphasizing that in a community policing scenario

> all members of the community become active allies in the effort to en-
> hance the safety and quality of neighborhoods. ... Reinvigorating com-
> munities is essential if we are to deter crime and create more vital neigh-
> borhoods. In some communities, it will take time to break down barriers
> of apathy and mistrust so that meaningful partnerships can be forged.
> Trust is the value that underlies and links the components of community
> partnership and problem solving. A foundation of trust will allow police
> to form close relationships with the community that will produce solid
> achievements. Without trust between police and citizens, effective polic-
> ing is impossible." (Department of Justice, 1994, p. vii)

Note that the term "trust" is repeated several times. Trust figures highly in all interaction between police and citizens, and it is a term that, along with other active terms that convey a strong sense of emotional commitment, like confidence, dependence, reliance, hope, and expectation, plays an important role in the communication of any organization's intentions. And in the borough of Lambeth in London, England, a 2000 report entitled "Policing Diversity in Lambeth (PDL)" found that while the relations between the community and police had improved over the previous 15 years, community confidence was below average for the time, due to a poor rating given police services by Black citizens, based on "a sense of being over-policed as crime suspects, and under-protected as crime victims. Stop-and-search, CS [riot control] spray, deaths in custody and the investigation of racially motivated crimes were all specific sources of concern." Added to that was low police morale, a perception by officers that the community didn't value their work, and feelings on the part of police personnel "that community concerns were overstated and based on rumour, anecdote and misunderstanding" (Spencer and Hough, 2000, p. v). A seeming bid to counter the low morale of police officers is the "Thin Blue Line/ Blue Lives Matter" movement, an effort by police unions and representative groups to instil pride in policing; within Canada's Royal Canadian Mounted Police, discussion and tension were triggered over the use of a symbol—in the form of a patch—worn by some officers that displays a thin blue line across a backdrop of a black-and-white Canadian flag. RCMP officials told members to stop wearing the patch symbol and the union gave its members the green light to wear it. Controversially, the symbol is "tied to the Blue Lives Matter

campaign, founded in the U.S. as a countermovement to Black Lives Matter....
[Blue Lives Matter] creates a "reverse discrimination narrative" that casts police as victims and shields them from accountability" (Beattie, 2020, October
13). According to York University researchers Mark Thomas and Steve Lufts,
the creation of "blue solidarity" movements among police officers serves to
repress efforts for racial justice and promotes the "othering" of marginalized
communities (Thomas and Lufts, 2020, January 23).

In Lambeth, a priority was placed on community and race relations training,
and the recruitment of People of Colour into police ranks, and the report recommended the development of a "coherent, organised, and effective communications strategy.... We have argued that poor communication and mutual misunderstanding lies at the heart of poor police/community relations. Strategies such
as PDL need to give attention both to internal communication within the police
and to communication between the police and community." Additionally, Spencer and Hough recommended the creation of a community and race relations
resource centre, underpinned by the work of the police services personnel actively connecting with spokespeople in the community who could help deliver the
message of understanding and cooperation (Spencer and Hough, 2000, p. 29).

Connecting with the community through diversity hiring has significant
consequences. Miles-Johnson (2019), in an Australian study of occupational
attitudes among police officers, found that "ethnic minority self-identified recruits are significantly more likely to be aware of negative influences on proper
conduct (such as lack of pride in their work, negativity of senior officers toward
policing diverse people, and likelihood of rule breaking) when policing members of diverse groups than other [white] recruits," pointing to (among other
findings) a conclusion that "recruitment of more ethnically diverse people into
policing is vital in Australia."

Community policing is difficult. It requires many meetings, much talk, and
plenty of sustained and repeated contact. It is not surprising perhaps that the
use of artificial intelligence has been suggested to either augment or even replace the *idea* of a community-focused policing infrastructure. Such a tactic
can lead to the "management" of populations through the use of electronic surveillance, an approach that was increasingly ratcheted up in terms of desire and
perceived wants-and-needs following the New York World Trade Center attack
of September 11, 2001. Since that time, the "Internet of things" (the interconnectedness of systems, surveillance, and data in a plethora of devices worldwide) has become a platform to design and activate instrumentarian systems,

which use data mined by artificial intelligence-driven infrastructure to develop models of the predictability of human behaviour, gather information for private sector and government clients, and manipulate the behaviour of people (Zuboff, 2019). Instrumentarian systems are widely marketed as a solution to crime, through the application of monitoring and tracking software:

In the U.S., local law enforcement has joined the queue of institutions seeking access to instrumentarian power. Surveillance-as-a-service companies eagerly sell their wares to local police departments.... One startup, Geofeedia, specializes in detailed location tracking of activists and protesters, such as Greenpeace members or union organizers, and the computation of individualized "threat scores" using data drawn from social media (Zuboff, 2019, pp 387–388).

We can now add Black Lives Matter protesters to the list that includes Greenpeace and unions, for U.S.-based Mobilewalla, "a marketing company that uses AI [artificial intelligence] to categorize phone users by race, gender and even religion, has now published a report using phone location data secretly collected during those protests" (Doffman, 2020, June 26).

While there is no mention of any accusations of criminality in tracking protesters, the point is: if artificial intelligence becomes the new face of law enforcement (or at least a major tool in its toolbox), what becomes of community policing? Does the "datafication of everything" create a more level playing field, or will it exacerbate already-existing tensions in communities? And what happens to people reaching out across cultures who seek to engender a genuine understanding of each other, and who seek to work together for the common good?

A TIP FOR CROSS-CULTURAL COMMUNICATION

Respect differences: "Just as you want to be respected for distinctive characteristics that you may bring to a group, others do as well.... Make it your business to learn at least one fact about every [group] member's culture. Assume a clear and welcoming tone when you communicate by phone. Demonstrate flexibility.... Respect different time zones when scheduling virtual meetings" (Zofi, 2017, June 6).

TRUSTWORTHINESS AND POLICING

When 62-year-old Ejaz Ahmed Choudry was confronted by police and shot dead while holding a knife in his apartment in Malton (a neighbourhood in the city of Mississauga, Ontario) on June 20, 2020, there were several facets to the situation that, had they come to light or been better understood, might have prevented Choudry's death: his history of schizophrenia, the fact that he spoke only Urdu and Punjabi, and the detail that the original call was made for mental health reasons, based on a family request to take Choudry to the hospital. His death led to calls for an inquiry into policing, especially in light of a 25 percent increase in mental health calls in Peel Region, the area where Choudry lived (White and Isai, 2020, June 22). Peel Police Chief Nishan Duraiappah delivered a clear statement of support for the family on social media:

I know and fully understand the grief within the community, and continue to extend my heartfelt sympathies to the family, friends and community of Mr. Ejaz Ahmed Choudry. The Service has been in constant dialogue with representatives of the family since the tragic events on June 20, 2020, that culminated in the death of Mr. Choudry. You have my commitment, as the Chief, and that of this entire organization, to continue to be accountable to the people we serve. ... We are also aware that there are issues regarding the mental health system and the appropriate response to individuals in crisis (Duraiappah, 2020, June 27).

Duraiappah's key phrases: "I understand the grief," "I extend sympathies," "constant dialogue," "you have my commitment," "you have the organization's commitment," "accountability." Also note that the police chief mentioned "community" twice.

Intersectionality was also at play in the death of Choudry. "Intersectionality addresses the inequalities, disadvantaged position and oppression of particular groups" (Merrill and Fejes, 2018, p. 7), and involves the tightly-interwoven confluence of factors that need to be disentangled (those factors often but not always created by the mainstream, white, dominant culture) in order to be understood fully (Carbado et al., 2013). In the education field, "most critical multicultural education discourses would consider the intersections of multiple social structures of race or culture, gender, class, sexual orientation, national origin, language and disability" (Tisdell, 2005, p. 164).

The intersectionality of the factors in the life and death of Ejaz Choudry (a

South Asian non-English speaking man with a history of mental illness) and the seeming unwillingness of the police services to understand and respond to these factors, created a scenario where the community's trust in the police was eroded, leading to a demonstration through the streets of Mississauga, demanding justice (Casey, 2020, June 23). Cao (2011), in a study of the confidence of People of Colour in police services, found that

> the impact of visible minorities and neighbourhood problems on confidence in the police should be of special concern to law-enforcement administrators. Even though many neighbourhood problems are not susceptible to control or even regulation by the police, citizens' perceptions of these problems provide salient information that appears to influence their confidence in the police. ... With several substantial visible minority groups in Canada nowadays, a single incident of injustice or even an incident of perceived injustice can have unexpected deleterious effects (pp. 18–19).

To say that racial profiling by police officers has been a contentious issue for decades would not be an understatement, and studies of the issue have been produced in quantity over the past several years. "In the policing context, concerns of racial profiling ... highlighted the contention that racial profiling in police work extends to many realms beyond the customary focus on traffic stop activity. Beyond police street checks there is concern that racial profiling is likely a factor in all areas of policing activity including surveillance, searches, charges, arrests, recruitment, and data retention," an invasive process that reaches deep into other areas of society, such as child welfare, education and health (Azmi, 2017, p. 7).

The collection of race-based data was denied in the past by colour-blind police departments, which served to hide—consciously or unconsciously, perhaps both—systemic racism. Foster and Jacobs (2017) found that

> race data collection efforts are an attempt to provide the tangible numbers that will enable police and community leaders to better understand their policing activities. Good data can help identify and verify issues, theories and perceptions ... proactively address issues ... measure progress and capitalize on opportunities ... gain trust, develop effective, respectful consultations, and secure the support of key decision-makers

and stakeholders. ... It is only with the collection of racial data by police that it will be possible to determine if racial profiling is a systemic problem for Canadian police services (p. 18).

Collecting data and proving what were once just unarticulated suspicions (or ignored pleas) gave credence to the lived experiences of People of Colour when encountering the police; "the thesis of police denial of racial profiling as a practice of deflection and neutralization embedded in a subculture of police and professionalism" (Reasons et al., 2016, p. 81) has been offered as a reason for discussion of this behaviour being suppressed. Meng et al. (2015), in a study of racial profiling of Black youth by police, found that in addition to stops for suspicion of gun-related crime and traffic infractions, "drug-related stop-and-searches of Black youth occur most excessively in neighbourhoods where more White people reside and are less disadvantaged, demonstrating that race-and-place profiling of Black youth exists in police stop-and-search practices" (p. 115). In a study of perceptions of police bias among Black youth, Owusu-Bempah (2014) found "perceptions of police bias to be particularly pronounced amongst Toronto's Black population ... marginalized Black youth in Toronto are treated as 'symbolic assailants' and thus subject to high levels of police surveillance, interrogation, harassment, and abuse. This is a sentiment shared not only amongst young Black men, but also amongst many of the Black police officers whose accounts are documented" in Owusu-Bempah's study (p. 226).

Police have a propensity for stopping Black youth who "look out of place" (also known as race-and-place profiling) and this speaks to the application of racial threat theory, which

> suggests that minority groups not only become a demographic threat to White people as their presence in the population grows, but also, in addition, if not in a subordinate position, they also threaten White socio-economic advantage, cultural and political dominance, and even feelings of superiority. The use of formal social control is therefore deemed necessary to reduce these threats (Meng et al., 2015, p. 136).

All of which calls to mind the situation with Dafonte Miller and Michael Theriault in Whitby in 2016: Miller looking "out of place" on a quiet suburban street in the quiet hours, the mostly white nature of the neighbourhood, and the suggestion of social control to reduce the implied threat.

Meng et al. (2015) stress that "police personnel should recognize that policing strategies should be based on sound research, have the support of the community, and ensure effective crime control while maintaining principles of democratic policing ... profiling or race-and-place profiling destroys public trust in and support for the police" (p. 139).

Citizen pressure and a wealth of effective studies (in Canada and elsewhere) offering proof of the effectiveness of race-based data collection led the province of Ontario's Special Investigations Unit to begin compiling such data in 2020: "Until now, the Special Investigations Unit (SIU)—which investigates interactions with police that involve serious injury, death or sexual assault—only collected and maintained data on the age and gender of people who were involved in investigations. But in April, the SIU was authorized to start collecting data on the race, ethnicity, religion and Indigenous identity of complainants and officers who are the subject of its investigations" (Carter, 2020, June 11).

In the wake of the trial of Michael Theriault and the death of George Floyd, then Toronto police chief Mark Saunders said in a *Toronto Star* article, speaking about the 2017 Transformational Task Force involving input from external and internal sources, that "I believe passionately that our [police] Service gets it right most of the time. We choose guardians, not warriors. Good policing starts with hiring the right people, but that's not enough" (Saunders, 2020, June 26). Saunders went on to list four areas of investment in change:

- The 2019 creation of an equity, inclusion and human rights unit, offering equity, diversity and inclusion training;
- A race-based data strategy, designed to identify systemic racism and assist in the creation of approaches to mitigate systemic discrimination;
- In-person training on race-based data, using curriculum drawing on a variety of expert resources;
- Anti-Black racism training, developed through a cooperative effort between the police force, academics and field experts (Saunders, 2020, June 26).

Additionally, police recruits must have a more rigorous academic education: American researchers Sereni-Massinger and Wood (2016) examined ways to improve cross-cultural competencies among police forces and found that given the rapidly-changing face of the U.S. social fabric, significant societal changes [are] demanding that law enforcement officers assume the role of problem solvers within their communities. ... To promote community and officer safety, officers should now be required to receive academy education focusing on critical thinking and interpersonal communication skills. Education focusing on problem solving should be required on an annual basis and be mandated for all continuing law enforcement certification purposes (p. 262).

Clearly, change is overdue. Szeto (2014), in research that examined policing diversity from the perspective of recruits of colour, found that "recruitment trends over the last 15 years reveal the continued lack of representation in the composition of Canada's population ... contrary to the popular belief that police services are aggressively diversifying. ... It is perhaps within this belief that a corporatized image embracing diversity has shaped the external perception of the organization" (p. 81).

There is an infrastructure within a society that continues to put a high value on whiteness. Historically, "in contrast to Blackness which symbolized dispossession, Whiteness symbolized freedom, meaning the ability to own one's own body and labor. Subsequently, Whiteness became among the most priceless of all properties" (Logan, 2011, p. 448). That has a profound effect on hiring and recruitment in police services; according to Szeto (2014), "the perceptions and experiences of minority police officers reveal cultural and emotional barriers towards the recruitment and experiences of visible minorities. Furthermore, minority police officers are challenged by a male, white, dominated police culture. Such a culture has led to experiences of heightened visibility, feeling devalued, stigmatization, isolation, sexism, and racism" (p. 81).

Going forward, the creation of a positive, fluid dialogue between police services and the communities they serve is essential and this can be helped through accommodation, a recognition of differences of culture, attitude and living that helps to bridge the gap between people; Barker et al. (2008) note that "accommodative practices should be sensitive to the values, customs, and needs of a wide variety of community members within a given culture (foreign, immigrant, mentally disturbed, elderly, homeless, executives, and so forth) without being stereotypical or adversarial. While community members often see 'the badge' rather than the person behind it, officers, too, should be person-centered" (p. 107).

THE CULTURE OF COMMUNICATION

How do police services communicate across cultures, and what has changed since the genesis of police forces in Canada in the late 1700s onwards, through the establishment of modern policing in 1829 and later, in Canada, the creation of a national police force, the Royal Canadian Mounted Police, in 1873, and on into the 21st century? Most importantly, what efforts are police services making to dialogue effectively with the publics they serve?

A U.S.-focused study by Gerspacher (2014) sees in some cases the police "subculture as one that glorifies aggressive and dogmatic tactics in policing, prioritizing crime fighting above order maintenance and service calls." Officers working within this subculture had little respect for the law, the court system and citizens, though these attitudes and behaviours were not reflected in *all* police officers (p. 7). This would suggest a communications milieu where messaging is delivered in a unilateral way, with little interchange or discussion between parties; such a means suggests an authoritarian state of action ("I know what is best for you. Trust me!") that is not synchronized with the expectations of communities seeking to provide input into how law and order is managed.

Such an approach runs counter to the textbook tenets of good policing. A 2001 British study by Jones and Newburn points to "policing by consent" as an effective (and accepted) means of reaching out to diverse cultural groups. Policing by consent is rooted in what are called "Peelian principles," criteria that established canons of modern policing and are usually attributed to Sir Robert Peel in the early 19th century, though their popularity is sometimes credited to policing textbooks developed in the early 20th century. Overall, the principles form a matrix for Anglo-American police comportment (Loader, 2014). These principles are centred on the idea that police actions should meet with (or be validated by) community approval. Sir Robert Peel, a parliamentarian and twice British Prime Minister, set the course for modern western policing with the establishment in 1829 of Britain's first police force (a model adopted by Commonwealth countries and the United States). Because "many British citizens feared that a standing police force would undermine democracy by enabling the state to suppress protest ... Peel sought to make a formal police force acceptable to the public by setting out nine principles that every new officer was to follow." These principles were focused on officers' understanding that their main responsibility was protecting the rights of citizens as well as fighting crime—essentially a means of curbing police powers through democratic responsibility (Adegbile, 2017, p. 2230).

Community-based policing has been a theme in police work for decades. In 1949, Cincinnati police department captain Raymond E. Clift wrote on police departments and public relations: "Of the many activities in police departments today few are more important than those which aim to better the press and public relations for the police service" (Clift, 1949, p. 667). According to Clift:

> The matter of maintaining good relations with the public involves … trying to satisfy all those elements of divergent likes and dislikes in the society. … One of the first of such classes the department must consider is the minority group or groups. Whether people in this category are Negroes, Asiatics, or Indians, or whether they are in a minority because of religious preference, they require careful consideration by the police and other public authorities. … This is not to say they are to be singled out and catered to, but only that they are to receive their equitable share of service from the public agencies. … It is only in emphasizing … equality that the police, or any other agency, can win and hold the support of minority groups" (p. 669).

For Jones and Newburn (2001) Peelian principles must engage community consultation within the framework of policing by consent, and consultation "needs to be seen as a process, rather than an event. The reality of police-community relations, indeed all social relations, is that they are in a continual process of negotiation and re-negotiation. Consultation has to be seen as a long term, ongoing process without an end-point" (p. x).

A focal point of optimism in Ontario is the Community Safety and Policing Act, an act that became a reality in April 2024 after years of dioscussion. The act's principles focused on eight key areas:

- The need to ensure the safety and security of all persons and property in Ontario, including on First Nation reserves.
- The importance of safeguarding the fundamental rights and freedoms guaranteed by the Canadian Charter of Rights and Freedoms and the Human Rights Code.
- The need for co-operation between policing providers and the communities they serve.
- The importance of respect for victims of crime and understanding of their needs.

- The need for sensitivity to the pluralistic, multiracial and multicultural character of Ontario society.
- The need to be responsive to the unique histories and cultures of First Nation, Inuit and Métis communities.
- The need to ensure that police services and police service boards are representative of the communities they serve.
- The need to ensure that all parts of Ontario, including First Nation reserves, receive equitable levels of policing (Government of Ontario e-laws, 2019).

The act was being praised and welcomed by various organizations, including the Ontario Association of Chiefs of Police, which issued a statement which read, in part:

Efforts to modernize the delivery of policing services to the people of Ontario are welcome and needed. We believe there are items in the new Community Safety Policing Act, 2019 that are welcome in that regard. As Ontario's police leaders, we look forward to continuing our work with the government, all MPPs, and other stakeholders, knowing that community safety is our absolute priority (OACP, 2020).

Police services and their public relations efforts are influenced by the concept of impression management, the process "by which people control how they are perceived by others … relevant to the attainment of desired goals. … When people are motivated to manage their impressions, the impressions that they try to convey are influenced by the roles that they occupy" (Leary, 2001). As such, impression management figures highly in police public relations work, and getting the message out the door, connecting with stakeholders, educating the public and ensuring effective internal and external communication falls to police service public relations officers. These personnel are engaged in "taking an active role in managing their [police service's] image in response to social and political forces" (Motschall and Cao, 2002, p. 152). Historically, "law enforcement's emphasis on community relations and the subsequent integration of more formalized communication/public relations activities was partly a response to major social and political events of the 1960s, including urban riots and civil rights protests" and recommendations by boards of authority included "community relations programs and more positive news media relations. ... Spin-off programs, such as press offices or public information units, were established to help police deal more effectively with the media and to appear more open with the public in communicating information" (p. 154). Social media's relevance has led to a rapid uptake by police departments. According to a U.S. study by Strom (2016):

> Social media has tremendous potential in modern-day law enforcement. Many [departments] have highlighted the importance of social media for building trusting relationships between police and the local community ... citizens from the community also have the opportunity to communicate with the police via social media, which can deliver valuable feedback and raise the department's awareness of community perceptions of local law enforcement ... [there is] potential for police departments' use of social media to promote public safety in times of unrest, and the potential for active social media use to humanize the local police force by showing that officers are also members of the community (pp. 4–8).

Sensitivity to public image also leads organizations toward a greater use of social media, and Fray (2017) in a study of the Rockford, Illinois, Police Department (RPD) and its use of social media to communicate and build relationships, found a growing amount of trust in the ability of social media to get messages across to the public. Four themes were clear in the Rockford Police Department's use of social media, in

> outing criminals, community events, crime reports, and public interest pieces. ... The RPD's use of social media relies heavily on the traditional DC citizenship paradigm [DC, or dutiful citizenship, emphasizes open, community-based participation in civic life]. This paradigm relies heavily on the traditional form of political engagement in which individuals rely upon the traditional authority and power structure to provide information and shape their attitudes and beliefs. ... [On Facebook] the RPD retains the typical authoritative control over the content shared. ... The RPD retains control of how the information is presented and the content is shaped in the perspective of the public. ... The repeated focus on the RPD's officers' involvement in the community and publicizing of events in local neighborhoods demonstrates the officers' willingness to meet the community in local neighborhoods and actively communicate create

opportunities for communication between the RPD and the community (Fray, 2017, p. 93)

Police departments are focusing on staying ahead of events by monitoring social media and focusing on transparency. Julie Parker, in "Hiding and hoping is not a PR strategy," outlines the necessary steps in writing about police response to a hypothetical crisis involving alleged use-of-force by officers in the field, captured on video and posted to Twitter. Parker writes of the need to identify issues, uncover facts, review social media constantly, draft strong, clear messages that present the organization's perspective and keep an eye on the clock—it is essential to share an organization's story as soon as possible after an event:

> Having the agency declare that its leaders are aware of the case, looking into it, and willing and able to share what they know once they've pieced together some critical pieces could help.... Silence on social media can lead some to believe that what's being said about the officers is true, or the agency or police leaders might be perceived as hiding from the incident (Parker, 2019).

If good communication comes down to a clear message, an explanation, and connectedness to stakeholders and the public, it makes sense that police departments are focusing on building trust in the community, especially in light of the reality of systemic racism. There is a need to confront this issue, build into police service infrastructures the means to acknowledge it, and work to eliminate it. This speaks to the accountability and transparency that is expected by the publics being served by police departments. Zamani et al. (2011), of the Center for Constitutional Rights, in an examination of the work being done to address police abuse, misconduct and racial profiling practices, made several recommendations to improve police oversight and accountability, including "transparency and availability of data concerning police practices, incidents and complaints" and establishing "a broad base of support around fair and just policing. Place impacted and community voices at the forefront of any demands, and include these voices in critical decisions" (p. 15).

THUNDER BAY

For years, the city of Thunder Bay's police force had a protracted, difficult, often violent relationship with its Indigenous citizens. That there was/is an unspoken segregation between peoples is apparent. On one occasion in the early 1990s, I visited that city for a division meeting during which (in the pre-PowerPoint era) I delivered a slide presentation. I was working for the Ontario government's transportation ministry, based in Toronto, and from my Thunder Bay colleagues there were the usual corny jokes about "another southerner" (as in people from southern Ontario) coming north to "the Lakehead," as Thunder Bay was known. I delivered my presentation, and later went to a local pub with a handful of regional office personnel for lunch. Regional offices of the provincial government are spread far and wide across the province, and the (at that time) largely white staffers worked on road and remote airport maintenance and the clearing of brush—even on occasion dynamiting beaver dams, though not blowing up the beavers themselves, to prevent flooding of local roads. The regional staff members worked closely with local First Nations communities and often developed strong and lasting relationships. But what happened in that pub was, to my mainstream, southern Ontario ("hey, we're a multicultural country!") eyes, inexplicable and troubling, though it did not really sink in until after I had left that city and had years to reflect on it. All of the people at our table were white and male. We were having our lunch of chicken wings, burgers and fries when a young First Nations woman appeared at the door of the pub, gesturing to one of my lunch companions, a burly guy in his twenties with a scruffy beard and baseball cap. He dutifully got up, went to the door and they stood outside talking. Clearly they were in a relationship and the young woman was the man's life partner, girlfriend, or wife. The men at the table talked in cheerful tones about the nature of the community the young man was from, and how there was a lot of "mixing up there," as in the mixing of cultures. But she hadn't come in the door of the pub, she stood frozen at the door, making hand gestures to get his attention in those pre-cellphone days. I wondered for some time why she didn't come into the restaurant, until thinking that maybe *she just wasn't welcome.* That was the silent evidence of the unspoken barrier between cultures in the community—*standing at a doorway and not being welcomed in.*

So it is equally troubling but not less surprising that the city and its police department (as a reflection of prevailing attitudes) have had a history of systemic discrimination against Indigenous people, either in their direct treatment of First Nations, or in their failure to deliver satisfactory investigations into the mistreatment and deaths of Indigenous People—and there have been many incidents, resulting in the city leading "the country in hate crimes against Natives in 2015. The hostility was so rampant that ... people started using the hashtag #ThisIsThunderBay to share stories of verbal attacks, racial slurs, police abuse, and physical assaults" (Jago, 2020, February 5).

Allegations "that systemic racism influenced investigations into the deaths of nearly forty people, most of whom were First Nations," resulted in two investigations into the Thunder Bay Police Service, or TBPS. The "investigations have been described as rushed and haphazard by members of the Indigenous community, who point to numerous examples of police declaring deaths accidental without waiting for an autopsy, pursuing testimony, or reaching out to witnesses" (Jago, 2020, February 5).

One of the fact-finding reports, written by a team led by Murray Sinclair, a First Nations lawyer and Canadian senator, documented that racist acts by the TBPS "have ranged from well-documented public mockery and the dissemination of racist stereotypes, to use of excessive force against and humiliation of Indigenous individuals, to disturbing deaths in custody" (Sinclair, 2018, November 1, p. vi). More Indigenous people were murdered in Thunder Bay than any other Canadian city. Thunder Bay accounts for 5 percent of Ontario's Indigenous population, but 37 percent of Indigenous murder victims province-wide; hate crimes against First Nations are widespread, and anti-Indigenous hate had been normalized (Jago, 2020, February 5).

A second report, by Gerry McNeilly, then Ontario's Independent Police Review Director, entitled *Broken Trust*, examined 37 investigations by the Thunder Bay Police Service involving sudden deaths of Indigenous People dating to 2009 (McNeilly, 2018, December, p. 5), and found missteps in several investigations so profound that McNeilly recommended reinvestigation; overall, a significant recommendation (among many) was to "focus proactively on actions to eliminate systemic racism, including removing systemic barriers and the root causes of racial inequities in the service" (p. 13), as well as initiating greater community outreach, and implementing Indigenous cultural competency and anti-racism training and proper screening of recruits. "Thunder Bay has the dubious distinction of having one of the highest rates of reported hate crimes in Canada. This means, among other things, that greater efforts have to be made to ensure that recruits and new officers are not already imbued with racist attitudes" (p. 17).

Sinclair's report had a total of 45 wide-ranging recommendations focused on accountability and transparency; in the area of communication, it recommended that the Thunder Bay Police Services Board (which oversees the police service):

Create its own website, use social media tools to encourage input, post information on police activities, and develop policies for representation, crisis communication and internal and external communication needs, strengthen its outreach to First Nations communities, create a statement "committing to the principle of openness and transparency in its communication" including open and accessible meetings, publication of meeting notices, video coverage of meetings and the adoption of principles of "reconciliation and recognition of Indigenous peoples" (Sinclair, 2018, November 1, pp. 107–108).

The board was later dissolved following the issuing of the reports and an administrator appointed in its place (Canadian Press, 2018, December 14). A month later, a civilian oversight board officially apologized to the Indigenous community for systemic racism during a reconciliation circle ceremony and promised to "work together with the entire community to move forward" (Prokopchuk, 2019, January 14).

CASE STUDY:
THE ROYAL CANADIAN MOUNTED POLICE (RCMP)
AND ALLAN ADAM
The historical relationship between the Royal Canadian Mounted Police and Indigenous Peoples is long and difficult. There have been many iterations of that relationship, starting with the autocratic treatment of Indigenous communities when the RCMP policed them for decades after the RCMP's creation in the 1870s as the North West Mounted Police, followed by the ensuing decades of oppressive systemic discrimination that became entrenched in the RCMP and other police services as well. Over time, some First Nations began establishing their own police forces; in the 1960s the RCMP started the process of withdrawing its police services on First Nations territory in Ontario and Quebec, completing the task in 1971 (Clairmont, 2006, September), although some territories in other provinces are still policed by the RCMP. As First Nations began policing

their own regions, many found success through autonomy; stories of achievement include the Nishnawbe Aski Police Service of northern Ontario, which, since its inception in 1994, "has never shot and killed anyone and no officer has died in the line of duty ... a record of which the Nishnawbe Aski Police Service (NAPS) is proud, especially in light of the recent uproar in North America over police killings and brutality" (Perkel, 2020, July 13).

But the contentious relationship between police services and Indigenous Peoples continues. Waves of increasing violence against Indigenous Peoples during the late 2010s galvanized First Nations and Inuk communities and drew sharp attention from government and the dominant culture, from the 2017 death of Dale Culver, a First Nations man in Prince George, British Columbia, by RCMP officers, to the June 3, 2020, brutal treatment of an Inuk man in Nunavut, again by an RCMP officer and, the following day, the death of Chantel Moore, an Indigenous woman in New Brunswick, shot by police during a wellness check, as well as the death by police shooting of Rodney Levi, a member of the Metepenagiag Mi'kmaq Nation (Beattie, 2020, June 13).

This welling up of violence and anger crystallized in the release of video showing the treatment of Athabasca Chipewyan First Nation Chief Allan Adam by an RCMP officer in Alberta. A dashcam video shot in the parking lot of the Boomtown Casino in Fort McMurray on March 10, 2020, shows Adam being "beaten during an arrest by Alberta RCMP over expired licence plates. Dashcam video of the incident was released Thursday [June 11], and shows an officer charging Adam, tackling him to the ground and punching him in the head" (Beattie, 2020, June 13). Images of Adam's bloody, bruised face swept across traditional and social media; members of the public were outraged that Adam was charged with resisting arrest and assaulting a peace officer, charges that were later withdrawn in court. Following court proceedings, Adam called for several changes to the justice system, including setting up Indigenous police forces, mitigating systemic discrimination practices and police brutality against Indigenous people, and implementing cross-cultural police training. Adam added that every commissioner and deputy commissioner in the RCMP should try to better understand Indigenous people. "I recommend that you go and take your sidearms off and you go in the bush with an Aboriginal elder for two weeks and learn to live with our people," said Adam (Canadian Press, 2020, June 24).

Prior to the release of the Chief Allan Adam video, Prime Minister Justin Trudeau delivered a statement in the House of Commons speaking to the need for change: "Unconscious bias is real. Systemic discrimination is real. For millions of Canadians, it is their daily, lived reality. The pain and damage it causes is real, too" (Trudeau, 2020, June 2). The violence also led the Black Parliamentary Caucus in Ottawa to produce a manifesto asking for major changes in policing across Canada, comprising a fundamental change in the approach of police, including an emphasis on de-escalation techniques, the use of race-based data, and the immediate banning of "carding" (the demand for identification) by police during random street checks (Ballingall, 2020, June 19). What followed was a head-turning display of shifting attitudes. After some stutter steps in responding to allegations of racism, the head of the RCMP, Commissioner Brenda Lucki, would admit that systemic racism was a reality, "just days after she questioned whether systemic racism exists in the national police force" (Ballingall, 2020, June 13). Lucki's official statement was clear and to the point:

I do know that systemic racism is part of every institution, the RCMP included. Throughout our history and today, we have not always treated racialized and Indigenous people fairly. Systemic racism isn't about the behaviour of a single individual or the actions of one person. It's in the institutional structures that reflect the inequities that persist in our society. And it shows up in policies, processes or practices that may appear neutral on the surface, but disadvantage racialized people or groups (Lucki, 2020, June 12).

As for the Black Caucus declaration, Prime Minister Justin Trudeau would later be criticized by some parliamentarians for his apparent slowness in acting on the recommendations, though he promised a work plan and policies that would "include reforms to the police and the justice system, improved protections for temporary foreign workers and legislation to expand First Nations policing of their own communities" (Ballingall, 2020, August 7).

Case Study Questions

1. What is the communications value of the statements that Trudeau and Lucki delivered? Are they sincere? What needs to be done in order for credibility to be maintained?
2. Think about what Chief Allan Adam said concerning Indigenous autonomy. If you were working for a policing organization, from a communications perspective, focus on two or three of the items Adams mentioned, and think about how your police service can respond to them. Then create three or

four key messages outlining cooperation with Indigenous communities on those items.

3. Look in the news. Find an additional source of information on the relationship between the RCMP and Indigenous people. Is it similar to the accounts we have been reading here? If not, how is it different? What ideas can you formulate regarding the way the media reports on events and issues in the community?

CONTINUED PRESSURE ON THE RCMP

Respect differences: The Royal Canadian Mounted Police continued to be the focus of intense investigation: on November 19, 2020, former Supreme Court Justice Michel Bastarache released a damning report, "Broken Dreams, Broken Lives," outlining the results of an investigation that found a toxic RCMP culture rife with sexism, homophobia and racism—and laced with resistant attitudes from senior personnel who essentially tolerated such behaviour (Haig, 2020, November 19). The report called for a serious external review of the force, and a *Toronto Star* reporter wrote that in an hour-long interview, Commissioner Lucki repeated the terms "learning" and "listening" no less than 12 times, suggesting that she had been gobsmacked by Bastarache's findings, even as she faced pushback from within and external criticism that the RCMP "needs to seriously consider overhauling itself from the ground up and rethink its mandate" (Quan, 2020, November 20).

PROFILE

DR. JAMES WALSH, PROFESSOR, FACULTY OF SOCIAL SCIENCE AND HUMANITIES, ONTARIO TECH UNIVERSITY

Dr. James Walsh is a specialist in academic research focusing on surveillance, security and social control; borders, mobility and migration; policing; law and society; and crime and media. A graduate of the University of California (M.A. and Ph.D., Sociology), he has served as a Visiting Assistant Professor at the University of Richmond in Virginia and Postdoctoral Fellow at the University of Pennsylvania's Social Science and Policy Forum.

What do you feel are the most serious issues that police departments face with respect to interacting with diverse cultures?
In North America, the most serious issue would be addressing the strained relations that have emerged as a result of the over-policing of particular communities. Various studies have shown that, whether in relation to 'carding' in places like Toronto or 'stop and frisk' in New York City, visible minorities are disproportionately subject to police attention and are considerably more likely to be cited, arrested, and potentially killed for what are generally low-level offenses—jaywalking, drug possession, panhandling etc. Additionally, as local police services have come to play a more prominent role in identifying and detaining those in breach of migration law—trends that are distinctly visible in the United States—those living in predominantly immigrant communities have come to view law enforcement with a great deal of fear and suspicion.

In addition to raising obvious concerns about injustice and rights violations, such outcomes threaten to erode the legitimacy of the police and legal authority itself. When communities view authorities as unfair, corrupt or cruel they are less likely to reach out and share information, outcomes that make it considerably more difficult to address crime problems. Public opinion surveys in both Canada and the U.S. reveal that there are pretty significant variations in views of the police, with racial and ethnic minorities possessing disproportionately negative perceptions.

These issues reveal that improving interactions with diverse communities requires altering the orientation of police services and not just diversifying their ranks. While hiring from a diverse pool of applicants and ensuring officers are from the communities they serve can help reduce the social and cultural distance between the police and local residents, without corresponding institutional change, doing so is unlikely to promote positive police-community relations.

Is there a future for community policing?
Yes, but only if it represents a true desire to improve police-community relations and not a superficial exercise in public relations as is oftentimes the case. Winning back support from diverse communities will be an uphill battle and is not something that will happen overnight, but the police should make every effort to listen to and engage with community members, take their interests seriously, and provide them with more expansive opportunities to influence police

priorities and steer decision making. At present, without winning back public trust, many police services will find themselves in a very difficult situation.

What effect is surveillance culture having on policing and how does this affect police services' relationships with diverse communities?

Surveillance culture is double-edged and has contradictory effects on policing. However, in the final instance, these effects are likely to adversely impact police services' interactions with diverse communities. On the one hand, new technologies ranging from crime-mapping software to algorithms that scrape and analyze social media data have been found to reinforce biased patterns of enforcement that disproportionately target minority communities. Such outcomes are compounded as growing emphasis on counterterrorism and immigration enforcement has produced an increase in racialized patterns of profiling and surveillance in the U.S. in particular. On the other hand, with the ubiquity of camera-equipped smartphones and social networking sites, it is significantly easier for activists and ordinary citizens to record and expose cases of police indiscretion and brutality, dynamics that have eroded public perceptions and generated significant outcry within immigrant and minority communities. Ultimately, these latter outcomes suggest the police have lost control of their public image and are emerging as targets and not just agents or practitioners of surveillance.

How do communications and public relations pertain to connecting with diverse communities?

While communications and public relations work should never be a substitute for good policing on the ground, they can help build trust and improve interactions. For the vast majority of individuals, their direct encounters with law enforcement are infrequent. Accordingly, perceptions are typically shaped through media coverage with police services, whether by hosting press conferences, hiring public relations officers, or other forms of impression management, investing considerable energy and resources in controlling their public image.

At present, the rise of digital platforms, in particular, ensures police services have a wealth of new opportunities for connecting with their constituents. Specifically, sites like Twitter and Facebook allow police services to bypass the mass media and directly and instantaneously reach members of the public. In terms of connecting with diverse communities, digital platforms can be used to convey police support of and involvement in the local community whether by hosting virtual town halls or circulating content about charitable events, ethnic and cultural festivals, and other community events and concerns. While these sorts of efforts are certainly important and can help build trust, they need to be viewed as a supplement, rather than substitute, to positive interaction and engagement in an offline environment.

LET'S CHECK IN!

In this self-assessment, reflect on the chapter (and use the statements provided to get you started) and think about how your viewpoint has changed with respect to the topics that were presented, or about how the discussion has generated new ideas or perceptions. Write a brief, bullet-pointed description of your thoughts and feelings. You are then encouraged to reflect on what you are thinking, and share it with your colleagues for a larger discussion.

KEY TERMS

Common good: the sense of camaraderie, compassion, empathy and commonality that assists in helping people feel a sense of community.

Goodwill: a core tenet of public relations: creating goodwill generates acceptance by your publics, and that results in social permission to continue operating.

Instrumentarian power: the use of data-mining, through artificial intelligence-driven systems, to develop models of the predictability of human behaviour, gather information for private sector and government clients, and manipulate the behaviour of people.

Internet of things: the interconnectedness of surveillance, systems and data collection in a wide variety of devices worldwide.

Intersectionality: the interconnected confluence of factors involved in inequalities and oppression of particular groups of people, including class, culture, disability, gender, national origin, race and sexual orientation.

Peelian principles: policing principles centred on the idea that police actions should meet with (or be validated by) community approval. Based on the ideas of Sir Robert Peel.

Racial profiling: action by police services that relies on stereotypes about ancestry, colour, ethnicity, race, religion, or place of origin, as a justification for greater scrutiny.

QUESTIONS TO EXPLORE

1. Why is the term "trust" so important in policing, and in the public relations work around policing?
2. If you were asked to write a brief communications statement about the three most important components of effective policing, what would you write? How would you define each of them?
3. Do you think the future of policing will be focused on greater surveillance (Zuboff's 'instrumentarianism') or by an emphasis on community policing? Are there benefits to either of these methods? Can they work effectively in combination?
4. Outline your thoughts on why Dafonte Miller rejected the interim police chief's apology and also state your opinion on the follow-up from the Toronto Police Service. How do you think statements like these are received by the public?

EXERCISE

CREATE A BRIEFING NOTE

In this hypothetical scenario, you will be asked to produce a briefing note for the executive members of your Police Services Board. Your job is to provide information. Re-read the sections on the Durham Regional Police Service and its equity and diversity program and prepare a briefing note on this topic. You may also take a look at the Durham Regional Police Service for more information. You will recall from Chapter 3 that the format for a briefing note is concise, and you should use the following subheads as you create it:

- Subject: the briefing note's title.
- Purpose: the "why" of the briefing note.
- Summary: the "who," the "where," and the "what." The facts of the matter at hand.
- Recommendations: the "how" and "where," offering a recommended course of action.
- Conclusion: a short, focused synopsis of what has been said.

EXERCISE

MIND-MAPPING AND WRITING A SHORT SPEECH

Think about the town or city you live in. Identify its police department by looking up its website. Take a look and see if it has plans and materials that deal with equity, diversity and inclusion. Now, consider that you work in communications for this police department. Your job is to develop a positive, two- to three-minute, good-will-focused speech to your city or town council that speaks to your work with the diverse communities that your organization serves. Good will is a core component of effective public relations; as Braun (2015) says in *Writing for Public Relations*, "The creation of goodwill is important because goodwill turns into public acceptance and public acceptance turns into social permission for the organization to continue operating" (p. 214).

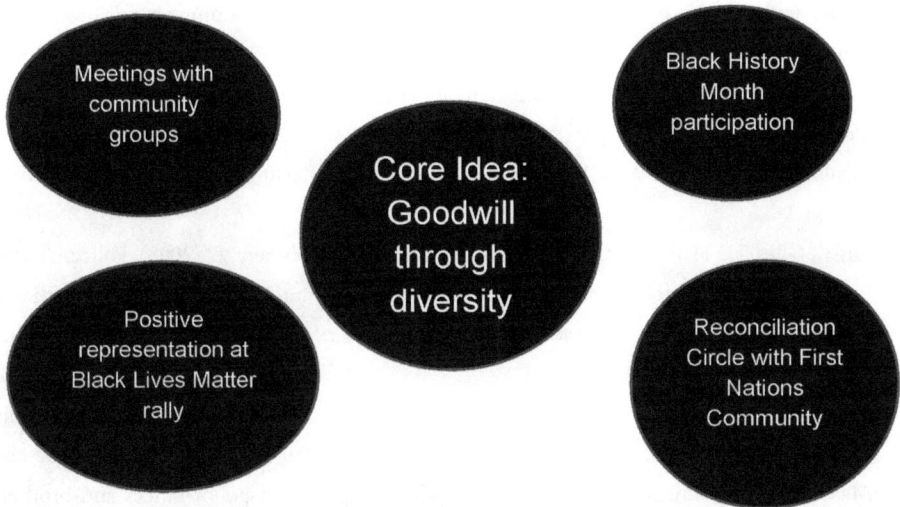

Start with a mind map. (Above is a hypothetical [and partial] mind map to help get you started.) A mind map is a diagram, a free-ranging set of connected ideas and word bubbles that "identifies a central word or concept or message … and then maps out other words associated with it.… [The writer works] outward in all directions to produce a structure of related thoughts, words or images" (Braun, 2015, p. 219). You can point to specific items that you find in your research that support the police department and its work. If there is no equity, diversity and inclusion plan, use the speech to talk about creating one. A good speech will have an opening that speaks to a specific need, desire or

John E. C. Cooper, EdD

goal, a middle that spells out how you are going to fulfill that need (or how you already managed to achieve the goal), and a conclusion that summarizes what you have already said. A two- to three-minute speech will be about 300 to 540 words (remember that while we read at the rate of about 250 words per minute, we speak at an average of 150 to 180 words per minute).

REFERENCES

Adegbile, D. (2017). Policing through an American prism. *The Yale Law Journal*, 126(8): 2222–2259. https://digitalcommons.law.yale.edu/cgi/viewcontent.cgi?referer=https://www.google.com/&httpsredir=1&article=5813&context=ylj

Alexander, M. (2012). *The new Jim Crow*. New York: The New Press.

Azmi, S. (2017). The human rights approach to addressing racial profiling: The activity of the Ontario Human Rights Commission. In *Canadian Diversity, Racial Profiling and Human Rights*, pp. 6–8. Ontario Human Rights Commission. http://www.ohrc.on.ca/sites/default/files/Racial%20Profiling%20and%20Human%20Rights_Canadian%20Diversity.pdf

Ballingall, A. (2020, August 7). Caucus head faults Trudeau as slow on systemic racism. *Toronto Star*, p. A11.

Ballingall, A. (2020, June 19). RCMP responds to racism manifesto from Black Caucus. *Toronto Star*, p. A6.

Barker, V., Giles, H., Hajek, C., Ota, H., Noels, K., Lim, T-S., & Somera, L. (2008). Police-civilian interaction, compliance, accommodation, and trust in an intergroup context: International data. *Journal of International and Intercultural Communication*, 1(2): 93–112. http://dx.doi.org/10.1080/17513050801891986

Bascaramurty, D. (2020, June 25). Toronto police officer and brother, accused of beating young Black man Dafonte Miller, face verdict on Friday: What you need to know. *The Globe and Mail*. https://www.theglobeandmail.com/canada/article-toronto-police-officer-and-brother-accused-of-beating-young-black-man/

Beattie, S. (2020, October 13). RCMP union tells officers to proudly wear controversial "thin blue line" symbol. *Huffington Post*. https://www.huffingtonpost.ca/entry/rcmp-thin-blue-line_ca_5f8609b9c5b6f53fff065118?ncid=fcbklnkcahpmg00000001&fbclid=IwAR2wh0ONysM90kGo_L5yWZu9ckvdd4gwP7HluK8myPbq11ZLTcySbWFUGrs

Beattie, S. (2020, June 13). Recent claims of police brutality In Canada are 'tip of the iceberg' for Indigenous People. *Huffington Post*. https://www.huffingtonpost.ca/entry/police-brutality-canada-indigenous_ca_5ee3dc4ec5b699cea5318697?ncid=fcbklnkcahpmg00000001&fbclid=IwAR1fbK9iEzwmR82t4oyoFjwfnzeSz4Y1tj5u9vWgiut12cGcF3LdIea_NZE&guccounter=1

158

Braun, S. (2015). Writing for public relations. In Carney, W., and Lymer, L. (Eds). *Fundamentals of Public Relations and Marketing Communications in Canada*, pp. 211–258. Edmonton: University of Alberta Press.

Broom (2019). Rethinking belonging in western nations: Theorizing the Public Commons as a shared pluralistic community. *Journal of International Social Studies*, (9)2: 75–93. https://files.eric.ed.gov/fulltext/EJ1236313.pdf

Buccola, N. (2019). *The fire is upon us*. Princeton, NJ: Princeton University Press.

Buford, T., Waldron, L., Syed, M., & Shaw, A. (2020, July 16). We reviewed police tactics in nearly 400 protest videos. Here's what we found. *ProPublica*. https://projects.propublica.org/protest-police-tactics/

Canadian Press (2020, November 5). Toronto cop sentenced to 9 months for beating in jail for beating Dafonte Miller. *HuffPost*. https://www.huffingtonpost.ca/entry/dafonte-miller-michael-theriault-case_ca_5fa42b90c5b623bfac4d148f?ncid=fcbklnkcahpmg00000001&fbclid=IwAR0-cUIn6ekf9tv75XygiFMVlJUS_ZCUb3uiJ8K3ju1rra2xnV-QoQO1p2I

Canadian Press (2020, June 26). Toronto cop convicted of assault in beating of Dafonte Miller; brother acquitted. *National Post*. https://nationalpost.com/pmn/news-pmn/canada-news-pmn/newsalert-toronto-cop-convicted-of-assault-in-beating-dafonte-miller-2

Canadian Press (2020, June 24). Charges dropped against First Nations Chief Allan Adam in violent arrest. *CBC*. https://www.cbc.ca/news/canada/edmonton/allan-adam-athabasca-chipewyan-first-nation-arrest-rcmp-assault-1.5624976

Canadian Press (2018, December 14). Thunder Bay police services board dissolved after scathing 'racism' report. *Global News*. https://globalnews.ca/news/4763969/thunder-bay-police-services-board-racism/

Cao, L. (2011, January). Visible minorities and confidence in the police. *Canadian Journal of Criminology and Criminal Justice*. doi:10.3138/cjccj.53.1.1

Carbado, D., Crenshaw, K., Mays, V., & Tomlinson, B. (2013). Intersectionality: Mapping the movements of a theory. *Du Bois Review: Social Science Research on Race*, 10(2): 303–312. doi: 10.1017/S1742058X13000349

Carter, A. (2020, August 10). Black people face 'disproportionately' high charge, arrest rates from Toronto police: report. *CBC*. https://www.cbc.ca/news/canada/toronto/black-people-human-right-commission-police-1.5680460

Carter, A. (2020, June 11). Provincial police watchdog to start collecting race-based data. *CBC*. https://www.cbc.ca/news/canada/toronto/siu-race-based-data-1.5606505

Casey, L. (2020, June 23). Demonstration continues in Mississauga over police shooting death of Ejaz Choudry. *The Globe and Mail*. https://www.theglobeandmail.com/canada/toronto/article-demonstration-continues-west-of-toronto-over-police-shooting-death-of/

CBC (2018, December 11). Toronto police chief acknowledges racial profiling challenges in wake of human rights report. https://www.cbc.ca/news/canada/toronto/saunders-ohrc-response-1.4940677

Clairmont, D. (2006, September). Aboriginal policing in Canada: An overview of developments in First Nations. Attorney General of Ontario. https://www.attorneygeneral.jus.gov.on.ca/inquiries/ipperwash/policy_part/research/pdf/Clairmont_Aboriginal_Policing.pdf

Clift, R. (1949). Police, press and public relations. *Journal of Criminal Law and Criminology*, 39(5): 667–674. https://scholarlycommons.law.northwestern.edu/cgi/viewcontent.cgi?article=3630&context=jclc

Coates, T. (2015). *Between the world and me*. New York: Spiegel & Grau.

Cole, D. (2015, April 21). The skin I'm in: I've been interrogated by police more than 50 times—all because I'm black. *Toronto Life*. https://torontolife.com/city/life/skin-im-ive-interrogated-police-50-times-im-black/

CTV News (2020, August 8). TPS statement in response to Dafonte Miller case. *CTV.* https://toronto.ctvnews.ca/video?clipId=2010400&cache=%3FcontactForm%3Dtrue

Delgado, R. & Stefancic, J. (2012). *Critical race theory*. New York: New York University Press.

Department of Justice, U.S. (1994). Understanding community policing: A framework for action. Bureau of Justice Assistance. https://www.ncjrs.gov/pdffiles/commp.pdf

Doffman, Z. (2020, June 26). Black lives matter: U.S. protesters tracked by secretive phone location technology. *Forbes*. https://www.forbes.com/sites/zakdoffman/2020/06/26/secretive-phone-tracking-company-publishes-location-data-on-black-lives-matter-protesters/#3592094d4a1e

Duraiappah, N. (2020, June 27). Statement by Peel Police Chief following death of Ejaz Ahmed Choudry. Peel Regional Police. https://www.peelpolice.ca/modules/news/index.aspx?newsId=24f4247c-71eb-41f4-8468-a5f394f2b551

Durham Regional Police Service (2020a). Mission/Core Value Statement. DRPS. https://members.drps.ca/internet_explorer/mission.asp

Durham Regional Police Service (2020b). Equity and Inclusion. DRPS. https://members.drps.ca/internet_explorer/our_organization/unit.asp?Scope=Unit&ID=70

Durham Regional Police Service (2020c). Equity and Inclusion Plan 2020–2022. DRPS. https://members.drps.ca/upload_files/20202022EquityandInclusionPlan.pdf

Enenajor, A. (2020, July 2). Criminal courts no place for needed policy changes. *Toronto Star*, p. A17.

Farooqui, S. (2020, August 7). Dafonte Miller rejects Toronto police apology after officer's assault trial. *Global News*. https://globalnews.ca/news/7257556/dafonte-miller-doesnt-accept-apology-toronto-police/

Fiddler, A. (2020, July 1). No cause for celebration in the Canada in which I live. *Toronto Star*, p. A17.

Flavin, B. (2018, October 12). Police officers explain why diversity in law enforcement matters. Rasmussen College. https://www.rasmussen.edu/degrees/justice-studies/blog/diversity-in-law-enforcement/

Foster, L. and Jacobs, L. (2017). Why police should collect racial data. In *Canadian Diversity, Racial Profiling and Human Rights*, pp. 16–18. Ontario Human Rights Commission. http://www.ohrc.on.ca/sites/default/files/Racial%20Profiling%20and%20Human%20Rights_Canadian%20Diversity.pdf

Francis, A. (2020, December 9). Police forces still largely white and male, report shows. *Toronto Star*, p. A8.

Fray, C. (2017). Narrative in police communication: The art of influence and communication for the modern police organization (MA Thesis). Illinois State University, Theses and Dissertations. https://ir.library.illinoisstate.edu/cgi/viewcontent.cgi?article=1754&context=etd

Funk, S. (2014). Community police in Durham Region: Implications for diverse ethnic groups (MA Thesis). University of Ontario Institute of Technology. File:///C:/Users/John/Downloads/Funk,%20Sheldon.pdf

Gerspacher, K. (2014). Communication culture in law enforcement: Perceptions from officers and supervisors (Master's thesis). Wright State University. https://corescholar.libraries.wright.edu/cgi/viewcontent.cgi?article=2368&context=etd_all

Gillis, W. (2020, August 8). Saunders wasn't told of Miller's beating. *Toronto Star*, p. A19.

Goodfield, K. (2020, August 6). 'Trust has been broken': Toronto's interim police chief apologizes to Dafonte Miller, promises transparency. *CTV News*. https://toronto.ctvnews.ca/trust-has-been-broken-toronto-s-interim-police-chief-apologizes-to-dafonte-miller-promises-transparency-1.5053280

Government of Canada Justice Laws Website, Section 139(1), Obstruction of Justice. (2020). Government of Canada. https://laws-lois.justice.gc.ca/eng/acts/c-46/section-139.html

Government of Canada Justice Laws Website, Section 268 (1), Aggravated Assault (2020). Government of Canada. https://laws-lois.justice.gc.ca/eng/acts/c-46/section-268.html

Government of Ontario e-laws (2019). Community Safety and Policing Act, 2019, S.O. 2019, c. 1, Sched. 1. Government of Ontario. https://www.ontario.ca/laws/statute/19c01

Grunig, J. (2013, May 27). The two-way symmetrical model of communication. James Grunig: Excellence Theory. https://excellencetheory.wordpress.com/2013/09/27/the-two-way-symmetrical-model-of-communication/

Haig, T. (2020, November 19). A scathing report calls out the RCMP's 'toxic' culture in dealing with women. *Radio Canada International*. https://www.rcinet.ca/en/2020/11/19/a-scathing-report-calls-out-the-rcmps-toxic-culture-in-dealing-with-women/

Hussain, W. (2018, February 26). The Common Good. *Stanford Encyclopedia of Philosophy*. https://plato.stanford.edu/entries/common-good/

James, R. (2020, July 2). Dangerous lessons from an unjust decision. *Toronto Star*, p. A14.

Jones, T. & Newburn, T. (2001). Widening access: Improving police relations with hard to reach groups, Paper 138. Home Office, London. https://www.researchgate.net/profile/Tim_Newburn/publication/240417389_Widening_Access_Improving_Police_Relations_With_Hard_To_Reach_Groups/links/53ce769c0cf2b8e35d1496a8/Widening-Access-Improving-Police-Relations-With-Hard-To-Reach-Groups.pdf

Leary, M. (2001). Impression management. *Science Direct.* https://www.sciencedirect.com/topics/psychology/impression-management

Loader, I. (2016). In search of civic policing: Recasting the 'Peelian' principles. *Criminal Law and Philosophy*, (10): 427–440. DOI 10.1007/s11572-014-9318-1

Logan, N. (2011) The White leader prototype: A critical analysis of race in public relations. *Journal of Public Relations Research*, 23 (4): 442–457, DOI: 10.1080/1062726X.2011.605974

Lucki, B. (2020, June 12). Statement by Commissioner Brenda Lucki. RCMP. https://www.rcmp-grc.gc.ca/en/news/2020/statement-commissioner-brenda-lucki

McIntosh, P. (1989). White privilege: Unpacking the invisible knapsack. *The National Seed Project.* https://nationalseedproject.org/Key-SEED-Texts/white-privilege-unpacking-the-invisible-knapsack

McNeilly, G. (2018, December). *Broken Trust.* Office of the Independent Police Review Director. http://oiprd.on.ca/wp-content/uploads/OIPRD-BrokenTrust-Final-Accessible-E.pdf

Meng, Y., Giwa, S. & Anucha, U. (2015). Is there racial discrimination in police stop-and-searches of Black youth? A Toronto Case Study. *Canadian Journal of Family and Youth*, 7(1): 115–148. DOI: https://doi.org/10.29173/cjfy24301

Merrill, B. & Fejes, A. (2018). Editorial: Intersectionality and adult education. *European Journal for Research on the Education and Learning of Adults*, (9)1: pp. 7–11. http://www.diva-portal.org/smash/get/diva2:1196383/FULLTEXT01.pdf

Miles-Johnson, T. (2019, July 19). Policing Diverse People: How Occupational Attitudes and Background Characteristics Shape Police Recruits' Perceptions. *Sage Journals.* https://journals.sagepub.com/doi/10.1177/2158244019865362

Motschall, M., & Cao, L. (2002, June). An analysis of the public relations role of the police public information officer. *Police Quarterly*, 5(2): 152–180. https://www.researchgate.net/publication/247748589_An_Analysis_of_the_Public_Relations_Role_of_the_Police_Public_Information_Officer

Ontario Association of Chiefs of Police (2020). Statement by the Ontario Association of Chiefs of Police (OACP) on the introduction of the Community Safety Policing Act, 2019. OACP. http://www.oacp.on.ca/news-events/news-releases/statement-by-the-ontario-association-of-chiefs-of-police-oacp-on-the-introduction-of-the-community-safety-policing-act-2019

Ontario Human Rights Commission (2020). What is racial profiling? (Fact Sheet). OHRC. http://www.ohrc.on.ca/en/what-racial-profiling-fact-sheet

Ontario Human Rights Commission (2018). *A Collective Impact: Interim report on the inquiry into racial profiling and racial discrimination of Black persons by the Toronto Police Service.* http://www.ohrc.on.ca/en/public-interest-inquiry-racial-profiling-and-discrimination-toronto-police-service/collective-impact-interim-report-inquiry-racial-profiling-and-racial-discrimination-black

Owusu-Bempah, A. (2014). Black males' perceptions of and experiences with the police in Toronto (Ph.D. thesis). Centre for Criminology and Sociolegal Studies, University of Toronto. https://tspace.library.utoronto.ca/bitstream/1807/68227/1/Owusu-Bempah_Akwasi _201411_PhD_thesis.pdf

Parker, J. (2019, August 21). Hiding and hoping Is not a PR strategy. *Police Chief Online.* https://www.policechiefmagazine.org/hiding-and-hoping-is-not-a-pr-strategy/?ref=00f53ceac0486 2725bfde685bfc02a8a

Perkel, C. (2020, July 13). Taking a different approach to policing. *Toronto Star*, p. A9.

Prokopchuk, M. (2019, January 14). Thunder Bay police board apologizes, pledges to improve police-Indigenous relations. CBC. https://www.cbc.ca/news/canada/thunder-bay/thunder-bay-reconciliation-circle-1.4976782

Putnam, R. (2000) *Bowling alone.* New York: Simon and Schuster.

Quan, D. (2020, November 20). Will RCMP's Lucki find cure for 'toxic' culture? *Toronto Star*, p. A1.

Reasons, C., Hassan, S., Ma, M., Monchalin, L., Bige, M., Paras, C., and Arora, S. (2016). Race and criminal justice in Canada. *International Journal of Criminal Justice Sciences*, 11(2). https://www.sascv.org/ijcjs/pdfs/reasonsetalijcjs2016vol11issu2.pdf

Regional Municipality of Durham (2018, April 13). Information report. Commissioner of Planning and Economic Development, Durham Region. https://www.durham.ca/en/living-here/resources/Documents/2018-INFO-53-2016-Census-of-Population.pdf

Reich, R. (2018). *The common good.* New York: Alfred A. Knopf

Saunders, M. (2020, June 26). Toronto police responding to urgent need for change. *Toronto Star*, p. A15.

Schweitzer, M., Wood Brooks, A., and Galinsky, A. (2015, September). The organizational apology. *Harvard Business Review.* https://hbr.org/2015/09/the-organizational-apology

Sereni-Massinger, C., & Wood, N. (2016). Improving law enforcement cross cultural competencies through continued education. *Journal of Education and Learning*, 5(2): 258–264. http://dx.doi.org/10.5539/jel.v5n2p258

Sinclair, M. (2018, November 1). Thunder Bay Police Services Board Investigation Final Report. Safety, Licensing, Appeals and Standard Tribunals Ontario. https://slasto-tsapno.gov.on.ca/

ocpc-ccop/wp-content/uploads/sites/5/2018/12/TBPSB_Investigation_Final_Report_-_EN-FINAL-1.pdf

Spencer, A. & Hough, M. (2000). Policing diversity: Lessons from Lambeth, British Home Office, policing and reducing crime. Washington and Lee University School of Law. https://scholarlycommons.law.wlu.edu/cgi/viewcontent.cgi?referer=http://scholar.google.ca/&httpsredir=1&article=1197&context=wlufac

Stenning, P. (2004). Policing the cultural kaleidoscope: Recent Canadian experience. *The Canadian Review of Policing Research.* http://crpr.icaap.org/index.php/crpr/article/view/27/24

Strom, K. (2016). Research on the impact of technology on policing strategy in the 21st century. National Institute of Justice. https://www.ncjrs.gov/pdffiles1/nij/grants/251140.pdf

Szeto, J. (2014). Policing diversity with diversity: Exploring organizational rhetoric, myth, and minority police officers' perceptions and experiences (M.A. thesis). Wilfrid Laurier University. https://scholars.wlu.ca/cgi/viewcontent.cgi?article=2762&context=etd

Thomas, M., & Lufts, S. (2020, January 23). Blue solidarity: Police unions, race and authoritarian populism in North America. *Work, Employment and Society*, 34(1). https://doi.org/10.1177/0950017019863653

Tisdell, E. (2005). Critical multiculturalism, in English, L. (Ed.). *International Encyclopedia of Adult Education*, pp. 162–165. New York: Macmillan.

Toronto Police Services Board (2020, June). Toronto Police Services Board statement regarding the decision in the Theriault trial. Toronto Police Services Board. https://www.tpsb.ca/mmedia/latest-news-release

Trudeau, J. (2020, June 2). Prime Minister's address in the House of Commons on anti-Black racism in Canada. Government of Canada. https://pm.gc.ca/en/news/speeches/2020/06/02/prime-ministers-address-house-commons-anti-black-racism-canada

Walsh, J., & O'Connor, C. (2019). Social media and policing: A review of recent research. *Sociology Compass*, pp. 1–14. DOI: 10.1111/soc4.12648

White, P. & Isai, V. (2020, June 22). 'We need justice': Brother of police shooting victim Ejaz Choudry demands answers. *The Globe and Mail.* https://www.theglobeandmail.com/canada/toronto/article-we-need-justice-brother-of-police-shooting-victim-ejaz-choudry/

Zamani, N., Head, I., Alexander, A., & Charney, D. (2011, July). Advocating for justice: Case studies in combating discriminatory policing. *The Center for Constitutional Rights.* File:///C:/Users/John/Downloads/Advocating_for_Justice_Case_Studies_in_C.pdf

Zofi, Y. (2017, June 6). 5 strategies for effective cross-cultural interactions. International Association of Business Communicators. https://www.iabc.com/5-strategies-for-engaging-in-effective-cross-cultural-interactions/

Zuboff, S. (2019). *The age of surveillance capitalism.* New York: PublicAffairs.

CHAPTER FIVE

Charting a Better Course for Diversity and Equity: Cross-cultural Teaching

OBJECTIVES OF THIS CHAPTER

This chapter investigates and discusses the teaching of diversity, equity and inclusion in both learning institutions and the corporate sector, with a focus on the following:

- Examining ideas of diversity, anti-racism, equity and inclusion;
- Examining the ways in which organizations are developing the means to deliver effective diversity training;
- Looking at two case studies of organizations and their experiences with diversity training;
- A Q&A with diversity trainer Dr. Pamela Heath.

HOW DO WE LEARN?

How do we learn? What is the difference between skills training and learning? And in a world that is focused on the importance of diversity learning, how will we continue to learn and how can we apply principles of effective communication to the practice of positive cross-cultural dialogue? Public relations is defined as "the strategic management of relationships between an organization and its diverse publics, through the use of communication, to achieve mutual understanding, realize organizational goals and serve the public interest" (Canadian Public Relations Society, 2020), and public relations courses have been taught for decades. According to Wright (2010), "the first university-level public relations course in the United States was called 'Publicity Techniques' and was taught at the University of Illinois in 1920," and it was designed to make the profession a more prestigious career choice (p. 454). In Canada, "the first university-based public relations course ... was taught by Leonard Knott at McGill University in Montreal in 1948. The next year, in 1949, the University of Toronto started teaching a public relations course with the assistance of the Public Relations Association of Ontario and the Advertising and Sales Club of Toronto" (p. 457). Today entire programs at universities and community colleges are dedicated to public relations, mass media, marketing communications and digital media, and similar studies.

The terms Diversity, Equity and Inclusion, usually grouped together as "DEI" or "DE & I," are generally defined as follows:

- **Diversity:** all the ways in which people differ, encompassing characteristics that make one individual or group different from another;
- **Equity:** the fair treatment, access, opportunity and advancement for all people, while at the same time striving to identify and eliminate barriers that have prevented the full participation of some groups;
- **Inclusion:** the act of creating environments in which any individual or group can be—and feel—welcomed, respected, supported and valued (Wallace and Lutrell, 2020, July 7).

Diversity training is "training delivered to make participants more aware of diversity issues in the workplace, their own beliefs on diversity, as well as provide skills to help them interact, collaborate and work more closely with people that have different qualities to their own. ... [For business,] diversity training is seen to have a number of benefits such as increased collaboration and relational skills, protecting against violations of discrimination legislation (therefore reducing the firm's risk profile) and empowering those from underrepresented groups to feel more confident and valued in the workplace" (HR Zone, 2020).

Diversity training in corporate settings dates back to the 1960s, and in the early years the training was compliance-based (for instance, in the U.S., to ensure compliance with the 1964 Civil Rights Act); the training grew over the next couple of decades to involve the improvement of relationships in the workplace (such as helping women and People of Colour assimilate into the corporate hierarchy), and today training is focused on leveraging the knowledge of diversity to improve business function (Anand and Winters, 2008). "Whereas early diversity training did not explicitly seek changes in behaviors but rather was designed to raise awareness, today it is very clear that the expected outcome is demonstrated behavioral competencies in diversity and inclusion" (Anand and Winters, p. 370). I will note here, as I did earlier in the text, that People of Colour (or Person of Colour) is a term that is met with acceptance by some and is frowned upon by others as it may be seen as an "aggregation" of people who are not white.

Anti-racism training looks at the "power imbalances between racialized people and non-racialized/white people ... [that] play out in the form of unearned privileges.... Anti-racism is the practice of identifying, challenging, and changing the values, structures and behaviors that perpetuate systemic racism.... Anti-racism is an active way of seeing and being in the world, in order to transform it" (Stand, 2020). Tackling the essence of racism by recognizing its position as a permanent or near-permanent part of society and taking measures such as forming, in the workplace, cross-racial caucuses or teams, are steps on the path to addressing issues in a very real and proactive way; according to DiAngelo and Flynn (2010, August), "a cross-racial team interrupts racism by providing a new model of leadership" (p. 4), and it is also essential to recognize that "a basic premise of antiracist education is that it is lifelong work; the process of identifying and challenging patterns of racism is always evolving and never finished" (p. 15).

A significant portion of diversity training focuses on 'microaggression,' a term created by African American professor Chester Pierce in the 1970s to describe "the slights, putdowns and invalidating remarks that racial minorities experience every day when interacting with people who unknowingly engage in implicit racism." The prevalence of such training is growing; "Google pulls up more than 8,000 mentions [of it] in professional papers, media and blogs. Some companies and institutions have initiated microaggression training as part of harassment-prevention policies. College campuses are awash in microaggression protests" (Hampson, 2016, July 8). Yet effective anti-racism learning and teaching must dig deeper, and "successful anti-racism training moves beyond awareness of the problem and how to take action against it.... For example, instead of educating employees about microaggression in the workplace, give them tools for how to respond to the behavior" (Lui, 2020, June 15). Acknowledging identity (Who I Am, How I See Myself, How I Am Seen, How I See Others) is a core component of anti-racism education, and it must be viewed in a collective way, not an individualistic one (and thus not limited to personal experience, but linked to the history of colonialism, capitalism and decolonization), such that "definitions of identity should ... make connections with the wider community. We cannot reject the politics of identity and difference. And we cannot simply engage in what can be called 'politics of the moment' or situational politics" (Dei, 2010, p. 21).

Diversity training is usually presented as upbeat, proactive, and engaging. However, there *are* criticisms of diversity training. According to Sloat (2019, April 1), researchers found that "short, one-off diversity training sessions that are commonplace across organizations are not likely to change most people's behaviors," yet on the other hand, "merely offering it in a workplace ... is an important signal that a company cares about establishing an inclusive, equal environment." Lui (2020, June 15), says that "research has shown compulsory diversity training can actually activate bias among workers who resent being told what not to do. By letting employees 'opt in' to equity training, they may come to the table with a more open mind to learn and change."

Clearly, the current climate is a churn of ideas. According to Sanchez (August 23, 2023), "With as many as 26 million people estimated to have participated in Black Lives Matter protests, it is the largest protest movement in American history" (https://www.brookings.edu/articles/americans-continue-to-protest-for-racial-justice-60-years-after-the-march-on-washington/). There have been both increased incidents of anti-Arab and Islamophobic bias in Canada and the U.S, as well as marches protesting against that bias, and efforts to combat antisemitism in the U.S., Canada and Europe. And organizations like the First Nations Land Defence Alliance have actively protested provincial efforts to establish mining operations on First Nations land (Erum, October 23, 2023, https://thevarsity.ca/2023/10/23/thousands-protest-demanding-ontario-government-stop-mining-on-first-nations-lands/).

These actions and others change attitudes in wholesale and incremental ways but it can take a long time to change attitudes, often resulting from a series of collective small pushes in the right places, *à la* Gladwell's *Tipping Point* (Gladwell, 2002). I recall spending time in diversity training sessions while working in the Ontario government; it was the early 1990s, the New Democratic Party (left-leaning politically) had been elected, defeating a Liberal government that itself had ended 30 years of Conservative rule in the mid-1980s, and among the NDP personnel within government there was a zeal to proactively refashion the workplace in an equitable way. One way was laying bare and actively addressing issues of systemic discrimination in order to effect change. What perhaps wasn't expected was the degree of resistance to change from within. The sessions—which organizers worked hard to make upbeat, inclusive and positive—were peopled by mostly white participants (between two-thirds and three-quarters of participants in of the sessions), and about a fifty-fifty male/female split, and most had started working for the government under the previous Conservative regime. They were not used to, nor would they accept, changes to the way they thought and acted in the workplace, although, to be clear, white privilege is not the bastion of conservatism—it exists across political lines. Participants were unwilling to challenge their own perceptions. They had lived in the bubble of white privilege, sometimes for decades (a bubble I have also lived in), enjoying a benefit that had coalesced as white institutional presence. White institutional presence gives those in white culture an ability to either dismiss issues of ethnicity, colour, or culture (in particular as they relate to socio-economic status), or to consider such matters from a distance, and this emotional, rational and social distancing is a means of dealing with troubling questions or ideas *by not dealing with them* (Gusa, 2010). And so when a white deputy minister in the ministry where I worked was asked to speak as part of a diversity panel discussion, and he was presented with the fact that 85 percent of administrative jobs (lower-paying secretarial or clerical work with limited upward mobility) were held by women of colour, he beamed and said, "That's great! It demonstrates that we do a good job *hiring minorities.*" He didn't get it, in that the issue at hand was the profound lack of representation by BIPOC representatives in management, not the hiring practices of the institution. Likewise, my colleagues in the diversity sessions didn't get it either. They were in denial, and the attitude was "We're not racist, so why do we have to attend these sessions?" Avoidance of difficult conversations and denying the marginalization of others is a form of resistance to diversity (Vaccaro, 2010). Canada often lauds itself on being different from the more visibly stratified social infrastructure of the U.S., where racism tends to be openly acknowledged; denial of racism north of the border is common, and "in Canada, it is hard even to reach this issue because of pervasive denial of the very existence of racism in Canadian society" (Aylward, 1999, p. 40). So, my fellow participants in our diversity sessions, with their occasional snickers, snide remarks, and general disrespect for the session trainers, felt justified in their belief that they were not living in a racist society, or they just didn't care to embrace change.

As for the process of learning, libraries are filled with books dedicated to the topic. The Genevan philosopher Jean-Jacques Rousseau, in *Emile* (written in 1762, it was a guide to the teaching of a hypothetical pupil named Emile), said that learning came from three sources: nature, other people, or things, and he urges the good teacher to:

teach your scholar to observe the phenomena of nature; you will soon rouse his curiosity, but if you would have it grow, do not be in too great a hurry to satisfy this curiosity. Put the problems before him and let him solve them himself.… Let us transform our sensations into ideas, but do not let us jump all at once from the objects of sense to objects of thought.… Let the senses be the only guide for the first workings of reason. No book but the world, no teaching but of fact (Rousseau, 2013, p. 156).

The American educational reformer and philosopher John Dewey held that students must engage with the world and develop their own interpretation of it; their education would be built on that foundation. This learner-centred approach recasts the classroom "as a social entity for children to learn and problem-solve together as a community. In these classrooms children are viewed as unique individuals; students can be found busy at work constructing their own knowledge through personal meaning" (Williams, 2017, p 93). The Brazilian educator and philosopher Paulo Freire took innovative approaches to teaching, and his focus was on working to raise the consciousness of the oppressed (*conscientização* or critical consciousness) so they would recognize the condition of their lives; learners "may discover through existential experience that their present way of life is irreconcilable with their vocation to become fully human. They may perceive through their relations with reality that reality is really a process undergoing constant transformation" (Freire, 2000, p. 75). Conscientização is "critical knowledge that becomes a source of hope. In that sense, the idea provides both a space to denounce social inequity and critically question society at large" (Mora, 2014).

Through engaging in critical consciousness, we all become learners, and in times of unrest and social questioning, we see protests, we walk in protest marches, see statues splashed with paint or torn down or their heads chopped off, engage in difficult dialogues, watch businesses change their corporate approach, logos, or marketing strategies (regardless of how much this might be incentivized by profit). All of this motivates people to change, and this paradigm shift changes the way people perceive privilege. It motivates people in a necessary way. Bivens (2005) notes that "white privilege is so pervasive that white people do not even notice that they end up together and in the same place: sharing power and privilege that structural racism denies people of color.… Ultimately, white people must come to their own understanding of why it is in their interests to dismantle a system that does not work for all humanity and commit to creating something better" (pp. 43–44).

In *Faces at the Bottom of the Well* educator, lawyer and well-known civil rights activist Derrick Bell mused on his own well-worn, traditional view that education would be instrumental to ending racism, in that "education leads to enlightenment. Enlightenment opens the way to empathy. Empathy foreshadows reform … whites—once given a true understanding of the evils of racial discrimination … would find it easy, or easier, to give up racism … but we fool ourselves when we argue that whites do not know what racial subordination does to its victims … they *know*" (Bell, 1992, pp. 150–151).

Teaching about racism was not lost on Jane Elliott, a white schoolteacher in the overwhelmingly white small town of Riceville, Iowa. She decided, following a student's question after the assassination of Martin Luther King, Jr., in April 1968 ("Why did they shoot him?" she was asked), to teach her third-grade pupils about racism with her now-famous Blue Eyes/Brown Eyes Exercise, in which blue-eyed children became a classroom "minority group" that suffered the indignities of discrimination. She told other teachers "how several of her slower kids with brown eyes had transformed themselves into confident leaders of the class. Withdrawn brown-eyed kids were suddenly outgoing, some beaming with the widest smiles she had ever seen on them." The next school day she reversed the process, and brown-eyed children were treated as the subordinate group. The students were allowed to join in—and some did with unbridled enthusiasm—building on the unverifiable generalizations that make up discrimination. "When the exercise ended, some of the kids hugged, some cried. Elliott reminded them that the reason for the lesson was the King assassination, and she asked them to write down what they had learned" (Bloom, 2005).

The way that the children, some of whom had formerly been friends, reacted to being in either a dominant or oppressed group, was shocking. "The arbitrary division among the students intensified over the course of the experiment, so much so that it actually ended in physical violence. Children often fight, argue, and sometimes hit each other, but this time they were motivated by eye color" (Exploring Your Mind, 2019, July 9).

While Elliott was vilified by many for her daring experiment (which would likely not be welcomed in classrooms today, perhaps for reasons of ethics and sensitivity to children's feelings rather than the implicit nature of bullying and discrimination), over the years she became a hero of cross-cultural awareness and teaching, and publisher "McGraw-Hill has listed her on a timeline of key educators, along with Confucius, Plato, Aristotle, Horace Mann, Booker T. Washington, Maria Montessori and 23 others" (Bloom, 2005).

Teaching about diversity and engaging in cross-cultural dialogue demands an approach that borrows from the ideas presented above: experiential, investigative, focused on the learner's own motivations and desired outcomes. So how do we teach cross-cultural awareness?

WHAT IS HAPPENING IN COLLEGES AND UNIVERSITIES?

In a college class that I teach to first-year public relations and communication foundations students, I have conducted an exercise that I call Culture Talk: Table for Two or Three. It is a ten-minute exercise, followed by a fifteen- to twenty-minute classroom discussion; students are told to find a partner or partners in the room "whose cultural background is different from your own." It is an exercise that is not original and no doubt is repeated in similar ways in countless other classrooms. Finding partners with a different cultural background is not difficult, for the classroom is a diverse place, especially given that up to a third of the students in the class are international students, from places like China, Colombia, India, Mexico, Pakistan and Russia. Students are asked to sit facing each other, take a sheet of paper, and generate a mind map of their ideas. The goal: "share *one* aspect of your culture with your partner (or partners), something that would be new or unknown to them." Students take to it with enthusiasm; they jot down ideas, sometimes sketch out pictures, talk about customs and religion and often about the foods they eat. There is no negativity to it. Afterwards, they use masking tape to put their mind maps on the walls around the room. There is discussion about differences, but it is done in a way that is not forced; students welcome the opportunity to talk. All of which makes sense, for this is, after all, the kind of "soft" dialogue (informal, unstructured, easygoing) that comes with our standard Canadian idea of multiculturalism, an idea enshrined in the Canadian Multiculturalism Act of 1988, which states that among its goals is recognition and promotion of "the understanding that multiculturalism reflects the cultural and racial diversity of Canadian society and acknowledges the freedom of all members of Canadian society to preserve, enhance and share their cultural heritage … [as well as] the understanding that multiculturalism is a fundamental characteristic of the Canadian heritage and identity and that it provides an invaluable resource in the shaping of Canada's future" (Government of Canada, 2020).

More difficult discussions are embarked on when we leave the classroom and go across campus to the college's First Peoples Indigenous Centre. There, we sit in a circle and are guided by Indigenous academic coaches, taken through a discussion about the colonial history of Canada, the genocide against First Nations children stolen from their parents and placed in residential schools, or fostered out into non-Indigenous families, and the near-extinction of cultures, languages and life practices. There are upsides to the discussion, too, about hope and faith and the future, and laughter about differences and attitudes, and students are encouraged to explore their own perceptions of Indigenous cultures. And it is understood that, as I find with my culture-connecting exercises, students like talking about food. Food connects us. As mentioned, it is a relatively easy cross-cultural experience, and we can appreciate the way it awakens all of the senses. It is part of creating a culture of learning, where "educators make a point of focusing on the cultural contribution of class members and develop a growing knowledge of respective cultures" (Chia, 2009). It is much harder, though (regardless of how well one person knows another), to talk about the granularity of racism, and discrimination based on gender, sexual identity and orientation. And so in college classrooms the more difficult discussions will come through the work of a coach, as with the Indigenous coaches at the college, or through open and honest dialogue, as with my Black students who will talk about the discrimination they experience in connection with police officers. Schools are broadening their approach to be more aware, and to work to ensure that these broad-based ideas that involve very pithy, focused, results-based language, will filter down into the classroom. Culturally Relevant Pedagogy (CRP) is a way that instructors can demonstrate a commitment to drawing on, synthesizing and most of all valuing the cultural life experiences of everyone in the classroom. "CRP occurs when a teacher shifts away from entirely ignoring student differences, or from viewing them as a burden to academic achievement, and instead embraces their contributions and capabilities. … [B]y utilizing CRP, instructors have the power to create an inclusive classroom climate and 'provide space' for divergent ideas" (Goethe and Colina, 2017, December 20).

This can be applied to public relations teaching in a direct way. Chia (2009) notes that "public relations educators need to be flexible and develop an understanding of public relations around the unique contributions of each cohort of students." An important way to trigger/urge/influence a greater awareness of diversity issues in students is to expose them to new and often innovative ideas that shift their focus from the traditional coursework they are studying in the public relations, communications and mass media fields, and to incorporate diversity, equity and inclusion examples into their work; there is a need to create a flow of ideas that reflect sometimes uncomfortable, challenging, outside-the-box thinking, moving learners from the position of neutrality (the white neutral norm) towards Freirean consciousness-raising. Otherwise there is the potential to reinforce oppression. MacPherson (2006) calls out current standards for education as methods "to propagate modern Western norms as educational outcomes and best practices ... arrived at without reference to alternative cultural practices. ... The ethnocentric failing is to see what is local and relative as universal, and to see what is normative as factual. When this failing combines with power and coercion, it is an error that can perpetrate great harm in the name of good" (p. 75).

Muturi and Zhu (2019, August 17), in a study of the perceptions of students of public relations work and how those perceptions are influenced by levels of diversity exposure, found that "despite the emphasis on diversity in the field ... [we] did not find diversity exposure to significantly influence how students perceived race/ethnicity issues in public relations. Overall, students had moderate exposure to diversity and a low level of perceptions about race/ethnicity-related issues in public relations practice. This is possibly due to the lack of focus on discipline-specific diversity issues in the courses taken or informally through participation in diversity-related events and activities during their academic career."

In my own doctoral research—a case study involving curriculum review and interviews and journaling with seven faculty members at Oshawa, Ontario's Durham College, where I teach, I found that

> practical, task-oriented coursework will take precedence over the engagement of critical thinking around racial diversity; teachers struggled to define and address issues of racial diversity; there was a desire to avoid talking about race, and a need to move into a rhetorical safe zone of discussing culture instead; there was an expressed need for more institutional involvement in helping prepare teachers to understand and embrace racial diversity; teachers need to play a key role in generating curriculum that addresses the topic (Cooper, 2016, pp 166–167).

The necessity for teachers to be involved in building effective diversity-focused curriculum is essential, say Muturi and Zhu: "From an education perspective, mass communication faculty play a vital role in influencing perceptions about the public relations field. Understanding their perspectives about diversity in the discipline and how they incorporate it into their courses and the overall curriculum is an area that requires research" (2019, August 17).

On an administrative level, taking pledges and committing to action (or reconfirming their commitments) is a route that many post-secondary institutions take. Durham College in Oshawa, for example, was one of 200 institutions that signed the CEO pledge of the BlackNorth Initiative, which commits Canada-wide organizational leaders to set targets and engage in actions to dismantle anti-Black systemic racism; a core component is generating opportunities for the underrepresented BIPOC community. The BlackNorth Initiative is the work of the Canadian Council of Business Leaders Against Anti-Black Systemic Racism and the signing of the pledge is representative of a range of organizations that is "extraordinarily diverse and spans companies of all sizes, industries and mandates, including: financial services, education, extractive industries, professional services, healthcare, online services, consulting, manufacturing, small to medium sized firms, business associations, private companies, and more. Notably, 30 percent of the companies on the TSX 60 have signed the pledge and the total market cap of all committed organizations exceeds \$1 trillion, representing almost one-third of the TSX's total market cap" (BlackNorth, 2020, July 21). Getting companies with an abundance of capital is essential to making change happen; change takes money, and the commitment of wealthy organization moves the focus of diversity and equity training from an ancillary function to a core component of business operations.

For Durham College, a range of five values in its 2020–23 strategic plan included diversity and inclusion, along with collaboration, excellence, integrity, respect, innovation, and social responsibility; the college has an Equity, Diversity and Inclusion Working Group, delivers unconscious bias training for students and employees and supports a DC Black Student Success Network (Durham College, 2020). Additionally, its Indigenization Protocol outlines its recognition of Indigenization as "a continuous process requiring each member of our campus community to actively commit to reconciliation with the goal of building respectful, reciprocal relationships that will contribute to better educational outcomes for all students. Inherent among this commitment is our pledge to uphold the seven principles of the Indigenous Education Protocol for Colleges and Institutes of which DC is a proud signatory" (Durham College, 2020). Colleges and Institutes Canada is a national body representing publicly supported colleges, institutes, and polytechnics and the creator of the Indigenous Education Protocol, which covers the following commitments:

1. Commit to making Indigenous education a priority;
2. Ensure governance structures recognize and respect Indigenous peoples;
3. Implement intellectual and cultural traditions of Indigenous peoples through curriculum and learning approaches relevant to learners and communities;
4. Support students and employees to increase understanding and reciprocity among Indigenous and non-Indigenous peoples;
5. Commit to increasing the number of Indigenous employees with ongoing appointments throughout the institution, including Indigenous senior administrators;
6. Establish Indigenous-centred holistic services and learning environments for learner success;
7. Build relationships and be accountable to Indigenous communities in support of self-determination through education, training and applied research (Colleges and Institutes Canada, 2020).

Cities, too, are taking the equity and diversity message seriously; the city of Oshawa, Ontario, formed a Community Diversity, Equity and Inclusion Committee in 2020, comprised of "15 community members from diverse backgrounds, representing a broad range of under-served and equity seeking groups." The representatives' mandate is the implementation of the city's diversity plan, though a commitment to "attend meetings, provide feedback, consultation and advice to city staff on the elimination of barriers within city programs, services and policies and on the creation of new programs or initiatives related to enhancing diversity, equity and inclusion in our community. The committee is also expected to liaise and work with other community partners including the city's accessibility committee and cultural leadership council in various initiatives to foster greater understanding and awareness of diversity, equity and inclusion matters" (City of Oshawa, 2020, July 8).

IN THE PUBLIC RELATIONS WORKPLACE

The essential nature of workplace diversity training is underscored by identities, and these are formed in the workplace, such that "workers figure out how to position themselves in an organization, how to perform identities that are acceptable to their immediate peers but also allow them freedom and some autonomy and control" (Fenwick, 2008, p. 22). These identities can change, and creating and delivering programming that affects identities, allowing workers to understand the need for greater dialogue, engagement, discussion, challenging their privilege and reshaping their understanding of others, is essential. In public relations, clarity of language and message are core components of the industry, focused on "efforts to reduce ambiguity and uncertainty in an ever smaller, yet more tightly networked world. It is this ambiguity and uncertainty that has allowed the practice of public relations to emerge as a valuable organizational communication function" (Kent and Taylor, 2011, p. 50). Public relations training that de-centres whiteness is essential, for

> the emergence of a White leader prototype in public relations seems inevitable because for so long only White people had access to positions that were able to prepare employees for public relations and leadership roles. Even after affirmative action granted African Americans access, perceptual barriers still limited their ascension. Nevertheless, African Americans and non-White people have risen to leadership positions in public relations contexts. This is progress. Yet more needs to be done to ensure professional leadership is determined by talent and skill instead of race (Logan, 2011, p. 451).

In professions such as public relations, traditional media, social media and mass communications in general, visibility ranks highly. Publics want to see that they are being represented, and to know that as clients, their needs are being served by people who reflect who they are in society; working with a diverse staff is a plus. As PR professional Rodney Pruitt wrote about undertaking a career in public relations, which he says he joined because of a love of writing and storytelling, "As a twenty-something person of color working in the PR industry, I often find myself drawn into conversations surrounding diversity, equity and inclusion (DEI), specifically the lack of racial and ethnic diversity in the field. … I wouldn't see many people who looked like me, which, whether you know it or not, can take a mental toll on an entry-level professional" (Pruitt, 2018). Ravazanni (2006) notes that "recruiting and retaining members of underrepresented groups and professionals from diverse backgrounds in organizations and in particular in public relations departments and associations give rise to advantages in both internal and external contexts" (p. 4). Internally, this happens through the attraction of a wider range of talents and boosting innovation through varied viewpoints and embedding "the theme of diversity deeply in the organizational culture and mission" (p. 4). Externally, it allows organizations to become more heterogeneous so that they may "effectively manage their respective and specific stakeholder relationship systems ... [provide an] effective response to reflect the market, to assimilate the attitudes and expectations of different stakeholders and sometimes to catch emergent or hidden trends" as well as promote overall diversity (p. 4). Successfully addressing issues of difference, and embracing diversity, demands a self-awareness, an understanding of the environment that people are in, and knowing *who they are* in that environment. This situationality leads to reflection and action. "Reflection upon situationality is reflection about the very conditions of existence; critical thinking by means of which people discover each other to be 'in a situation.'" Only when people encounter others, and see the reality around them and around others (seeing and knowing their situation), can they begin to emerge from the dense entanglement of their existence by applying *conscientização*, or consciousness-raising, "the deepening of the attitude of awareness characteristic of all emergence" (Freire, 2000, p. 109). In this way, effective diversity training brings people together to understand their situationality and act on it.

Comprehending situationality is essential, and many organizations work to understand their positionality and take proactive measures to move forward. For example, changing the literal face of public relations is a focus of the Code Black Manifesto; the manifesto was created by the Code Black Communicator Network and outlined "barriers that have prevented Black communications professionals from entering and succeeding in the field, as well as actions that can create a more equitable working environment" (Kolm, 2020, July 13). For organizations, engaging with employees who, in their behaviours and approaches to the workplace, trend towards egalitarian attitudes can be a positive, and "actions such as simply looking for explicitly egalitarian people to hold places of influence (e.g. policy and initiative-makers, managers and other leadership), publicly endorsing and affirming company members who demonstrate pro-diversity, and providing self-regulatory training for management, can go a long way" (Willard et al., 2015, p. 105). Overall, there is a more focused effort to comprehend "how culture affects our understanding of public relations programming" (Zaharna, 2009, p. 90). The personal influence model of public relations (Grunig et al., 1995), which emphasizes the development of interpersonal (networking-focused) relations between practitioners and their contacts in government, media, and elsewhere, all in order to achieve specified aims, "turns the goal of public relations on its head, in that relations for relationship[s'] sake—without a visible or measurable outcome—can be a valid and primary goal" (Zaharna, 2000, p. 90). This view shifts the practitioner's goal from being immediately results-based and, especially in a cultural context, practitioners may see their work as long and sustained, with the results being accrued over time, rather than in a series of "one-offs."

Wallace and Lutrell (2020, July 7), say that "rather than making DE&I add-on elements of strategic communication campaigns and messages, practitioners should make conscientious decisions to put DE&I considerations at the forefront of their planning." For instance, in planning public relations campaigns, they recommend combining factors of national origin, race, ethnicity, age, physical qualities/abilities, and gender, and then further assessing these elements against elements such as religious background, job, language, mental health and wellness, learning and thinking styles, political background, and personal habits—in total a range of 17 attributes. In this way, practitioners get down to the minutiae of people's lives and get to know and understand their audiences in a comprehensive way.

Accountability in creating more diverse workforces is becoming essential in Canada. A signal of the move to greater responsibility and transparency was the enactment, in January 2020, of an amendment to the Canada Business Corporations Act; it requires federally incorporated companies (more than half of Canadian firms) to report to "shareholders with information on the corporation's policies and practices related to diversity on the board of directors and within senior management, including the number and percentage of members of the board and of senior management who are women, Aboriginal persons, members of visible minorities and persons with disabilities," making Canada the first jurisdiction to require reporting on race and ethnicity in addition to gender (Jeffrey et al., 2019, July 30). The requirement came at a necessary time; according to Cukier et al. (2020), in a report designed to "provide a holistic view of diversity on [corporate] boards through a quantitative analysis of diverse representation on boards and a qualitative deep dive that explores diverse individuals' experiences with pursuing and/or holding board positions" (p. i), found that women were underrepresented on boards, at just under 41 percent, and "For racialized people, the situation is far worse. While racialized people represent 28.4 percent of the population across the jurisdictions studied, they occupy only 10.4 percent of board positions overall" (p. iii).

As workplaces change, workers will demand to see things from a perspective that they understand, welcome and promote. In a study of the responses of 22 university-level public relations students to issues of diversity in the course of engaging in client work as part of their studies, Place and Vanc (2016), found that "when considering diversity in the context of client work, students appear to reference their own diverse identities first, then engage in meaning-making of diversity as they consider individuals and the world around them ... though not articulated explicitly, participants appeared to understand for the most part that 'diversity' was more complex than racial or ethnic diversity, as they often identified elements of religious, cultural, racial, class, or ethnic diversity that they associated with themselves."

Sometimes diversity teaching holds cautionary tales. In the headlong rush for multicultural and diversity awareness and teaching in post-secondary classrooms, Tavares (2007) sees potential hazards in applying western scientism to the topic, such that "multicultural teacher education becomes, intentionally or not, an educational practice that contains diversity and difference, fixes subjectivity, and creates a desire for order and mastery of difference.... While there have been many discursive shifts in the deployment of diversity over the past several decades by educational researchers, educational practice and its research publications remain wedded to the scientific code." As we hurry toward what one of my own thesis-study participants described as "getting those [diversity] check-boxes filled" (Cooper, 2016), we yearn for a sense of enrichment and inclusivity, believing that by proverbially dotting the *i*'s and crossing the *t*'s of diversity education we will achieve everything we need, yet it may have the effect of reinforcing an assumption that "multicultural education and cultural diversity are licensed or authorized discourses that provide the right inventory of cultural norms of different cultural groups. This assumption leaves unchallenged the social relations and political and historical forces which sustain distinctions and differences" (Tavares, 2007).

Diversity training also needs to respond effectively to changing workforce demographics. Public relations professor Aerial Ellis, in a Plank Center panel discussion on millennials and diversity within the public relations industry, said that, from the perspective of being a millennial, "millennials [those born between 1981 and 1996] are redefining the space of diversity and inclusion ... we have a very serious need for expression and acceptance. We're less concerned about the traditional way in which diversity is considered—race, age, and gender. That is an absolute for us. We are accustomed to and must see spaces where there are various races, gender, ethnicity, et cetera. We're now more concerned about how those things then show up in the space of thoughts, ideas, and philosophies" (Ellis, 2017, October 19).

Clearly, more exposure to diversity, through practice in actual workplaces during academic training, offers positive benefits. According to Place and Vanc (2016), "public relations students ... often have difficulty identifying or addressing their personal biases, assumptions, or stereotypes regarding diversity, which holds serious implications for how students, as future public relations professionals, might carry over those biases or assumptions into the workplace ... public relations students may struggle with notions of diversity but can benefit greatly from the exposure to diversity, preparedness and personal growth that client work with diverse publics can offer."

An open, receptive workplace welcomes new ideas, commits to taking employees through a challenging change process by engaging in diversity training, and is open to planning. It involves itself with external and internal diversity and will be well-positioned for future success. According to practitioners, the days of thinking of DEI as an "add-on" function of the business process are numbered—the most important step forward is to embrace change in a straightforward way.

Cukier et al. (2020) call for legislation that "can inform the current values, beliefs, and cultures that impact underrepresented communities' lived experiences" along with rigorous research that informs legislation, the stronger and more rigorous promotion of diversity within organizations, embedding diversity in a way that challenges "potentially exclusionary behaviours, such as recruitment through networks, and provide mentorship and sponsorship opportunities to individuals from underrepresented groups." Coupled with these positive changes are mentoring, more efforts by organizational members from the dominant culture to become effective allies, and the sharing of "stories of success, which can help combat the perception that some organizations or sectors are impossible to enter for leaders from underrepresented communities" (p. 72).

Heath (2020, June 24) argues for inclusivity versus integration (integration being the tendency to hire a more culturally diverse workforce without consideration for the dynamics within the workplace), such that "it's not just enough to hire a diverse group of people and expect they will flawlessly integrate into your company. ... Fostering inclusion in the workplace matters. Not only does it reduce employee turnover because staff feel more valued and included, but it reduces absenteeism, attracts skilled workers and enhances creativity. Different people with different perspectives can drive positive change as everyone works together to build a positive employee culture." Neil Foote, president of the National Black Public Relations Society, Tracey Wood Mendelsohn, CEO of the Black Public Relations Society–New York, and Simon Erskine Locke, founder and CEO of CommunicationsMatch (2020), cite several actions that will assist communications companies to succeed in a world that is increasingly aware of, and working towards, greater DEI, including:

Celebrate Difference: To communicate effectively, companies need diverse perspectives. … When difference and diversity are celebrated and based on respect, rather than imposed, the dynamics are very different.

Build Relationships: It's important on an ongoing basis to seek out and build relationships with Black and diverse PR professionals at agencies or companies.

We Are All PR Professionals: We need to celebrate the talents of inspiring communicators from all backgrounds. … But, if we fail to recognize Black, Hispanic or other diverse professionals among the industry's leading "communicators", the industry is not looking hard enough at the talent within it.

Understand Your Unconscious Bias: The path to changing behaviors starts with self-awareness. Understanding unconscious bias needs to start with each of us.

When Hiring Professionals, Increase the Number of Diverse Candidates: If only one or two of your interview candidates are from diverse backgrounds, you are not trying hard enough (Foote et al., 2020).

What are the elements necessary to create the ideal diversity training program? We can think of the need for inclusivity, engagement and discussion. Organizations will talk often about their bottom line: diversity is going to be important in terms of demonstrating to clients, stakeholders and their industry that they are not just focusing on integration—the hiring of BIPOC professionals—but on inclusion.

Trainers and analysts stress that there can be no "shying away from" the challenges of difficult conversations. "Imparting cultural awareness is only half the battle. … The best training programs should also teach employees how to act in cultural situations that make them uncomfortable" (Chebium, 2015, January 7). Allen and Montgomery (2001, November) outline a top-down organizational approach to diversity, necessitating a "thaw" in resistance and most importantly, support from top-level management. This is a planning-focused corporate approach aimed at entrenching diversity values in order to position the organization for success. They suggest the following stages for diversity-focused change in organizations—Unfreezing, Moving, and Refreezing:

> **Unfreezing:** the forces advocating change must be increased to the point that they overcome the forces resisting change.... It may be a gradual realization on the part of top management that diversity is necessary to be competitive in the present or near term future;
>
> **Moving:** An organization ... must then move through a number of steps to achieve a complete organizational culture change. This movement toward diversity should include such practices as recruiting and outreach programs, co-op and internship programs, training and educational programs, and mentoring and career development programs;
>
> **Refreezing:** Finally, the organization must insure the changes of the moving stage are institutionalized ... by aligning the organizational policies, procedures and the reward system to perpetuate the new culture (Allen and Montgomery, 2001, November).

Research by psychology professor Alex Lindsey and colleagues found that "walking in another's shoes," and setting workplace diversity goals, are proactive ways to conceptualize diversity; the result is a constructive behavioral change through the expression of greater social support and a more empathetic attitude toward the oppressed:

> Taking the perspective of LGBT individuals or racial minorities—by writing a few sentences imagining the distinct challenges a marginalized minority might face—can improve pro-diversity attitudes and behavioral intentions toward these groups ... [as does] asking diversity training participants to set specific, measurable, and challenging (yet attainable) goals related to diversity in the workplace. For example, a trainee might set a goal to challenge inappropriate comments about marginalized groups when overhearing them in the future (in combination with receiving information about how best to handle such situations) (Lindsey et al., 2017, July 28).

Medical schools have embraced the concept of cross-cultural training, by establishing core elements that embed diversity dialogue and teaching into the curriculum and the learning environment practices. These include:

- Creating a diversity and human rights education institutional policy;
- Ensuring a safe and unthreatening learning environment;
- Developing concise learning outcomes;
- Ensuring that content reflects diverse human experiences;
- Building awareness of students' prejudices and biases, with a focus on critical self-examination;
- Integrating cultural diversity in the curriculum;
- Forming multi-disciplinary teams of educators with experience in a variety of communities (Dogra et al., 2009, November 12).

According to Heath (2020), some of the stumbling blocks in moving to an inclusive work environment include:

- Getting stuck in deficit thinking: "This is how it's always been done" or "They need our help to understand our way";
- Assuming "sameness" in everyone: "I treat everyone the same" or "I don't see colour";
- Non-verbal communication: "Why don't they look me in the eye?" Never assume common gestures have the same meaning;
- Stereotypes based on judgement and/or faulty assumptions: "That's just what those people do." Out of stereotypes comes a tendency to evaluate, approving or disapproving against the backdrop of our own cultural views (Heath, 2020).

A TIP FOR CROSS-CULTURAL COMMUNICATION

No judgment: "Respecting others means suspending judgment." If encountering behaviour outside your cultural norm, take "the time to reflect before saying or doing something that you may regret and consider several interpretations of the behavior or situation in question ... [and be] aware of your personal biases. For example, in business situations, you may prefer to communicate in a direct manner rather than to smooth over differences without confronting an issue. Be aware that different cultures handle areas of disagreement in a much more circumspect manner" (Zofi, 2017, June 6).

CASE STUDIES
TEXACO AND STARBUCKS

How does diversity training impact an organization, and what are the outcomes? The following case studies provide a brief examination of the effects of efforts to improve the cross-cultural environment at two major organizations: the oil company Texaco, and the coffee chain Starbucks.

Texaco

In late 1996, the behaviour of senior management at Texaco, engaging in racist jokes about Black employees while in the midst of a discrimination suit, resulted in a significant court settlement of $176 million (Coombs and Schmidt, 2009). During the course of the suit, the company had hired a diversity "guru" to train executives in diversity, and yet its most senior management faltered, not seeming to take the issue seriously (Bierema, 2010, July), such that "after investing heavily in the training, and recruiting minorities into top level executive positions, white executives at the company were caught on tape mocking the diversity training and making racial slurs" (p. 3).

The outcome of the discrimination suit saw a portion of that settlement ($35 million) directed to fund a diversity training program and create a task force of high-profile experts to oversee it (Levit, 2008). The outcome was that "Texaco revamped training, expanded feedback to managers through diversity audits and diversity evaluations, and set up mentoring programs and affinity networks for women and minorities" (Dobbin et al., 2007, p. 21).

According to Bierema (2010, July), a fundamental failure of diversity training is that while it is often well-intended, "such programs fail to address structural power relations that protect white males in organizations and prevent the development and advancement of marginalized workers based on race, gender, class, sexuality, or other positionalities." As such, human resource personnel fail to embrace it, seeing it as unidirectional, not contextual, and "because it demands that asymmetrical power relations be challenged, and traditional ways of conceptualizing diversity be questioned" (p. 10).

In Texaco's case, "some diversity experts dismissed training, arguing that attitudes are difficult to alter but that behavior can be changed with feedback. Instead they supported performance evaluations offering feedback on managers' diversity efforts. Laboratory experiments support this idea, showing that subjects who are told that their decisions will be reviewed are less likely to use stereotypes in assigning people to jobs. ... Texaco's settlement called for a new Leadership Performance Factor (LPF) system for evaluating each manager's progress on diversity. Bonuses were tied to the LPF score" (Dobbin et al., 2007, p. 24). Within a few years, the company had:

- set up seven company affinity networks (such networks are targeted to specifically identified culture groups within an organization, from Black to Latinx, Asian or Gay, and allow for activities such as general discussion, socializing, and speaker presentations);
- established a mentoring program; and
- hired a diversity manager (Dobbin et al., 2007).

Though, as Coombs and Schmidt (2009) note, Texaco was able to rebuild its *public image* through carefully-managed public relations efforts, "at the end of 2000, total minority employment (at Texaco) was equal to its 1996 number at twenty-three percent, whereas the percentage of African-American employees had risen only from nine to ten percent and the percentage of females dropped"; as well, the 2001 merger of Texaco and Chevron made further assessment of any "further progress in diversity" at the organization difficult (Levit, 2008, p. 394).

Starbucks

In April 2018, two Black men, Donte Robinson and Rashon Nelson, were sitting in a Philadelphia Starbucks coffee shop; staff accused them of loitering and called the police; the men were arrested—six officers arrived to carry out the arrests—and escorted from the shop. A video of the incident created uproar as it lit up social media networks. As it turned out, the men were waiting for their business partner to arrive. And therein lay the makings of a public relations crisis, and diversity action by a company whose brand is based on social skills, engagement and a sense of community. Starbucks quickly apologized, then promised change (Stewart, 2018, April 15).

The company announced the closure of all of its 8,000 U.S. outlets for a single afternoon in order to engage in diversity training for its 175,000 employees, the curriculum for which "placed an emphasis on encouraging some employees to become 'color brave' instead of 'color blind'" and meditated on Starbucks' responsibility as the "third place for some members of the community, akin to a home and workplace" (Calfas, 2018, May 30). The company recruited high-profile anti-racism figures to assist, and in small self-guided groups of three to five employees "they reflected by themselves, in pairs and as a group, on the meaning of bias. They privately jotted down thoughts in a customized notebook outfitted with prompts about identity and race. They ran through scenarios that may elicit a biased reaction" (Wiener-Bronner, 2018, May 29).

A sampling of solicited opinions from Starbucks employees post-training ranged from "too much talking on the videos (training was delivered via iPads) and too little group discussion," to the delivery of personal journals for employees to jot down their thoughts, evoking a response of "I don't need to reconfirm what I already know," to a desire for more training, and a criticism that the training focused on a white/Black dynamic without giving consideration for other cultures (Calfas, 2018, May 30).

The shutdown of operations cost the company $12 million in revenue (Calfas, 2018, May 30), and there were questions about the efficacy of the one-day program. "Researchers and social scientists recently told *Time* magazine that a one-time education program isn't enough to combat racism and eradicate the use of racial biases. Hours before the programs began … Starbucks Executive Chairman Howard Schultz said the company plans to globalize these efforts and make similar initiatives part of the on-boarding process for new employees" (Calfas, 2018, May 30).

In July 2018, Starbucks reported on its website that it would roll out a series of training module-based initiatives that would focus on leadership as well as diversity. According to Dahlstrom (2018, July 2), "Some of the topics include cultural perspectives, engaging with empathy, gratitude, building diverse teams and more. … The company is also in the early stages of planning a conference next year [2019] for more than 15,000 store managers and leaders to continue conversations about bias and look for ways to be more inclusive." In January 2019, *Restaurant Business* reported that "Starbucks is testing a new process that allows employees to report worrisome in-store incidents electronically, instead of over the phone, to speed the time it takes to get help to a store. That's one of several changes underway at the Seattle-based coffee giant in the wake of a racially charged incident last spring at a Philadelphia unit that made international headlines, according to a Starbucks-commissioned report on the chain's progress" (Lalley, 2019, January 24). The company reported in 2021 that its efforts included an "Intentional Inclusion & Diversity learning and development plan for Canada focusing on raising awareness of bias and racial inequities, including a Courageous Conversations series to listen and learn from I&D

guest speakers and practitioners" and "partnering with external organizations and experts to support learning and development" (Starbucks, April 13, 2021, https://stories.starbucks.ca/en-ca/stories/2021/starbucks-commitment-to-anti-racism/).

Case Study Questions

1. In thinking about the actions of Texaco executives, how would you categorize their behaviours, based on the readings so far? Were they engaging in white privilege?

2. Do you think that, as Bierema (2010) notes, Texaco's diversity efforts failed "to address structural power relations that protect white males in organizations?" Can you suggest ways to help change attitudes in that kind of situation?

3. What danger does a systemic environment steeped in white privilege present for a company?

4. What are the differences between Texaco's situation and the situation at Starbucks?

5. What do you think of the efforts that Starbucks made to address their issues? Were they effective?

6. How effective will Starbucks be in handling diversity issues over the long term?

PROFILE
DIVERSITY, EQUITY AND INCLUSION CONSULTANT
DR. PAMELA HEATH
As Principal of Calgary-based Heath Consultancy, Dr. Pamela Heath assists organizations to embrace and develop diversity with empathy, genuineness and unconditional respect. She works to help people understand and accept the universality of bias, and to shape that understanding into a means of improving workplace culture and productivity.

A graduate of the University of Calgary with a doctorate in education, Heath has worked at the Southern Alberta Institute of Technology (SAIT), where she was associate director in the office of Learner Services; previously, she worked as academic chair of SAIT's English Language Foundations department.

What should organizations be looking to do in order to develop an inclusive workplace?

Organizations need to see the development of an inclusive workplace as an iterative process; they need to be flexible and willing to take a step back, see the big picture, and implement changes over time. It's not a one-off process. In working with organizations, I usually start with assessments in order to see where people are in terms of their awareness of issues and especially with respect to their own identity and attitudes. You cannot change a structure if there is no real willingness for change to happen; otherwise the underlying white power structure stays in place. Ideally, you want to focus on creating an environment where all employees feel a sense of respect and belonging.

Organizations should be looking at a multiplicity of areas in order to foster such an inclusive environment. It starts with leadership, and asking yourself how you will engage your employees. You have to look at internal practices and hiring procedures, and you especially have to make a commitment to attach resources to new processes in order to get it done properly. It's not a quick fix, and it's not like saying "at the end of the summer we'll get everybody diversity-trained."

The human resources department is a great place to embed those ideas of inclusivity, but too many times senior management will overrule things. Many organizations have this idea of political correctness, you hear people say "I'm really nice to those people," suggesting a built-in denial, and there is an unwillingness to address uncomfortable situations. But you have to be comfortable with being uncomfortable, and there must be recognition that we all carry bias. There are white men I have dealt with who are just enraged with the thought that they have bias. They can't, and won't, accept it, and this is the kind of behaviour that derails productive discussion. We need to assess what is happening, take a step back, and then move forward in a way that engages everyone at the discussion table, taking the time to implement positive change. There is no quick fix.

Why is it important now for companies to be inclusive?

If the workplace isn't inclusive, then how are you encouraging employees to speak up? How do they know if it's okay to speak openly about what they see happening around them? How do you address negative behaviours? Trust has to be built into the structure of your workplace.

If you look at the general statistics, 23 percent of new Canadians grow up not speaking English as a first language; you have issues of gender, race, ethnicity and sexual orientation, and it is vital to look at making your workforce diverse. In fact, engaging in workforce diversity can be quite lucrative for companies—it sends a really positive message to clients, stakeholders and the public. When I look at my life, I am surrounded by diversity. And if you look at the demographics and the next generation coming up, they seem to be a bit bolder about challenging attitudes. They have expectations that the workforce will reflect them. They are a lot more aware than previous generations and they are very tuned in to what's going on around them.

What are some of the inclusivity "stumbling blocks" you have encountered?
I think the biggest one really is that lots of people are not aware of a culture of whiteness; they don't see it. They apply policies equally, and they are trapped in a "policy of equality" which doesn't reflect the realities of the workplace. Equality implies sameness, whereas equity suggests fairness. They are not the same thing. You can have equal policies in a workplace, but there is no equity. We seem to want to apply equity in the same way as equality. We are stuck in the idea that we are not racist. In many workplaces, this Canadian concept of "niceness" pervades, and there is a lack of understanding on the part of white Canadians as to the privilege they enjoy. There is a desire in organizations to put together beautifully worded statements that speak to equity, but there has to be more than that. There is the idea that somehow the words are enough, yet we put up barrier after barrier in front of people with respect to fairness. There is a difference in perspective, in that somehow People of Colour should be grateful for being in Canada, and we expect people to thank Canada for its implied "goodness." Here immigrants are expected to always be thanking us for being here.

In what ways has Diversity, Equity and Inclusion training changed over time?
I think it's moved a lot from intercultural training—the ways in which people communicate between cultures—but really not attending as much to issues of identity. Gender-based analysis is becoming important, and it asks questions about policies that are based on various identity factors beginning with gender. But I don't think the workplace has caught up yet. A lot of what I am seeing, it's focused on integrative models of helping people to fit in. One of the things I worry about, I am getting the sense that whiteness feels it's under attack,

and this is an example of white fragility. Diversity learning has moved from intercultural to inclusive training, but when I look at the courses, they often talk about intercultural learning, but it's really based on an integrative model, there's no anti-racism training, there's no discussion of white privilege, it's just to generally help people fit in. Sometimes people from diverse communities "go along to get along" but we don't think about what happens to a person when they continually have to be someone they're not in the workplace.

What are the top things that organizations need to think of when working toward inclusivity?

First, they need to decide to what extent they want to diversify and become inclusive. If all they're looking to do is a small amount of training, then they need to give an explanation to staff and outline the rationale behind what they are doing. But if they are serious about inclusivity they need to do the work ahead of time and accept that it is going to be a long process; they have to do an assessment, an equity audit, to give them an idea of where they want to start. That in itself can be a bit overwhelming. If you're going to begin the process, you have to have the time and the accountability to go through it—and understand that it is going to get rough before it gets better; you have to have the determination to go through with this and to really make space for other people to be comfortable.

Sustainability is also important and you need a sustainable model for workplace diversity. You can't have just one person doing the diversity work, because if this person goes away, then things fall apart. You need to plan for sustainability and understand how this is going to become the core of the workplace. Right now diversity is very much in vogue, everybody is resilient and determined to do things right now, but where will we be in six months' time? Will organizations be able to sustain that level of commitment?

Finally, you need deep and sustained leadership. Leadership can't just be this passive lip service where you hire a diversity coordinator and say, "Okay, this is your responsibility." Senior leadership has to be driving the bus, because if they're not, it's not going to work. I look to essential elements: leadership, engagement, resources, training and policy. Leaders have to weigh in and be ready to make decisions to make diversity, equity and inclusivity a long-term part of an organization—a leader's job is not to be liked, it is to push the company forward.

In this self-assessment, you will be asked to think about your attitudes toward, and knowledge of, the subject matter discussed in this chapter. On a scale of 1 to 10 (1 being low/disagree/doesn't apply, 10 being high/fully agree/fully applies) rate your knowledge of, and comfort level with, each of the statements presented. These statements may also be used as dialogue starters in group discussions.

Statement	Score
Anti-racism training should be a requirement in every workplace.	
Public relations practitioners are adept at understanding issues of cultural significance.	
I have experienced situations in workplaces or in the classroom where prior anti-racism training would have been effective.	
Organizations will make mistakes based on race and culture but they are easily corrected.	
Cultural sensitivity is something that cannot be taught from a textbook.	
An inclusive workplace is one where people are encouraged to talk about their differences.	

KEY TERMS

Anti-racism: the examination of power imbalances between racialized people and non-racialized/white people that create unearned privileges.

Diversity: the ways in which people differ; the characteristics making individuals or groups different.

Diversity training: training designed to make participants more aware of workplace diversity issues, allow them to understand their own beliefs on diversity, and offer skills to assist them in interaction and collaboration with others.

Equity: access, advancement, fair treatment, and opportunity for all and the focus on eliminating barriers that prevent participation.

Inclusion: creating environments in everybody can feel respected, supported and valued.

White institutional presence: the ability of white people in a given environment to dismiss issues of ethnicity, colour, or culture through emotional, rational and social distancing.

QUESTIONS TO EXPLORE

1. Zaharna (2000) talks about Grunig's "personal influence model of public relations" and the idea that "relations for relationship sake," turns public relations "on its head." Why might this be a good approach to cross-cultural public relations?
2. Think about the examples of diversity training that have been discussed in the text. Then consider an organization that you have worked in—what kind of approach would work? If your organization doesn't need diversity training, what is it doing now that works?
3. What are potential negatives of diversity training?

EXERCISE
CREATE A PLAN AND A MEMO

The scenario: You are working for a medium-size technology company of 250 employees. You are embarking on diversity training for employees. Your job as communications manager, in tandem with the human resources department and an external diversity trainer, is to put together a plan with some basic ideas for training. The training is not in response to any incidents, and your company has what is considered to be a reasonably balanced representation of diversity (it reflects Canadian society) at all levels of responsibility within the company. However, your president feels a responsibility to demonstrate a commitment (internally to employees and externally to clients, stakeholders and the public) to an inclusive workforce, and feels that delivering one or more diversity training sessions is the right thing to do.

Your job:
- Based on what you know and have read, develop some ideas around a diversity training program. What will work? What should you avoid?
- Write a 300-word memo to staff announcing the diversity training initiative.

Think of the 5W's when you write the memo—make it positive, clear and direct. Be sure to explain why the organization is creating and delivering this training.

REFERENCES

Allen, R., and Montgomery, K. (2001, November). Applying an organizational development approach to creating diversity. *Organizational Dynamics.* DOI: 10.1016/S0090-2616(01)00049-3 http://scholar.google.ca/scholar_url?url=https://www.researchgate.net/profile/Richard_Allen11/publication/247142385_Applying_an_organizational_develop ment_approach_to_creating_diversity/links/56b25f0308ae795dd5c7b661/Applying-an-organizational-development-approach-to-creating-diversity&hl=en&sa=X&scisig=AAGBf m1Xp1bET1bEKBmtPECQiod3XASvBg&nossl=1&oi=scholarr

Aylward, C. (1999). *Canadian critical race theory: Racism and the law.* Halifax: Fernwood Publishing.

Anand, R., and Winters, M. (2008). A retrospective view of corporate diversity training from 1964 to the present. *Academy of Management Learning and Education,* 7(3): 356–372.

Bell, D. (1992). *Faces at the bottom of the well.* New York: Basic Books.

Bierema, L. (2010, July). Resisting HRD's resistance to diversity. *Journal of European Industrial Training,* 34(6). https://www.researchgate.net/publication/235286357_Resisting_HRD %27s_resistance_to_diversity

Bivens, D. (2005). What is internalized racism? In Potapchuk, M., Leiderman, S., Bivens, D., and Major, B. *Flipping the script: White privilege and community building,* pp. 43–52. Silver Spring, MD: MP Associates Inc. https://www.racialequitytools.org/resourcefiles/potapchuk1.pdf

BlackNorth (2020, July 21). Canadian CEOs commemorate launch of the BlackNorth Initiative. *BlackNorth Initiative.* https://www.blacknorth.ca/Press-Releases/The-BlackNorth-Initiative-Summit-Launches-With-(1)

Bloom, S. (2005). Lesson of a lifetime. *Smithsonian.* https://www.smithsonianmag.com/science-nature/lesson-of-a-lifetime-72754306/

Calfas, J. (2018, May 30). Was Starbucks' racial bias training effective? Here's what these employees thought. *Time.* https://time.com/5294343/starbucks-employees-racial-bias-training/

Canadian Public Relations Society (2020). Public relations definition. CPRS. https://www.cprs. ca/About.aspx#:~:text=CPRS%20Public%20Relations%20Definition,and%20serve%20 the%20public%20interest.

Chebium, R. (2015, January 7). How to create an effective cross-cultural training program. SHRM. https://www.shrm.org/hr-today/news/hr-magazine/pages/010215-cross-cultural-training.aspx

Chia, J. (2009). Intercultural interpretations: Making public relations education culturally relevant. *Journal of University Teaching and Learning Practice*, 6 (1). https://ro.uow.edu.au/cgi/viewcontent.cgi?referer=&httpsredir=1&article=1085&context=jutlp

City of Oshawa (2020, July 8). Oshawa announces first-ever Community Diversity, Equity and Inclusion Committee. News release. City of Oshawa. https://www.oshawa.ca/Modules/News/index.aspx?feedId=0e765813-d33e-4ba5-b464-3e0fff61eab4&newsId=65245a4e-ca49-4aa5-a30f-f9a4e5a33a3f

Colleges & Institutes Canada (2020). Indigenous Education Protocol for Colleges and Institutes. *CiCan*. https://www.collegesinstitutes.ca/policyfocus/indigenous-learners/protocol/

Coombs, T. and Schmidt, L. (2009). An empirical analysis of image restoration: Texaco's racism crisis. *Journal of Public Relations Research*, 12(2): 163–178.

Cooper, J. (2020, July 30). Interview with Pamela Heath.

Cooper, J. (2016). Community College Instructors and Race: Learning about Teaching a Dimension of Diversity (doctoral thesis). University of Calgary. https://prism.ucalgary.ca/bitstream/handle/11023/3321/ucalgary_2016_cooper_john.pdf?sequence=1

Cukier, W., Latif, R., Atputharajah, A., Parameswaran, H., and Hon, H. (2020). Diversity Leads 2020. Ryerson University. https://www.ryerson.ca/diversity/reports/DiversityLeads_2020_Canada.pdf

Dahlstrom, L. (2018, July 2). Beyond May 29: Lessons from Starbucks anti-bias training—and what's next. *Starbucks Stories and News*. https://stories.starbucks.com/stories/2018/beyond-may-29-lessons-from-starbucks-anti-bias-training-and-whats-next/

Dei, G. (2010).The intersection of race, class and gender in the anti-racism discourse. In Zawilski, V. (Ed.), *Inequality in Canada*, pp. 3–24. Don Mills, ON: Oxford University Press.

DiAngelo, R. and Flynn, D. (2010, August). Showing what we tell: Facilitating antiracist education in cross-racial teams. *Understanding and Dismantling Privilege*, 1(1).

Dobbin, F., Kalev, A., and Kelly, E. (2007). Diversity management in corporate America. *Contexts*, 6 (4): pp. 21–27. DOI: 10.1525/ctx.2007.6.4.21

Dogra, N., Reitmanova, S., and Carter-Pokas, O. (2009, November 12). Twelve tips for teaching diversity and embedding it in the medical curriculum. *Medical Teacher*. https://doi.org/10.3109/01421590902960326

Durham College (2020). Strategic Plan 2020–2023. Durham College. https://durhamcollege.ca/strategic-plan

Ellis, A. (2017, October 19). In "Millennials, diversity and inclusion in the public relations industry" (panel discussion). The Plank Center for Leadership in Public Relations. http://plankcenter.ua.edu/resources/webinars/millennials-diversity-and-inclusion-in-the-public-relations-industry/

Exploring Your Mind (2019, July 9). Blue eyes and brown eyes: The Jane Elliott experiment.

Exploring Your Mind. https://exploringyourmind.com/blue-eyes-and-brown-eyes-the-jane-elliott-experiment/

Fenwick, T. (2008). Workplace learning: Emerging trends and new perspectives. In Merriam, S. (Ed.), *Third Update on Adult Learning Theory*, pp. 17–26. San Francisco, CA: Jossey-Bass.

Foote, N., Wood Mendelsohn, T., and Locke, S. (2020). Diversity in public relations: Eight things communicators & agencies can do today to make a difference. *CommPro.* https://www.commpro.biz/diversity-in-public-relations-eight-things-communicators-agencies-can-do-today-to-make-a-difference/

Freire, P. (2000). *Pedagogy of the oppressed.* New York: Bloomsbury Publishing.

Gladwell, M. (2002). *The tipping point.* New York: Back Bay Books.

Goethe, E., and Colina, C. (2017, December 20). Taking advantage of diversity within the classroom. *Journal of Chemical Education.* https://doi.org/10.1021/acs.jchemed.7b00510

Government of Canada (2020). Canadian Multiculturalism Act. Government of Canada, Justice Laws website. https://laws-lois.justice.gc.ca/eng/acts/c-18.7/page-1.html

Grunig, J., Grunig, L., Sriramesh, K., Huang, Y. and Lyra, A. (1995). Models of public relations in an international setting. *Journal of Public Relations Research*, 7 (3): 163–186. https://doi.org/10.1207/s1532754xjprr0703_01

Gusa, D. L. (2010). White institutional presence: The impact of whiteness on campus climate. *Harvard Educational Review*, 80(4): 464–489.

Hampson, S. (2016, July 8). Derald Wing Sue on microaggression, the implicit racism minorities endure. *The Globe and Mail.* https://www.theglobeandmail.com/life/relationships/derald-wing-sue-on-microaggressions-racism/article30821500/

Heath, P. (2020, June 24). Integrative vs. inclusive: Diversity in the workplace. LinkedIn. https://www.linkedin.com/pulse/integrative-vs-inclusive-diversity-workplace-pamela-heath-edd/?trackingId=t1LZqGgmAZ9nei9%2BfA6XqQ%3D%3D

HR Zone (2020). What is diversity training? Diversity training definition. *HR Zone.* https://www.hrzone.com/hr-glossary/what-is-diversity-training

Jeffrey, J., MacDougall, A., and Valley, J. (2019, July 30). Canada is first jurisdiction worldwide to require diversity disclosure beyond gender; Diversity disclosure rules will apply to federally incorporated public companies effective Jan. 1, 2020. Osler. https://www.osler.com/en/resources/regulations/2019/canada-is-first-jurisdiction-worldwide-to-require-diversity-disclosure-beyond-gender-diversity-disc

Kent, M., and Taylor, M. (2011). How intercultural communication theory informs public relations practice in global settings. In Bardhan, N., and Weaver, C. (Eds)., *Public Relations in Global Cultural Contexts*, pp. 50–76. New York: Routledge

Kolm, J. (2020, July 13). A manifesto against racism in PR. *Strategy Online.* https://strategyonline.ca/2020/07/13/a-manifesto-against-racism-in-pr/

Lalley, H. (2019, January 24). Report: Starbucks making systemwide changes following racial-bias incident. *Restaurant Business.* https://www.restaurantbusinessonline.com/operations/report-starbucks-making-systemwide-changes-following-racial-bias-incident

Levit, N. (2008). Megacases, diversity and the elusive goal of workplace reform. *Boston College Law Review,* 49(2): 367–429. https://lawdigitalcommons.bc.edu/cgi/viewcontent.cgi?referer=http://scholar.google.ca/&httpsredir=1&article=2382&context=bclr

Lindsey, A., King, E., Membere, A., and Cheung, H. (2017, July 28). Two types of diversity training that really work. *Harvard Business Review.* https://hbr.org/2017/07/two-types-of-diversity-training-that-really-work

Logan, N. (2011) The White leader prototype: A critical analysis of race in public relations. *Journal of Public Relations Research,* 23(4): 442–457. DOI: 10.1080/1062726X.2011.605974

Liu, J. (2020, June 15). Companies are speaking out against racism, but here's what it really looks like to lead an anti-racist organization. *Make It, CNBC.* https://www.cnbc.com/2020/06/15/what-it-means-to-be-an-anti-racist-company.html

MacPherson, S. (2006). To STEAL or to TELL: Teaching English in the global era, in Yatta, K. (Ed.), *Curriculum as cultural practice: Postcolonial imaginings,* pp. 71–94. Toronto: University of Toronto Press.

Mora, R. (2014). Conscientização. Center for Intercultural Dialogue. https://centerforinterculturaldialogue.files.wordpress.com/2014/11/key-concepts-conscientizaccca7acc83o.pdf

Muturi, N. and Zhu, G. (2019, August 17). Students' perceptions of diversity issues in public relations practice. *Journal of Public Relations Education.* https://aejmc.us/jpre/2019/08/17/students-perceptions-of-diversity-issues-in-public-relations-practice/

Place, K. & Vanc, A. (2016). Exploring diversity and client work in public relations education. *Journal of Public Relations Education.* https://aejmc.us/jpre/2016/12/14/exploring-diversity-and-client-work-in-public-relations-education/

Pruitt, R. (2018). On diversity in PR … I want to see more people who look like me. *Medium.* https://medium.com/@WeberShandwickSTL/on-diversity-in-pr-i-want-to-see-more-people-who-look-like-me-6308d835b190

Ravazzani, S. (2006). 2nd World Public Relations Festival, "Communicating for Diversity, with Diversity, in Diversity." Institute for Public Relations. https://www.instituteforpr.org/wp-content/uploads/Ravazzani_Diversity_Summit.pdf

Rousseau, J. (2013). *Emile.* Mineola, NY: Dover Publications.

Sloat, S. (2019, April 1). Diversity training study uncovers an unexpectedly positive behavior shift. *Inverse.* https://www.inverse.com/article/54513-diversity-training-results-gender-bias

Stand (2020). Anti-racism defined. Alberta Civil Liberties Research Centre. http://www.aclrc.com/antiracism-defined

Stewart, E. (2018, April 15). Two black men were arrested in a Philadelphia Starbucks for doing nothing. *Vox.* https://www.vox.com/identities/2018/4/14/17238494/what-happened-at-starbucks-black-men-arrested-philadelphia

Tavares, H. (2007). Making diversity desirable: Scientism and the fetishizing of difference. *College Quarterly*, 10(4). http://collegequarterly.ca/2007-vol10-num04-fall/tavares.html

Vaccaro, A. (2010). What lies beneath seemingly positive campus climate results: Institutional sexism, racism, and male hostility toward equity initiatives and liberal bias. *Equity and Excellence in Education*, 43(2): 202–215. doi: 10.1080/10665680903520231

Wallace, A. and Lutrell, R. (2020, July 7). 4 steps for adopting a 'diversity first' practice in PR. *Ragan's PR Daily.* https://www.prdaily.com/4-steps-for-adopting-a-diversity-first-practice-in-pr/

Wiener-Bronner, D. (2018, May 29). How Starbucks' racial bias training went down. *CNN Business.* https://money.cnn.com/2018/05/29/news/companies/anti-bias-training-starbucks/index.html

Willard, G., Isaac, K-J., & Carney, D. (2015, May). Some evidence for the nonverbal contagion of racial bias. *Organizational Behavior and Human Decision Processes*, (128): 96–107. http://faculty.haas.berkeley.edu/dana_carney/bias.contagion_finalpublished.OBHDP.pdf

Williams, M. (2017). John Dewey in the 21st century. *Journal of Inquiry and Action in Education,* 9(1): 91–102.

Wright, D. (2010, July). A critical analysis of the history and development of public relations education in the United States and Canada. First International History of Public Relations Conference, Bournemouth University. https://www.academia.edu/4705454/THE_PROCEEDINGS_OF_THE_FIRST_INTERNATIONAL_HISTORY_OF_PUBLIC_RELATIONS_CONFERENCE?email_work_card=title

Zaharna, R. (2000). Intercultural communication and international public relations: Exploring parallels. *Communications Quarterly*, 48 (1): 85–100. DOI: 10.1080/01463370009385582

Zofi, Y. (2017, June 6). 5 strategies for effective cross-cultural interactions. International Association of Business Communicators. https://www.iabc.com/5-strategies-for-engaging-in-effective-cross-cultural-interactions/

CHAPTER SIX

Making the Conversation Make Sense: Addressing Issues of Oppression, Anger, Violence and Crisis Affecting 2SLGBTQI+ Communities

OBJECTIVES OF THIS CHAPTER

This chapter is designed to help develop an understanding of:

- The historical role Canada has played in opposing, and then embracing, same-sex marriage;
- Attitudes relating to the acceptance of 2SLGBTQI+ communities;
- A "community to community" approach to cross-cultural dialogue;
- The role of communications and public relations in understanding and embracing 2SLGBTQ+ communities;
- An examination of Hallmark's corporate blunder in rejecting the realities of 2SLGBTQ+ communities;
- Allyship and activism in supporting 2SLGBTQI+ People.

SAME-SEX MARRIAGE

To most Canadians, the controversy around same-sex marriage might seem to have moved on, after much debate, from outlawed status through resistance and finally to acceptance. With same-sex marriage legal in Canada since 2005, it is becoming entrenched in Canada's legal system and, to a large extent, the country's shared values. There is a history to that approach: former prime minister Pierre Trudeau, when he was justice minister in 1967, in an appeal for the decriminalization of homosexuality, declared that "there's no place for the state in the bedrooms of the nation … what's done in private between adults doesn't concern the Criminal Code" (CBC Digital Archives, 2020); and while one in four Canadians still oppose same-sex marriage, 75 percent of the population are strongly in favour of it (Little, 2019, August 1).

It wasn't always that way, and in some places you will still find opposition. According to *NorthReach*, the first men convicted of consensual homosexual sex in Canada were Patrick Kelly and Samuel Moore in 1842, and until 1869, Canada imposed death penalties on those convicted of sodomy. In 1949 Jim Egan became the first person in Canada to write as an openly gay man, denouncing discrimination against the gay community; starting in the 1950s, members of 2SLGBTQI+ communities were seen as a threat to security and government, and a 1953 amendment to the Immigration Act banned homosexuals from entering Canada. The first gay-positive organization, ASK, was started in 1964, and "the 'We Demand' protest held in Ottawa in 1971 [became] the first major demonstration of its kind in the country—protestors demanded an end to anti-gay laws and police harassment" (NorthReach, 2020). Throughout the 1970s there were raids on bathhouses and clubs—popular and often clandestine gay hangouts, and in 1981,

"Operation Soap," also known as the Toronto Bathhouse Raids, took place. … [It] is considered to be a turning point in Canadian LGBTQ+ civil rights history. Toronto police raided four bathhouses and arrested over 250 gay men[;] the next night, over 3000 people protested to the arrests and the raids. This is often referred to as "Canada's Stonewall" [the Greenwich Village Stonewall Riots of 1969 were violent protests by the gay community in response to police raids at the Stonewall Inn] (NorthReach, 2020).

Hundreds of gay men were arrested. According to *Canada's Human Rights History*, Operation Soap was the "largest police action since the October Crisis" of 1970, and "The *Globe and Mail* characterized the raids as an "ugly action" and a clear case of discrimination against homosexuals: "This flinging of an army against the homosexuals is more like the bully-boy tactics of a Latin American republic attacking church and lay reformers than of anything that has a place in Canada" (Clément, 2020). Discrimination against 2SLGBTQI+

People continued into the twenty-first century; in September 2000, Toronto police raided a lesbian event at the Club Toronto bathhouse; it was an act condemned as bullying, harassing and homophobic, with critics calling for the resignation of then-police chief Julian Fantino (Nolen, 2000, September 22). Fantino, who, following retirement, would become a Conservative Member of Parliament and cabinet minister in Ottawa, was considered by many to be anti-gay; during his tenure as police chief for the city of London, Ontario, in the 1990s, he was responsible for "Project Guardian, which police hailed as the largest pedophile investigation up to that time but which some people viewed as a hunt for gay men" (Freeze, 2000, June 22).

Apologies for past police behaviour would take some time. Fantino reached out to Toronto's 2SLGBTQI+ communities in the early 2000s; in 2016, then police chief Mark Saunders expressed "regrets on behalf of the Toronto Police Service for the 1981 Bathhouse Raids" (Toronto Police Service, 2020). And in the 2010s, organizations like Pride Toronto took issue with the Toronto Police Service, stemming from the seeming indifference of the police before and during the investigation into multiple serial murders in the gay community committed by Bruce McArthur, characterized by what community representatives called an environment and relationship typified by over-policing and under-protecting 2SLGBTQI+ People. In 2018, it was requested that police withdraw an application to take part in the annual Pride Parade (which annually attracts more than a million visitors); the "community's frustration over the way that police have handled the investigation into alleged [now convicted] serial killer Bruce McArthur might have been the final straw, so to speak, but it's exacerbated by a decades-long struggle for fair treatment from police." This included accusations that a racialized double standard in policing exists, and the "Alliance for South Asian AIDS Prevention has argued that there is a different standard of justice for racialized and LGBTQ2 people in Canada, and ... has called for an independent review into the recent missing persons cases [in 2SLGBTQ+ communities]" (Hooper, 2018, April 16).

It's clear that events like the Stonewall Riot, Operation Soap, and complaints against the alleged lack of protection by police were essential in galvanizing 2SLGBTQI+ communities, triggering a greater push for recognition, acknowledgement and human rights. And it should be acknowledged that gains made by 2SLGBTQI+ People came, not due to the largesse of governments, but through the activism of individuals and groups pushing for change. In our repressively tolerant society, where the status quo always seeks to maintain its equilibrium—

to essentially have things its own way—change is not something that those on the margins can sit and wait for; it has to be sought out in a kinetic exercise of changing the process of how we think and behave and, in due course, how we enact legislation. As Marcuse (2007) notes, "the tolerance which is ... the token of a free society, will never be the gift of the powers that be; it can, under the prevailing conditions of tyranny by the majority, only be won in the sustained effort of radical minorities, willing to break this tyranny" (p. 59).

In the years following Operation Soap, provinces and territories saw the need for change and responded to it, creating their own legislation prohibiting sexual orientation-based discrimination. In 1971, Pierre Trudeau had announced his intention to implement a federal multiculturalism policy; that came to fruition in 1988, with the Canadian Multiculturalism Act. Among its tenets, the Act was designed to

> recognize and promote the understanding that multiculturalism reflects the cultural and racial diversity of Canadian society and acknowledges the freedom of all members of Canadian society to preserve, enhance and share their cultural heritage ... recognize and promote the understanding that multiculturalism is a fundamental characteristic of the Canadian heritage and identity and that it provides an invaluable resource in the shaping of Canada's future ... promote the full and equitable participation of individuals and communities of all origins in the continuing evolution and shaping of all aspects of Canadian society and assist them in the elimination of any barrier to that participation (Justice Laws Website, Government of Canada, 2020, August 6).

Work continued at the federal level to recognize human rights, and "in 1996, Bill C-33, An Act to amend the Canadian Human Rights Act, was enacted, which included sexual orientation. ... The amendment brought the federal Act in line with the provinces and territories, except for Alberta which did not have sexual orientation as protected at that time" (NorthReach 2020).

Over the years, Canada has continued working to burnish its reputation as a 2SLGBTQI+-friendly country. In the U.S., 2SLGBTQI+ rights issues followed a slightly different track:

- Henry Gerber's creation of the Society for Human Rights in 1924 (the first gay rights association);

- The 1950 formation by activist Harry Hay of the Mattachine Society, which promoted social acceptance for gays;
- The banning of gays from working for the U.S. federal government in 1953 (as alleged security risks);
- In 1961, the decriminalizing of sodomy by the state of Illinois;
- Also in 1961, the first televised documentary on homosexuality (CNN Editorial Research, 2020, June 17).

Changes to the law, reflecting societal inclusion of 2SLGBTQI+ rights, continued over the decades, and in June 2020, the U.S. Supreme Court ruled "that federal law protects LGBTQ workers from discrimination. The landmark ruling extends protections to millions of workers nationwide and is a defeat for the [Donald] Trump administration, which argued that Title VII of the Civil Rights Act that bars discrimination based on sex did not extend to claims of gender identity and sexual orientation" (CNN Editorial Research, 2020, June 17). According to Robinson (2015),

> pioneering research done in the mid to late twentieth century helped the field [of gay rights] emerge and set the foundation of the timeline of gay and lesbian activism history. The scholarship published in the twenty-first century relies heavily on this foundation. Scholars in the twentieth century had to prove homosexuals were a minority group, had to combat the belief by many scholars and gay and lesbian activists that the movement had a history before the Stonewall Riots, and studied the most well-known gay and lesbian organizations on the West and East coasts (p. 34).

A STRUGGLE FOR FAIRNESS

The struggle for fairness, recognition and equity was hard fought both in the U.S. and Canada. I am reminded of the time when I worked as a senior communications manager for the Ontario government. As part of our semi-regular "lunch and learn" sessions, I invited the head of one of the civil service's 2SLGBTQI+ alliances—representing and supporting the rights of 2SLGBTQI+ civil servants (there are approximately 60,000 public service employees in the province, and most of the positions of authority continue to be held by white males)—to come and speak to our group. She was white, a lesbian, a nurse. She stood before us in a wood-paneled corporate boardroom, the 40 or so people from the communications branch, most of us cisgender, a handful from 2SLGBTQI+ communities. The speaker's voice was a bit tentative (maybe trying to get a read of our group—*how will they respond*?) but strong as she unfolded her story and the history of her association. She told in heartbreaking detail of watching friends die of AIDS-related illnesses (she said that for a period of about three years, she was attending an average of one funeral a month), of coming to terms with discrimination and oppressive social networks within the Ontario Public Service, how the gains being made were small, incremental, and necessary, and how the voice of the province's 2SLGBTQI+ employees became stronger, more focused—and, finally, heard. I also recall a staff member—white and female—chafing at having to go to this event during the workday, though refreshments were provided and it wasn't outside of regular hours; this staff member argued that having to attend the event threatened her right of refusal, and she said so to myself and another manager. Was it a case of someone saying "you are denying me my right to be bigoted?" Perhaps. Yet how else to reach people? If you are within a community, and have gone through the bumps and trials and heartaches and challenges that living a life within that community represents, how else can you begin to get people from outside the community to understand what you have experienced, except by telling them in as straightforward a way as possible, through having a difficult conversation that would lay out all the potholes and cracks and faults along the road to understanding? It may have helped at the time that we had an openly gay premier, Kathleen Wynne (the first openly gay provincial premier in Canada, in office from 2013 to 2018), and had openly gay cabinet ministers like Glen Murray (a former mayor of Winnipeg, and the first openly gay mayor of a large North American city, a Liberal at the time and later a member of the Green Party). But figureheads can be a way for a repressively tolerant society to simply say "hey, look at us—we're being open and accepting!" while below the surface, discrimination continues. However, there was in Ontario, in the first couple of decades of the 21st century, along with large parts of the entire country, a sense of growing *normativity* to gay rights. This normativity was becoming part of the social and workplace landscape, though commentators such as Smith (2019, January 10), see *homonormativity* as representative of

> advances in LGBTQ rights … [that] privilege same-sex couples who are just like straights except for their sexual orientation. They are thus 'normative' but 'homo' and, hence, 'homonormative'. Some discussions

of homonormativity also emphasize the link to neoliberalism, seeing the domesticated same-sex couples as contributing to neoliberal values (Smith, 2019, January 10).

Yet the growing strength of implied tolerance and acceptance—at least at face value—was also part of larger gains being made across the country. At the federal level, in late November 2016, Prime Minister Justin Trudeau stood in the Legislature and delivered a formal apology to 2SLGBTQI+ People, a speech in which he said the word "sorry" 13 times:

> Today, we finally talk about Canada's role in the systemic oppression, criminalization, and violence against the lesbian, gay, bisexual, trans-gender, queer, and two-spirit communities.... Since arriving on these shores, settlers to this land ... brought rigid gender norms—norms that manifested in homophobia and transphobia. Norms that saw the near-destruction of Indigenous LGBTQ and two-spirit identities ... dis-crimination against LGBTQ2 communities was quickly codified in crim-inal offences like "buggery", "gross indecency", and bawdy house provi-sions.... It is with shame and sorrow and deep regret for the things we have done that I stand here today and say: We were wrong. We apologize. I am sorry. We are sorry (Trudeau, 2017, November 28).

Justin Trudeau, after taking office in 2015, embarked on a very clear agenda to build links to 2SLGBTQI+ communities. In 2017, Graeme Reid, director of the Lesbian, Gay, Bisexual and Transgender Rights Program at Human Rights Watch, lauded Canada for safely resettling almost 30 victims of an anti-gay purge in Chechnya. Those victims had suffered persecution by security forces under the aegis of Chechen Republic leader Ramzan Kadyrov, who was widely criticized for a variety of human rights abuses. Said Reid: "Canada deserves praise for standing up—in word and deed—to Kadyrov's gruesome purge by publicly condemning his actions, pressing the Russian government to inter-vene, and now providing safe haven in Canada to individuals who were strand-ed in Russia, at risk from Chechen security forces and even their own families" (Reid, 2017, September 3).

Statistics on the number of Canadians who identify with 2SLGBTQI+ com-munities vary widely. According to Statistics Canada, in 2014, those who iden-tified as gay or lesbian (ages 18–59) comprised 1.7 percent of the population, and those who identified as bisexual in the same age range accounted for 1.3 percent of the population; in 2011, there were 64,575 same-sex couple families (Statistics Canada, 2017, September 25). Yet a cross-Canada survey by Montreal-based Fondation Jasmin Roy found that 13 percent of Canadians belong to 2SLGBTQI+ communities. About half of all respondents reported that fear of bullying or harassment kept them from coming out to either workplace or academic colleagues in the classroom; a hopeful sign from respondents was that "eighty-one percent of LGBT respondents say that Canadian society has shown a willingness to make efforts to integrate people from LGBT communities" (Fondation Jasmin Roy, 2017, August 9).

Fondation Jasmin Roy also provided a glossary of terms for sexual orientation:

- Heterosexual: A person who is sexually attracted to individuals of the opposite sex.
- Homosexual: A person who is sexually attracted to individuals of the same sex.
- Bisexual: A person who is sexually attracted to men and women.
- Trans: A person whose gender does not correspond to the sex they were assigned at birth.
- Pansexual: A person who is sexually or emotionally interested in other people regardless of their gender.
- Asexual: A person who is not interested in or does not desire sexual activity, either within or outside of a relationship.
- Binary: Defines gender as either male or female.
- Non-binary: Defines genders that fall outside the male/female binary.

The term "Two Spirit" generally refers to "Indigenous people who are gay, lesbian, bisexual, transgender, queer, other gendered, and third/fourth gendered individuals who walk carefully within the worlds and between the genders" (Canadian Centre for Gender + Sexual Diversity, 2020), although Two Spirit is not always used by Indigenous people who identify as 2SLGBTQI+ and so there is a fluidity to it in terms of its adoption. According to Enos (2017, March 28), Two Spirit "has been present in Native communities for countless generations that predate LGBTQ terminology. For generations, Two Spirit Native culture went underground to avoid detection and persecution."

The term "gay" is sometimes ubiquitously used to refer to any relationship within 2SLGBTQI+ communities, "to refer to all people, regardless of sex, who have their primary sexual and or romantic attractions to people of the same sex. The term can also exclusively refer to men who are emotionally, romantically, sexually, affectionately, or relationally attracted to other men, or who identify as members of the gay community. Lesbians, bisexuals, and transgender individuals may feel excluded by the term 'gay'" (Montclair State University LGBTQ Center, 2020). "Queer" is a term that "describes sexual and gender identities other than straight and cisgender. Lesbian, gay, bisexual, and transgender people may all identify with the word queer" (Planned Parenthood, 2020a).

It is important to understand that even the use of the term "community" (as in "the 2SLGBTQI+ community") or "communities" can be problematic, and my use of the term "communities" in this chapter refers to the many communities that make up these spheres of being and is meant to recognize that these communities are multilayered, pluralistic, and diverse. However, it should also be noted that researchers such as Eleanor Formby (2017, August 8) find that the term "community" may be too inclusive of people with widely disparate states of personal understanding and experience. During the course of research, Formby found that study participants

spoke about their quest to find this [2SLGBTQI+] "community"—with many trying and failing to discover such a thing. The idea of an LGBT community suggests that people who identify in this way should feel part of something. If they don't it can compound negative experiences. Many participants in my research also talked about experiencing discrimination from other LGBT people relating to their age, body, disability, ethnicity, faith, HIV status, or perceived social class. So although the phrase implies that LGBT people somehow automatically belong to a ready-made community—this is simply not the case … using "LGBT people" would be more accurate—and would not risk alienation felt by an already (at times) marginalised group of people (Formby, 2017, August 8).

At the federal level, Canada continued to be outwardly supportive of 2SLGBTQI+ People, and in 2019 announced $500,000 to support two projects: the Canadian Trans Network (bringing trans and non-binary people together to work on forward-facing advocacy projects), and Egale Canada Human Rights Trust, an initiative to develop an LGBTQI2S (lesbian, gay, bisexual, trans, queer, intersex, and two-spirit) research lab and hub (Government of Canada, 2019, August 1). As one of 30 countries to recognize same-sex marriage, the Canadian government made it clear, in its legislation and in its public relations and communications approach, that it strongly supports the rights of the 2SLGBTQI+ People, citing the Universal Declaration of Human Rights to underscore the position that

> Canada stands up for the protection and promotion of the human rights of lesbian, gay, bisexual, transgender, queer, 2-spirit and intersex (LGBTQ2I) people globally. The human rights of all persons are universal and indivisible. Everyone should enjoy the same fundamental human rights, regardless of their sexual orientation and their gender identity and expression (Government of Canada, 2020, July 7).

OPPOSITIONAL VALUES

Yet some factions appear to figure highly in opposition to those values. There is a school, Redeemer University College, located in Ancaster, near Hamilton, Ontario, imbued, as it proudly says, with Christian moral standards, and promising on its website that "Redeemer students are being shaped by the Reformed Christian commitment to see faith woven through all aspects of learning and life ... a degree from a Christian university is about what you do on the one hand, and who you are on the other. That changes everything. Starting with you" (Redeemer University College, 2020). All straightforward, so far; Christian values can vary considerably between churches. The United Church, for example, talks about Faith, Marriage ("we welcome all people to the full life of Christian community, including marriage"), Social Justice, Baptism and Communion, Relationship and Inclusion, and Giving, Generosity and Gratitude (United Church of Canada, 2020). All of which appears to be fairly all-encompassing. The Reformed Christian Church (of which Redeemer is a part) doesn't mention any outright ban on, or exclusionary policies toward, 2SLGBTQI+ communities.

Yet within Redeemer's Student Conduct and Accountability Policy was a provision: any behaviour that falls outside the biblical "norms" of heterosexuality is against school policy, and will be dealt with harshly, given that it falls under the school's definition of "sexual misconduct." It appears to be a stalemate between human rights—those of LGBTQ (Lesbian, Gay, Bisexual, Transgender and Queer, which may also be expressed as LGBTQ+ to include orientations such as Two-Spirited and Intersex) students—and the rights of the school to set its own policy, protected, as the school's president told CBC News, under sections 18 and 24 of the Ontario Human Rights Code (Hristova, 2020, August 4). According to the Ontario Human Rights Commission, section 18 recognizes the rights of association for groups to carry out joint activities, and section 24 allows for the application of "creed-based qualifications" to their policies (OHRC, 2020); essentially it means that groups can set their own rules outside of those that apply to other organizations.

The school's stance was challenged by a Toronto human rights lawyer as being discriminatory against 2SLGBTQI+ students, several of whom told the Canadian Broadcasting Corporation that they quit going to the school because of its policies. This might not be an issue if the school were solely privately funded, "but it can still access taxpayer money through grants and funds [and did receive federal grants for infrastructure]. Human rights experts say the government giving money to a school found to discriminate would contravene the Canadian Human Rights Act and potentially the Charter of Rights and Freedoms" (OHRC, 2020). The stance of Redeemer University College represented a rigidity and an unwillingness to shift from a set of "traditional" practices and beliefs, and yet at the same time there was a tacit willingness to accept money from a government that clearly accepts and appears to embrace and certainly endorse 2SLGBTQI+ rights. The government has made this position clear through legislation: in 1996, the Canadian Human Rights Act was amended to specifically include sexual orientation as one of the prohibited grounds of discrimination. This inclusion was a clear declaration by Parliament that gay, lesbian and bisexual Canadians are entitled to

> an opportunity equal with other individuals to make for themselves the lives they are able and wish to have … The Canadian Human Rights Commission, which is responsible for monitoring the application of the Act, gives further information about human rights and sexual orientation. … Within the Canadian Charter of Rights and Freedoms, section 15 states that every individual is to be considered equal regardless of religion, race, national or ethnic origin, colour, sex, age or physical or mental disability (Government of Canada, 2020).

Redeemer University continued to make headlines when, in 2022, the death by suicide of a transgender student resulted in the school working to "finalize a report and recommendations that many are hoping will improve support for students, especially in the LGBTQ community." (Hristova, 2023, May). The resulting recommendations were called "insulting" by the chair of Hamilton's LGBTQ advisory committee; the report made "no mention of the LGBTQ community" (Hristova, 2023, June).

The question is "where do the rights of one end and the other begin?" If an organization is permitted to exercise its rights through exclusion, can this be allowed/forgiven/accepted in an inclusive world? Do we give a pass to those who say "within the confines of this particular infrastructure (office, school, building, club, business) we will do as we please, even if that means discriminating against other people," or do we seek to establish guidelines (as governments do) that lean toward acceptance of all viewpoints, orientations, identifications, and backgrounds?

As we discussed in the first chapter, the Canadian Public Relations Society's first code of conduct is that members "shall practice public relations according to the highest professional standards. Members shall conduct their professional lives in a manner that does not conflict with the public interest and the dignity of the individual, with respect for the rights of the public as contained in the Constitution of Canada and the Charter of Rights and Freedoms" (CPRS, 2020). For public relations practitioners, it makes things clear in terms of their expected professional behaviour.

This idea of respect for the *dignity of the individual* calls to mind the words of writer James Baldwin, who was both Black and gay, and his struggles with defining himself while growing up in the racist, homophobic world of the United States in the middle of the 20th century:

> Loving anybody and being loved by anybody is a tremendous danger, a tremendous responsibility. … The terrors homosexuals go through in this society would not be so great if the society itself did not go through so many terrors which it doesn't want to admit. The discovery of one's sexual preference doesn't have to be a trauma. It's a trauma because it's such a traumatized society. … It seems to me simply a man is a man, a woman is a woman, and who they go to bed with is nobody's business but theirs. I suppose what I am really saying is that one's sexual preference is a private matter. I resent the interference of the State, or the Church, or any institution in my only journey to whatever it is we are journeying toward (Baldwin, quoted in Goldstein, 2018, June 22).

According to researcher Miriam Smith, there are inherent problems with Canada's public-facing support for 2SLGBTQI+ rights while at the same time allowing for legislation that continues to discriminate against members of the community. In a way similar to the "white neutral norm" and its effect on race issues, issues of sexuality are influenced by "the persistence of political homophobia alongside of homonationalist celebration of queer normativity" (Smith, 2019). This duality of thinking (outward community support but legislative disapproval) means that "Canadian progress in the legal recognition of LGBTQ rights has been accompanied by homophobic public policy that sanctions the symbolic and actual criminalization of anal sex" and "the development of legal prohibitions against discrimination on the one hand versus the ongoing symbolic and actual criminal regulation of gay sex on the other hand" (Smith, 2019). Although in 2016, legislation was proposed to remove Section 159 from the Criminal Code of Canada (regarding the legality of anal intercourse), the 1969 decriminalization of homosexuality

> existed as an exception in the criminal law prohibition outlawing gross indecency.... The government's inability and unwillingness to change the law entails an ongoing stigmatization in which gay sex continues to be singled out for criminal regulation, even though the law has repeatedly been found to be unconstitutional. This alerts us to the idea that, even in jurisdictions that can be considered homelands of queer progress [as Canada fashions itself], homophobia remains. Homonationalist celebration coexists with the ongoing encoding of second class legal status for queers" (Smith, 2019).

COMMUNITY TO COMMUNITY IN CROSS-CULTURAL DIALOGUE

There can be a widening gap between understanding and supporting communities, and misreading, misinterpreting and tearing down, rather than building and strengthening open, receptive and supportive lines of communication. This leads to a vast misunderstanding and a lack of proper interpretation of what might be said, written, or delivered in any form, whether it is a speech, a news release, or a social media post.

Communities connecting with other communities is essential—an exclusionary community (like the private Christian college mentioned above) may set its own rules, but even the exclusionists are still functioning within larger communities, and this demands an ability to (as I recall my kindergarten teacher saying) "get along well with others." According to Gomez (2013), "inclusion really means accepting, embracing, and celebrating the gifts, talents, and differences in all of us as a means of shaping communities that are welcoming places for all people ... inclusion has evolved from an aspiration linked to place to one tied to participation, choice, and relationships. ... In inclusive communities, people belong" (Gomez, 2013, June 1).

Inclusion demands empathy, but it must be sincere, and driven by feelings that go beyond being merely transactional. "Empathy helps connect people, moving them toward each other in a helping and/or healing capacity. ... As we live our lives at work and at home, we are continually interacting and balancing relationship dynamics. When we lack empathy, we are unable to develop and nurture those interpersonal connections" (Clarke, 2020). Empathy can be approached in different ways, and Clarke cites cognitive and emotional empathy as two essential approaches to connecting with others. Cognitive empathy connects us through being able to see the world through another's eyes or experiences and to understand the feelings of another person; with emotional empathy, we feel another person's distress, we share in their experience, and we are willing to take on a burden to help another person; other empathic responses include affective empathy (understanding someone else's emotions and responding in kind) and somatic empathy, involving a physical reaction, such as blushing, in response to another person's experience (Clarke, 2020).

Yeomans (2016), in a study of empathy in public relations, found that "while empathy in PR is discursively framed as a desirable skill for practitioners, reinforcing neo-liberal notions of the self-enterprising individual and emotional competence/capital, the type of empathy suggested within a business context is inevitably instrumental and codified in its pursuit of business goals" (p. 21).

Yeomans (2016) goes on to say that

I question the desirability for practitioners to engage in other-centred emotional empathy using intercultural communication conceptualisations and call for a re-framing of empathy, for example, as "role-taking" or "social perspective taking" to emphasise cognitive definitions of other-orientated practice. These concepts do not exclude the possibility of emotional empathy and feelings of genuine human concern in professional relationships, but neither do they connote the commodification of feeling, with which the concept of empathy is inexorably loaded within a commercial context" (pp. 21–22).

Reaching out and challenging the business world to be inclusive is part of the Human Rights Campaign's (HRC) Corporate Equality Index, "the national benchmarking tool on corporate policies, practices and benefits pertinent to lesbian, gay, bisexual, transgender and queer employees" (Human Rights Campaign, 2020). The HRC is the largest political lobbying organization and biggest supporter of 2SLGBTQI+ rights in the U.S., and was the result of a merger between the Gay Rights National Lobby and the Human Rights Campaign Fund. Through 11 comprehensive programs and a variety of resources, the HRC Foundation supports 2SLGBTQI+ individuals, allies, and institutions. The Corporate Equality Index allows anyone to find the points rating of private companies, municipalities and health care facilities in the U.S. For instance, a search for "Buffalo, New York," found that the city had perfect scores (5 out of 5) in non-discrimination laws for sexual orientation and gender identity in employment, housing and public accommodations.

CHANGING THE VIEW: THE ROLE OF COMMUNICATIONS

Media and communications have been essential in helping to change public perception of 2SLGBTQI+ communities. And it appears to be clear that good government support is necessary to backstop the messaging that is delivered in support of communities. In a study of the effect of transnational media on boosting mainstream acceptance of 2SLGBTQI+ People, Ayoub (2018, May 24), writes of the popularization of openly gay characters in television shows through the 1990s and into the twenty-teens; a pivotal moment in particular was the coming out of Ellen Degeneres in 1998 in her sitcom, *Ellen:*

> Media portrayals of new issues and previously marginalized people are an understudied dimension of the ways ideas, values, and principles are spread—transnationally as well as within countries ... as the liberalization of attitudes towards gays and lesbians has occurred in many countries across the globe since the 1980s, change has been encouraged in part by communications climates—within and across nations—that allow for the free transmission of minority viewpoints. Yet gaps in tolerance and freedom of expression remain between free countries and those that restrict the sharing of controversial content or minority viewpoints. To close gaps in tolerance and cultural change, movements and leaders must encourage various forms of media to tell more accurate stories about lesbian and gay people (Ayoub, 2018, May 24).

Pride parades began the year after the Stonewall events, and the first parades, in Chicago, San Francisco, Los Angeles and New York, soon inspired similar events elsewhere. Despite the fact that today there are more than 150 Pride parades worldwide, discrimination against members of 2SLGBTQI+ communities continues, with one in five lesbian, gay or bisexual employees being discriminated against, and up to 47 percent of transgendered employees facing discrimination. And in the public relations industry, the "cool factor" of 2SLGBTQI+ employees can lead to exploitation. "LGBT practitioners in public relations were frequently asked to help plan campaigns and design message strategies that would attract LGBT audiences while not offending mainstream heterosexual audiences for certain brands while simultaneously being asked for advice on how to make niche campaigns over the top for brands targeting the LGBT community," suggesting that the industry lacks a deep or serious view of a major part of its workforce (Waters, 2014, June).

The work of gaining mainstream acceptance has been an uphill, but ultimately—depending on how you look at it—successful battle; according to Noah Berlatsky, in a review of Leigh Moscowitz's *The Battle Over Marriage: Gay Rights Activism Through the Media,* advocacy groups worked hard to normalize the life of gay people through proactive public relations campaigns, shifting the focus away from the trite or exoticized early-years photographs and accounts (as well as mainstream perceptions) of community members as denizens of "seedy bars" or bathhouses and shifting the emphasis toward "wholesome" images featuring more "conventional" behaviours. "They sent video tapes of gays and lesbians in domestic settings—walking their dog, cooking dinner, coming home from work—to the TV networks for use as background, or 'b-roll,' footage for related news stories. They worked to get LGBT-friendly religious leaders in front of the cameras. The campaign against negative representation, particularly in the gay marriage debate, was effective," though it also started to shift the mainstream news media in the direction of images that were as heteronormative as possible (aligned with heterosexual stereotypes) and also forced other issues (such as workplace discrimination) to the margins (Berlatsky, 2013, November 15). And public relations firms may offer jobs for creative, enthusiastic members of 2SLGBTQI+ communities, but they sometimes fall short of demonstrating an all-engaging, complete approach to these communities—for instance, they may hire, promote and nurture the careers of gay communications practitioners, but they don't always listen to their advice when it comes to diversity matters, or, while being accepting of a practitioner's sexual orientation, the organization may expect them to conform to a "look" that smacks of heteronormativity, says Thomas Moore, who interviewed six public relations professionals who are also 2SLGBTQI+ People. Overall, the marks given to the industry ranged from a C to a B+ (Moore, 2019, June 4).

The 2SLGBTQI+ communities in the U.S. are worth a lot of money. According to Schneider and Auten (2017, April 4), "the purchasing power of the queer community in the U.S. is near $1 trillion. The pink dollar [a term widely used to describe 2SLGBTQI+ spending] was approximately 14 percent of all disposable income in the U.S. in 2016. Gay and lesbian couples earn more than straight couples." In Canada, according to a 2015 Nielsen Survey

the pink dollar … accounts for $3.8 billion in consumer packaged goods (CPG) sales across Canada. That translates to $5,400 per household annually, which is less than the $5,835 the average household spends. But hold on to your seats! While LGBT consumers may be spending slightly less than the average, they shop more often. In fact, they make 170 trips per year—10 more than the average Canadian household. That means marketers have many more opportunities to directly interact with a ready-to-spend consumer in a trip-declining industry (Nielsen, 2015, June 29).

And a 2017 survey by advertising agency Ogilvy found that "nearly two-thirds of Americans (65 percent) believe that LGBT-inclusive brands/businesses are good for the economy, and a similar number (64 percent) believe that these initiatives reflect our country's diversity. However, the majority (68 percent) report that in order to be an LGBT ally, brands/businesses need to "walk the talk," following through on promises and plans" (Carufel, 2017, July 10).

Given that kind of economic—and by extension, social—power, there are public relations and marketing firms that focus almost solely on 2SLGBTQI+ People, including OutNow (banking, tourism, insurance); Popular Publicity NY/Penetration Inc. (websites, blogs, video, events); Outbrands (ecommerce, lifestyle marketing, web design); and Flip @ Radarworks, Inc. (specializing in connecting Fortune 500 companies with the LGBT community) (Tannahill, 2015, April 27).

The economic clout extends deep into the private sector. Can a T-shirt or sweatshirt trigger discussion, activism, a difficult conversation? Perhaps. A clothing company, Self Sovereignty, https://sovereigntyofself.com/ "is run by

Queer Indigenous womxn of color who are proud intersectional feminists (click click) fighting for Self Sovereignty. We are passionate about fighting for what's right and looking confident while doing so. We want badass people everywhere to wear their resistance, creating conversations, one t-shirt at a time. We ARE the resistance" (Self Sovereignty, 2020). The clothing is adorned with phrases like "The American Dream is a Pyramid Scheme," "Protectors Not Protestors," "I Stand with Indigenous" and "Indigenize." According to Tovar (2020, July 22), the Aotearoa (New Zealand) based company is aiming to "critique and dismantle" colonization, and the clothing pays tribute to the cultural lineages, values and perceptions of creators Laura (Ngāpuhi and Ngāti Kahu Ki Whangaroa) and Jonie.

HALLMARK'S BLUNDER

There are times when mainstream corporations blunder, and they don't listen carefully to what is being said, or they provide a knee-jerk reaction response instead of thinking critically about the issue, and they then have to take the time to make things right.

When crises happen to organizations, they have to consider what Coombs and Holladay (2014, January) refer to as the "rhetorical arena," and within the rhetorical arena, "sub-arenas."

According to Coombs and Holladay, "a rhetorical arena opens around a crisis and is where the various crisis voices are heard. Those voices are not limited to those representing the organization. The rhetorical arena is the space where numerous crisis actors talk about the crisis. … Sub-arenas consist of 'spaces' where crisis publics may express and hear ideas about the crisis" (2014, January, p. 41).

For Hallmark Cards, Inc., an error it made in December 2019 was measured not only in lost revenue, but also in loss of trust—along with major pushback from significant action groups in the "rhetorical arena" that was created. A purveyor of soft-edged, relaxed romance movies—many targeted to viewers during the holiday season—Hallmark Cards, Inc., which oversees Crown Media Family Networks, found itself in the middle of a controversy after it bent to conservative pressure and removed a Zola commercial from a broadcast—the commercial featured a lesbian couple getting married. To say that Hallmark movies, to date, have been heteronormative would be an understatement, so there was little for conservatives to complain about. But when the company caved in and removed "one-stop" wedding-planning company Zola's ad from a broadcast in December 2019, the roar was deafening, and resulted in the resignation of the chief executive of Crown Media Family Networks, along with key changes to the company's policies and approach. "The Hallmark Channel first removed the wedding company's pro-2SLGBTQI+ ad after it was mentioned in a blog post by One Million Moms, which bills itself as a group of parents working to stop the 'exploitation of children' by entertainment media" (Madani and Atkinson, 2020, January 22); as well, the conservative Catholic group LifeSiteNews had compiled an anti-gay-material-on-Hallmark petition of 40,000 names. Hallmark then felt backlash from the Human Rights Campaign, which admonished Hallmark for not showing leadership in working to increase the visibility of 2SLGBTQI+ communities (Aviles, 2019, December 10).

Pressure was on for Hallmark to do two things: reinstate 2SLGBTQI+-positive advertising (which it did, quickly), and also "greenlight an LGBTQ script ASAP … (and) Hallmark said it would work with GLAAD to further ensure LGBTQ consumers felt represented" (Dry, 2019, December 17). GLAAD, formerly the "Gay & Lesbian Alliance Against Defamation" (since 2013 it has expanded its mandate to include bisexual and transgender issues, shortening the name to just GLAAD) was founded in 1985 by 2SLGBTQI+ representatives in the media; as a non-governmental media monitoring organization, it "tackles tough issues to shape the narrative and provoke dialogue that leads to cultural change" (GLAAD, 2020).

Hallmark responded to the crisis in a detailed news release that underscored its contrition and its commitment to change:

> Hallmark is, and always has been, committed to diversity and inclusion—both in our workplace as well as the products and experiences we create. It is never Hallmark's intention to be divisive or generate controversy. We are an inclusive company and have a track record to prove it. We have LGBTQ greeting cards and feature LGBTQ couples in commercials … [we] have been recognized as one of the Human Rights Campaigns Best Places to Work, and as one of Forbes America's Best Employers for Diversity. … Hallmark will be working with GLAAD to better represent the LGBTQ community across our portfolio of brands. The Hallmark Channel will be reaching out to Zola to reestablish our partnership and reinstate the commercials (Hallmark, 2019, December 15).

GLAAD responded to Hallmark's decision with a message from GLAAD President and CEO, Sarah Kate Ellis:

The Hallmark Channel's decision to correct its mistake sends an important message to LGBTQ people and represents a major loss for fringe organizations, like One Million Moms, whose sole purpose is to hurt families like mine. LGBTQ people are, and will continue to be, a part of advertisements and family programming and that will never change. GLAAD exists to hold brands like The Hallmark Channel accountable when they make discriminatory decisions and to proactively ensure families of all kinds are represented in fair and accurate ways (GLAAD, 2019, December 15).

In the summer of 2020, Hallmark continued to deliver on its promise of change, "taking a small step forward in its strive for inclusivity and diversity in its storytelling. Their latest original movie … *Wedding Every Weekend*, features the first same-sex wedding on the network. … While Hallmark has, in the past, included LGBTQ characters and couples in its original movies, they have often been supporting characters. This is the first time a gay wedding ceremony has been featured in a Hallmark movie" (Ng, 2020, August 15).

This crisis began—and the rhetorical arena opened up—not necessarily due to the Zola commercial but with the *reaction to it* (from One Million Moms) and then the reaction by Hallmark to One Million Moms, followed by *responses from stakeholders* like the Human Rights Campaign and GLAAD. "Crisis managers need to consider sub-arenas into their crisis communication efforts. As part of monitoring the effects of a crisis communication effort, crisis managers need to map the various sub-arenas, assess how people are reacting in the various sub-arenas, and adapt their crisis messaging to those reactions" (Coombs and Holladay, 2014, January 1, p. 53). Hallmark, sensitive to the influence of its stakeholders, responded quickly and decisively, and managed to reestablish a position of trust with them; in the early 2020s it began releasing an increasing number of gay-themed movies.

ALLYSHIP, ACTIVISM, POLICE AND 2SLGBTQI+ COMMUNITIES

What works in the 2SLGBTQI+ community in terms of activism—the kind of energy-laden, people-driven influence that drives societal change? How are social media initiatives used to help guide people in establishing their identity and their place in the world?

Identity, and how individuals come to understand themselves against the background of, and within, society, is a slow and steady process of change. Ac-

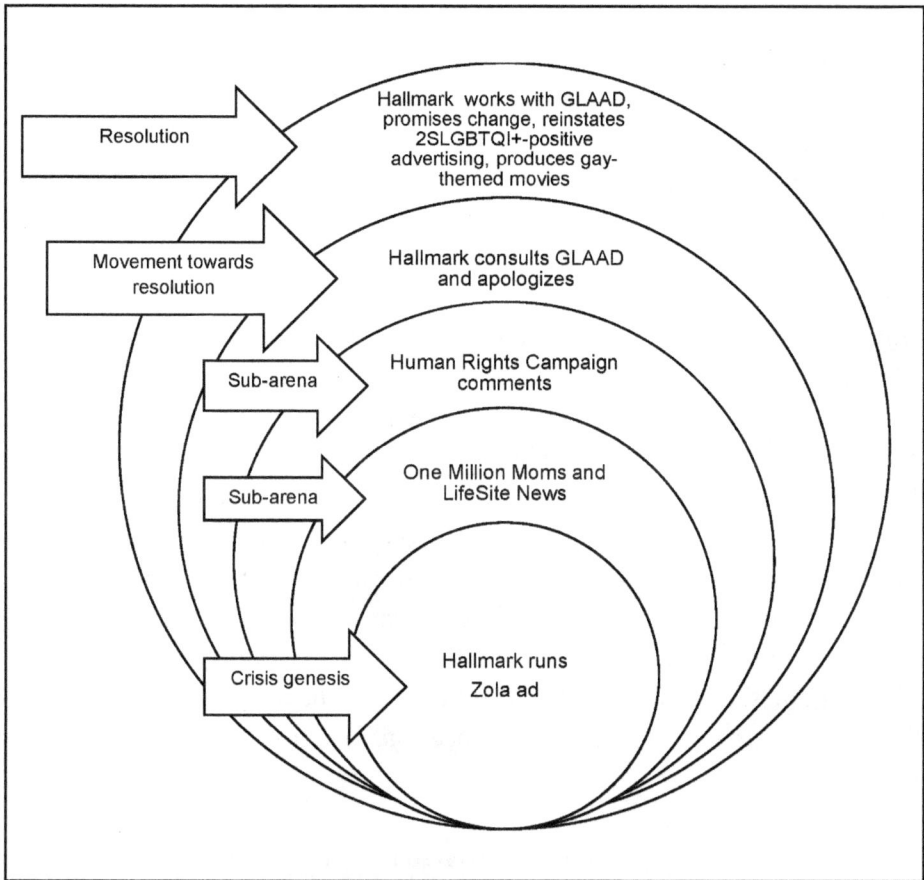

Hallmark's Zola Crisis: Rhetorical Arena

cording to Pożarlik (2013), identity is both a process and symbolic—it comes to symbolize what is expected by the individual with respect to their relationship within a community. "The social is the space where the individual and the collective gain concrete meaning as they emerge as a consequence of social role playing.... Thus, 'self as reflection of society' finds ... explanation in the symbolic construction of identity as a process negotiating meanings attached to concrete forms of behaviour" (p. 79).

Ciszek (2014), in a study of activism and advocacy among youth in the not-for-profit It Gets Better Project, found that "strategic communication has been instrumental in construction of LGBT as a cohesive collective identity and has played a vital role in the early stages of the gay rights movement ... the construction of identity is the result of a dynamic process between producers and consumers in which power is localized and does not simply belong to an organization or its public" (pp. iv).

The It Gets Better Project describes itself as "a nonprofit organization with a mission to uplift, empower, and connect lesbian, gay, bisexual, transgender, and queer youth around the globe. Growing up isn't easy, especially when you are trying to affirm and assert your sexual orientation and/or gender identity. It can be a challenging and isolating process—but, the good news is, no one has to do it alone" and its vision message states that "The It Gets Better Project envisions a world where all LGBTQ+ youth are free to live equally and know their worthiness and power as individuals" (It Gets Better Project, 2020). Among its corporate partners are Arizona Iced Tea, Converse, Jack & Jones, Riot Games, Tik Tok and Zenni.

According to Ciszek, The It Gets Better Project, as a social media-driven entity, unfolds in a space that while purporting to be democratic (open to posts from individuals) uses a measure of control over what is put on its site and, as such, "identities are produced and consumed as part of the cycle of production/consumption, in which meanings arise through articulations" (p. 138); despite the articulation of identity in different cultural spheres, identities are temporary, though stereotypes such as the culture of homophobia endure, and Ciszek found that these engrained identities are difficult to deconstruct. Ciszek further found that unlike the in-your-face confrontation that typified past protests,

> contemporary activism, as demonstrated here [in the It Gets Better Project], uses strategic communication and strategic decision making to carry out organizational objectives in ways that entangle them in marketplace considerations. The It Gets Better Project, activism, and public relations are not in separate camps but occupy a more fluid environment that is informed by cultural-economic forces. Market forces and economic need can lead to the co-opting of activist organizations, pulling them into the mainstream as they align with corporations and major funders to keep themselves afloat (Ciszek, 2014, pp. 147–148).

It is essential to recognize that while traction has been made to push for the recognition and acknowledgment of 2SLGBTQI+ rights, 2SLGBTQI+ People continue to deal with issues of discrimination and violence such as physical assault, sexual assault, and robbery. According to Simpson (2018, May 31), citing the 2014 General Social Survey on Canadians' Safety (Victimization), lesbians, gays and bisexuals were two times more likely than their heterosexual counterparts to be victims of violent crime … bisexual individuals were almost nine times more likely to be sexually assault-ed [in the previous year]. … Among those who reported experiencing discrimination in the five years preceding the survey, lesbian and gay individuals were significantly more likely (79 percent) than their bisex-ual (35 percent) and heterosexual (2 percent) counterparts to perceive the discrimination as being based on their sexual orientation (Simpson, 2018, May 31).

In 2022, and based on the continuing challenges faced by 2SLGBTQI+ com-munities, in that they encounter "higher rates of harassment and violent vic-timization as well as poorer economic outcomes than their heterosexual and cisgender counterparts," the federal government launched "Canada's first Fed-eral 2SLGBTQI+ Action Plan … a suite of measures that seek to advance eq-uity and protect hard-earned rights, while also tackling discrimination against 2SLGBTQI+ individuals" (Statistics Canada, 2023, August 16).

2SLGBTQI+ People have taken, for countless years, the brunt of brutal be-haviour, driven by what is known as the Dark Tetrad of bullying: "Machiavel-lianism … a tendency to calculatedly manipulate others for your own good; psychopathy, an attribute that includes a lack of empathy … sadism, the pro-pensity to derive pleasure from inflicting pain on someone else; and narcis-sism, an obsession with self and feeling that you are better than other people" (Bernstein, 2020, July 14). For bisexual youth, being bullied, and not being able to find an avenue for dealing with it, along with a lack of support (coupled with rejection from gay, lesbian and heterosexual communities—which may in some cases see bisexual youth as hypersexualized, a perpetuating stereotype in itself) means that many victims of crime are unwilling to report incidents to police, and the "result is a group of individuals experiencing violence more fre-quently, but reporting it less. … One potential reason for this is the stipulation that reporting these crimes means sharing personal, often secret information." Responses from Canadian police and social service departments to provide safety to members of 2SLGBTQI+ communities include the Regina Police Ser-vice; it started a campaign called "Safe Place" to make members of 2SLGBTQI+ communities feel safe and supported when they contact authorities to report a crime; in Saskatoon, a group called OUTSaskatoon operates a safe-haven shel-ter for 2SLGBTQI+ youth (Praill, 2018, June 5).

Support and assistance are necessary, for the history of violence toward

2SLGBTQI+ People is long and severe, and actions to educate the public as well as curb systemic discrimination against these communities are still on-going. George Washington University professor Bonnie Morris cites the June 12, 2016, mass shooting at the Pulse nightclub in Orlando, Florida, where 49 people died and 58 were injured, as a turning point in attitudes of officials and institutions towards 2SLGBTQI+ People. The dance club was popular with the gay community and

> the immediate, caring response from mayors, police and FBI authori-ties, local and national politicians, and the President of the United States [Barack Obama], who reached out to express outrage and concern, demonstrates the enormous shift toward acceptance and public support for the LGBT community. Although the LGBT community and individ-uals remain targets for hate violence and backlash throughout the world, the hard work of activists and allies made it possible to reach this era, where the perpetrators of violence, not the victims, are condemned as sick (Morris, n.d.).

In the year following the shooting, there was a greater sense of community between the mainstream and 2SLGBTQI+ communities in Orlando, and while Orlando citizens continued to express concerns over the violence, its long-term effects, and the continuing challenge of confronting homophobia, positive ac-tions did take place, such as the launch by Orlando Police of "a Safe Place ini-tiative which encourages businesses and organizations to display decals stating their commitment to sheltering gay, lesbian or transgender people who are victims of hate crimes or are feeling threatened … many in Orlando's gay com-munity say that over the past year they have felt a welcoming communal spirit in the city that makes them stand a little taller and feel a little … well, prouder" (CNNwire, 2017, June 12). The kind of support that reaches across cultures is what allyship is about. Allies are essential to the 2SLGBTQI+ community; an ally "is a member of the dominant group who works to end oppression in his or her own personal and professional life by supporting and advocating with the oppressed population" (University of Illinois, 2020). As an essential and proac-tive supporter of 2SLGBTQI+ People, bringing fairness, mutual respect and eq-uity to the process of building links between the mainstream and 2SLGBTQI+ communities (GLAAD, 2020a), an ally "adopts an identity as someone in a social position of moral responsibility to advocate for members of a group …

adopts moral obligations to that group in virtue of taking up a social position as an ally; and … actively works against the oppression that harms individuals within the group. When adopting this identity, an ally assumes some power to act in a group's interest and to speak on its behalf" (Trent University, n.d.)

Support has continued to come through the efforts of social support organizations and government channels and this has been seen in areas such as opposition to conversion therapy. According to GLAAD, "Conversion therapy is any attempt to change a person's sexual orientation, gender identity, or gender expression. … Proponents of conversion therapy often intentionally conflate the attempted altering of sexual orientation, gender identity or gender expression with the treatment of an actual condition such as sexual addiction." It has also been variously described or promoted using terms such as "reparative therapy," "sexuality counseling" or "sexual orientation change efforts" (GLAAD, 2020b). Writer Peter Gajdics described the painful process of undergoing conversion therapy in a magazine article in 2018:

[The] therapy meant to help me overcome past trauma had turned into a form of "conversion therapy" meant to "correct the error" of my homosexuality. … Over the next six years, the doctor prescribed near fatal dosages of various concurrent psychiatric medications … directed me to "release my pain" and to "feel my rage" during prolonged sessions of primal scream therapy; he injected me weekly with ketamine hydrochloride … before "reparenting" sessions where I would lie in his lap like a newborn baby so he could nurture me as my new "daddy…" The truth of the matter is that practitioners of conversion therapies—whether religious-based or, as in my case, secular—prey on the vulnerable and those in need of relief from suffering by turning the desire to belong into a desire to change one's sexuality" (Gajdics, 2018, June 6).

In March 2020, Canada's federal government introduced Bill C-8, which would amend the Criminal Code to outlaw conversion therapy, either delivered to an adult against their will, or the administration of conversion therapy to any child under any circumstances; it also criminalizes the advertising of conversion therapy and the taking of profits from such therapy (Open Parliament, 2020).

Digging into the roots of issues such as transphobia often falls to academics, activist groups, and medical and mental health practitioners. Transphobia "is the fear, hatred, disbelief, or mistrust of people who are transgender, thought to be transgender, or whose gender expression doesn't conform to traditional gender roles" and it can be expressed through any number of ways, from bullying and the expression of irrational fears to name-calling and violence (Planned Parenthood, 2020b). In March 2020, British journals announced the Transphobia Project, an initiative spearheaded by transgender activist Andrea James and designed to build, through an examination of written pieces on gender identity, "an interactive data visualisation platform mapping people and media outlets that publish biased content about gender identity and expression." Through examining the use of language that leans toward transphobia, the project is focused on identifying bias, and James noted that "when a journalist writes about trans issues for a news outlet known to publish transphobic content, it is likely that the article would have a similar tone ... these attitudes cross political divides, in what [James] described as 'islands of intolerance'" (Green, 2020, March 17). Even famed author J. K. Rowling showed a perceived lack of awareness and understanding of trans issues when she created a Twitter-storm by expressing "her unfounded befuddlement over an opinion article titled, 'Creating a More Equal Post-COVID-19 World for People Who Menstruate,' pushing back against the headline for not referring to those who get their periods as just 'women.' The tweet sparked a wave of backlash from the 2SLGBTQI+ community and its supporters, who were quick to remind Rowling that transgender people, non-binary people and gender-nonconforming people can also menstruate" (Delbyck, 2020, June 7). Social media is the platform on which much discussion plays out. For instance, digital media consumer intelligence company Brandwatch, which scans billions of consumer data-focused insights online, joined with Ditch the Label, an anti-bullying charity, to create a transphobia report that resulted from the analysis of 10 million social media posts over more than three years, exposing 1.5 million transphobic comments (Brandwatch, 2019). The joint study found that the results pyramided in severity, from transphobic comments at the bottom, through acts of trans bias, discrimination and violence, up to comments on trans genocide. In the U.S., trans abuse comments spiked when U.S. President Donald Trump proposed a military ban on trans people in July 2017, and in September 2018, proposed defining gender biologically. The study did note that it found that "constructive, pro-trans conversation far outweighs the negative ... [yet although] Transphobic conversation is in the minority ... it's still very loud and very damaging" (Brandwatch, 2019).

The challenges confronting transgender individuals are distinct; a study by

Abramovich et al. (2020, August 28), found that by comparison to cisgendered people (those who identify with the gender that is assigned to them when they are born), transgender people face much higher rates of poverty, threats of violence, and discrimination in education and in the search for employment. The research found

> that transgender individuals were more likely to live in lower-income neighborhoods, experience chronic physical and mental health conditions, and have higher health service use compared with the general population. Specifically, our study found higher rates of asthma, COPD, diabetes, and HIV and greater rates of mental health comorbidity ... transgender individuals experienced high rates of depression, anxiety disorders, post-traumatic stress disorder, schizophrenia, and other psychotic disorders. Transgender individuals experience major challenges accessing health care because of a lack of transgender-competent and inclusive health services, lack of practitioners with sufficient transgender inclusion training, and systemic discrimination (Abramovich et al., 2020, August 28).

So protracted can the lack of understanding be (and so great the degree to which 2SLGBTQI+ issues are politicized) that in the U.S., former federal education secretary Betsy DeVos made a promise to hold back on $18 million in grants to Connecticut schools "unless they withdraw from an athletic conference that allows transgender students to compete on teams 'that correspond with their gender identity' ... in May [2020], the Education Department's Office of Civil Rights claimed that the Conference violated the [federal government] Title IX rights of women and girls to receive equal opportunities in education and athletics" if they had to compete against transgender girls. Called "extortion" by critics of the education director's decision (Court, 2020, September 18), it was an example of the right-wing Republican Trump government using cisgender privilege and reverse discrimination to uphold historically embedded discrimination against transgender people.

Pushing back against intolerance is a focus of organizations like Pflag Canada, which   concentrates on giving support to families of 2SLGBTQI+ People, especially during the process of their children "coming out." Pflag Canada, established in 1994 with 70 chapters or representatives in nine Canadian provinces, was "founded by parents who wished to help themselves and their family members understand and accept their LGBTQ2S children." It has been described as Canada's "only national organization that offers peer-to-peer support striving to help all Canadians with issues of sexual orientation, gender identity and gender expression" through the provision of resources and education (Pflag Canada, 2020). As a proponent of fairness and advocate for positive change, Pflag Canada offers commentary on social issues that affect 2SLGBTQI+ People. In summer 2020, when the town of Aurora, in the Region of York, north of Toronto, decided to repaint a crosswalk in its downtown core in the colours of the rainbow flag, it was hailed as a very gay-positive gesture in a suburban area (on a side note, the Rainbow Flag was created by artist and drag queen Gilbert Baker in 1978—the rainbow as a symbol of 2SLGBTQI+ People had ties to gay community icon Judy Garland, her role in the movie *The Wizard of Oz* and the song "Somewhere Over the Rainbow"; its multiple colours formed a graphic representation of diversity, and according to Baker, "a flag is a more powerful symbol than a seal or a sign, since it is flown to represent a nation, people or country" [Swanson, 2015, June 29], and has a universality to it that transcends borders).

In general, small towns and suburbs are not known for being communities with strong support for gay rights, and many 2SLGBTQI+ People living outside of large cities will be closeted, or they will find other ways to fly under the radar of communities where the physical and emotional bullying directed toward those who live outside the heteronormative standard can be staggering. The regional association Pflag York Region was outspoken in its support for the gesture, and while some opposed it (though it was paid for by an anonymous donor), an Aurora town councilor "argued the crosswalk supports council's recent adoption of an inclusion charter, which welcomes and promotes diversity" (Queen, 2020, July 16). The crosswalk was painted, a media event walk-across was held, and all was well for a few days, until one person in a truck deliberately left skid marks on the crosswalk, and someone used black spray paint to deface it. And arrest was made, and the community strongly condemned the acts (Rodrigues, 2020, August 22). Pflag York Region President Tristan Coolman offered a public thank-you to the town of Aurora and York Regional Police:

There will always be hate in every community big and small. But these acts of hate are just a small example of the hate that is woven through LGBTQ2 history and our daily lived experiences. … We thank the Town of Aurora and York Regional Police for their swift action, which also

shows our community that acts of hate are not tolerated. The bright colours which represent our Pride, our resiliency and our resolve will always shine much brighter than any form of hate (Coolman, August 23).

Note how the statement connects the "acts of hate" with the history of
2SLGBTQI+ communities ("a small example of the hate that is woven through
LGBTQ2 history") and the "daily lived experiences" of 2SLGBTQI+ People.
There is an immediacy to the statement, and the statement works to enhance
a sense of greater community by thanking the Town of Aurora and York Regional Police for showing that "acts of hate are not tolerated," bringing Pflag
solidly within the greater community, and serving, in turn, to de-marginalize
the groups represented by Pflag. The final portion of the statement brings it
to a positive, forward-looking conclusion ("our resiliency and our resolve will
always shine much brighter").

On the flip side, a case of small-town bigotry was demonstrated by the
town of Emo in northwestern Ontario, on the Ontario-Minnesota border,
where local businesses and churches supported Pride efforts but politicians
vetoed positive acts of tolerance, acceptance and understanding. Journalist
Emma Teitel wrote in the *Toronto Star* of a gay lawyer's efforts to promote
2SLGBTQI+ diversity and inclusion through the Borderland Pride initiative,
linking communities on both sides of the border, and yet "Emo's town council [citing conservative 'Christian values'] voted to reject Borderland Pride's
resolution to officially declare June Pride month and display a rainbow flag
outside the town council, a decision that provoked media attention in the
wider community and expressions of anger and disappointment on social
media" (Teitel, 2020, June 1).

Reaching out successfully to 2SLGBTQI+ People, especially young people,
who may feel marginalized, alone and powerless, hinges on sound information
campaigns. In an examination of public relations and 2SLGBTQI+ activism,
Ciszek (2017, May) established that a thorough understanding of target groups
is essential in order to conduct successful campaigns, and this knowledge will
drive communications efforts with respect to planning, messaging and strategic communications overall (Ciszek, 2017, May). According to Fleming (2015),
audience analysis ("Who are we trying to reach," "What are their preferences?"
"What do they already know?" "What are their needs?" and "How will we fulfil
those needs?") plays a significant role in planning, and involves a close look at
demographics (age, gender, occupation, income, education), psychographics

(lifestyle preferences, personality and interests); and geographics (looking at where the target audience lives and examining how this affects preferences, political views, and choices), as "in-depth information on audience lifestyles, education, age, and attitudes better prepares the practitioner to develop strategies that guarantee success" (p. 183).

Ciszek (2017, May) found that 2SLGBTQI+ campaigns will be formulated as

an intervention designed to stop young people from spiraling downward, because LGBT people are commonly the victims of bullying and experience suicidal thoughts. [In Ciszek's research] several activists perceive navigating identity as an LGBT young person as dangerous. From this perspective, the campaign functions as a lifeline for young people (p. 4).

Activist "gatekeeping" of stories and messaging (some allowed in, others not) helps to shape the dialogue and in turn "builds an agenda for LGBT issues, often focused on bullying and suicide prevention. In this way, the project sets a public agenda for LGBT issues that helps define the contemporary LGBT movement" (Ciszek, 2017, May, p. 4).

CASE STUDY

TORONTO'S PRIDE PARADE, BLACK LIVES MATTER TORONTO AND CONNECTIONS BETWEEN COMMUNITIES

In the summer of 2016, Black Lives Matter Toronto (BLM-TO) was invited to take part in the Toronto Pride Parade, a major event organized by non-profit Pride Toronto, an organization with "a mission to support our communities in the pursuit of our unequivocal rights to be known, be heard, be understood, be accepted, be respected, and to celebrate the beauty of who we are" (Pride Toronto, 2020). When the parade got to its two-thirds-completed point, BLM had a sit-down protest, demanding that Pride parade organizers sign a list of BLM-generated demands. The demands included a provision to not include parade floats from police forces in future parades.

According to the CBC, a BLM Toronto news release said "Pride Toronto 'has shown little honour to black queer/trans communities, and other marginalized communities. Over the years, Pride has threatened the existence of black spaces at Pride that have existed for years.' The group released a list of demands, including a commitment to increase representation among Pride Toronto staff, and to prioritize the hiring of black transgender women and indigenous people" (CBC News, 2016, July 3). After some discussion, Pride officials signed the demands in order to get the parade moving again and organizers and Black Lives Matter Toronto representatives discussed providing more space and funding for Pride events focused on 2SLGBTQI+ Black youth and Indigenous representatives. The following year, at the 2017 Pride Parade (at which uniformed police were banned), BLM Toronto representatives—though not scheduled to take part in the parade—inserted themselves into the parade route towards the end of it; holding placards, "they chanted and repeatedly stopped the parade for a few seconds at a time" in order to "refocus the "narrative" on the [anti-Black] issues the group aims to confront" (Gray, 2017, June 25).

Academic and writer Rinaldo Walcott said the debate continued to rage

between those who believe all gay rights are now secure and those who understand that rights are parsed out according to privileged identities. On the one side, many are white male queers, and on the other side many are Black, Indigenous and bisexual people of colour (BIPOC), including poor queers, sex workers and people with disabilities. Those in the second group are still collectively fighting for fully accorded rights to be their full queer selves; to them, the police still represent a clear and present danger (Walcott, 2017, June 28).

The intersectionality of the issue was impactful for 2SLGBTQI+ communities. According to Pannu (2017, August 14),

the more minority groups one identifies with, the more discrimination and stigma that person may experience. One could assume that a black, queer woman would, in essence, have a more difficult life experience than a heterosexual white male just by virtue of her experiences as a woman, compounded with her experience as a black person, and topping it off with her queer identity. ... She would have to work that much harder to be taken seriously in today's heteronormative, white, male-dominated world.

Recognizing the connectedness between BIPOC communities, 2SLGBTQI+ communities and global health issues, a live-streamed event called Global Pride

2020 was held in June 2020 as a response to the effect of the COVID-19 pandemic on marginalized communities and especially its role in forcing the cancellation of Pride events worldwide. It was estimated that 300 million people tuned into the event, which was organized through an international collaboration of Pride associations and 2SLGBTQI+ organizations. As "the first-ever worldwide gathering of the LGBT+ community … (Pride 2020) announced it will put Black Lives Matter at the centre of their event … the event will be a ray of light amid the global coronavirus pandemic that is disproportionately affecting LGBT people" (Wareham, 2020, June 13). And in the same month, a New York rally brought together representatives of 2SLGBTQI+ communities and Black Lives Matter "when 15,000 people came together for the Brooklyn Liberation march and rally for Black Trans Lives. …These coalitions draw strength from one another. It is this sense of community that keeps us going. We know we're a part of a larger, shared experience. It's a community where people are accepted, and where you are supported through tough times" (Kai, 2020, June 22).

PROFILE

ACTIVIST, SPOKESPERSON, PUBLIC SPEAKER:
RAHIM THAWER WALKS MANY PATHS

As a social worker, psychotherapist, mental health and EDI consultant, lecturer, writer and therapy podcast host, Rahim Thawer knows well the intersectionality that exists in Canada's 2SLGBTQI+ communities. He's been a counsellor at the AIDS Committee of Toronto, Hassle Free Clinic, 519 Church Street Community Centre and Sherbourne Health. At the time of writing, he was an instructor at the University of Alabama School of Social Work. He has also been an organizer with Salaam Canada and Ismaili Queers: Advocates for Pluralism; both groups focus on creating space for people identifying as both Muslim and queer and trans. As a gay Muslim, Thawer speaks with ease and clarity about the changing face of being gay in Canada and, especially, the challenges of cross-cultural engagement.

While navigating the mainstream heteronormative culture growing up, Thawer's formative years in the Toronto suburb of Etobicoke brought him into contact with Communities of Colour as well as enclaves within Canada's 2SLGBTQI+ communities. It was an experience that occasionally left Thawer in a position of defending his culture and religion while coming to terms with being a gay Person of Colour; as such, it made for a granular, pragmatic, sometimes fragmented but wholly enlightening upbringing. Following graduation from the University of Waterloo and resettling in Toronto, he finally, as he noted in an online article, "found the intersectionality I sought in a number of places: working for a South Asian AIDS organization and through co-founding Ismaili Queers (IQ), a queer Muslim organization. It seemed that once I met a few queer people of colour, I could set myself up to meet more. … I felt ready to be with my people and to live at the intersections of my many identities" (Thawer, 2021).

What are some of the challenges in being queer and Muslim, and how do multiple identities allow you to strike a balance with the communities around you?
I grew up in a close-knit Muslim community, and looking for representations of queerness within my community was difficult. They were there, but they just weren't visible.

It really isn't about how progressive a community is; when you grow up in a community that's close-knit, you experience and anticipate the possibility of loss and rejection in a unique way because you worry that if you come out or put words to your identity, you're at risk. You may also internalize an idea about "being bad" or understanding yourself as being "against nature." The developmental trajectory of understanding myself started with pride in my Muslim identity and then calling into question for years how a religion that wasn't for me could create space for me. While I was grieving this loss and anticipating implications of potential rejection, I sought out community resources and groups that were LGBTQ-focused; I felt out of place there too, but the distance from my origins was needed. I could sit with myself and explore what it meant to me to be a gay man. I could ask "What does my sexual orientation mean for my life? Who do I want to be in the world? What might my future look like? How will relationships look in my journey? Do I want to pray in a congregation again? Can I be culturally Muslim? What if I want to be an atheist Muslim?" You have to take time to explore these layers of your identity.

Moving back to Toronto post-undergrad I saw such a visible community of LGBTQ Muslims, and that put me at ease. I recognized that a lot of religion is culturally influenced or ritual-based and that alone is a legitimate way to engage with the world (with the absence of theological teachings and beliefs). I started to think about the nuances of being a Muslim in a largely white society. In a Eurocentric society like this one, lots of people have ways to engage with rituals like Easter or Christmas with varying degrees of religiosity. That was not readily afforded to me as a racialized Muslim living in Canada. I decided that I wanted to choose what fits for me in a way that's neither in opposition to my religious community nor adherent to any rigid belief system. This is something lots of white folks get to do without scrutiny. And giving myself permission to do this has helped me reconcile the multiple layers of my identity.

How does cross-cultural dialogue work in helping you with an intersectional reality?

Cross-cultural dialogue is important but challenging: we cannot make assumptions about which group of people is more progressive and accepting and which groups of people are backwards and regressive. Both in Muslim and non-Muslim communities, in racialized and white communities, there's going to be a range of acceptability of LGBTQ+ individuals, some accepting and some not. This can range based on exposure to ideas and dreams, economic status, or educational background. Don't get me wrong: you can have money and formal education and not be open-minded. For example, there's a common assumption that in small communities there is less acceptance compared to big cities. However, I've met a number of people who grew up in smaller places where everyone knew each other and while it wasn't all rainbows and confetti, they talk about how people accommodate for you—sometimes even defend you—because they know your whole family.

I am someone who is South Asian and Muslim but Canadian-born, and we (including myself) often think of coming out as being a very explicit thing. There is something about being "out and proud" that gives many of us a sense of liberation; but we have to recognize that it also contradicts values in some cultures around showing pride. For some, life is governed by humility so the language of pride or proudness can feel a bit antithetical to how authenticity and coming into one's true self is conceptualized in the west. There's a tension there that we need to reconcile so that we allow people to show "pride" in multiple expressions.

What about the concept of homonormativity? How does it play out in your life and in your work?

I would be inclined to say that having access to dominant spaces is an experience of power, and power feels good, and if you have proximity to power it can be easier to lose sight of other people who are still struggling, and it can be easier to submerge oneself in a dominant view or lens. This is the threat of a new normativity—one that begins with a cis and straight worldview and is upheld by mostly binary gay men and queer women who have fought to fit in instead of for the right to stand out. Fitting in always means excluding others; it's this system that makes capitalism and white supremacy so successful.

I think it's important to be vigilant about what it might mean to get comfortable with our progress or our individual acceptance and celebrations that focus on gains; it's so important to think about who's being left out and how some people benefit from others' exclusion. For example, a double-income gay male couple might really appreciate being able to own a home and adopt children in a neighbourhood that makes them feel comfortable—especially years after enduring homophobia. But, how do they respond when newcomers to Canada move into that area and/or the municipality makes plans for supportive housing projects to be developed nearby? Their homonormative life—a supposed symbol of collective progress—erases the intersectional needs of others. It shows up in their concerns of real estate property value, fear-mongering around safety, and sudden ideas about scarce resources in their neighbourhood.

In what ways are you critical of the politicization of gay rights?
Canada has benefited from homonationalism; its track record on gay rights has made the country overall seem progressive, which only serves to try to erase the past and present inequities that exist. We are not a stand-alone community defined only by who we love—though people like to say that a lot. For example, Canada fails queer and trans people when it continues to fail Indigenous communities, and it is a leader in criminalizing people with HIV; Canada also routinely turns away LGBTQ asylum seekers who face death when not given refuge. Similarly, the Canadian government is not interested in defunding those police services that have shown again and again that they cannot be reformed and simply do not protect the most vulnerable. Both the government of Canada and police services across the country have tried to "apologize" for the ways queer and trans people have been criminalized but they continue to surveil people of colour, harass trans women, and brutalize Black men—that's not progress, that's pinkwashing.

How do members of the media treat the topic of LGBTQ+ Muslims?
I think in the last five years there has been more positive media coverage and the opening of LGBT-affirming prayer spaces or mosques in various places in Canada, the United States and Europe, and I think there's one in Australia as

well. Having coverage in mainstream media is important. I have seen queer and trans Imams being featured in stories and op-eds as well. Researchers are increasingly interested in the queer/trans Muslim experience; it's positive but tiring as well. I worry about how people in our communities will participate and how this research will actually help them in future.

When there is a news piece about Muslims—whether as victims of Islamophobic violence or extremist perpetrators of something—the media exists as a source of fear and anxiety for LGBTQ+ Muslims. Our worldviews, our identities, our rage and grief, often all get disenfranchised.

As a therapist, activist and teacher, the work you are doing is really important. What does the future hold?

People ask me, "Why do I want to support religion, which might represent institutionalized kinds of homophobia?" and I say, "Look, I think many religious institutions have done harm to LGBTQ people but we can't see them [the institutions] as static or fixed, but rather as organisms that change over time." If someone comes to a queer Muslim space, it doesn't matter if they want to pray or if they are atheist, they belong in that space, so that if they have an experience of growing up in a Muslim community, have struggled or embrace that identity, they belong in this space and what people need is space where they can figure out who they are without having to deal with Islamophobia or homophobia or transphobia. They can make meaningful connections with people without worrying about their safety or who is talking about them. That is the kind of space I am interested in cultivating. Hopefully, the future has a lot more space for racialized queer and trans Muslim voices.

LET'S CHECK IN!

In this self-assessment, you will be asked to think about your attitudes toward, and knowledge of, the subject matter discussed in this chapter. Think about the statements in each of the boxes in the diagram on the next page, and indicate whether you: agree strongly; agree somewhat; are neutral; disagree somewhat; or disagree strongly (but try to avoid a "neutral" answer). Then prepare to explain your thoughts as you share your results with your colleagues.

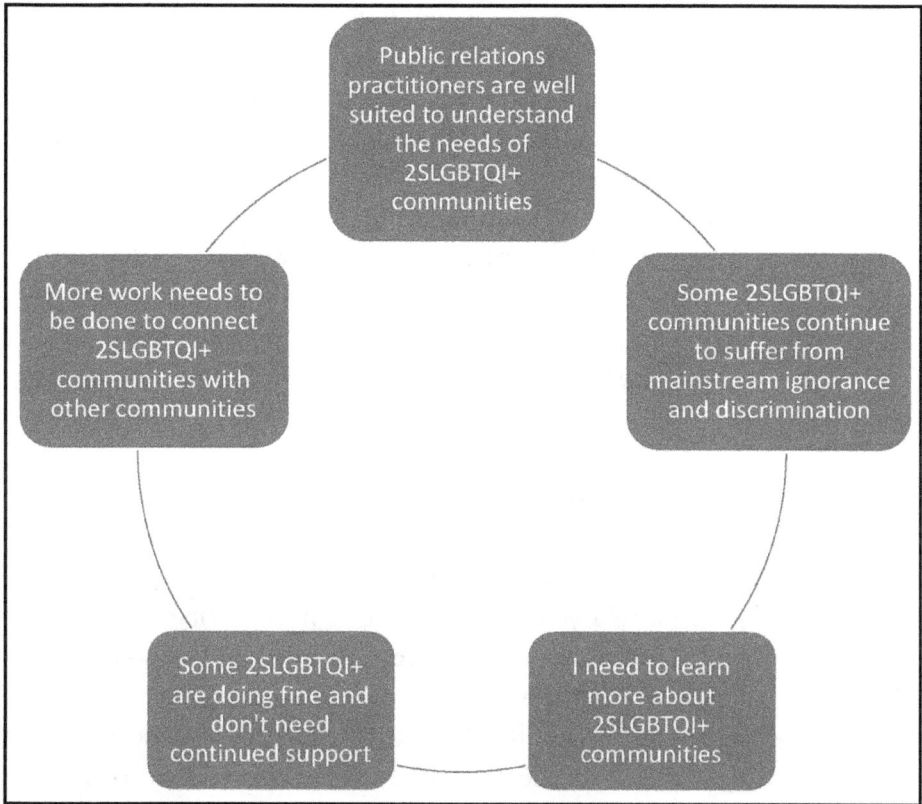

```
                    ┌─────────────────┐
                    │ Public relations│
                    │practitioners are well
                    │ suited to understand
                    │   the needs of  │
                    │   2SLGBTQI+     │
                    │   communities   │
                    └─────────────────┘

┌─────────────────┐                    ┌─────────────────┐
│ More work needs to│                  │ Some 2SLGBTQI+  │
│ be done to connect│                  │communities continue
│   2SLGBTQI+     │                    │  to suffer from │
│ communities with│                    │mainstream ignorance
│ other communities│                   │ and discrimination│
└─────────────────┘                    └─────────────────┘

┌─────────────────┐                    ┌─────────────────┐
│ Some 2SLGBTQI+  │                    │ I need to learn │
│ are doing fine and│                  │   more about    │
│   don't need    │                    │   2SLGBTQI+     │
│ continued support│                    │   communities   │
└─────────────────┘                    └─────────────────┘
```

KEY TERMS

Ally: a member of the dominant group working to end oppression by advocating with, and supporting, the oppressed population.

Asexual: A person who is not interested in or does not desire sexual activity, either within or outside of a relationship.

Binary: Defines gender as either male or female.

Bisexual: A person who is sexually attracted to men and women.

Cisgender: identifying with the gender that is assigned to an individual at birth.

Heteronormative: a position or view that promotes heterosexuality as the ideal standard for behaviour and orientation.

Heterosexual: A person who is sexually attracted to individuals of the opposite sex.

Homosexual: A person who is sexually attracted to individuals of the same sex.

Non-binary: Defines genders that fall outside the male/female binary.

Pansexual: A person who is sexually or emotionally interested in other people regardless of their gender.

Rhetorical arena: the space that opens up around a crisis; the space is filled with crisis voices that occupy sub-arenas. Public relations practitioners must examine, understand and respond to the concerns that are expressed in each sub-arena in order to effectively manage the crisis.

Transgender: A person whose gender does not correspond to the sex they were assigned at birth.

Two-spirit: a term used generally (though not always) by Indigenous people who are gay, lesbian, bisexual, transgender, queer, other gendered, and third/fourth gendered.

QUESTIONS TO EXPLORE

1. What does the term "normativity" mean to you? If you were writing a newsletter article on gay marriage, how would you treat this idea of normativity? Is it okay for heterosexual people to think that gay marriage means 2SLGBTQI+ People can be "just like us"?
2. You work for an organization that is providing corporate support for Pflag Canada. Create five major messages that you would want to deliver to a meeting between Pflag representatives and your organization.
3. Why do you think Hallmark made the initial decision it did in pulling the Zola ad from its broadcast? What does Hallmark's subsequent apology and recommitment to 2SLGBTQI+ People say about the position corporations are taking with respect to 2SLGBTQI+ communities?

EXERCISE

MIND MAP THE REASONS WHY

In early 2021, the Toronto Catholic District School Board (TCDSB) was involved in an action that earned it a strong measure of disapproval before it sought to correct the situation. In an article in the newspaper *Corriere Canadese*, complaints were lodged against the board for offering a link on its website to the website for the LGBTQ YouthLine organization, an online resource for 2SLGBTQI+ youth; there were suggestions that the site hosted "pornographic" content. The TCDSB removed the link to the site. YouthLine responded with a strong statement condemning the newspaper article, stating that its site is a key resource for marginalized 2SLGBTQI+ youth, and adding that the "rhetoric [in the newspaper article] is harmful, unacceptable, and is overt homophobia and transphobia. ...What's extremely concerning is that the TCDSB felt it appropriate to remove our much-needed service from their resources based on an article that is homophobic, transphobic, and racist" (LGBT YouthLine, 2021, January 11). After a meeting with board representatives, TCDSB reestablished the link on its website (Lavoie, 2021, January 15).

Your job: Mind map the issues around the decision to remove the link to the YouthLine website.

Questions:
1. Why do you think the TCDSB responded so quickly?
2. What might have been a more effective way of handling the situation regarding the newspaper article?
3. From a communications perspective, what does the TCDSB need to do in future to ensure greater inclusiveness?

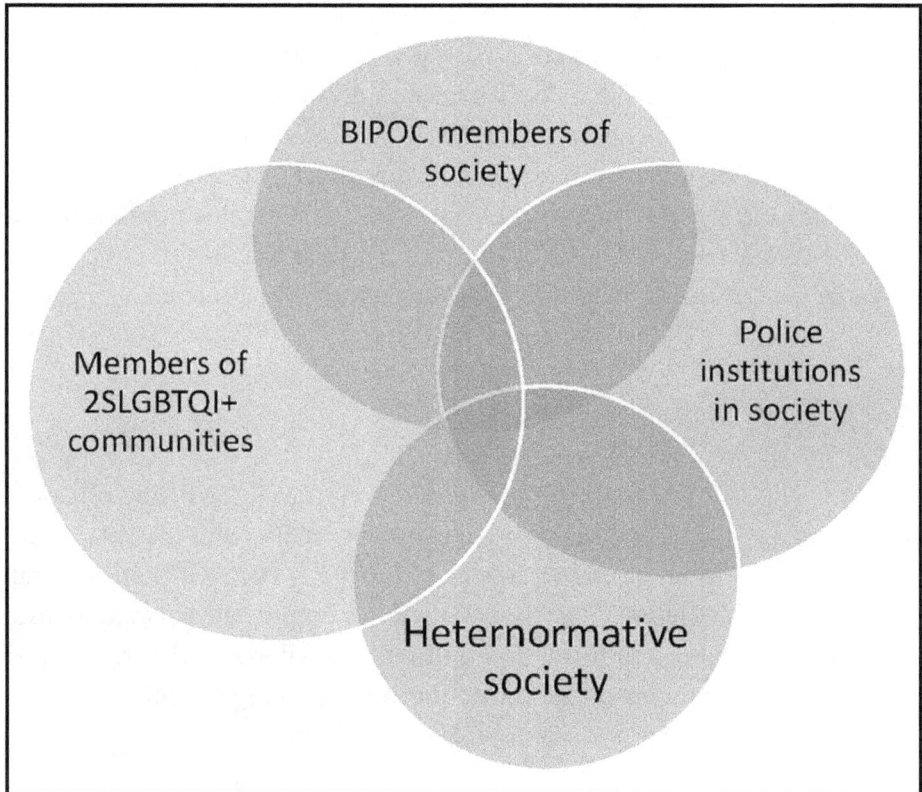

EXERCISE

CROSS-CULTURAL CHALLENGES

1. Take a look at the Venn diagram below. Think about, and list, the major social, cross-cultural challenges facing each of the communities in their interactions with one or more of the other communities.

	Heteronormative society	Police institutions	BIPOC communities
LGBTQ+ communities			
Heteronormative society			
Police institutions			
BIPOC communities			

2. Taking the list you compiled under Question 1, identify the specific communications challenges involved for each community. What are some of the difficulties they may encounter when getting their messages across to the other communities? What do they need to do to be effective communicators? What mechanisms/approaches may help them succeed?
3. If you were coordinating communications efforts for the Toronto Police Service, and you were approached for your organization's position on the Pride Parade and BLM, what would your response be?
4. What are the major, long-term effects of events like Pride 2020? How do they serve to link ideas and people together?

EXERCISE

CREATE A NEWS RELEASE

You work in communications for K & L Enterprises, a large, diversified company that makes and markets a variety of products (think of Procter & Gamble, Nestlé or Kraft Heinz). Your organization has become a corporate sponsor for an initiative designed to support anti-bullying efforts in the transgender community. You have been tasked with the job of creating a media plan and a news release to promote this initiative. Here are the details:

1. The initiative is a joint effort that draws on the knowledge and expertise of organizations like Pflag Canada as well as the corporate support of major Canadian banks, the Canadian Marketing Association, and the federal and provincial governments.
2. It is a $10 million initiative that will involve advertising, campaigns in schools, colleges and universities, hospitals and social service agencies.
3. Your company is contributing $2 million to the cost of the initiative.
4. Create a media plan. Look for target audiences—who are you trying to reach? Then develop a list of media that serve those audiences, focusing on traditional (print, radio, television), as well as social media.
5. In your plan, identify your objectives (i.e. "to develop positive media response to K & L Enterprise's involvement with this initiative").
6. Develop your key messages. Ensure that they are representative of your company and its outside partners.
7. Write your news release. Use an inverted pyramid style, and put the 5Ws+H (who, what, when, where, why, and how) as close to your introductory paragraph as possible.

A QUICK QUIZ
MATCH THE MESSAGE WITH WHO OR WHAT DELIVERED IT

[I offer] regrets on behalf of the Toronto Police Service for the 1981 Bathhouse Raids.	Neilsen Survey
There's no place for the state in the bedrooms of the nation ... what's done in private between adults doesn't concern the Criminal Code.	Government of Canada
It is with shame and sorrow and deep regret for the things we have done that I stand here today and say: We were wrong.	GLAAD president and CEO Sarah Kate Ellis
The human rights of all persons are universal and indivisible. Everyone should enjoy the same fundamental human rights, regardless of their sexual orientation and their gender identity and expression.	Pierre Trudeau
[T]he pink dollar ... accounts for $3.8 billion in consumer packaged goods (CPG) sales across Canada.	Police Chief Mark Saunders
LGBTQ people are, and will continue to be, a part of advertisements and family programming and that will never change.	Justin Trudeau

REFERENCES

Abramovich, A., de Oliviera, C., and Kiran, T. (2020, August 28). Assessment of Health Conditions and Health Service Use Among Transgender Patients in Canada. *JAMA Network Open.* https://jamanetwork.com/journals/jamanetworkopen/fullarticle/2769915

Aviles, G. (2019, December 10). 'LGBT indoctrination agenda'? Petitions want to keep Hallmark 'family-friendly.' *NBC News.* https://www.nbcnews.com/feature/nbc-out/lgbt-indoctrination-agenda-petitions-want-keep-hallmark-family-friendly-n1099161

Ayoub, P. (2018, May 24). How the media has helped change public views about lesbian and gay people. Scholars Strategy Network. https://scholars.org/contribution/how-media-has-helped-change-public-views-about-lesbian-and-gay-people

Berlatsky, N. (2013, November 15). What the gay community lost while it was winning gay marriage. *The Atlantic.* https://www.theatlantic.com/national/archive/2013/11/what-the-gay-community-lost-while-it-was-winning-gay-marriage/281525/

Bernstein, E. (2020, July 26). Why it seems like bullies are everywhere, and how to stop them. *The Wall Street Journal.* https://www.wsj.com/articles/why-it-seems-like-bullies-are-everywhereand-how-to-stop-them-11594743348?mod=e2fb&fbclid=IwAR0D2m1AKI-SYIv27V8dlnGN4VUQdwbRJEaap1-f5P1pAA9sAO2vMi7O5y0&fbclid=IwAR2ky0-LxDlqICFZusWBTBhyCnx0AwdyDp3pgNWAieQK3CPzInOVxFkLS08

Brandwatch (2019). Exposed: The scale of transphobia online. *Brandwatch/Ditch the Label.* https://www.brandwatch.com/reports/transphobia/

CBC Digital Archives (2020). Trudeau: 'There's no place for the state in the bedrooms of the nation.' *CBC.* https://www.cbc.ca/archives/entry/omnibus-bill-theres-no-place-for-the-state-in-the-bedrooms-of-the-nation

CBC News. (2016, July 3). Black Lives Matter Toronto stalls Pride parade. *CBC.* https://www.cbc.ca/news/canada/toronto/pride-parade-toronto-1.3662823

Canadian Centre for Gender + Sexual Diversity (2020). Who are Two Spirit people? Canadian Centre for Gender + Sexual Diversity. https://ccgsd-ccdgs.org/1-who-are-two-spirit-people/

Canadian Public Relations Society (2020). Code of professional standards. CPRS. https://www.cprs.ca/About/Code-of-Professional-Standards#:~:text=A%20member%20shall%20practice%20the,and%20words%20not%20their%20own

Carufel R. (2017, July 10). PR pulse: Authentic LGBT-inclusive communications are driving business. *Agility PR.* https://www.agilitypr.com/pr-news/public-relations/pr-pulse-authentic-lgbt-inclusive-communications-driving-business/

Ciszek, E. (2017, May). Public relations, activism and identity: A cultural-economic examination of contemporary LGBT activism. *Public Relations Review, 43*(4): 1–8.

Ciszek, E. (2014). Identity, culture, and articulation: A critical-cultural analysis of strategic LGBT advocacy outreach (Ph.D. dissertation). University of Oregon. https://scholarsbank.

uoregon.edu/xmlui/bitstream/handle/1794/18364/Ciszek_oregon_0171A_10974.pdf?sequence=1&isAllowed=y

Clarke, J. (2020, April 7). Cognitive vs. emotional empathy. *Verywell Mind.* https://www.verywellmind.com/cognitive-and-emotional-empathy-4582389

Clément, D. (2020). Sexual orientation. *Canada's Human Rights History.* https://historyofrights.ca/encyclopaedia/main-events/sexual-orientation/

CNN Editorial Research (2020, June 17). LGBTQ rights milestones fast facts. *CNN.* https://www.cnn.com/2015/06/19/us/lgbt-rights-milestones-fast-facts/index.html

CNNwire (2017, June 12). One year after Pulse nightclub shooting: 'Hearts and minds changed.' *Fox 8 News.* https://fox8.com/news/one-year-after-pulse-nightclub-shooting-hearts-and-minds-changed/

Coolman, T. (2020, August 23). Vandalism and Hate Will Not Shake Our Resolve. Pflag York Region. https://mailchi.mp/dc27a5e204ce/mayors-and-pflag-in-york-region-support-lgbtq2-people-and-raising-the-pride-flag-4117109

Coombs, T. and Holladay, S. (2014, January). How publics react to crisis communication efforts: Comparing crisis response reactions across sub-arenas. *Journal of Communication Management,* 18(1): 40–57.

Cooper, J. (2021, January 14). Interview with Rahim Thawer.

Court, A. (2020, September 18). Education Secretary Betsy DeVos vows to pull $18 million in grants from Connecticut schools unless they pull out of an athletic conference that allows transgender girls to compete in female sports. *Daily Mail.* https://www.dailymail.co.uk/news/article-8748833/Betsy-DeVos-vows-pull-18-million-Connecticut-schools-transgender-sports-row.html

Delbyck, C. (2020, June 7). J. K. Rowling spent her Saturday pissing off the Internet with anti-trans tweetstorm. *Huffington Post.* https://www.huffingtonpost.ca/entry/jk-rowling-transphobic-tweetstorm_n_5edcff1cc5b6ee18dce14381?ri18n=true&ncid=fcbklnkcahpmg00000001&fbclid=IwAR38mtu0GISSr0datP11d8yuAoHgJXvtCT316A7HS1xbbPoT7rqCxcVP_YY

Dry, J. (2019, December 17). Hallmark Channel's latest LGBTQ mistake is why we need a gay Hallmark movie. IndieWire. https://www.indiewire.com/2019/12/gay-hallmark-movie-zola-commercial-channel-lgbt-1202197961/

Enos, T. (2017, March 28). 8 things you should know about Two Spirit People. *Indian Country Today.* https://indiancountrytoday.com/archive/8-things-you-should-know-about-two-spirit-people-294cNoIj-EGwJFOWEnbbZw

Fleming, A. (2015). The communications plan. In Carney, W., and Lymer, L. (Eds). *Fundamentals of Public Relations and Marketing Communications in Canada*, pp. 175–206. Edmonton: University of Alberta Press.

Fondation Jasmin Roy (2017, August 9). 13% of the Canadian population belongs to the LGBT community. Fondation Jasmin Roy. https://www.newswire.ca/news-releases/according-to-lgbt-realities-the-first-pancanadian-survey-on-lgbt-communities-conducted-by-crop-for-the-benefit-of-the-fondation-jasmin-roy-13-of-the-canadian-population-belongs-to-the-lgbt-community-639432223.html

Formby, E. (2017, August 8). Why you should think twice before you talk about 'the LGBT community.' *The Conversation*. https://theconversation.com/why-you-should-think-twice-before-you-talk-about-the-lgbt-community-81711

Freeze, C. (2000, June 22). Fantino mends fences with gay community. *Globe and Mail*. https://www.theglobeandmail.com/news/national/fantino-mends-fences-with-gay-community/article4165060/

Gajdics, P. (2018, June 6). I experienced 'conversion therapy'—and it's time to ban it across Canada. *Maclean's*. https://www.macleans.ca/opinion/i-experienced-conversion-therapy-and-its-time-to-ban-it-across-canada/

GLAAD (2020a). *GLAAD website*. https://www.glaad.org

GLAAD (2020b). Conversion Therapy. *GLAAD*. https://www.glaad.org/conversiontherapy?response_type=embed

Goldstein, R. (2020, August 18). James Baldwin on being gay in America (originally published in 1984). *The Village Voice*. https://www.villagevoice.com/2018/06/22/james-baldwin-on-being-gay-in-america/

Gomez, S. (2013, June 1). The vision for inclusion. *Inclusion*. https://meridian.allenpress.com/inclusion/article/1/1/1/461/The-Vision-for-Inclusion

Government of Canada (2020). Rights of LGBTI persons. Government of Canada. https://www.canada.ca/en/canadian-heritage/services/rights-lgbti-persons.html

Government of Canada (2019, August 1). Government of Canada invests in LGBTQ2 communities. Government of Canada. https://www.canada.ca/en/status-women/news/2019/08/government-of-canada-invests-in-lgbtq2-communities.html

Gray, J. (2017, June 25). Black Lives Matter Toronto makes surprise appearance at Pride Parade. *Globe and Mail*. https://www.theglobeandmail.com/news/toronto/black-lives-matter-toronto-makes-surprise-appearance-at-pride-parade/article35460305/

Green, D. (2020, March 17). Transphobia Project uses data visualisation to zoom in on outlets that spread biased transgender content. *Journalism.co.uk*. https://www.journalism.co.uk/news/transphobia-project-aims-to-encourage-newsrooms-to-work-with-trans-communities-for-better-coverage/s2/a753238/

Hallmark (2019, December 15). Hallmark affirms its commitment to diversity and inclusion (news release). Hallmark. https://corporate.hallmark.com/news-article/hallmark-affirms-its-commitment-to-diversity-and-inclusion/

Hooper, T. (2018, April 16). The gay community has long been over-policed and under-protected. The Bruce McArthur case is the final straw. *CBC News*. https://www.cbc.ca/news/opinion/pride-police-1.4618663

Hristova, B. (2023, June 6). Recommendations by Redeemer University after trans student's death are 'insulting': LGBTQ advocate. *CBC News*. https://www.cbc.ca/news/canada/hamilton/redeemer-university-recommendations-bekett-noble-1.6865634

Hristova, B. (2023, May 5). Redeemer University says it needs more time to deliver report promised after student death. *CBC News*. https://www.cbc.ca/news/canada/hamilton/bekett-noble-death-mental-health-recommendations-1.6829363

Hristova, B. (2020, August 8). Private Christian university says no sex outside heterosexual marriage. LGBTQ alumni say that discriminates. *CBC News*. https://www.cbc.ca/news/canada/hamilton/redeemer-university-discrimination-lgbtq-1.5651627

Human Rights Campaign (2020). Corporate Equality Index 2020. Human Rights Campaign. https://www.hrc.org/resources/corporate-equality-index

It Gets Better Project (2020). Website. https://itgetsbetter.org/about/

Justice Laws Website, Government of Canada (2020, August 6). Canadian Multiculturalism Act. Government of Canada. https://laws-lois.justice.gc.ca/eng/acts/c-18.7/page-1.html

Kai (2020, June 22). The deep connections between Pride and Black Lives Matter. *NYCLU*. https://www.nyclu.org/en/news/deep-connections-between-pride-and-black-lives-matter

Lavoie, J. (2021, January 15). TCDSB reinstates LGBTQ website. *Toronto Star*, p. A14.

LGBTQ YouthLine (2021, January 11). Public statement. LGBTQ YouthLine. https://www.youthline.ca/news/tcdsb-jan-11/

Little, S. (2019, August 1). 1 in 4 Canadians still oppose full same-sex marriage rights: poll. Global News. https://globalnews.ca/news/5713172/canadians-same-sex-marriage-rights-poll/

Madani, D., and Atkinson, C. (2020, January 22). Hallmark Channel parent's CEO out after same-sex marriage ad backlash. *NBC News*. https://www.nbcnews.com/feature/nbc-out/hallmark-channel-parent-ceo-out-after-same-sex-marriage-ad-n1120616

Marcuse, H. (2007). Repressive tolerance, in Feenberg, A., & Leiss, W. (Eds.), *The essential Marcuse*, pp. 32–59. Boston: Beacon Press.

Montclair State University LGBTQ Center (2020). Terminology. Montclair State University. https://www.montclair.edu/lgbtq-center/lgbtq-resources/terminology/

Moore, T. (2019, June 4). Is PR making the grade when it comes to LGBTQ acceptance? *PR Week*. https://www.prweek.com/article/1586196/pr-making-grade-when-comes-lgbtq-acceptance

Morris, B. (n.d.). History of lesbian, gay, bisexual and transgender social movements. American Psychological Association. https://www.apa.org/pi/lgbt/resources/history

Ng, P. (2020, August 15). Hallmark Channel features its first same-sex wedding in latest original movie. *ET Online*. https://www.etonline.com/hallmark-channel-features-its-first-same-sex-wedding-in-latest-original-movie-151375

Nielsen (2015, June 29). Pink power: The state of LGBT spending in Canada. Nielsen Company. https://www.nielsen.com/ca/en/insights/article/2015/pink-power-the-state-of-the-lgbt-community-in-canada/#:~:text=The%20pink%20dollar%2C%20the%20term,%245%2C835%20the%20average%20household%20spends

Nolen, S. (2000, September 22). Angry crowd decries raid on lesbians. *Globe and Mail*. https://www.theglobeandmail.com/news/national/angry-crowd-decries-raid-on-lesbians/article25471706/

NorthReach (2020). A brief LGBTQ+ Canadian history timeline. NorthReach. https://northreach.ca/education-2/lgbtq/a-brief-lgbtq-canadian-history/

Ontario Human Rights Code (2020). Ontario Human Rights Commission. http://www.ohrc.on.ca/en/ontario-human-rights-code

Open Parliament (2020). Bill C-8, an Act to amend the Criminal Code (conversion therapy). Open Parliament, Government of Canada. https://openparliament.ca/bills/43-1/C-8/

Pflag Canada (2020). Website. https://pflagcanada.ca/about/

Planned Parenthood (2020a). What does Queer mean? *Planned Parenthood*. https://www.plannedparenthood.org/learn/teens/sexual-orientation/what-does-queer-mean

Planned Parenthood (2020b). What's transphobia. *Planned Parenthood*. https://www.plannedparenthood.org/learn/gender-identity/transgender/whats-transphobia

Pożarlik, G. (2013). Individual, collective, social identity as (most) contested social science concept in the symbolic interactionism perspective. In Tamcke, M., de Jong, J., Klein, L., and van der Waal, M., (Eds.), *Europe—Space for transcultural existence?*, pp. 77–88. Universitätsverlag Göttingen. https://library.oapen.org/bitstream/handle/20.500.12657/37030/SE1_space.pdf?sequence=1#page=79

Pride Toronto (2020). Pride Toronto Mission. *Pride Toronto*. https://www.pridetoronto.com/

Praill, C. (2018, June 5). LGBTQ Canadians disproportionately affected by violence according to Stats Canada survey. Global News. https://globalnews.ca/news/4255599/lgbtq-canadians-disproportionately-affected-by-violence-according-to-stats-canada-survey/

Queen, L. (2020, July 16). 'Means the world': Pflag pleased Aurora approves rainbow crosswalk. *Aurora Banner*. https://www.yorkregion.com/news-story/10076777--means-the-world-pflag-pleased-aurora-approves-rainbow-crosswalk/

Redeemer University College (2020). About Redeemer University College. Redeemer University College. https://www.redeemer.ca/about/

Reid, G. (2017, September 3). Canada sets international example in LGBT rights. *The Globe and Mail*. https://www.theglobeandmail.com/opinion/canada-sets-international-example-in-lgbt-rights/article36157300/

Robinson, L. (2015). The modern gay and lesbian civil rights movement in the United States (M.A. thesis). The College at Brockport: State University of New York. https://digitalcommons.

brockport.edu/cgi/viewcontent.cgi?article=1596&context=ehd_theses

Rodrigues, G. (2020, August 22). Man charged after rainbow crosswalk in Aurora, Ont., spray-painted black. *Global News*. https://globalnews.ca/news/7292562/aurora-rainbow-crosswalk-damaged-spray-paint/

Schneider, J., & Auten, D. (2017, April 4). Why we need to talk about queer money. *Forbes*. https://www.forbes.com/sites/debtfreeguys/2017/04/04/talk-about-queer-money/#4b434e8780b2

Self Sovereignty (2020). Website. https://sovereigntyofself.com/

Simpson, L. (2018, May 31). Violent victimization of lesbians, gays and bisexuals in Canada, 2014. *Statistics Canada*. https://www150.statcan.gc.ca/n1/pub/85-002-x/2018001/article/54923-eng.htm

Smith, M. (2019, January 10). Homophobia and homonationalism: LGBTQ law reform in Canada. *Social and Legal Studies*. https://journals.sagepub.com/doi/10.1177/0964663918822150

Statistics Canada, 2023, August 16). Improving data on 2SLGBTQ+ populations. Statistics Canada. https://www.statcan.gc.ca/o1/en/plus/4313-improving-data-2slgbtq-populations

Statistics Canada (2017, September 25). Same-sex couples and sexual orientation ... by the numbers. Statistics Canada. https://www.statcan.gc.ca/eng/dai/smr08/2015/smr08_203_2015

Tannahill, J. (2015, April 27). The four leading LGBT PR agencies. *Everything PR*. https://everything-pr.com/lgbt-public-relations/

Teitel, E. (2020, June 1). Recognizing Pride crucial, especially in small towns. *Toronto Star*, p. A11.

Thawer, R. (2017). Defending uncritical art has consequences. *Marvellous Grounds*. http://marvellousgrounds.com/blog/defending-uncritical-art-has-consequences/

Toronto Police Service (2020). "It's in our hands." Toronto Police Service. http://www.torontopolice.on.ca/churchstmural/

Tovar, V. (2020, July 23). Apparel brand Self Sovereignty sees extended sizing as part of their goal to Indigenize. *Forbes*. https://www.forbes.com/sites/virgietovar/2020/07/22/apparel-brand-self-sovereignty-sees-extended-sizing-as-part-of-their-goal-to-indigenize/#3f8a1deb5c9f

Trent University (n.d.). What is an ally? Trent University. https://www.trentu.ca/colleges/sites/trentu.ca.colleges/files/documents/Ally%20Allies--editted.pdf

Trudeau, J. (2017, November 28). Remarks by Prime Minister Justin Trudeau to apologize to LGBTQ2 Canadians. Office of the Prime Minister. https://pm.gc.ca/en/news/speeches/2017/11/28/remarks-prime-minister-justin-trudeau-apologize-lgbtq2-canadians

United Church of Canada (2020). What We Believe. United Church. https://www.united-church.ca/community-faith/welcome-united-church-canada/what-we-believe

University of Illinois Springfield (2020). LGBT and ally terms and definitions. University of Illinois. https://www.uis.edu/gendersexualitystudentservices/students/ally-guide-uis/lgbt-ally-terms-and-definitions/

Walcott, R. (2017, June 28). Black Lives Matter, police and Pride: Toronto activists spark a movement. *The Conversation*. https://theconversation.com/black-lives-matter-police-and-pride-toronto-activists-spark-a-movement-79089

Wareham, J. (2020, June 13). Global Pride to focus on Black Lives Matter at first worldwide LGBT event. *Forbes*. https://www.forbes.com/sites/jamiewareham/2020/06/13/global-pride-to-focus-on-black-lives-matter-at-first-worldwide-lgbt-event/#4d1e1db569b5

Waters, R. (2014, June). Overcoming persistent stereotypes: the battle against LGBT discrimination. IPRA. https://www.ipra.org/news/itle/overcoming-persistent-stereotypes-the-battle-against-lgbt-discrimination/

Yeomans, L. (2016) Imagining the lives of others: Empathy in public relations. *Public Relations Inquiry, 5* (1). http://eprints.leedsbeckett.ac.uk/2207/9/Imagining%20the%20Lives%20of%20Others_Empathy%20in%20Public%20Relations.pdf

CHAPTER SEVEN

Disasters, Pandemics and the Racialization of Catastrophe

OBJECTIVES OF THIS CHAPTER

This chapter is focused on working towards an understanding of:

- The COVID-19 pandemic and its effect on cross-cultural understanding with respect to diverse communities;
- The racialization of major disasters; and
- The role of public relations in pandemics and disasters.

COVID-19, RACISM AND HEALTH

I recall well the last day I taught in a college classroom before the COVID-19 pandemic really took hold. It was Thursday, March 12, 2020, and the small college campus where I taught—built in the 1950s, it looked more like a high school, built around a quadrangle with a reflecting pool and evergreen trees, with brightly painted lockers and a cozy cafeteria and shiny terrazzo flooring, and the facility in fact was formerly the Toronto Teachers College, where aspiring teachers were trained from the 1950s through the 1970s—was wiped down regularly, handrails and doorknobs thoroughly cleaned, and though masks were not mandatory and physical distancing still a nascent idea, cautions were being urged. The talk in my crisis communications class focused on the ominous discussions about the pandemic, but at that point COVID-19 was still something that was happening "out there" to other jurisdictions. Then Friday, March 13 came, the school closed, and for months public spaces were inaccessible, businesses and schools locked tight, police caution tape wrapped around playground equipment, people sequestered in their homes, and there were runs on Lysol wipes and toilet paper and bottled water at Walmart outlets, people engaged in nervous wide-arc neighborhood distancing when walking their dogs, some people wearing face masks nearly 24/7. Face-masking become the new norm, and if you were in public without a mask it was certain to earn you scowls and nasty comments. There was a fear that escalated as the list of deaths grew; I finished the semester doing online work with that course and the two others that I taught at another college, and then (along with just about everyone else) consumed the news over the next several months, watching as the medical and scientific side of the equation did battle with the hysteria-mongers, the conspiracy theorists and the racialists. This was especially so with the racialists—those whose beliefs came into bas-relief clarity as they spouted theories or simply enforced their views—society's views, oftentimes— through their behaviours: COVID-blaming the Chinese ("will Chinese food give you COVID?"), suggesting that people of African descent were somehow immune to COVID, and ignoring the plight of First Nations People and their legitimate concerns over the pandemic sweeping through their communities.

American president Donald Trump was quick to blame the Chinese government for the virus, calling it variously the "Chinese virus" or the "Wuhan virus," and this helped to provoke "a wave of anti-Asian sentiment, including over 1,500 racist incidents nationwide between mid-March and mid-April" (Lempinen, 2020, May 15).

The months following saw a churn of news, from medical updates to COVID restrictions, from masks to sanitation to social distancing and limits to the size of groups. As well, it was reported that African Americans and Latinos were dying of COVID-19 at a higher rate than whites; in some places, Blacks accounted for up to 70 percent of deaths while accounting for only a quarter of the population (Thebault, Ba Tran and Williams, 2020, April 7). Media reports were quick to link the health problems faced by African-Americans to poor economic status, rather than genetic factors, as had happened in the past:

African Americans are ... more likely to be uninsured and live in communities with inadequate health-care facilities. ... [A]s a result, African Americans have historically been disproportionately diagnosed with chronic diseases such as asthma, hypertension and diabetes ... [and] might have been more exposed [to the virus] because many held low-wage or essential jobs, such as food service, public transit and health care, that required them to continue to interact with the public (Thebault, Ba Tran and Williams, 2020, April 7).

The clarity that is gained when linking health issues to economic and social oppression is in contrast to the blurring of information that takes place when arguments are racialized and false genetic arguments enter the equation, as happened in the past with the dominant culture's application of scientific racism and social Darwinist arguments. According to Social Darwinism, "human groups and races are subject to the same laws of natural selection as Charles Darwin perceived in plants and animals in nature. According to the theory, which was popular in the late 19th and early 20th centuries, the weak were diminished and their cultures delimited while the strong grew in power and cultural influence over the weak" (Britannica, 2020). Social Darwinism was used politically to justify the oppression of African Americans as well as Indigenous Peoples in both Canada and the U.S. The Social Darwinist suggestions of mental and physical inferiority among those outside the dominant culture were refuted by activist academics like DuBois in the early 20th century: "As DuBois saw it, scientific racism was a closed system which reached untenable conclusions by weak methodology in the hands of biased researchers. ... Social Darwinists argued that racial antagonism [antipathy between the races] was an avoidance of poor racial traits, such as poor health and low ability. There was no evidence, DuBois replied, that whites were innately more healthy than blacks" (Taylor, 1981, p. 455).

It seems like the use of the word "outrageous" carries little weight at the time of writing this—given the hyperbole seen in the media—yet it is hard not to use it when examining the race-baiting attacks by Conservative member of Canadian parliament and party leadership candidate Derek Sloan on Theresa Tam, Canada's top medical expert during the COVID crisis. Sloan suggested that Tam was repeating advice from the World Health Organization (WHO), and that WHO was in turn disseminating what Sloan called misinformation from the Chinese government. The language was hardly guarded as Sloan openly stated that Tam, Canada's Chief Public Health Officer, was putting the interests of the World Health Organization and China over Canadians' health—in other words, working for China:

[Sloan] posted a message and video on Facebook and Twitter claiming Tam had "failed Canadians" through her performance during the pandemic and asking if she works "for Canada or for China." "Dr. Tam must go! Canada must remain sovereign over decisions," Sloan continued. "The UN, the WHO and Chinese Communist propaganda must never again have a say over Canada's public health!" (Zimonjic and Cullen, 2020, April 29).

Sloan called for Tam to leave her post; his comments were widely denounced by political writers and members of his own party, to the point that Conservative Party members voted in favour of kicking him out of office if he didn't apologize (Boutilier, 2020, April 30), though his ideas clearly represented a wedge issue that opened up discussion—much of it online—allowing (encouraging, sometimes) commentators and observers to unleash volleys of stereotypical anger, something considered more than "garden-variety anti-globalist conservatism, which is ironically at least partly an American import.... Sloan is a crank on the fringe, but if he isn't repudiated by leadership, where is the fringe?" (Arthur, 2020, April 24). A poll conducted in Montreal, Toronto and Vancouver by the Chinese Canadian Council for Social Justice found that one in five Canadians felt unsafe sitting next to an Asian person on public transportation; the poll followed calls to action after Canadians of Asian descent became victims of physical attacks and the target of online hate campaigns (Li, 2020, April 28). Schools took a strong stand against anti-Asian racism during the pandemic; Centennial College in Toronto published an online Anti-Asian Racism Social Action Card outlining three steps to working to end bias: "Educate Yourself (consider what biases you have and how they are connected to a history of anti-Asian racism); Check Your Behaviour (consider the content you share and choose your words thoughtfully as it is incorrect to refer to COVID-19 as a "Chinese virus"); Speak Up (call out acts of racism and ask groups you are part of to denounce anti-Asian racism)" (Centennial College, 2020). In October 2020, the city of Toronto announced a social media initiative to combat "anti-East Asian racism," the racist acts directed at citizens of actual or perceived Chinese descent. The campaign focused on stereotypes, and video footage shone a light on "the impact racism has on Torontonians of East Asian descent who share their experiences with racism prior to and during the pandemic.... Since the beginning of the pandemic, 26 per cent of more than 600 reported anti-East Asian racism incidents in Canada took place in Toronto, according to the Chinese Canadian National Council" (Wilson, 2020, October 13). In Brampton, home to a large number of Sikhs and Hindus, COVID-related news reporting focused largely on social gatherings and attendance at temples and parties celebrating events like Diwali, and there were suggestions that loosely enforced social distancing practices led to a higher number of COVID cases; in November 2020, the city posted Canada's highest positivity rates (Kerr, 2020, November 13). The Region of Peel (within which Brampton is the region's second most-populous municipality) has the Greater Toronto Area's (GTA's) highest percentage of People of Colour; Peel's Sikh population is the highest in the GTA, and more than half of Brampton's population is South Asian (NHS, 2013, May). But the underlying reason for the high numbers was a combination of factors, in particular a lack of health care resources and the fact that many residents didn't have the option of staying home from work—many work in factories and in the trucking industry; as such, according to civic experts interviewed by the *Globe and Mail*, "city residents are being unfairly maligned, victims of government underfunding and circumstances beyond their control ... many criticisms of Brampton's COVID-19 situation are based on stereotypes and racism," and leaders blamed a lax health care system for not doing a better job of reaching People of Colour in the community (Kerr, 2020, November 13).

ANGST AND PREJUDICE

Widespread calls to ban wet markets (markets where fresh meat and vegetables are sold in the open air) in China in the wake of COVID-19 were considered a mixture of angst and prejudice: "Attacks and calls to ban 'wet markets' because of their potential for spreading diseases such as Covid-19 may be missing the point, say experts. ... While the markets may be considered unsanitary by western standards, most wet markets in China do not sell live animals other than fish in tanks, or sometimes in open pools" (Standaert, 2020). A University of Cambridge case study of wet market reform found that changing demographics (wet markets being frequented mainly by the middle-aged and elderly) and threats from the advent of "mobile payment and online shopping APPs developments, the improvement of cold chain transportation and delivery efficiency, and the convenience of all-day contactless service" (all hallmarks of western business culture) created conditions for necessary change that could include transforming wet markets from simply places to purchase food to community hubs, service and logistics centres and "healthy diet campaign" icons (Mintz-Habib, 2023, March).

Looked at from the perspective of a different culture, proposed bans might be seen as an example of ethnocentrism, the idea that what is "good" for one culture (in this case, western culture) is equally applicable to other cultures—that one's cultural values are an acceptable yardstick for measuring the worth of others. The "concept of ethnocentrism is a subjective emotion or attitude where an individual or a group places his/their culture at the centre … [for example] eating habits and clothing that do not conform to their own cultural norms [are seen] as abnormal, invaluable [sic; likely "unvalued" is the intended meaning] and even immoral. Such an approach contains subjective behaviours and attitudes that are full of common stereotypes and biases and greatly harm intercultural communication" (Aslantas, 2019, March, p. 320). The scientific community made calls for the creation of "more-than-human geographies" in the analysis of COVID-19, moving toward a greater understanding of the connectedness between humans and other animals in the transmission of zoonotic diseases, and

> better recognition of and support for theoretically informed approaches to public health that open consideration of the diverse ways in which humans and other critters live with viruses and infectious disease. Public health and biomedicine have long been informed by a humanist ethos that places a premium on human life and that separates humans from other nonhuman entities (Blue and Rock, 2020, June 17).

These calls showed the potential for rational, step-by-step approaches that could reduce the abject, politically driven race-and-culture-blaming that was taking place during the pandemic. White privilege raised its head high during the pandemic, and cultural misappropriation—in this case, the appropriation of a historical symbol—was prevalent; in April 2020, media reported that White House officials conflated the actions of white protesters (acting out in public against government orders to continue self-isolating in the face of the pandemic) with those of civil rights icons like Rosa Parks (Murphy, 2020, April 18). This served to underscore the acquisitiveness of the dominant culture, along the lines of the ways in which white supremacists will focus on saying "All Lives Matter" when confronted with "Black Lives Matter" commentary or will say "Blue Lives Matter" in reference to police services (following police violence against BIPOC citizens). This steers the discussion towards white nationalism, which is "an attempt to cloak white supremacist ideas in the more respectable language of racial separatism, just as the alt-right has tried to repackage fascist thought in a more modern form. All these variants are built on common notions of a white identity and racial superiority. They promote hate and violence as valid political tools, rejecting values of equality, coexistence, and the rule of law in favor of raw power and ethnic division" (Clark, 2020, July 1).

The language of white nationalism—and the appropriation of ideas, practices and beliefs from other cultures by mainstreamers—represents an attempt to further muddy the distinction between, and understanding of, the issues at play in civil rights actions as well as to deconstruct the arguments for civil rights. The arguments against fairness comprise layers of thought drawn from the white cultural cornerstones of rugged individualism (attributed to Depression-era U.S. president Herbert Hoover, and embracing the notions of independence and laissez-faire self-reliance), the Protestant work ethic (focused on the benefits of hard work and discipline) and the scientific method (using science to support theories focusing on the differences between people), though the creation of these white "American" values and the notion of "White culture —indeed the idea that any set of cultural practices belongs to any race—ignores or repudiates the defining development of the modern world: the cosmopolitan mixing of older, face-to-face cultures made possible by the expansion of communication and migration" (Ford, 2020, August 18). Underpinning these ideas is the language of genetic superiority, stated outright or implied. In September 2020, Donald Trump congratulated a crowd of white Minnesotans on their "good genes," which "prompted alarm on social media and comparisons to the Nazi obsession with the "master race" and eugenics" (Haltiwanger, 2020, September 21). Here we have a confluence of white-privilege outlooks in action: the white person as "victim," the deconstruction of what civil rights is really about, and the reinforcement of dominant white attitudes in Trump congratulating Minnesota (the state is 79 percent white) for its "genetic makeup"—and the "image" is what captures the attention.

ZERO-SUM GAME

The notion of white superiority is a zero-sum game. It can only be accomplished if someone else is subjugated. In *Stony the Road: Reconstruction, White Supremacy, and the Rise of Jim Crow*, professor Henry Louis Gates, Jr., details the combination of racism, political will, and technology in the post-Civil War era in the U.S., when the use of newly advanced techniques in chromolithography (a multi-colour print process used in pictures and posters) allowed people to spread negative stereotypes of African Americans, creating a seeming justification for the slavery that had been abolished in 1863 and the subjugation of American Blacks into the 20th century and beyond, such that virtually anywhere a white person saw an image of an African American, she or he was encoded in one of these stereotypes as somehow laughably ignorant, subhuman, devoid of thought and reason. ... The collective image of the black person in American popular culture functions like a visual mantra reinforcing the negativity of difference (Gates, 2019, p. 132).

Racist attitudes have been engrained in Western consciousness since the Industrial Age began in the 1700s, and were used in conjunction with Darwinism (the evolution of "superior" Caucasians over others) and scientism (everything from weighing brains and measuring skull shapes and body proportions to observations of health while disregarding individual differences and economic/social inequalities) to justify slavery and racial ranking, and the "biological justification [of prejudice] imposed the additional burden of intrinsic inferiority upon despised groups, and precluded redemption by conversion or assimilation. The 'scientific' argument has formed a primary line of attack for more than a century" (Gould, 1981, p. 63). White doctors could be caustically indifferent to the needs of patients of colour; in the late 1800s, Canadian doctor William Osler (often held up as paragon of medical insight and a father of modern medicine), while working in a segregated ward at a hospital in Baltimore, Maryland, dismissed an intern's concerns over the health of Black patients by saying that most of them were alcoholic and syphilitic (Oved, 2020, November 9). So entrenched have been the presumptions of racial difference—and white cultural indifference to suffering so pronounced—that researchers with the U.S. Public Health Service watched over decades as African-American men infected with syphilis died painful deaths in the Tuskegee syphilis study, "even after they realized penicillin could cure them. ... The researchers chose black subjects because they, like many whites at the time, believed black people were 'a notoriously syphilis-soaked race.' ... The news [of the study, uncovered in the 1970s] spread like pox through black communities: doctors were doing research on black people, lying to them, and watching them die" (Skloot, 2011, p. 50).

Such beliefs, supported and encouraged by media of the day and the continual flow of negative stereotypes, actively etched into the collective consciousness a set of racist attitudes that have continued well into the 21st century. And in the area of health, and especially access to health services and general standard of living, "social exclusion is generalized and reflects the inheritance of past racial discrimination and the experience of continuing discrimination.

Whether in developed countries, such as the United States, Australia or Canada, or developing countries, such as Brazil, South Africa or Colombia, ethnic/racial minorities, immigrants and refugees suffer disadvantages in their living conditions and health status, independent of their level of education, income, age or gender" (Parodi, 2005, p. 68).

COVID-19 (as well as the killing of George Floyd in May 2020) had a dramatic effect on mental health and well-being. In August 2020, the HR technology service provider Morneau Shepell reported spikes in depression and isolation during the COVID-19 lockdown period, resulting in negative mental health scores, according to the organization's Mental Health Index. The index provides scores based on replies from thousands of American respondents. A news release from the company, which provides health care services to a range of private and public sector clients, indicated that in July 2020, "feelings of isolation and financial risk (continue) to be the top drivers of American employees' mental health" and "the Mental Health Index saw anxiety scores worsen for most people of color in June during the initial awareness and response to the killing of George Floyd. July showed some signs of improvement as the dialogue on racism continued and early indication of change began" (Morneau Shepell, 2020, August 5). And the COVID lockdown generated ill-effects in children of BIPOC families in Canada, according to a study by public engagement organization Maximum City. By comparison to children in white families, children in racialized families were concerned with getting COVID-19 as well as worrying over having adequate food and shelter, a situation exacerbated by major impacts in income losses during the pandemic (Kopun, 2020, September 30).

In a *Scientific American* article, Wallis (2020, June 12) found that "COVID-19 is cutting a jarring and unequal path across the U.S. The disease is disproportionately killing people of color, particularly Black Americans, who have been dying at more than twice the rate of white people" and the impacts of racism—from economic inequities to social marginalization, reduced nutritional options and toxic air and water, as well as the preponderance of frontline worker jobs held by People of Colour—left People of Colour at the mercy of chronic diseases and the COVID virus, pointing to racism as a leading cause of illness. Acknowledging the fact that COVID-19 was attacking people of all ages, racial backgrounds, cultures and financial circumstances (even Donald Trump and his wife Melania tested positive for the virus in October 2020, after the president had spent months downplaying its seriousness and attended political rallies with thousands of unmasked, cheek-by-jowl-packed devotees) author Calvin Baker in *The Atlantic* said the "virus doesn't discriminate, but the world we occupy does. In addition to the damage wrought by environmental pollution—higher in communities of color—and discrepancies in quality of care, there is also the stress of racism on the black body, most obviously manifest in the greater frequency of conditions such as high blood pressure" (Baker, 2020, June). By July 2020, the city of Toronto, with a population of approximately three million, was reporting that outside of long-term care homes, COVID-19 had infected racialized citizens at rates far out of proportion to their populations; in Toronto from May to July 2020, 83 percent of cases were among racialized people, despite their accounting for just over half of the total population, with Black people and South Asian/Indo-Caribbean People topping the list at 21 percent and 20 percent respectively (Seucharan and Bascaramurty, 2020, July 31). The previous month, the *Toronto Star* reported that the northwest corner of the city was particularly hard-hit, with rates of infection "more than 10 times higher in some of these neighbourhoods than in the least-affected areas, which are wealthier and more central. ... [Community advocates] fear the pandemic is having a disproportionate impact on the Black community and is yet another spotlight on the pernicious effects of systemic racism: the city's northwest neighbourhoods also have the city's largest proportion of Black residents" (Yang et al., 2020, June 28). Various sectors responded to the racialization of the virus by creating ways to study how COVID-19 affects the marginalized; at the Hospital for Sick Children in Toronto, a coalition of medical researchers, Black community groups and universities embarked on a study to examine the effect of the virus on racialized populations. The study, which its proponents said would represent the "crystallization" of medical science, socio-economic factors and demographic indicators, was focused on observing "how prevalent COVID-19 was and the extent to which Black Canadian communities may be protected from a second wave in the fall [of 2020]" (Francis, 2020, September 21).

Racialized attitudes have shaped the response to the coronavirus, and they include the belief that Blacks are somehow inured to pain and more prone to disease; Chotiner (2020, May 7), in an interview with Harvard University History of Science Chair Evelynne Hammonds, noted that by May 2020, African Americans made up more than a third of American COVID-19 deaths, despite their comprising just 13 percent of the population. Inequities and systemic bias in the health care infrastructure were blamed for the differences in the way

Black patients were being treated. These attitudes date back to the 18th century and outbreaks of yellow fever to which white doctors believed Blacks were
immune, through the 19th century and the isolating of Black citizens during a
smallpox outbreak (instead of being vaccinated) and the 20th century Tuskegee
study mentioned earlier, as well as the development of an "extinction thesis"
(the belief that, because they were "more prone" to diseases, they would eventually die out). The extinction thesis was created by a Frederick L. Hoffman, an
insurance statistician whose May 1896 journal article, *Race Traits and Tendencies of the American Negro*, was an attempt to denounce efforts to end insurance
discrimination against Blacks; Hoffman's treatise, loaded with racist theories
and speculation, deemed African Americans uninsurable due to health and
social issues and helped to promote continued discrimination against Blacks
(Wolff, 2006, January-February).

A HISTORY OF PREJUDICE

The vast majority of doctors in the 19th century and into the 20th century were
white and working in accordance with white neutral norms; as such, the medical community was immersed in the attitudes of the dominant culture. They
were not used to working with "difference," and they were steeped in a belief
system that held that African American physiology was different, the culture
itself was dissimilar and the cultural attitudes disparate, and as the medical
community adopted the attitude that some in society (i.e. those in the dominant white culture) were "destined" to survive, there was less political will to
invest in infrastructure to help the most vulnerable. Those at the margins of society ended up suffering the most, which is what was seen with the COVID-19
pandemic (Chotiner, 2020, May 7). The promotion of "herd immunity" by the
White House in the days leading up to the November 2020 U.S. election can be
linked to an interpretation of the extinction thesis; in the face of failed U.S. efforts to curb the outbreaks, and with 8 million people infected with COVID-19
and more than 200,000 deaths, the re-election campaign of Donald Trump focused on telling people that herd immunity was a valid "option"—i.e., enough
people get the virus and survive, society as a whole will be safeguarded, and os-
tensibly economies can continue functioning as close to normally as possible,
which is a goal in a capitalist system. This proposal was captured in the "Great
Barrington" declaration, in which a group of epidemiologists and medical professors called for the "focused protection" of herd immunity (Great Barrington
Declaration, 2020). The declaration was supported by the right-wing Ameri-

can Institute for Economic Research (which is funded by conservative magnate Charles Koch) and stated "that lockdowns are more damaging than the alternative" (Arthur, 2020, October 16, p. A1); it was roundly denounced by 80 public health and epidemiology scientists who "said relying on immunity among people who have recovered from Covid-19 is a flawed strategy. …While some research backs the theory, other research finds no evidence of pre-existing immunity from other coronaviruses," and it could lead to unnecessary exposures for the most vulnerable (Edwards, 2020, October 14). While COVID-19 death rates "are low …there is more than death to COVID, too. Everyone understands that the pandemic, and restrictions, have adverse consequences. That's why people encourage government support to people who need it, until vaccines arrive" (Arthur, 2020, October 16, p. A7).

On the positive side, during the pandemic there was considerable reaching out across cultures in displays of understanding, such as the decision by the City of Mississauga's council to support its Muslim community (through a temporary adjustment to noise bylaws) allowing "local mosques to broadcast the [five-minute-long] evening call to prayer during the month of Ramadan …the decent thing to do at a time when everyone is trying to make the best of a tough time" (*Toronto Star*, 2020, May 7); though that decision was met with anger, hatred and social media outrage, the council stuck to its decision, underscoring its support for Muslims who were unable to get together at mosques during the pandemic. Elsewhere in the world, such as in Latin America, the news was not so positive: the pandemic crushed the decades-long, slow movement toward income equality and better living conditions, erasing many advances; over "the past 20 years, millions of families had marched out of poverty in one of the most unequal regions on earth. … Now, the pandemic is threatening to reverse those gains … potentially upending politics and entire societies for years to come" (Turkewitz and Villamil, 2020, July 18).

As for blame ("Who caused it? Who spreads it?") the field was an open one; just about anyone outside the dominant culture could and often did become a target of hate. In Europe, the Roma (pejoratively referred to as "Gypsies" in the past) became the collective object of scorn and anger, much of it state-driven and involving police checkpoints and interrogation, and focused on viewing (and reinforcing the attitude of) Roma as vectors of the COVID-19 virus. Media played a role in reinforcing this hatred, suggesting that Roma were both spreaders of the virus and immune to it: "Across Europe, a range of media outlets have been broadcasting similar narratives blaming Roma, especially

those recently returning from other countries, for spreading COVID-19....
[In Romania,] local and national newspapers have raged a racist, hateful, and
life-threatening campaign of anti-Roma propaganda ... countless anti-Roma
dehumanizing, degrading, and deeply offensive fake posts and 'news' on Facebook remain unaddressed by that platform" (Matache and Bhabha, 2020, June),
although, following backlash from major advertisers pulling advertising, and
subsequent Facebook corporate waffling, the tech giant "announced it would
add various labels to political posts ... and [would be] expanding its definition
of hateful content that warrants removal. It also committed to an audit over its
approach to hate speech from the Media Review Council" (Bort, 2020, July 1).

In Canada, following the lockdowns of March 2020, some workers (health
care workers, grocery store clerks, retail and service sector employees, personal
support workers and nurses in long-term care homes) were expected to continue showing up for their shifts; they did not have the opportunity or benefit
of being able to work from home. This denial of distance-work was seen to
be racialized—many workers in areas such as those mentioned were BIPOC
employees; the Canadian Centre for Diversity and Inclusion cited the example
of a call centre where desperate-for-work immigrants, most of them People
of Colour, were expected to continue showing up for work, placing them "in
greater danger of contracting COVID-19" (Canadian Centre for Diversity and
Inclusion, 2020, April 6). Civil liberties were impacted: the Canadian Civil Liberties Association joined with other groups to question the province of Ontario's establishment of a virus database allowing police and others to access citizens' contact information, like addresses, full names and birthdates; there was
a fear that emergency powers gave authorities too much access to information
deemed private (Powell, 2020, April 25). This led to the question of biopolitics, a term coined by French philosopher Michel Foucault; biopolitics deals
with the "strategies and mechanisms through which human life processes are
managed under regimes of authority over knowledge, power, and the processes of subjectivation" (Garrison, 2013, January 21). Since the 1970s, biopolitics
has run in tandem with neoliberalism, which, though it might sound "liberal,"
is in fact focused on loosening government controls and regulations on prof-
it-making and taxes, making the concept a part of right-wing political agendas.
Neoliberalism demands that "the market mechanism should be allowed to direct the fate of human beings. The economy should dictate its rules to society,
not the other way around" (George, 1999, March). Neoliberal policies see the
monetization of all things related to humanity; it explains the drive to mark-up

prices on sanitizing products, tissues, hand wipes and masks during the pandemic and, though we might think that the race to create a COVID-19 vaccine was driven by altruism, there was also a serious financial bottom line involved for the pharmaceutical industry.

The pandemic put the mainstream-dominated power structure of systemic racism into hyper-drive; according to Concordia University professor Yasmin Jiwani, the pandemic "intensified public attention to the unequal vulnerability of Indigenous and Black people and amplified other racialized inequalities inherent in society. … The pandemic ushered kaleidoscopic frames mediated by a white gaze," with reports of anti-Asian physical violence during the pandemic, and an intense focus on police violence against Blacks and Indigenous People" (Jiwani, 2020, June 30). A report by the Toronto Foundation (a registered charity and grant-funding organization) found that racialized Torontonians and those on the lower end of the income-earning scale had far higher rates of infection during the COVID pandemic. "Black, Latin American and Arab, Middle Eastern or West Asian Torontonians have COVID-19 infection rates at least seven times higher than white residents … [the report] also finds people earning less than $30,000 a year are just over five-times more likely to catch the virus than those making $150,000 or more" (680 News Staff, 2020, November 12).

There was little escape for anyone during the pandemic, and this highlights the plight of those with the fewest options: inmates of Canadian prisons were found to be at a much higher risk of contracting COVID-19. Correctional Services Canada delivered almost 1,800 COVID tests (to September 29, 2020), and there were hundreds of illnesses and two deaths (Correctional Services Canada, 2020); federal and provincial prisons took the unprecedented move of releasing hundreds of low-risk inmates in order to reduce crowding and lessen the risks associated with transmission, but there were also complaints of a lack of soap and sanitizers, sick prisoners being locked up in solitary confinement, medical shortages and a lack of social distancing (Bradley, 2020, August 14). It is important to also see the COVID-and-prison scenario within a cultural context: more than a third of inmates are Indigenous, though they make up only 5 percent of Canada's population (Cecco, 2020, January 22), and there are numerous reports of abuses against Indigenous inmates in federal and provincial penal systems. Canada's Indigenous communities, already coping with matters of land claims, reconciliation and systemic bias, have seen dramatic upticks in mental health issues relating to the COVID-19 pandemic, with increased calls to crisis centre lines and hundreds of reported COVID-19 cases on reserves. The federal government promised $305 million for Indigenous communities "to help Indigenous communities prepare for emergencies and prevent the spread of the new coronavirus" (Wright, 2020, August 13), and the government also promised $82.5 million in funding for the "mental health needs" of Indigenous communities, acknowledging that the pandemic layered additional stressors on top of existing issues such as child welfare abuses and residential school trauma (Barrera, 2020, August 25).

Indigenous communities' relations with the federal government, especially in the area of health care, have been strained, violent, difficult and at times explosive. Canadian history is built on the near-annihilation of Indigenous communities; for instance, pandemics in the 1800s, coupled with reduced food provisions to First Nations communities, were used to manipulate and control those communities on the prairies. In a bitter, perfect storm that combined the forces of wild game reduction (especially the near-extinction of the buffalo) with diseases like smallpox, measles, tuberculosis and influenza, the forced relocation of First Nations communities to reserve lands, and the manipulation of local economies, John A. Macdonald's federal government decimated Indigenous communities. Deprived of food, essentially prevented from leaving their reserves, and under the thumb of the Canadian government, First Nations' survival was severely threatened, and these activities presaged the cultural genocide that followed as Indigenous children were forced into residential schools. As James Daschuk notes in *Clearing the Plains*, during a whooping cough outbreak in 1889, even media outlets that had traditionally been less-than-friendly towards Indigenous groups showed compassion; the *Saskatchewan Herald* called on the federal authorities to act during the outbreak: "The newspaper, seeing infection take hold among the relatively affluent Denesuliné (Chipewyan), knew that the disease would be far more dangerous for the poor and hungry reserve population of the plains, where 'it would not fail to be fatal to an appalling extent'" (Daschuk, 2019, p. 167). Such scenes repeated themselves over time in Canadian history, and so it is not surprising that the Liberal government of Justin Trudeau would make gestures to assist Indigenous communities during the COVID-19 pandemic. However, given Canada's "abysmal" record of support, Indigenous communities were at great risk during the pandemic, and in addition to facing discrimination when trying to obtain health services, "many First Nations communities lack access to clean water and inadequate funding for on-reserve housing has led to severe overcrowding, making social distancing difficult. In urban settings, Indigenous people are also overrepresented in populations at heightened risk of Covid-19: populations experiencing homelessness, prison populations, and people living in poverty" (Carling and Mankani, 2020, June 9). The strained relationship between Indigenous Peoples and the health care system was further brought to light with the death of Joyce Echaquan, an Atikamekw woman in Quebec, who died in a Joliette hospital in September 2020; Echaquan used her cellphone to provide a graphic Facebook video record of her treatment by nurses, who made racist comments as she lay dying. Nurses' comments ranged from calling Echaquan "stupid" and saying that she was "only good for sex" to stating that tax dollars were paying for her health care (Barrera, 2020, October 1). "Her death has called attention to a health-care system that Indigenous medical workers say has been failing to serve Indigenous people for years. ... [W]hen racist stereotypes are in the [health care] mix, the result can be deadly in the form of misdiagnosis, overlooked symptoms or failure to treat" (Francis, 2020, October 2). In response, Québec's provincial nursing body, the L'Ordre des infirmières et infirmiers du Québec, denounced the racism that was directed at Echaquan, and said it would investigate (Barrera, 2020, October 1).

In addressing COVID-19 and First Nations, the federal government had reported by the end of July 2020 that:

- The percentage of First Nations individuals living on reserve testing positive for COVID-19 was currently one-quarter the rate of the general Canadian population;
- The COVID-19 case fatality rate for First Nations individuals living on reserve was about one-fifth that of the fatality rate in the general Canadian population;
- More than 80 percent of those testing positive for COVID-19 had recovered; and
- Almost 2,000 orders for personal protective equipment had been sent to First Nations communities (Government of Canada, 2020, October 2).

Jolene Banning, in the journal of the Canadian Medical Association, noted that despite "poverty, overcrowding, limited health infrastructure and poor access to clean water—ideal conditions for the spread of disease ... Indigenous communities have fared better than the rest of Canada in the first wave of the COVID-19 pandemic" (Bannon, 2020, August 24), attributable to a fresh awareness of past, deadly epidemics, and a proactive community approach that stressed self-isolation, proper hygiene practices and the use of personal protective equipment. Then the next wave arrived. In late October 2020, there was a surge of COVID-19 cases on reserves in Alberta, Saskatchewan and Manitoba; according to health officials, "Manitoba's test positivity among First Nations stands at 11 per cent. It's 8.6 per cent for the rest of the province." On October 30, the federal government announced an additional $200 million in COVID-19 funding earmarked for Indigenous communities (Malone, 2020, October 31).

Some hard-learned lessons were coming to light. The dangerous, negligent and often presumptuous approach to medical treatment of Indigenous Peoples has historically been based on assumptions and stereotyping, and in fact there were predictions (which eventually came true) that Canada's First Nations, Inuit and Métis populations would be hard hit by COVID-19 (Richardson and Crawford, 2020, September 21). Past experience showed a pattern of Indigenous suffering combined with government negligence; James Daschuk notes that issues like an increase in tuberculosis among First Nations in the 19th century were caused by disruption of environment and ecology (Daschuk, 2019, p. 178). In combination with social disorder, overcrowding and lack of food, the introduction of any new disease had devastating effects. Yet medical specialists at the time chose to overlook the social and economic causes and instead chose to "interpret the chronic bad health of the Indigenous population as a condition of their race, claiming that tuberculosis was largely hereditary. By the early twentieth century, the notion that First Nations people were biologically more susceptible to disease than the mainstream population was medically and politically orthodox" (Daschuk, 2019, p. 185). These attitudes naturally supported and reinforced feelings of white Eurocentric superiority.

Today, thanks to a growing understanding of (and refutation of the mainstream attitudes connected to) that history, Indigenous communities have focused on preparedness (note that these efforts have not been 'handed to' Indigenous communities by federal authorities, but have been self-generated):

In Canada, almost all Indigenous communities have pre-existing emergency preparedness plans, and they have been updated and implemented to deal with the current pandemic. Furthermore, innovative educational materials and public health campaigns have been created by many different First Nations, Inuit and Métis communities. These materials build on prevention, isolation and containment measures put forward by public health institutions but are grounded in the local context of each community, including its language, culture, and physical and social environments (Richardson and Crawford 2020, September 21).

Incarceration of the "other" during a pandemic proved to be problematic for governments in power. In the U.S., the locking up of Latin American refugee adults and children by ICE (the Immigration and Customs Enforcement agency) was halted, at least in some detention centres, by a federal judicial decree in June 2020. "The ruling is part of an ongoing effort to release immigrants held in detention who are particularly susceptible to the coronavirus given the confined settings at facilities and the potential for spread" (Alvarez, 2020, June 27). But the ill treatment of refugees by the authorities took another turn during the pandemic as media reported a high number of unnecessary, forced hysterectomies on Spanish-speaking women at an ICE detention centre in Georgia, drawing "parallels to America's clouded history of forced sterilization targeting Black and Brown communities" (Fowler, 2020, September 15).

One group hit hard by the pandemic was migrant farm workers. Every year, Canada welcomes thousands of workers from Jamaica, Guatemala, Mexico and other countries under the Canadian Seasonal Agricultural Worker Program. "In 2019, the federal government says it approved 46,707 positions," and most of those workers went to Ontario (40 percent), Quebec (32 percent) and BC (18 percent) (Pazzano, 2020, August 28). In 2020, many stayed home because of the pandemic; for those who made the trip the Canada, the pandemic had devastating consequences. Overworked and without access to outlets to buy masks, many were defenseless. According to Basok and George (2020, April 26), "migrant workers (were) left unprotected from the spread of COVID-19 and its social and emotional spin-offs. Their housing conditions constitute the greatest threat to these workers," with up to 60 living in houses divided up into bunk-bed quarters, and "workers have little time in the day and week to meet their own basic needs, including shopping for food, a task that has generated considerable anxieties." In the U.S. some migrant farm worker crews were forced into lockdown, where they were required to "remain either in the camps, where they are housed, or the fields, where they toil … [causing] many workers to complain that their work site has become like a prison" (Jordan, 2020, October 24). An outbreak of COVID-19 in a farming community in Kelowna, B.C., created serious concerns for the safety of migrant farm workers, according to health safety researchers:

> Without a coordinated plan for enforcement, federal government advice to employers on how to prevent the spread of COVID-19 among migrant workers is risky and toothless. Public health experts, rather than industry groups or individual employers, should oversee protocols to safeguard migrant workers' health in light of the pandemic (Weiler et al., 2020, April 1).

The lack of rights and freedoms prompted Leah Vosko, a York University political science professor, in an interview with Deirdre Kelly, to call on the federal government to offer migrant farm workers "permanent residency status. Redefining their status in this country would give the migrant workers standing and recognition as essential workers meriting fair compensation and full access to occupational health and safety protections" (Kelly, 2020, Fall). And in a major legal win for migrant farm workers, the Ontario Labour Relations Board found that Scottlyn Growers, a farming operation in Norfolk County, Ontario, "broke the law when it terminated [migrant worker] Gabriel Flores Flores shortly after he spoke out about poor living and working conditions at the farm. Some 199 migrant workers at the multimillion-dollar operation tested positive for COVID, including Flores himself" (Mojtehedzadeh, 2020, November 12). The ruling, which served to confirm and support the fact that firing or disciplining employees on the basis of safety and health issues is illegal, was considered a first in Ontario.

THE RACIALIZATION OF DISASTERS: HURRICANES KATRINA AND MARIA AND THE HAITI EARTHQUAKE

It may seem like a cliché that disasters can bring out the worst and the best in people, but, in stripping away artifice and bringing human behaviour down to its essentials during chaos, they do have that effect. Hurricane Katrina is a sound example: pounding the American coast from Texas to Florida in August 2005, it was a Category 5 hurricane that caused three-metre-high storm surges along the coastline, bursting through poorly engineered levees, affecting the lives of 15 million citizens and killing 1,800, and resulting in "more than $160 billion [U.S.] in damage" (Britannica, 2024, Jan. 4); it displaced thousands of residents, and left them without food, water, shelter and communications. The economic impact made it the costliest natural disaster to hit the U.S. Many in New Orleans were supposed to evacuate, but "tens of thousands of people remained in the city—not necessarily by choice, but rather because they were too poor to afford a car or bus fare to leave" (Lopez, 2015, August 28). People helped: professional emergency personnel and ordinary citizens saved lives, people found sanctuary (50,000 divided between the New Orleans Convention Center and the Superdome), and there were food drives—but it was also a highly racialized disaster, bringing to light "the confluence of race and poverty [which] has become part of a new and more insidious set of forces based on a revised set of biopolitical commitments ... [that] have embraced an emergent security state founded on cultural homogeneity" (Giroux, p. 11).

In the aftermath of the hurricane, the graphic images were compelling: people wading through the flooded streets of New Orleans, messages chalked on rooftops ("Please Help Us!"), a lone man holding an infant, wandering through waist-high water, looking for help, hospitals having to choose who would live or die (and evacuating the lucky ones), dead bodies bagged and tagged by emergency workers and left on porches, and the tide of humanity swamping the public spaces, especially the Superdome. The vast majority of the victims were African Americans. This was a disaster that impacted the working poor and devastated them. For leaders, it was a political disaster marred by misunderstanding, missteps, failed public relations campaigns and misguided "help." While the federal government was warned of impending disaster three days before it happened and was begged by the governor of Louisiana for more assistance as Hurricane Katrina made landfall (Lopez, 2015, August 28), then president George W. Bush continued taking a month-long vacation in Texas, then cut his vacation time short and embarked on what his aides thought would be a feel-good "flyover" of the disaster; this sense of being distanced from the disaster was underscored by slow response by federal and state authorities (Walsh, 2015, August 28). The Federal Emergency Management Agency (FEMA) got involved much later than needed and expected; Bush would sign an initial aid package for more than $10 billion four days after landfall, "and ordered 7,200 National Guard troops to the region. A few days later, he requested—and Congress approved—an additional $51.8 billion in aid" (Robillard, 2012, October 3). Ultimately the federal government would spend $120 billion on assistance (Alpert, 2015, August 21).

It became clear to many on the ground that the response was tainted by racism, in particular the environmental racism that does not give consideration to marginalized communities when government policy is developed; in the case of Katrina, "the government's failure to maintain infrastructure and organize evacuation plans led up to the disadvantages that poor and racial minorities [experience] when natural or human disasters occur. ... [R]acial discrimination played a role in the safety of minority communities and their [government's] negligence to prevent the potential damages, such as building neighborhoods that are next to poorly maintained flood levees," which were swamped by the hurricane (ESRI, n.d.). It took a week for flood survivors to be evacuated.

In writing about the social effects of Hurricane Katrina, scholar and culture critic Henry Giroux noted the growing authoritarianism that "dominates popular culture, the media and the culture industry" (Giroux, 2006, p. 69), which explained the racialized media coverage of the event that, in combination with slow responses from government authorities, served to paint a picture of chaos; stories were written of the Superdome becoming a "hell hole" of murder, rape and sniper attacks, and there were stories of citizens being stubbornly unwilling (rather than unable) to leave the city (Lopez, 2015, August 28). This continuing trend deepens the rift between peoples in a society. According to Cheryl Harris in the *California Law Review*, polls showed that more than "two-thirds of Blacks believed that the federal government would have responded more quickly if the victims had been White, while over three-quarters of Whites believed the response time would have been the same" (Harris, 2006, May, p. 910).

Kaiser et al. (2008) examined the attitudes of white and Black subjects with respect to questions of a) the disaster response being due to racism, or b) the disaster response being linked to simple government incompetence. "Whites exposed to video clips arguing that the Hurricane Katrina disaster response was due to racism displayed greater racial ingroup attachment and ingroup love compared to Whites exposed to videos conveying that the government's incompetence was to blame for the disaster response. In contrast, Blacks displayed strong levels of ingroup attachment and ingroup love across both video conditions." As such, white subjects were threatened by implications of racism as it threatened their hierarchy status, causing them to adhere more closely to their group identity. According to Giroux (2006), the "stifling and dangerous anti-democratic tendencies that transformed a natural disaster into a human and social tragedy are still at work in American society, prompting a collapse of the public and leaving no place for individual and social agency that is responsive to the deepest social conflicts and problems of our time" (p. 77).

In September 2017, racialization of "the other" was reinforced during Hurricane Maria, which swept across the U.S. territory of Puerto Rico, causing almost $100 billion (U.S.) in damage and creating a humanitarian crisis (there was a lack of water and power for months afterwards) that was underscored by an overriding attitude of "Us" vs "Them," and led to the exodus of 130,000 of the island's 3.4 million residents (Mercy Corps, 2020, September 9). So pronounced was the anti-Latinx sentiment of the U.S. White House that President Trump suggested "selling off" the island as the hurricane approached (Choma, 2020, July 11). According to a study by Rodriguez-Dias and Lewellen-Williams (2020, May 22), the colonial relationship between Puerto Rico and the United States served to underscore extant racism. Racism "is perceived as a barrier to proper response in the aftermath of natural disasters" and the conditions in Puerto Rico created "a perfect storm caused by major hurricanes [the island was also hit by Hurricane Irma two weeks before Maria] and a human-made financial crisis manufactured by bankers and a predatory class of investors" (Rodriguez-Diaz and Lewellen-Williams, 2020, May 22). A year after the hurricanes, a poll of Puerto Ricans affected by the damage found that "83 percent reported either major damage to their homes, losing power for more than three months, employment setbacks or worsening health problems, among other effects of the storm," and they blamed the slow and uninspiring recovery work by the federal government, as well as disrespectful photo-ops such as Donald Trump making jokes and casually tossing rolls of paper towels to a gathered crowd in Guaynabo, Puerto Rico, after the hurricane (Clement et al., 2018, September 12). Rodriguez-Diaz and Lewellen-Williams said the structural racism triggered a greater community effort—a "coming together," as it were, of island citizens in a show of local philanthropy, which helped to a degree, but ultimately because of the "colonial status of PR (Puerto Rico) ... [r]acism was a detrimental determinant for emergency and recovery response" (2020, May 22). Da Silveira, in a study of racialized media coverage of Hurricane Maria, found that:

journalists decontextualized, decentered, and distanced Puerto Rico and the people of Puerto Rico and reinforced the white racial frame [the "white neutral norm" discussed earlier]. ... [Journalists'] anti-Other and pro-white subframes function to center whiteness and exclude Puerto Ricans from a conversation where they are the ones with the first-hand narratives. As a way to almost make up for their avoidance of the topic, they overcompensate with almost theatrical language that reduces Puerto Rico and the people in Puerto Rico as "ravaged" or "pummeled" (Da Silveira, 2019, p. 54).

Three years later, the island was still recovering, and while water and electricity were restored, outages still occurred; Puerto Rico suffered an earthquake in January 2020 and the problems were exacerbated by COVID-19, which put strains on recovering businesses and forced schools to go virtual (Mercy Corps, 2020, September 9). It wasn't until September 2020 that Trump—commentators say that he was influenced by the upcoming November federal election—decided to approve $11.6 billion in funding to help rebuild, money that was held back for three years (Wilner, 2020, September 19). Still, the political damage was done, and in the run-up to the election, the leading Puerto Rican newspaper *El Nuevo Dia* lambasted the administration of Donald Trump, stating that

in the last four years, the administration of President Donald Trump has shown an overwhelming amount of inattention, disdain and prejudice against our people. President Trump charged at the dignity of Puerto Ricans, to the extreme of throwing paper towel rolls when he visited the island while our people still suffered the worst horrors of the hurricane´s aftermath. He has suggested exchanging our island for Greenland, as if both were merchandise and we had little value. These acts show his disassociation from the great Puerto Rican contributions to democracy and world peace, as well as to the society and economy of the United States (*El Nuevo Dia*, 2020, October 18).

Five years after Maria, Puerto Rico would be hit by Hurricane Fiona; the September 2022 hurricane would cover parts of the island in 75 centimetres of rain, leaving close to a million residents without power and a quarter-million without water (Sanchez, 2022, September 24).

Or consider the 2010 Haiti earthquake, which killed somewhere around 300,000 (estimates vary depending upon the report, but later academic analysis suggested the number was closer to 160,000), caused extensive damage, displaced hundreds of thousands and, with the country's electricity disrupted, made it difficult for relief workers to reach the survivors and provide aid, including medical assistance and helping to uncover people buried under the rubble of destroyed buildings (Pallardy, 2010). Eleven years later, a 7.2 magnitude earthquake would kill more than 2,500 and have an economic impact of U.S. $1.6 billion, almost 10 percent of the country's GDP (Cavallo, E. et al., 2021, September).

What made the 2010 earthquake stand out was not just its effect on well over 2 million citizens, and the international relief money totalling more than $13.3 billion that flowed to the country over the next decade (CNN Editorial Research, 2020, June 2) but the social chaos. Distressingly evident was the looting, the violence, and the search for family members. And the shooting of a 15-year-old girl. Fabienne Cherisma was a pragmatic young person, spending mornings selling knick-knacks in the family's stall in Port-au-Prince, and afternoons in school. In the rubble of the buildings Fabienne had joined others, looking for items that could be reused and sold. The accounts are scanty as to whether she joined looters and scavenged the two plastic chairs and three framed pictures she was carrying home days after the January 12 earthquake or whether she had purchased them—iffy, too, is the question of whether the police deliberately shot her or whether they were simply shooting in the air; regardless, she was killed by a police bullet (Carroll, 2010, January 26) and lay across the rubble, blood forming a rivulet under a painting of a flower in a vase. What happened next spoke to the dynamics of the social and narrative power of the dominant culture. Photojournalists, most of them white, saw an opportunity to create a dramatic photo, gathering to take in the vivid image of Fabienne, a Black girl clad in bright pink, her lifeless body strewn face down on the concrete, and they not only gathered, a flock of them jockeying for position, camera flashes popping, to take her picture, they also allegedly took the time to rearrange her body to "improve" their shots, some of the shots being taken after Fabienne's family had arrived on the scene (Reel Foto, 2013, May 30). One of the photographers, Paul Hansen, would win an international photography award for his picture. Critics were quick to call out the subtext of the event itself, deeming it everything from the biopolitical subjugation of Black bodies (Itagaki, 2016, March 9), to an example of poverty porn, "a tactic used by nonprofits and charity organizations to gain empathy and contributions from donors by showing exploitative imagery of people living in destitute conditions. … A distinct mark of poverty porn advertisements and photographs made by non-African photographers is the lack of decency, dignity, virtuous character, or that it shows the subjects' most vulnerable moment" (Dortonne, 2016, December 8). According to Jeffrey Maciejewski, the existence of two pictures of Fabienne in different "poses," appeared "to make it clear that someone, maybe even Hansen himself, moved Cherisma's body so as to make it more compelling and to make her identity more visible. The ethics here are such that news photographers are not to alter what they see; they are to merely document news events with the aid of their cameras" (Maciejewski, 2013, February 8).

THE ROLE OF PUBLIC RELATIONS DURING THE PANDEMIC

It is understood that public relations is a means of communicating the economic and the political, and as such, PR may play "a role in the ways in which race and racialized groups are presented in these political and economic contexts … as part of a system that racializes disadvantage by creating and circulating meanings that thrust a White worldview on to the reality of a racialized existence" (Munshi and Edwards, 2011, p. 354). That having been said, PR can also push back against stereotypes and, through its accessibility to, and connection with, the world in "real time," it can set precedents and establish agendas for positive social behaviour that links people across cultures. Public relations practitioners play a focused role in any organization, and especially so during crisis times like pandemics, producing effective key messages and generating sound crisis plans to help their organizations navigate the uncertainty of the times. According to Alton (2020, April 8), the COVID-19 pandemic was a chance for practitioners to clarify the identity of their audiences, establish/reestablish their communication goals and work on strengthening business and stakeholder relationships by "striking the right tone" with messaging in order to effectively connect with their key audiences. The public relations industry responded strongly in the face of the COVID-19 pandemic, essentially either ramping up (those serving the pharmaceutical, food/grocery and health care sectors) or, in the case of hospitality, retail, sports and recreation during lockdown, winding things down, putting work on hiatus or temporarily halting work (Rabaey, 2020, May 11). Sudhaman (2020, April 17) noted that public relations practitioners were essentially given a green light to be creative in helping to build links to a greater understanding of the "new normal" that clients and the public were facing while living and working through the pandemic, and this ability to pivot would be grounded in a greater understanding of "realtime cultural insight." Public relations CEO Deborah Geiger (2020, March 23) noted that in "a time of crisis, it's all about human connection and meaning over the transactional. Public relations is an important function, but it has to be authentic to work effectively … a PR consultant can proactively engage with journalists, ensure positive and influential media coverage for you and your business and handle content creation." And when the COVID-19 vaccine began to become available in December 2020, effective PR also had a role to play in convincing reluctant recipients to roll up their sleeves. A study by Newhagen and Bucy (2020, October 23) noted the position of politically hard-right "anti-vaxxers" in refusing to get a shot, and saw that their resistance was rooted (not surprisingly) in emotion, rather than logic; they were driven by "trust factors" such as social trust (how much do you trust other people, especially strangers, those speaking another language, or journalists?), trust in science, and trust in government; falling low on those trust factors would mean people refusing to get a shot, focused as they were on "anger and fear … denial and alarm. These responses occur within an increasingly distorted and fractured media ecology characterized by hyper-polarization, where preferred information channels act as preprocessing filters to organize information into ideologically familiar frames." In other words, people opt for social media sites that block out the messages they don't want to see and hear. There was also a sense of mistrust that many BIPOC community members felt toward the vaccine, and while the historical record of medical discrimination (and the high incidence of COVID-19 infection among Persons of Colour) led to calls in the U.S. for Blacks, Indigenous and Latinx communities to be prioritized in the early rounds of COVID-19 vaccinations, "it's also what has made many people of color distrust the medical establishment developing and disseminating such vaccines" (Samuel, 2020, October 28). To boost acceptance of the vaccine's safety, many news outlets rolled out footage of prominent members of BIPOC communities getting their shots.

RESOURCES DURING THE PANDEMIC

The U.S.-based Institute for Public Relations provided a guide to COVID-19 resources during the pandemic, including a site focused on "Diversity, Equity, and Inclusion," which offered up articles outlining the effect of the virus on marginalized populations, from rates of infection and job losses to the virus's intersections with initiatives like Black Lives Matter (Institute for Public Relations, 2020). The PR/marketing firm Purpose Brand found that PR agencies were focusing during COVID-19 on providing information to the public and traditional media (Purpose Brand, 2020, June 25).

Many communications personnel are found in the public service; the United Nations Department of Economic and Social Affairs, in a policy brief, noted that public service employees were front-and-centre in ensuring the continuity of services during the pandemic, and the roles of public relations practitioners are often reflected in the goals established for public service employees, including effective and ongoing communications to various publics, with a focus on:

- Comprehensive public service capacity development;
- The institutionalization of early warning, emergency planning, preparedness and ensuring fast, well-coordinated and appropriate, time-sensitive responses;
- Networking, collaboration and information sharing;
- Sustained development of responsible, responsive, accountable and people-focused leadership (United Nations Department of Economic and Social Affairs, 2020, June 11).

From a communications perspective, it is necessary in a crisis, such as the pandemic, to:

- Establish a leadership team, each member knowing their specific functions;
- Properly assess the situation and its impact on the organization;
- Identify the audiences you need to reach, including your internal audiences (employees of the organization) and external audiences (public, stakeholders, media, government officials);
- Create a timetable for issuing statements, key messages, guidelines and other information to internal and external audiences;
- Update your communications materials;
- Conduct research on the crisis and update your information so that it is current;
- Develop and maintain contacts with your audiences on an ongoing basis (Cooper, 2016).

LET'S CHECK IN!
In this self-assessment, you will be asked to think about your attitudes toward, and knowledge of, the subject matter discussed in this chapter. Spend 10 or 15 quiet minutes and choose the most impactful idea that crystallized in your mind, based on your reading of this chapter and the feelings that flowed from it. Write your idea down and set down the major thoughts that flow from it as bullet points. Prepare to discuss with your colleagues.

KEY TERMS

Ethnocentrism: a subjective position in which an individual or group places their own culture at the centre, positioning it as the "norm" and measuring or subjugating other cultures as a result.

Extinction thesis: the belief that, because they are "more prone" to diseases (without taking into consideration health and social factors), some groups of people will eventually die out, leaving the "stronger" to survive.

Herd immunity: The idea that if a large proportion of a society is immune to a disease, their collective immunity will stop its spread.

Poverty porn: a tactic used to generate sympathy by exploiting the images of destitute people and distinguished by a lack of dignity and decency.

Protestant work ethic: a viewpoint that focuses on the idealization of the benefits of hard work and discipline.

Rugged individualism: a point of view embracing the notions of independence and laissez-faire self-reliance.

Social Darwinism: A now-debunked theory of the 19th and early 20th centuries suggesting that human groups and races were subject to laws of natural selection, with the weak eventually dying out and the strong surviving.

White nationalism: efforts to wrap white supremacist ideas in the "respectable language" of racial separatism.

QUESTIONS TO EXPLORE

1. What responsibilities do media and public relations practitioners have toward BIPOC communities during a pandemic?

2. If you were asked to compile a briefing note comparing the Great Barrington proposal to the standard COVID-19 approach of social distancing, hygiene, and mask-wearing while a vaccine was being developed, what major points would you emphasize?

3. Think about the situations that occurred during Hurricane Katrina, Hurricane Maria and the Haiti earthquake, and take a look at some of the video of the devastation of each on YouTube. What were some of the cultural issues that showed up in each of them, and how could agencies and communicators have dealt more effectively with these issues?

EXERCISE

Your organization, which is in the food processing industry and produces a variety of food products including jams, nut-based spreads and peanut butter, is a medium-sized business with approximately 475 employees. You have a very diverse workforce, and BIPOC employees comprise 35 percent of your shop floor workers and 20 percent of management. You have large contingents of Filipino Canadian and Chinese Canadian workers. During a pandemic, your company continued to work on the basis of rotating shifts, following established guidelines for social distancing, the use of personal protective equipment, and proper hygiene practices.

Your job in the communications department is to provide information to employees through a company newsletter and the company website. There have been concerns raised about the spread of COVID-19; some anonymous comments online and postings around the plant suggest that your workers of Asian background are putting other segments of your internal workforce at risk. Your vice-president of communications has asked you to provide a briefing note for the company president to help them manage the communications around this situation; as well, you need to provide a brief written statement that can be delivered through the company's internal newsletter and in company meetings.

You will recall our discussion about briefing notes in Chapter Three. Focus on the five basic components:

Subject: the briefing note's title;

Purpose: the "why" of the briefing note;

Summary: the facts of the matter at hand, and explanations that support the briefing note's purpose;

Recommendations: the briefing note will provide a recommended course of action;

Conclusion: a summary of what has been said; it is short and is focused on providing an accurate synopsis of the points that have been covered.

The task: Create a 750-word briefing note that will help your organization tackle this situation, and a 500-word statement that supports the company's position on inclusion, fairness and equity, and gives assurances of continued adherence to health guidelines.

EXERCISE

Henry Giroux said in *Stormy Weather*: "The aftermath of Hurricane Katrina provided a glimpse of the dire consequences that can befall a society when it succumbs to the notions that neoliberal capitalism and democracy are synonymous, that the highest values in society can be measured only in economic terms, and that some groups in society are disposable because they are not productive consumers" (2006, pp 113–114).

Analyze this statement from the perspective of a professional communicator. What are the important points that you take from this statement, and how does this affect your job as a communications practitioner?

Could a disaster like Katrina affect a Canadian city? Are there areas of a city such as Toronto that would be considered largely BIPOC communities?

Here is a scenario: you are working for the City of Toronto. Develop a vision, mission, and values statement that reflects the diversity of the city and positions the city in terms of awareness of, and responsibility to, the diverse communities contained within it.

REFERENCES

680 News Staff (2020, November 12). Racialized, lower-income Torontonians bearing heavier burden during pandemic: report. *680 News*. https://www.680news.com/2020/11/12/racialized-lower-income-torontonians-bearing-heavier-burden-during-pandemic-report/

Alpert, B. (2015, August 21). $120 billion in Katrina federal relief wasn't always assured. Nola.com. https://www.nola.com/news/article_338b3dd9-30e5-576d-b52a-d91ee07a499a.html

Alton, L. (2020, April 8). How to create a crisis communication plan during coronavirus pandemic. *National Funding*. https://www.nationalfunding.com/blog/how-to-create-a-crisis-communication-plan-during-coronavirus/

Alvarez, P. (2020, June 27). Judge rules migrant children in government family detention centers must be released due to coronavirus. *CNN*. https://www.cnn.com/2020/06/26/politics/children-released-from-immigration-detention-centers/index.html

Arthur, B. (2020, October 16). Anti-lockdown memo is unrealistic and irresponsible. *Toronto Star*, pp. A1–A7.

Arthur, B. (2020, April 24). Ugly smear reveals an infection in politics. *Toronto Star*, p. A8.

Aslantas, (2019, March). The effect of intercultural education on the ethnocentrism levels of prospective teachers. *International Electronic Journal of Elementary Education*, 11(4): 319–326. DOI: 10.26822/iejee.2019450790

Baker, C. (2020, June). In a pandemic, all some people see is your color. *The Atlantic*. https://www.theatlantic.com/magazine/archive/2020/06/coronavirus-racism/610609/

Banning, J. (2020, August 24). Why are Indigenous communities seeing so few cases of COVID-19? *CMAJ*. DOI: https://doi.org/10.1503/cmaj.1095891

Barrera, J. (2020, October 1). Criminal investigation needed into death of Joyce Echaquan, say 2 legal experts. *CBC News*. https://www.cbc.ca/news/indigenous/joyce-echaquan-death-lawyers-investigations-1.5745587

Barrera, J. (2020, August 25). Ottawa announces $82.5M to help Indigenous communities deal with COVID-19 mental health fallout. *CBC News*. https://www.cbc.ca/news/indigenous/marc-miller-funding-mental-health-1.5699204?utm_source=TVO&utm_campaign=6b11e47871-EMAIL_CAMPAIGN_1_17_2019_10_56_COPY_01&utm_medium=email&utm_term=0_eadf6a4c78-6b11e47871-24187777

Basok, T., and George, G. (2020, April 26). Migrant workers face further social isolation and mental health challenges during coronavirus pandemic. *The Conversation*. https://theconversation.com/migrant-workers-face-further-social-isolation-and-mental-health-challenges-during-coronavirus-pandemic-134324

Blue, G., and Rock, M. (2020, June 17). Genomic trans-biopolitics: Why more-than-human geography is critical amid the COVID-19 pandemic. *Dialogues in Human Geography*. https://doi.org/10.1177/2043820620935660

Bort, R. (2020, July 1). Advertisers are fleeing Facebook over its failure to moderate hate speech. *Rolling Stone*. https://www.rollingstone.com/politics/politics-news/facebook-advertisers-fleeing-content-moderation-1023186/

Boutilier, A. (2020, April 30). MP refuses to apologize to Tam. *Toronto Star*, p. A4.

Bradley, J. (2020, August 14). Canada's correctional institutions released thousands of inmates in the early days of COVID-19. *National Post*. https://nationalpost.com/news/canadas-correctional-institutions-released-thousands-of-inmates-in-the-early-days-of-covid-19

Britannica (2024, January 4). Hurricane Katrina. *Encyclopedia Britannica*. https://www.britannica.com/event/Hurricane-Katrina/Aftermath

Britannica (2020). Social Darwinism. *Encyclopedia Britannica*. https://www.britannica.com/topic/social-Darwinism

Canadian Centre for Diversity and Inclusion (2020, April 6). CCDI emphasizes the importance of diversity and inclusion in the workplace during the COVID-19 pandemic. CCDI. https://ccdi.ca/media/2119/20200406-communications-importance-of-di-during-covid-19-pandemic-en.pdf

Carling, A., and Mankani, I. (2020, June 9). Systemic inequities increase Covid-19 Risk for Indigenous People in Canada. *Human Rights Watch*. https://www.hrw.org/news/2020/06/09/systemic-inequities-increase-covid-19-risk-indigenous-people-canada

Carroll, R. (2010, January 26). Haiti earthquake. He had not picked her up since she was a toddler. Last week he carried her home. *The Guardian*. https://www.theguardian.com/world/2010/jan/26/haiti-earthquake-shooting-girl-story

Cavallo, E., et al. (2021, September). Estimating the Potential Economic Impact of Haiti's 2021 Earthquake. *Inter-American Development Bank*. https://publications.iadb.org/en/estimating-potential-economic-impact-haitis-2021-earthquake

Cecco, L. (2020, January 22). 'National travesty': report shows one-third of Canada's prisoners are Indigenous. *The Guardian*. https://www.theguardian.com/world/2020/jan/22/one-third-canada-prisoners-indigenous-report

Centennial College (2020). Anti-Asian racism social action card. Centennial College. https://www.centennialcollege.ca/centres-institutes/centre-for-global-citizenship-education-and-inclusion/social-action-cards/anti-asian-racism/

Choma, R. (2020, July 11). Trump allegedly suggested selling Puerto Rico as Hurricane Maria approached. *Mother Jones*. https://www.motherjones.com/politics/2020/07/trump-allegedly-suggested-selling-puerto-rico-as-hurricane-maria-approached/?fbclid=IwAR2vaP8SDEhN FWZu9DY8fdlFr4Jhg2pYeFc-GtJ67nwELWaLWWxsFDIgszc

Chotiner, I. (2020, May 7). How racism is shaping the coronavirus pandemic. *The New Yorker*. https://www.newyorker.com/news/q-and-a/how-racism-is-shaping-the-coronavirus-pandemic

Clark, S. (2020, July 1). How white supremacy returned to mainstream politics. Center for American Progress. https://www.americanprogress.org/issues/security/reports/2020/07/01/482414/white-supremacy-returned-mainstream-politics/

Clement, S., Zezima, K., and Guskin, E. (2018, September 12). Residents see a failure at all levels of government. *The Washington Post*. https://www.washingtonpost.com/news/national/wp/2018/09/12/feature/residents-see-a-failure-at-all-levels-of-government/

CNN Editorial Research (2020, June 2). Haiti Earthquake fast facts. *CNN*. https://www.cnn.com/2013/12/12/world/haiti-earthquake-fast-facts/index.html

Cooper, J. (2016). *Crisis communications in Canada: A practical approach*. Second edition. Toronto: Centennial College Press.

Correctional Services Canada (2020, September 29). Inmate COVID-19 testing in federal correctional institutions September 29, 2020. CSC. https://www.csc-scc.gc.ca/001/006/001006 -1014-en.shtml

Daschuk, J. (2019). *Clearing the Plains*. Regina, SK: University of Regina Press.

Da Silveira, María Manuela Méndez (2019). In the eye of the colonizer: The white racial frame of media coverage on Hurricane Maria. Student Research, DePauw University. https://scholarship.depauw.edu/studentresearch/119

Dortonne, N. (2016, December 8). The dangers of poverty porn. *CNN*. https://www.cnn.

com/2016/12/08/health/poverty-porn-danger-feat/index.html

Edwards, E. (2020, October 14). Covid-19 herd immunity, backed by White House, is a 'dangerous fallacy,' scientists warn. *NBC News*. https://www.nbcnews.com/health/health-news/covid-19-herd-immunity-backed-white-house-dangerous-fallacy-scientists-n1243415

El Nuevo Dia (2020, October 18). Editorial: Joe Biden's plan for Puerto Rico. *El Nuevo Dia*. https://www.elnuevodia.com/opinion/editorial/joe-bidens-plan-for-puerto-rico/

ESRI (n.d.). Aftermath of Katrina: A time of environmental racism. ESRI. https://www.arcgis.com/apps/Cascade/index.html?appid=2106693b39454f0eb0abc5c2ddf9ce40

Ford, R. (2020, August 18). Opinion: There is no 'White culture.' *CNN*. https://www.cnn.com/2020/08/18/opinions/american-culture-and-race-ford/index.html

Fowler, H. (2020, September 15). Reports of forced hysterectomies at Georgia ICE facility stir dark memories for some. *The Telegraph*. https://www.macon.com/news/state/georgia/article245747515.html

Francis, A. (2020, October 2). Treatment of dying Atikamekw woman 'not unique.' *Toronto Star*, p. A2.

Francis, A. (2020, September 21). Study targets virus's effect on Black people. *Toronto Star*, p. A11.

Garrison, L. (2013, January 21). Biopolitics, an overview. *Wordpress*. https://anthrobiopolitics.wordpress.com/2013/01/21/biopolitics-an-overview/

Gates, H. (2019). *Stony the road: Reconstruction, white supremacy, and the rise of Jim Crow*. New York: Penguin Books.

Geiger, D. (2020, March 23). Public relations in a pandemic. *Entrepreneur*. https://www.entrepreneur.com/article/347948

George, S. (1999, March). A short history of neoliberalism. Conference on Economic Sovereignty in a Globalising World, Transnational Institute. https://www.tni.org/my/node/11938

Giroux, H. (2006). *Stormy weather: Katrina and the politics of disposability*. Boulder, CO: Paradigm Publishers.

Gould, S. (1981). The *mismeasure of man*. New York: W.W. Norton & Co.

Government of Canada (2020, October 2). Coronavirus (COVID-19) and Indigenous communities. *Indigenous Services Canada*. https://www.sac-isc.gc.ca/eng/1581964230816/1581964277298

Great Barrington Declaration (2020). *Declaration*. https://gbdeclaration.org/

Haltiwanger, J. (2020, September 21). Trump told a crowd of nearly all white supporters that they have 'good genes.' *Business Insider*. https://www.businessinsider.com/trump-told-crowd-of-white-supporters-they-have-good-genes-2020-9

Harris, C. (2006, May). Review: Whitewashing Race: Scapegoating Culture. *California Law Review*, 94(3): 907–943. DOI: 10.2307/20439052

Institute for Public Relations (2020). COVID-19 resources for PR professionals. Institute for Public

Relations. https://instituteforpr.org/covid-19-resources-for-pr-professionals/#Diversity

Itagaki, L. (2016, March 9). Proximal subjects: framing the bystander and the visuality of vulnerability. *Prose Studies*. https://doi.org/10.1080/01440357.2016.1155970

Jiwani, Y. (2020 June 30). How racism works and shifts during the COVID-19 pandemic. *The Conversation*. https://theconversation.com/how-racism-works-and-shifts-during-the-covid-19-pandemic-141440

Jordan, M. (2020, October 24). "I never expected to lose my freedom." *Toronto Star*, p. IN8.

Kaiser, C., Eccleston, C., & Hagiawara, N. (2008). Post-Hurricane Katrina racialized explanations as a system threat: Implications for whites' and Blacks' racial attitudes. *Social Justice Research: Springer*. DOI 10.1007/s11211-008-0065-0

Kelly, D. (2020, Fall). Farm aid. *The York University Magazine*, 6(1).

Kerr, J. (2020, November 13). Why Brampton has become a hot spot for COVID-19. *The Globe and Mail*. https://www.theglobeandmail.com/canada/article-why-brampton-has-become-a-hot-spot-for-covid-19/

Kopun, F. (2020, September 30). Racialized children hit hardest by COVID-19. *Toronto Star*, p. A6.

Lempinen, E. (2020, May 15). Most Californians blame China for COVID-19, reject 'racialized' labels, poll finds. *Berkeley News*. https://news.berkeley.edu/2020/05/15/most-californians-blame-china-for-covid-19-but-reject-racialized-labels-poll-finds/

Li, W. (2020, April 28). Poll finds increase in racist attitudes. *Toronto Star*, p. A6.

Lopez, G. (2015, August 28). Hurricane Katrina, in 7 essential facts. *Vox*. https://www.vox.com/2015/8/23/9191907/hurricane-katrina

Maciejewski, J. (2013, February 8). When photographs (and photographers) lie. *Media Ethics Report*. https://mediaethicsreport.com/2013/02/08/can-a-photograph-lie/

Malone, K. (2020, October 31). COVID-19 cases are surging in First Nations communities. *HuffPost*. https://www.huffingtonpost.ca/entry/first-nations-covid-second-wave_ca_5f9d8d97c5b658b27c3ae33c?ncid=fcbklnkcahpmg00000001&fbclid=IwAR2wqenLesvteDNDI-ki6lVFn7zu-V-DAKrUmo_7q6OY7FlK0Yyoxvg8KZw

Matache, M., & Bhabha, J. (2020, June). Anti-Roma racism is spiraling during COVID-19 pandemic. *Health and Human Rights Journal*, 22(1): 379–382. https://www.ncbi.nlm.nih.gov/pmc/articles/PMC7348427/

Mercy Corps (2020, September 9). The facts: Hurricane Maria's effect on Puerto Rico. Mercy Corps. https://www.mercycorps.org/blog/quick-facts-hurricane-maria-puerto-rico

Mintz-Habib, N. (March 2023). Wet market reform in Nanjing, China: A case study. University of Cambridge. https://www.landecon.cam.ac.uk/sites/default/files/2023-07/case_study_china_nanjing_wet_market_reform_final_formatted.pdf

Mojtehedzadeh, S. (2020, November 12). Migrant farm worker wins historic ruling after being fired illegally. *Toronto Star*, p. A1.

Morneau Shepell (2020, August 5). COVID-19 and heightened attention to racism affect American workers' mental health and relationships. Cision. https://www.prnewswire.com/news-releases/covid-19-and-heightened-attention-to-racism-affect-american-workers-mental-health-and-relationships-301106039.html

Munshi, D., and Edwards, L. (2011). Understanding 'race' in/and public relations: Where do we start and where should we go? *Journal of Public Relations Research*, 23(4): 349–267. https://doi.org/10.1080/1062726X.2011.605976

Murphy, T. (2020, April 18). Trump advisor compares conservative anti-quarantine protesters to Rosa Parks. *Mother Jones*. www.motherjones.com/coronavirus-updates/2020/04/stephen-moore-donald-trump-coronavirus-rosa-parks/?fbclid=IwAR3PhpQjK4Om2AxuTv1EFI7Tp7OXbGbwNabHdsH4yOBhfkNlwrlkg1oFHnA

Newhagen, J., & Bucy, E. (2020, October 23). Overcoming resistance to COVID-19 vaccine adoption: How affective dispositions shape views of science and medicine. *Mis/information Review*, Harvard Kennedy School. https://misinforeview.hks.harvard.edu/article/overcoming-resistance-to-covid-19-vaccine-adoption-how-affective-dispositions-shape-views-of-science-and-medicine/

NHS (2013, May). NHS Bulletin, Ethnic Diversity and Religion. *National Household Survey*. https://www.peelregion.ca/planning/pdc/pdf/Ethicity_Religion_Bulletin.pdf

Oved, M. (2020, November 9). Sir William Osler's revered status in medicine shaken as racist views revealed. *Toronto Star*, p. A1.

Pallardy, R. (2010). 2010 Haiti earthquake. *Britannica*. https://www.britannica.com/event/2010-Haiti-earthquake/Humanitarian-aid

Parodi, C. (2005). Racism and health. In Office of the United Nations High Commissioner for Human Rights (Ed.), *Dimensions of Racism*, pp. 67–81. https://www.ohchr.org/Documents/Publications/DimensionsRacismen.pdf

Pazzano, J. (2020, August 28). Coronavirus: Canada's migrant farm workers face fatal COVID-19 outbreaks, alleged mistreatment. Global News. https://globalnews.ca/news/7301324/coronavirus-canadas-migrant-farm-workers-alleged-mistreatment/

Powell, B. (2020, April 25). Provincial virus database considered a major privacy invasion. *Toronto Star*, p. A2.

Purpose Brand (2020, June 25). Purpose Brand Business Tracker: PR's COVID-19, Racial Equity Response. Purpose Brand. https://purposebrand.com/news/purpose-brand-business-tracker-prs-covid-19-racial-equity-response/

Rabaey, J. (2020, May 11). What are PR agencies doing during the COVID-19 lockdown? Canadian Public Relations Society. https://cprstoronto.com/2020/05/11/what-are-toronto-pr-agencies-doing-during-the-covid-19-lockdown/

Reel Foto (2013, May 30). Fabienne Cherisma: A picture of a dead Haitian girl surrounded by photographers. *Reel Foto.* http://reelfoto.blogspot.com/2013/05/fabienne-cherisma-picture-of-dead.html

Richardson, L. and Crawford, A. (2020, September 21). COVID-19 and the decolonization of Indigenous public health. *CMAJ.* DOI: https://doi.org/10.1503/cmaj.200852

Robillard, K. (2012, October 3). 10 facts about the Katrina response. *Politico.* https://www.politico.com/story/2012/10/10-facts-about-the-katrina-response-081957

Rodriguez-Diaz, C. and Lewellen-Williams, C. (2020, May 22). Race and racism as structural determinants for emergency and recovery response in the aftermath of Hurricanes Irma and Maria in Puerto Rico. *Health Equity,* 4(1). https://doi.org/10.1089/heq.2019.0103

Samuel, S. (2020, October 28). Should people of color get access to the Covid-19 vaccine before others? *Vox.* https://www.vox.com/future-perfect/2020/10/2/21493933/covid-19-vaccine-black-latino-priority-access

Sanchez, R. (2022, September 24). Misery, yet again, for Puerto Ricans still recovering from Maria. *CNN.* https://www.cnn.com/2022/09/24/us/puerto-rico-hurricane-fiona-aftermath/index.html

Suecharan, C., and Bascaramurty, D. (2020, July 31). 83% of COVID-19 cases in Toronto among racialized people from May-July, data suggest. *The Globe and Mail.* https://www.theglobeandmail.com/canada/article-torontos-marginalized-communities-disproportionately-affected-by/

Skloot, R. (2011). *The immortal life of Henrietta Lacks.* New York: Random House.

Standaert, M. (2020, April 15). 'Mixed with prejudice': calls for ban on 'wet' markets misguided, experts argue. *The Guardian.* https://www.theguardian.com/environment/2020/apr/15/mixed-with-prejudice-calls-for-ban-on-wet-markets-misguided-experts-argue-coronavirus

Sudhaman, A. (2020, April 17). 'PR's moment to shine': Creativity in the Covid-19 era. *Provoke Media.* https://www.provokemedia.com/long-reads/article/'pr-s-moment-to-shine'-creativity-in-the-covid-19-era

Taylor, C. (1981). W. E. B. DuBois's challenge to scientific racism. *Journal of Black Studies,* 11(4): 449–460. https://pdfs.semanticscholar.org/f878/e535e4efbd4150b40567abef6de83b1b0db7.pdf

Thebault, R., Ba Tran, A., and Williams, V. (2020, April 7). The coronavirus is infecting and killing black Americans at an alarmingly high rate. *Washington Post.* https://www.washingtonpost.com/nation/2020/04/07/coronavirus-is-infecting-killing-black-americans-an-alarmingly-high-rate-post-analysis-shows/?arc404=true

Toronto Star (2020, May 7). Standing against intolerance. *Toronto Star,* p. A16.

Turkewitz, J., and Villamil, S. (2020, July 18–19). In Colombia, hope 'over.' *The New York Times International Weekly,* p. 1.

United Nations Department of Economic and Social Affairs (2020, June 11). UN/DESA Policy

Brief #79: The role of public service and public servants during the COVID-19 pandemic. *UNDESA.* https://www.un.org/development/desa/dpad/publication/un-desa-policy-brief-79-the-role-of-public-service-and-public-servants-during-the-covid-19-pandemic/

Wallis, C. (2020, June 12). Why racism, not race, is a risk factor for dying of COVID-19. *Scientific American.* https://www.scientificamerican.com/article/why-racism-not-race-is-a-risk-factor-for-dying-of-covid-191/

Walsh, K. (2015, August 28). The Undoing of George W. Bush. *U.S. News & World Report.* https://www.usnews.com/news/the-report/articles/2015/08/28/hurricane-katrina-was-the-beginning-of-the-end-for-george-w-bush

Weiler, A., McLaughlin, J., Caxaj, S., & Cole, D. (2020, April 1). Protecting the health and rights of migrant agricultural workers during the COVID-19 outbreak should be a priority. *Policy Note: A Progressive Take on BC Issues.* https://www.policynote.ca/migrant-workers/

Wilner, M. (2020, September 19). Trumps shifts on Puerto Rico, releases aid. *Toronto Star,* p. A26.

Wilson, K. (2020, October 13). Toronto launches campaign to confront anti-East Asian racism. *CP24.* https://www.cp24.com/news/toronto-launches-campaign-to-confront-anti-east-asian-racism-1.5142853

Wolff, M. (2006). The myth of the actuary: Life insurance and Frederick L. Hoffman's race traits and tendencies of the American Negro. *Public Health Reports,* 121(1): 84–91. doi: 10.1177/003335490612100115

Wright, T. (2020, August 13). Ottawa pledges extra $305M for Indigenous communities. *Toronto Star,* p. A8.

Yang, J., Allen, K., Mendleson, R., & Bailey, A. (2020, June 28). Toronto's COVID-19 divide: The city's northwest corner has been 'failed by the system.' *Toronto Star.* https://www.thestar.com/news/gta/2020/06/28/torontos-covid-19-divide-the-citys-northwest-corner-has-been-failed-by-the-system.html

Zimonjic, P. & Cullen, C. (2020, April 29). Derek Sloan ignores calls to apologize for attack on Canada's top doctor. *CBC News.* https://www.cbc.ca/news/politics/tam-sloan-china-caucus-apology-ontario-1.5550103/play/1797537698

CHAPTER EIGHT

Unpacking Cultural Baggage

OBJECTIVE OF THIS CHAPTER

Through a series of case studies, concepts, questions and exercises, this chapter is designed to present a series of recent events where intercultural communication was tested and challenged.

THE ATTACK ON THE MI'KMAQ FISHERY

In a small Nova Scotian community of snug houses, hardy fishing boats and even hardier fisher-people, situated on a spit of land jutting out into the ocean, the Bay of Fundy on one side, St. Mary's Bay on the other, what one might expect to be a place typified by long-held traditions of alliance and cooperation was instead the scene of anger that raged in the autumn days of 2020. It was an argument, a stand-off, a scene of small-scale destruction: members of the local Sipekne'katik First Nation, exercising their rights to fish outside of the government-sanctioned lobster season, versus the community of non-Indigenous commercial fishers. There was a standoff outside a Sipekne'katik lobster storage facility, an operation that had been damaged the previous night by a vandal; a vehicle was set on fire, there were physical skirmishes and rock-throwing, and more than 200 angry non-Indigenous fishers confronted 30 members of the First Nation. Complaints focused largely on the standoffishness of the local RCMP, essentially standing by while destruction was taking place, ignoring a 1999 decision by Canada's Supreme Court allowing Indigenous fishers to operate on their own. Mainstream fishers had accused First Nations fishers of depleting commercial stocks: "It's a conflict that is increasingly played out in grassroots flare-ups between Indigenous and non-Indigenous residents of southern Nova Scotia towns that rely on the fishing industry, instead of at round tables facilitated by the federal department responsible" (McKinley and McKeen, 2020, October 15). The Sipekne'katik fishers felt a sense of intimidation, a betrayal by government officials, and an all-too-familiar bullying by the dominant culture. Following the standoff, government officials expressed their dismay. Federal Fisheries Minister Bernadette Jordan said on Facebook:

I am appalled by the reported events in Digby County last night and I strongly condemn the actions of every individual who destroyed property, committed violence, or uttered threats. There is no place for this kind of violence or intimidation. I am particularly disturbed to hear reports of racist comments and actions made towards First Nations peoples. This is unacceptable and we all have a responsibility to call out and condemn this kind of behavior and language. I am very relieved that no injuries have been reported. Right now, I am calling on everyone involved to take a step back, and bring calm and understanding to the situation. Our Government is seized with the issue, and we will continue to work with both First Nations and industry leadership to find a path forward. Our conversations to date have been positive, and we must ensure they continue that way (Jordan, 2020, October 14).

Colin Sproul, the head of the local fishers' association, condemned the action while acknowledging the frustration commercial fishers were feeling (McKinley and McKeen, 2020, October 15). The leader of the Sipekne'katik, Mike Sack, later complained about the lack of enforcement by the RCMP, "which many say might have nipped the conflict in the bud," and Sack also directly asked Prime Minister Justin Trudeau to send more police reinforcements to protect Indigenous fishing rights, as the issue grew to embrace open accusations of racism, hate crimes, and a lack of federal commitment to reconciliation and an open process to bring both sides to the discussion table (McKinley, 2020, October 16). Joel Comeau, the (non-Indigenous) leader of the union local of the Maritime Fishermen's Union, who was conciliatory towards the Sipekne'katik fishers, stepped down after threats and intimidation in the community, given that "tensions are so high in his community of Meteghan, N.S., that he no longer feels he or his family are safe" (*As It Happens*, CBC, 2020, October 16).

Then the Fire

Then came a fire that destroyed a commercial building used to store lobster; according to CTV News, condemnation of the violence came from the Assembly of First Nations National Chief Perry Bellegarde as well as Nova Scotia senators, and Sipekne'katik leader Mike Sack

> confirmed in a statement Saturday morning that the building was "owned by a friend and ally of Sipekne'katik. … The devastating fire at the lobster pound in Middle West Pubnico further illustrates the need for greater police presence in the region," wrote Sack in an emailed statement. "This should never have happened, and the people responsible should be brought to justice. I do believe with the proper police presence, however, this could have been avoided" (Young and April, 2020, October 17).

Prime Minister Justin Trudeau said on Twitter: "I'm appalled by the acts of violence, intimidation, and destruction taking place in Nova Scotia. The perpetrators will be held accountable. We've approved a request to provide more support to the @RCMPNS [Royal Canadian Mounted Police Nova Scotia], and we're focused on keeping people safe" (Trudeau, 2020, October 17). Canada's Indigenous Services Minister Marc Miller said the RCMP had let down the Indigenous fishers, and called for calm to be restored in an environment of ongoing discrimination; Miller also lauded the Sipekne'katik for their resilience (Maloney, 2020, October 19). Trudeau further emphasized his support for the Indigenous community by reconfirming Sipekne'katik fishing rights as established by the Supreme Court in 1999 and, while acknowledging the challenges faced by commercial (non-Indigenous) fishers, said the government would ensure conservation while respecting Indigenous rights. As the issue grew, Sipekne'katik leader Mike Sack called for the military to come and restore peace (Boutilier, 2020, October 20); within a week, a Nova Scotia Supreme Court judge had issued an injunction to the Sipekne'katik prohibiting threats, blockades and interference against the Indigenous fishery (Renic, 2020, October 21), and as the confrontation heated up, Bellegarde issued a call for RCMP Commissioner Brenda Lucki to resign following her expression of support for the actions of RCMP officers in the dispute (Jones, 2020, October 23). According to fisheries expert and economics professor James Wilson, the issue must be seen as "a legitimate debate over the efficiency and justice of access rights distribution as presently executed by DFO (Department of Fisheries and Oceans).

Failing that, fisheries management will continue to be fraught by conflicts and by unsustainable exploitation of these public goods, thus undermining the very precepts of conservation DFO claims to uphold" (Wilson, 2020, October 23). And in an interesting footnote of sorts to this story, in November 2020, the Sipekne'katik became a partner (one of seven Mi'kmaq communities) in an Indigenous business coalition with an interest in purchasing a 50 percent stake in food giant Clearwater Seafoods Inc. (Rubin, 2020, November 10). The sale was completed the following year, with Premium Brands Holding Corporation acquiring the other 50 percent of Clearwater. So the Mi'kmaq ended up carving out a bigger slice of the seafood industry than their detractors might have anticipated.

The Messages

Federal fisheries minister Bernadette Jordan	I strongly condemn the actions those who destroyed property. We have a responsibility to call out this kind of action. We will continue to work with all parties to find a path forward.
Prime Minister Justin Trudeau	I am appalled by these acts of violence and intimidation. The perpetrators will be held accountable.
Federal Indigenous services minister Marc Miller	The RCMP let the Indigenous fishers down. Calm must be restored. The Sipekne'katik are to be congratulated for their resilience in the face of ongoing racism.
Colin Sproul, Bay of Fundy Inshore Fishermen's Association	I understand the feelings of the Indigenous fishers. The commercial (non-Indigenous) fishers are frustrated.
Sipekne'katik leader Mike Sack	The RCMP didn't do their job. Indigenous fishing rights need to be protected. The military need to come in to ensure peace.

Questions

1. What do you think of the messages delivered by the Minister of Fisheries and by the prime minister? Are they effective? Why or why not?
2. Beyond ensuring more police presence, what does the

federal government need to do to make things right? What kinds of communication efforts should be made?

3. What roles do the fishers' union, the Sipekne'katik First Nation, and the RCMP play? What should they be saying and doing?

4. What were the major "sticking points" between Indigenous and non-Indigenous stakeholders in this dispute?

5. Looking back at this story, what was the outcome? Did it make sense?

Exercise

In this scenario, we see the escalation of tensions where several parties have messages that appear to seek agreement. We also see that it requires some effective critical thinking to understand the relative positions of each group. Holladay and Coombs (2013) argue that public relations literacy—"identifying, analyzing and evaluating" the communication products that are delivered by organizations and individuals, as well as understanding the role of those messages in society—is essential for empowering consumers of public relations information, and "public relations messages are not limited to those messages produced by the 'PR industry' but also include those messages produced by social movements, organizations, and individuals seeking to persuade others through all forms of media as well as in interpersonal and public contexts" (Holladay and Coombs, 2013, p. 126). Using this statement as a basis, identify the consumers who would take an interest in the Nova Scotia fishing dispute story and consider the impact of the major messages that were delivered by the principals in the story. Then prepare a 500-word communications audit of the issue. A good audit will capture the essential information in a report format: an introduction, a summary of the salient facts, and a conclusion.

GOODBYE JOHN A. MACDONALD?

As we have seen in the text, the year 2020 was a year of intensive social and attitudinal change. One major upheaval has been the change in attitude toward Canada's first prime minister, Sir John A. Macdonald, whose statue in Montreal was pulled down by activists during a BIPOC protest in late August, though it had been toppled before, during protests in 1992 (CBC News, 2020, August 29). Macdonald's policies toward Indigenous Peoples have been called into question by academics, political commentators and the media.

Macdonald's role in the cultural genocide against Indigenous Peoples is well documented. During Macdonald's three decades as prime minister, his government created the residential school system, attacked First Nations and Métis and jailed their leaders, hanged Métis leader Louis Riel and amended the Indian Act of 1876 to implement policies that focused on oppressing and starving First Nations communities (Innes, 2018, August 13). As we saw in Chapter Three, the Indian Act was focused on the idea of "gradualism," which implied a steady "civilizing" of First Nations, and was "a consolidation of previous colonial ordinances that aimed to eradicate First Nations culture in favour of assimilation into Euro-Canadian society" (*Canadian Encyclopedia*, 2020). The attention paid by Macdonald to First Nations communities became especially intense in the 1880s, given the growing influx of European settlers and the transcontinental Canadian Pacific Railway. It appeared no action was too severe, as his government sought to criminalize the activities of Indigenous Peoples, remove them from desired agricultural lands and expel them from the route of the Canadian Pacific Railway; government agents "were merciless in their use of food to control the First Nations population after the decision to use the southern route [through the prairies and the reserves in Cypress Hills] for the CPR" and Macdonald openly spoke of starving out the First Nations in order to achieve the government's goal of making the area "safe" for both the railway and incoming Europeans (Daschuk, 2019, p. 123).

Is Presentism Involved?

Some might say that actions against Macdonald are a form of presentism, the stance of self-satisfied moral superiority that present-day viewers take of past people and events (CBC Radio, 2016, March 18). If we don't acknowledge Macdonald's role in creating Canada, then what does it mean when it comes to understanding the country and any positives—out of a myriad of social negatives—that have been gained? And yet there are demands that a definitive justice be served by spelling out clearly what Macdonald's attitudes and actions meant to Canada—and the diversity of humanity living here *before* the arrival of Europeans—and to those, like the Chinese who built the Canadian Pacific Railway, who were "imported" to work in the country and denied many rights accrued to "Canadians." Seeing the historical record with a clear eye also means understanding that decades of textbooks lauding Macdonald's policies, his personality and political motivations, have served to assist in raising generations of Canadians with a skewed and distorted view of what the man was all about—a view that demands correction.

While the pulling down of Macdonald's statue in the summer of 2020 resulted in a strong measure of Conservative Party chest-thumping, regrets from the prime minister, numerous calls from pundits and commentators about the role of Macdonald in Canadian history, and pleas from municipal leaders to respect the past, Macdonald's treatment of Indigenous Peoples—and a desire by officials to make good on promises of reconciliation—have sparked a variety of responses over the years, including the City of Victoria's removal of Macdonald's statue from its city hall steps, the protest-driven tying-up of a Macdonald statue with ropes in Regina, and the decision by the city council of Charlottetown to open up talks with local Indigenous groups on how best to present a still-standing Macdonald statue (CBC News, 2020, August 29).

As well, there was a decision by Queen's University to rename its law school building, changing it from Sir John A. Macdonald Hall following "mounting calls across the country to remove monuments commemorating its first prime minister, who is also recognized as the architect of the residential school system;" more than 4,600 signatures were collected on an online change-the-name petition (Glowacki, 2020, October 19). Mark Walters, dean of Queen's law school, said on the current affairs show *The Agenda* (when challenged on the reasons for removing the name, and being accused of engaging in presentism), the original decision to name the building after Macdonald in 1960 presented a "one-dimensional view of the person" and hence a celebration of the individual, and "it's not a really effective method at ... developing a rich and balanced view of history.... [W]e could put a little footnote or asterisk beside the name ... [but] is that going to be effective in the long run? I would ask, would it be effective to address the concerns of Indigenous students for examples or members of racial or ethnic minorities or not? And the answer we got was 'No.'" (Walters, 2020, November 2). The building is now simply called the Law Building.

There is also a push on by academics, critics and journalists to update official biographies, and pressure was put on Library and Archives Canada to edit and amend online profiles of leaders like Macdonald and Wilfrid Laurier (Laurier was prime minister from 1896 to 1911, and known for implementing head taxes on Asian immigrants as well as promoting a ban on the immigration of Black Americans into Canada): "Scholars and advocates say the [online] profiles—which mention nothing about residential schools or the Chinese head tax—amount to a whitewashing of history on a federal agency's widely consulted website." A variety of agencies and sources, from people dealing with

Indigenous child welfare to professors in university faculties of history, have called on the federal government for several years to make changes to better reflect the truth of Canadian history (Gallant, 2020, October 15).

Question

Valparaiso University's Dr. Bonita Neff said in 1994 that "public relations majors should be required to have a course in interpersonal communication which stresses a multicultural and international point-of-view. This also suggests that interpersonal communication should have a larger role of importance in the public relations function ... all of us need to be aware of the cultural trappings we carry with us. Then one can be challenged to think about a cross-cultural test to see how prepared one is to cross into another culture" (Neff, 1994, April 8). Thinking of the proposed changes to official biographies and public perception of leaders like Sir John A. Macdonald, how should teaching institutions approach these changes, especially in public relations and related communication courses? What can be done to better prepare communicators for a more diverse discussion on culture?

Exercise

Find several online sources of information on Sir John A. Macdonald, and write a 500-word biography of Canada's first prime minister, incorporating the details of his political position regarding residential schools as well as his government's policies on the treatment of First Nations on the Canadian prairies. Think in particular of how you would present this information if you were working for a government department, a school, a museum, or an encyclopedia-focused website.

THE POPE BACKS SAME-SEX UNIONS

It was a surprise to some and a welcome relief to others when Pope Francis, leader of the world's billion-plus Catholics, made a statement during a documentary interview to "endorse same-sex civil unions ... sparking cheers from gay Catholics and demands for clarification from conservatives, given the Vatican's official teaching on the issue." The church's teaching states that gay people "must be treated with dignity and respect but that homosexual acts are 'intrinsically disordered'" (Winfield, 2020, October 22); the Pope revised the church's position, saying in the documentary *Francesco* that members of the gay community are "children of God" with a "right to be in a family," and calling for a civil law to legalize such unions (Pullella, 2020, October 21).

The stance the Pope has taken on issues relating to religion and 2SLGBTQ+ communities (he has become more relaxed and progressive on the issue since being named pontiff in 2013) has been fraught with division, with some conservative hardline Catholics "waiting for the Pope to die and even, as grim as it may sound, hoping and praying for that day. They question whether he is a valid pontiff ... and are depending on his successor being less progressive" (Coren, 2020, October 22). Response from 2SLGBTQ+ communities was generally positive, and the Pope's message was met with a feeling that progress was being made since he first said, in 2013, that he "couldn't pass judgement" on the sexual orientation of a priest (and the Pope, while archbishop of Buenos Aires from 1998 to 2013, was a supporter of civil unions, though not of gay marriages sanctified by the church), and that in the years leading up to his statement on the documentary, the church had moved away from setting a moral standard and toward a greater sense of inclusion (White, 2020, October 21).

How will the Pope's comments affect disaffected and marginalized 2SLGBTQ+ Catholic communities? And how important is "endorsement" by religious authorities in affirming the state of "acceptance" by the church? Researchers found that in some cases there is a continual sense of being pulled in two directions; according to Wedow et al. in a paper examining the crisis of identity in being both gay and Catholic, post-secondary institutions with a religious basis for their teachings can be problematic in terms of helping a gay person establish their identity: "University atmospheres with anti-gay norms [the case with some post-secondary institutions] can produce fear of one's own sexual identity and create a number of challenges for LGBTQ students... Although religious university settings can be particularly challenging for sexual minorities, these minorities frequently face discrimination and heteronormativity in secular university settings as well" (Wedow et al., 2017, June 28). Pietkiewicz and Kołodziejczyk-Skrzypek (2016, May 24), found in a study of gay Polish students that "internalization of the principles taught by the Roman Catholic Church triggered a conflict when participants became aware of their homosexuality. They used a number of strategies to reconcile conflicting identities, including limiting their religious involvement, questioning interpretation of the doctrine, undermining priests' authority, trying to reject homosexual attraction, putting trust in God's plan, using professional help, and seeking acceptance from clergy." It appears clear that strong friendships, unbiased acceptance and an "OK" from authority figures count, and "support from peers and (re)interpretations of official Church doctrine are key factors in the development, negotiation, and sometimes integration of sexual and religious identities" (Wedow et al., 2017, June 28).

Question

Identify the issues that might flow from the comments the Pope made. What are they with respect to 2SLGBTQ+ communities?

How might the Pope's new position affect: (a) the Catholic Church; (b) 2SLGBTQ+ communities; (c) the mainstream community; (d) other Christian denominations?

Exercise

You are a public relations officer working in a social enterprise firm that has operations in several countries (most with very conservative religious ideals) where the Catholic Church has a significant presence, and your organization plays a significant role in providing assistance to 2SLGBTQ+ people who are oppressed in their own nations. Your CEO has asked for a briefing note on this issue: what it means for 2SLGBTQ+ communities, its effects on the Catholic Church, and how this might affect the work of your organization, and the church, going forward. Prepare a 400-word briefing note encapsulating what you know of this issue. Use any additional resources that you can find online. Remember the format for briefing notes:

Subject: the briefing note's title;

Purpose: the "why" of the briefing note;

Summary: the facts of the matter at hand, and explanations that support the briefing note's purpose;

Recommendations: the briefing note will provide a recommended course of action; and

Conclusion: a summary of what has been said; it is short and is focused on providing an accurate synopsis of the points that have been covered.

TRUDEAU: BLACKFACE, BROWNFACE

In the days leading up to the Canadian federal election of October 2019, Prime Minister Justin Trudeau was riding high, expecting to breeze to a second majority government in Ottawa. Then came the release of damning images of the prime minister in blackface and brownface—images that served to tilt public opinion of Trudeau, if only for a short time. The prime minister acknowledged his regret and said that he had changed as a person (suggesting, though not stating outright, maturity and greater intercultural awareness) since the images—two photos and a video—were produced in 2001; Trudeau said that the racist history of blackface was unacceptable, addressed racialized Canadians and apologized for the distress he caused. He told Global News: "Darkening your face, regardless of the context of the circumstances is always unacceptable because of the racist history of blackface. ... I never should have done it" (Global News, 2019, September 19). The first image that came to light was a brownface picture ("brownface" referring to the application of makeup in order to appear Middle Eastern, Latinx or South Asian) of Trudeau at an "Arabian Nights" party at the private school where Trudeau was teaching; then came images of Trudeau in blackface in high school, singing the Harry Belafonte hit "Day-O" before a third image, a scratchy video, was revealed with Trudeau, again in blackface, gesturing to the camera, hands in the air (Kambhampaty and Carlisle, 2019, September 19). Based on the content of the images, Trudeau, who has openly acknowledged that he comes from a background of white privilege, was clearly enjoying himself in each of these situations, with the impunity of one whose social status and financial security offer a measure of protection from censure or penalty—at least while one is *not* in a position of service to the people of a diverse, multicultural and multiracial nation. (Trudeau also found himself in some political/social/cultural hot water when, in India in February 2018, he donned traditional Indian clothing during official events and showed the crowd his "bhangra dance moves" at a public event, causing some cringing angst on the part of his hosts for apparently trying to appear too "Bollywood," and resulting in the cold shoulder from several high-ranking Indian officials [CTV News, 2018, November 26]. So it clearly appears that he is either tone-deaf or unaware of the impacts of his behaviour until "after the fact.")

For many commentators Trudeau's attitude with respect to delivering abject apologies in the blackface/brownface scandal was seen as a tendency toward virtue signaling (CBC News, 2019, September 19), virtue signaling being defined as "an attempt to show other people that you are a good person, for example by expressing opinions that will be acceptable to them, especially on social media" (Cambridge Dictionary, 2020). And as Trudeau later said to the media, he was not even aware that he could be causing any harm—though because of the staggering of the release of the images (they came to light over the course of two days) it was clear that he was aware of, but not being open about, all of the times that he had appeared in blackface/brownface. As commentator Ola Ojewumi of Project ASCEND (a non-profit education organization) noted, the

> difference between white liberals and white conservatives is that when conservatives are racist, they are upfront, honest and unapologetic about it ... white liberal racism is covert, casual and harder to detect. ... White people can do explicitly racist things and still believe they're not racist in part from conditioning that teaches racism is synonymous with white hoods, burning crosses and lynchings but often little more, and for people of color to think otherwise is a misunderstanding or overreaction (Ojewumi, 2019, September 20).

What Is "Blackface"?

"Blackface" was the practice of white entertainers applying makeup—sometimes burnt cork or shoe polish—to make themselves up to look like what amounted to white culture's stereotypical image of an African American. "By distorting the features and culture of African Americans—including their looks, language, dance, deportment, and character—white Americans were able to codify whiteness across class and geopolitical lines as its antithesis. ... Popular American actors, including Shirley Temple, Judy Garland and Mickey Rooney donned blackface, bridging the minstrel performance across generations" (National Museum of African American History and Culture, 2020). Minstrel shows, featuring jokes, singing, dancing and exaggerated pratfalls, were popular in the U.S. and Canada for well over a hundred years, before eventually falling out of favour in the mid- to late 20th century, although the practice is said to continue in private clubs. Blackface and brownface portrayals are especially offensive because they are more than just a means of cultural appropriation, defined as "the adoption or co-opting, usually without acknowledgment, of cultural identity markers associated with or originating in minority communities by people or communities with a relatively privileged status" (Dictionary.com, 2020). Blackface and brownface are blatantly racist, underscoring the replacement of entire communities of citizens with skewed, simplistic, demeaning and untrue portrayals of humanity, and they demonize and depersonalize Black and Brown individuals (Gollom, 2019, September 19).

It should be noted that cultural identity appropriation (outside of parties or other activities) also came to be a workplace/lifestyle issue, with some white activists and scholars appropriating, through makeup, hairstyles and false autobiographies, "Black" identities. For example, university professor Jessica Krug admitted in the summer of 2020 that she had adopted a "Black Caribbean identity" while teaching at George Washington University; calling herself a "culture leech," Krug called her own conduct "wrong, unethical, immoral, anti-Black and colonial" (Asmelash, 2020, September 4). Around the same time, CV Vitolo-Haddad, a Ph.D. candidate and teaching assistant at the University of Wisconsin, admitted to passing as a Person of Colour (Flaherty, 2020, September 14). And in 2015, white activist Rachel Dolezal was revealed to be living as a Black woman for years, arguing in interviews that she was Black even after her biological parents—both white—told the media that their daughter was indeed white. Dolezal was unrepentant in her stance. "Dolezal's claim on black womanhood still seems to be non-negotiable. Even in conversation with an actual black woman on the other end of the line or sitting in her cozy home, Dolezal unequivocally identifies as black. ... Dolezal spent years researching and then perfectly molding her black identity" (Samuels, 2015, July 19). Krug and Vitolo-Haddad resigned from their teaching positions, while Dolezal was dismissed from a part-time instructorship at George Washington University. She later became a teacher in Arizona, but in February 2024 was fired by the school district because she had posted adult content on the website OnlyFans, thus violating district policy (Willingham, February 15, 2024).

As for Trudeau, he was roundly criticized by race relations organizations, cultural groups and leaders of Canada's other political parties—his major rivals, the Conservatives, were smelling political blood, though it was evident that they were largely using the issue as a political weapon. Trudeau's open admission of guilt and remorse, followed by repeated apologies to major multicultural groups and associations, appeared to assuage some of the anger felt toward him. In many public relations disasters, organizations often think in terms of the possibility of having to pay out reparations for damage in addition to rebuilding connections with stakeholders; the loss is largely a financial one. In the case of Trudeau, the damage was done to his own reputation, and the loss would be to himself and his party (especially the potential loss of an election), so there was little else to do except apologize, demonstrate that change had taken place (i.e., stating his "epiphany" about his wrongful behaviour, his awareness of the need for change, and his dedication to doing better in future), throw himself on the mercy of a voting public that he hoped would understand and accept his remorse, and move on. Such an approach is becoming increasingly standard, and "organizational publics and other members of the society value apology because it acknowledges that social norms were disrupted, shows respect to the victims, and is the first step toward the rebuilding of relationships" (Kiambi and Shafer, 2016).

A Blip in the Process?

Not too surprisingly (given the colour-blind nature of the dominant culture), a significant number of Canadians treated the blackface/brownface scandal as a blip in the election process, and while the event was serious, it soon lost traction in the public consciousness; though it continued for months as a "comedy bit" for late-night television hosts, it may have been only one small element that tipped Trudeau's Liberal party from majority to minority status in the federal legislature (there are 338 seats in the Canadian Parliament; a party with more seats than all other parties combined can form a majority government, while a minority government is formed when no one party holds the majority of seats). According to *The Manitoban*, the issue seemed to make it clear that most white Canadians were unaffected by the scandal:

Disturbingly, a new report from McGill University, which looked at tweets from Sept. 17 to Sept. 28, found that within three days of the initial release of the photos, discussion online diminished significantly. Basically, people stopped caring. Furthermore, polling from Abacus Data taken during the week of the scandal has shown Canadians' voting intentions remain entirely unchanged. … It is no secret that Canada has a deeply racist history, but Canadians have been slow to accept the residual aftermath of the past (Ingram, 2019, October 16).

In the documentary *Margin of Error*, about the market research firm Advanced Symbolics Inc. (ASI), a company that uses the artificial intelligence algorithm "Polly" to crunch public data and forecast consumer attitudes, ASI co-founder and CEO Erin Kelly allowed that while the Trudeau debacle was a political bombshell, the data collected by Polly on public response to the blackface/brownface scandal only "knocked him [Trudeau] from majority territory into minority territory" (Kelly, 2020, October 21), and Trudeau would go on to win a minority government in the October 21 election.

In February 2020, Trudeau would revisit the scandal, telling guests at a Black History Month reception that coming to terms with his racist past was eye-opening and affirming, and that it galvanized his intent to work harder to build positive relationships across cultures. "Trudeau said all Canadians need to stop avoiding difficult questions and take a hard look at systemic discrimination against black Canadians.... [H]e said black leaders across the country encouraged him to turn the mortifying disclosure into something positive for race relations in Canada" (Canadian Press staff, 2020, February 24).

Questions

1. A Google search of the phrase "Justin Trudeau black-face" returns hundreds of thousands of hits, years after the incident. Even comedian Sacha Baron Cohen, in the second of his "Borat" movies, mocked Justin Trudeau's blackface scandal. How seriously do you think members of the public take this issue? Do they treat it as an important social concern, or as a joke? Why do you think people felt the way they did, and how should communications practitioners approach this topic?

2. Re-read the quote from Ojewumi about the differences between white liberals and white conservatives. What is your opinion of it? What gets in the way of white liberals understanding and changing their own behaviour?

3. What actions need to be taken to change public perception of issues like blackface and brownface?

4. Do you think Justin Trudeau was sincere in his handling of the scandal? Explain why or why not.

Exercise

You are a communicator for one of the major chartered banks. At a Halloween party the previous year, a white bank employee was reprimanded and suspended following the release of photographs showing them in blackface. It was an embarrassing situation that caused the bank considerable public relations challenges, including commentary on social media of a perceived culture of systemic discrimination at the bank, and allegations of discrimination in hiring practices; the outcome was a promise to customers, stakeholders and the public that the bank would examine its hiring practices (since done and made public), and the creation of a policy banning racist conduct by any bank employee, either while at work or at any other time. You are tasked with the job of writing a 500-word internal memo to all employees (to be sent via email), signed by the vice-president of communications, outlining the bank's policy prohibiting cultural appropriation and the use of blackface/brownface makeup, either at company functions or off-site. Keep in mind that memo format follows an inverted pyramid journalistic style: most important information at the top, least important information below, with a focus on the 5Ws and the H—Who, What, When, Where, How, and *very importantly*, Why. There should be clear headings in the memo:

To: Recipient's name (or names, in this case, "To all employees").

From: Sender's name (in this case, the vice-president, communications, with full name and title indicated).

Subject: Four or five words, clear and concise.

The body text follows the subject line. Open with the most important one or two points that the recipient needs to know. Keep your sentences short and to the point, and use paragraphs to your advantage to make the memo an easy, simple read. At the end, summarize your points with a short synopsis—a "recap"—of what you have said in the memo.

ISLAMOPHOBIA

Much dialogue has been generated on the topic of Islamophobia, and rightfully so. Western society chooses its "others," generalizes about them, condemns them for behaviours that are outside its white, mainly-Christian neutral norm, and persecutes them, even when they are successful and when they espouse ideals that reflect the core values that western society embraces, like caring about the importance of education, espousing the ideals of working hard and being successful, and adhering to family values—all because of differences that cannot be accepted, because of a fear of the "outsider." Media have been unwittingly, sometimes actively, complicit in spreading hate, through publishing stories focusing on allegations of mosques being centres for terror training and extremism, often a situation with "media outlets not properly vetting self-proclaimed experts on Islam—and research that implicates mosques as dangerous sites of radicalization – and then shrugging their shoulders after the damage is done" (Mastracci, 2017, June 27). Muslims comprise 3.2 percent of the Canadian population (Statistics Canada, 2017), yet are viewed as a "threat" to Canadian stability, and the hatred directed against the community has been devastating. Crimes against the Muslim community have often been explosive,

angry, lethal, and driven by white rage; in January 2017, Alexandre Bissonnette shot killed six men at the Islamic Cultural Centre of Quebec City; it was
considered "one of the deadliest mass shootings in Canadian history.... [The]
search history on his [Bissonnette's] internet browser showed he was an avid
follower of radical right-wing figures in the United States.... In the days before carrying out the attack, Bissonnette also repeatedly visited the Twitter feed
of US president Donald Trump, who had just imposed a controversial entry
ban on travelers from Muslim-majority countries" (Montpetit, 2019, April 25).
Vandalism of mosques increased in the twenty-teens and became a significant
problem in 2020, with some Toronto mosques suffering repeated attacks resulting in broken windows, damage to property and racist graffiti (Katawazi,
2020, August 19); in September 2020, Mohamed-Aslim Zafisa, a 58-year-old
caretaker at a mosque in Toronto, was stabbed to death by a follower of an anti-Semitic, Hitler-worshipping hate group who had "shared what appears to be
content from a satanic neo-Nazi group in social media posts, according to an
organization that tracks online extremism" (CBC News, 2020, September 21).

Hate crimes have risen dramatically in Canada in recent years, 253 percent
from 2012 to 2015, most of them Ontario and Quebec incidents focusing on
Blacks, Jews and Muslims (Zine, 2019, January 28). In particular, "Muslims have
been constructed as the 'enemies within' and represent the new folk devils that
threaten the stability of the nation. According to a 2017 Radio Canada poll, most
Canadians (74 percent) favour a Canadian values test for Muslim immigrants,
while 23 percent favour a ban on Muslim immigration, a level of support that ris-
es to 32 percent in Québec" (Zine, 2019, January 28). Islamophobia as a concept
and term dates back to the 1970s and Edward Said's *Orientalism* (a text that positions the attitudes of Western culture toward Islam against background themes
of politicization, power and exoticization), and is essentially defined as the dread
and hatred of, and unfounded prejudice against, Muslims (Bleich, 2011). For
many, particularly those on the political far right, Islamophobia is a charged
word, and there have been myriad discussions among political scientists and academics about its use, with some saying that it limits the ability of researchers
to critique aspects of the religion, while others find that it is a correctly used
descriptor of bigotry and the phobia that arises from it (Basu, 2014, October 15).

Clothing and Attitudes

Western societies have historically had issues with the custom of Muslim wom-
en wearing certain garments, generally in terms of viewing their garments as:

- Objects of oppression rooted in a male-dominated culture [though the same people might be reluctant to talk about, for instance, the widespread, consumer-focused sexualizing of young females in largely male-dominated North American society];
- As a form of exoticism;
- As objects of isolation and separation from the mainstream (Posetti, 2006).

Garments include the hijab (which covers the hair), the niqab (covering the head and part—or sometimes all—of the face), and the burka, which covers the head, face and body (Posetti, 2006, p. 37). The "hijab debate has come to symbolize the clash of cultures fanned by links between Islamic extremism and 21st century terrorism ... a backlash against Muslim culture has seen such clothing banned, along with the much more common hijab, in the interests of secularism" (Posetti, 2006, p. 1).

While in office, the Stephen Harper government (Harper was prime minister from 2006 to 2015) implemented a range of anti-Islam policies, from its "Zero Tolerance for Barbaric Cultural Practices Act" ("barbaric" was later removed) to a proposed ban on the wearing of the niqab at citizenship ceremonies (Zine, 2019, January 28); Harper said it was necessary for a person to show their face during swearing-in events (this in spite of assurances that identity could be verified outside of the public-facing courtroom in the presence of a court official). The niqab ban, originally introduced in 2011, was overturned in federal court, although as we saw in an earlier chapter, it has continued to be an issue in the province of Québec. Essentially a niqab ban is a refusal of "reasonable accommodation to specific women based on their cultural and religious beliefs while stripping them of their fundamental ability to choose what they want to wear" (Rabble, 2020), and "Canada's Charter of Rights And Freedoms would seem empty if Muslim women do not have as much right to wear the regalia of their religion as Orthodox Jewish and Catholic women and men have to wear theirs" (Gopnik, 2015, October 9).

According to Posetti's (2006) study of media attitudes towards Islam, in the post-9/11 years, western media served to promulgate a negative image of Islam, emphasizing links to terror and currying fear among the mainstream populace and portraying Muslims as untrustworthy, sneaky, oversexualized and dangerous (p. 3). Muslim women wearing traditional garb were seen as exoticized or dangerously extremist in Europe (p. 4), while Canadian media tended towards presenting traditionally garbed Muslim women as "oppressed outsiders," and "because of the media's cultural fixation on Muslim women's dress as a symbol of oppression, Muslim women often have to focus on that aspect of their identity as well" in discussion (Posetti, 2006, p. 5). Hussein (2007) in examining the issue within the context of Australian society, noted the complexities of coming to terms with what exactly a head/face covering means and, in any case, it appears to come down to it being interpreted as anti-western: "Anti-hijab rhetoric seems to be shifting away from a simplistic representation of hijab as a symbol of patriarchal control, and towards rhetoric about hijab as a symbol of religious separatism, 'chosen' by women themselves. ... The complex terrain of this issue does not translate easily into media soundbites" (Hussein, 2007, p. 14). Media representation of Islam has heightened dangerously negative perceptions of Muslims, despite research by the Noor Cultural Centre showing that while 0.01 percent of Muslims are involved in militant groups, Christians were responsible for 98 percent of violent deaths around the world in the 20th century, and in Canada since 1960, "three times as many people have been killed for being Muslim than by a Muslim. In the United States in 2016, an individual was 6 times as likely to be killed for being Muslim than [to be killed] by Muslim 'extremists'" (Noor Cultural Centre, 2017, December).

Harper's Leveraging Act

Stephen Harper appeared to try and leverage anti-Muslim sentiment in his favour as the country moved toward the October 2015 federal election, calling hijabs oppressive against women and stating that the wearing of the niqab during Canadian citizenship swearing-in ceremonies was "offensive," a position his political opponent Justin Trudeau (who won a majority government in that election) said amounted to fear-mongering; Trudeau suggested that telling people what to wear was a form of government-driven repression (Canadian Press, 2015, March 11). And as the country drew closer to the election, Harper brought forward his idea to ban the niqab during citizenship ceremonies, floated the idea of banning civil servants from wearing the niqab, and suggested the establishment of a "tip line" for people to snitch on what the Harper government called "barbaric cultural practices," moves that "have led some to accuse the party of engaging in identity politics and fueling anti-Muslim sentiment" (CBC News, 2015, October 6). The issue of identity politics, defined as "politics in which groups of people having a particular racial, religious, ethnic, social, or cultural identity ... [and] promote their own specific interests or concerns without regard to the interests or concerns of any larger political group" (Merriam-Webster, 2020), has grown in the last several decades, and while it was once seen as a tool of left-leaning social activism, it is now used equally by the far right in promoting a particular agenda, as was seen extensively in American politics following Donald Trump's election in 2016 (Lopez, 2017, August 17). As for the niqab issue, response to Harper's polarizing political stance was strong; Zunera Ishaq, the focus of the issue after fighting in court for her right to wear the niqab (the niqab ban was overturned by the federal Appeals Court in September 2015), said the issue pointed to disinformation from the federal government and the perpetuation of stereotypes, such as the niqab being viewed as "a symbol of female repression that is forced upon poorly educated women being dominated by their male family members" (Canadian Press, 2015, October 8). Quebec would pass the provincial Bill 62 (fostering adherence to State religious neutrality) in October 2017 and follow with Bill 21 (An Act respecting the laicity of the state) in 2019. Justin Trudeau, two years after becoming prime minister, would state that the federal government had no business in telling women what to wear, but he would not wade into the issue in the province of Québec and its ban on full-face coverings in public (Day, 2017, October 25). It should also be noted that Trudeau is the member of parliament for the riding of Papineau, in the city of Montréal, so he might have been biting his political lip in this situation.

Questions

1. As we saw in this case study, former Prime Minister Stephen Harper appeared to attempt to use anti-Muslim sentiment to sway an election. In your view, what should be the proper role of politicians, especially national leaders, in shaping or influencing public opinion? What are their responsibilities towards inclusion and how can communicators help them define and deliver on their responsibilities?

2. Robert Sapolsky, a professor of biology and neurology, wrote in his book *Behave* (2017) about similarities between humans, including the independent development of "agriculture, writing, pottery, embalming, astronomy and coinage" (p. 271). Sapolsky also references anthropologist Donald Brown's "cultural universals" (Brown, 2004), of which there is a wide range, a partial list of which includes everything from aesthetics and marriage to body adornment, murder, kinship terms, cooking, distinctions between

right and wrong, empathy, reciprocity, concepts of fairness, gossip, humor and symbolism (Sapolsky, 2017, pp 271–272). Given the similarities that are apparent between groups of people, what do you think accounts for the differences of opinion between cultures, and what are the reasons for cultures to (often intensely) dislike each other?

Exercise

Using available information, create a mind map of the relationship between the mainstream Canadian culture and Islamic Canadian culture. Then use this to develop ideas for three public relations initiatives to build a communications bridge between the two cultures. What would work and why?

MISOGYNY: THE PELOTON BIKE AD

Sometimes people are just tone-deaf—they don't listen to advice, perhaps, or to their own better instincts when devising the means to, for instance, sell products. They don't think about how the public might respond and they forge ahead, convinced that what they are doing is the right thing. That was the case for a televised advertisement that ran in late 2019, featuring a lean and fit young woman receiving a Peloton exercise bike from her husband as a Christmas gift. She begins working out on it, documenting her exercise journey over the next few months via selfie videos, looking longingly into her cellphone, anxious, nervous, happy, and *ever so thankful* to her husband, as if her existence revolves around being even thinner than she already is, and all for her husband's approval, then showing her husband at the end of her "journey" how much fitter she is. Reaction to the ad was overwhelmingly negative, many calling it a dystopian and sexist piece of trashy marketing that demeaned women. Despite the response of public relations and marketing specialists who frequently use the trite phrase "any publicity is good publicity" (the ad had almost a million views within the space of a day and racked up two million within a short time), it caused problems for the company; stock in Peloton nosedived, and criticism ran especially high toward an initially unrepentant company president. The unapologetic stance of the company was seen by some as simply a reinforcement of its focus on embracing "snarky" and pretentious social-elitist attitudes (Rivenbark, 2019, December 10). The company would lose up to $1.5 billion in value as a result of its tone-deaf marketing, though it tried to defend its position: "In a statement to CNBC, Peloton said it was disappointed by how some people had misinterpreted the advert, but was 'encouraged by—and grateful for—the outpouring of support we've received from those who understand what we were trying to communicate'" (Belam and Partridge, 2019, December 4), which, as Jason Aten noted in *Inc.*, is "about as passive-aggressive as a non-apology can be. It's a bad response because it's basically saying, 'We're sorry you feel that way.' Which ... is the absolute worst possible way you can ever respond to a customer or a critic" (Aten, 2019, December 5).

Questions

1. Go to YouTube and find the Peloton ad. What message does this send about the perceived notions around the relationships between women and men?
2. Think about the response of Peloton to its critics. What errors did the company make in its response? What do you think would have been a better response?

HOMELESS CULTURE

It appears ubiquitous: everywhere the homeless population seems to be growing, due to a changing economy and the downward trend in the number of well-paying, long-term jobs (a situation captured in the term "gig economy"), as well as social and income inequities, the outcome of COVID-19-related job losses and systemic discrimination.

What is "homeless culture?" It is the set of attitudes that both go with being in a state of homelessness, as in the lack of social structure, the suffering, the absence of stability, the violence, drug use, sexual harassment and abuse, alienation, disruption, lack of economic opportunity, coupled with the perception of homelessness as a "life choice" by the media and the political sphere, and tied to a generalized attitude that homelessness is an accepted component of the social infrastructure (Flaskerud and Strehlow, 2009, July).

According to a Nanos Research poll, up to 5 percent of Canadians (1.6 million) have experienced homelessness at some point in their lives, and a third of Canadians know someone who has been through it (Cousins, 2020, August 12). Homelessness has increased significantly, and BIPOC communities and youth are especially affected—Indigenous peoples are eight times more likely than the general population to be homeless and 20 percent of homeless people are between the ages of 13 and 25 (Fred Victor Mission, 2020). Hidden homelessness ("couch surfing" or otherwise staying in someone else's home—relatives, friends, neighbours—without any access to, or plans for one's own housing in the immediate future) has been a problem, affecting anywhere from 500,000 to a million Canadians, and more than half of racialized people living in poverty reside in Ontario (Colour of Poverty, 2019, March). In 2016, Canada's 995 shelters (including shelters for those escaping domestic violence) held 22,190 residents, 70 percent of them having no fixed address (Statistics Canada, 2019, April 15), and on "any given night in Toronto, 10,000 people are homeless" (Haven Toronto, 2020). According to Toronto street nurse Cathy Crowe, who has provided health care to the homeless for decades, "over the course of this year (2020) in Canada, an estimated 235,000 people (including families with children), will be homeless. … Across Canada, shelters are full and overcrowded, violence against women and family shelters report waiting lists, and new tiers of emergency shelter in the form of soccer-like domes and empty buildings have been opened to house homeless people. In some cases, 100 people sleep in one space with no separation between cots" (Crowe, 2020, March 22) and the Canadian Alliance to End Homelessness called for the spending of $52 billion in COVID-19 economic recovery funds in order to end homelessness by 2030 (Cousins, 2020, August 12).

Indigenous communities have been hard hit, and many people have suffered as a result of the instability caused by the residential school system, the disruption of stable home lives, the effects of systemic racism, and the violence and mental health and addiction issues linked to these outcomes (Homeless Hub, 2019). Also a part of this pattern of disruption and separation from home and culture was the Sixties Scoop, which saw the removal of Indigenous children from their homes and their subsequent adoption to non-Indigenous families during the 1960s; it was based on the paternalistic culture of the federal government toward Indigenous Peoples, and was an experience that "left many adoptees with a lost sense of cultural identity. The physical and emotional separation from their birth families continues to affect adult adoptees and Indigenous communities to this day" (Sinclair and Dainard, 2020, September 11). In a study that researched the root causes of homelessness based on researching the lives of homeless participants, Mabhala et al. (2017) found that homelessness was consistent with conditions of poverty, and was typified by "an abusive environment, poor education, poor employment or unemployment, poor social connections and low social cohesion … the social conditions in which [the participants] were raised and their references to maladaptive behaviours which led to them becoming homeless, led us to conclude that they believe that their social condition affected their life chances" (p. 15).

How do media view, assess and scrutinize homelessness? Schneider et al. (2010) wrote a very focused analysis on the ways in which Canadian media present the issue of homelessness, finding that expert testimony was being valued over the actual voices of the homeless, readers were strongly encouraged to feel sympathy for the homeless and that inherent in dealing with/writing about the homeless is a sense of regulation and control; that "narrative of control and regulation positions people as legitimate objects of scrutiny, regulation, and control. … [I]t is likely that it contributes to an ongoing estrangement of homeless people from domiciled people and therefore decreases the likelihood of the development of effective national policies in Canada to address homelessness" (p. 168).

Just about every reasonably sized town or city across Canada has a "homeless action plan," and these usually lay out courses of action to help the homeless. They are often developed and delivered in concert with private and public sector organizations—from donations of money to provision of food and clothing as well as shelter infrastructure; for example, the Canadian Alliance to End Homelessness, with a mandate to "prevent and end homelessness in Canada" to ensure that "all Canadians have a safe, decent and affordable home with the support necessary to sustain it" (CAEH, 2020), lists over 160 partners, from shelter organizations to social service agencies and civic associations. At the local level, municipalities will strike committees to investigate homelessness, develop plans for change, and take these plans through the fruition. The 2016 Saskatoon Homelessness Action Plan, for example, outlined a series of steps and consultations to address the problem, from discussions with Indigenous service providers to plans for the provision of adequate housing, all while gaining a better understanding of the "common systemic issues, such as poverty, colonialism, racism and discrimination, which impact particular groups in our community" (Saskatoon Homelessness Action Plan Steering Committee, 2016, p. 41). The committee was focused on a five-year strategy to "house 150 people experiencing chronic and sporadic homelessness by 2019" (James, 2016, November 22). The City of Toronto, with 75 base shelters and 24-hour respite sites for the homeless, announced in October 2020 that it would open 40 temporary facilities that would accommodate social distancing requirements during the COVID-19 pandemic, with the city offering up "more than 6,700 spaces through the City's base shelter system and approximately 560 new spaces" (City of Toronto, 2020, October 6). Street outreach in Toronto was also an ongoing initiative, with outreach staff handing out sleeping bags, blankets, and offering wellness checks on the homeless, with the goal of getting people into warm spaces during the cold weather.

Questions

1. What do you think public attitudes are towards homelessness?
2. What are the attitudes of media toward the issue?
3. Why might homelessness seem like a difficult problem to solve?

Exercise

You work for a small social enterprise firm that is involved in locally produced food products—you work with small-scale farmers to get their produce to restaurants and specialty stores, and you have your own line of organic, raw honey. The goal of your organization is "to do good in the community, for the community, by members of the community at the grassroots level." Among other initiatives, you work with a local community college as a participant in its Small Business diploma program and its Food Service Worker program, where students can gain hands-on experience as part of their academic training. A decision is made to join with a local food bank—along with other partners—in the provision of food and shelter for the homeless. This requires an outlay of money ($50,000 per year) and the use of your bricks-and-mortar facility for packaging and distributing goods for the homeless. Your task is to write a 500-word news release on this initiative, especially outlining the motivation behind your involvement.

WHAT ABOUT THE KIDS?

Few words say "family-friendly kids' entertainment" like "Disney." The media giant is worth somewhere in the neighbourhood of $200 billion at time of writing, and has become so well-branded since its inception in 1923 that it is synonymous with scrubbed-clean, wholesome American values ... except, of course, when one dips into the history vaults and finds that those values were neither all-inclusive, diversified nor particularly equitable over the years. Disney movies were chockfull of stereotypes that reflected not just mid-20th century thinking, but a continual, decades-long flow of typecast impressionism as seen through a white cultural lens: the Black centaur "Sunflower" in *Fantasia* (exaggerated facial features); caricatures of Japanese soldiers in World War II cartoons starring Donald Duck (facial features and accents in fractured English); the African American-rooted "jive talk" of King Louie in the *Jungle Book* movie; the Arabian Nights song in *Aladdin* (following complaints, producers replaced a line in the song); a plethora of cringe-worthy Indigenous stereotypes in *Peter Pan*; the outrageously insensitive, racist portrayals of Siamese cats, "Si" and "Am" in *Lady and the Tramp*, and Shun Gon in *The Aristocats;* the black crows (an homage to Jim Crow minstrel shows) in *Dumbo*; and Uncle Remus in *Song of the South,* a movie that reinforced images of passive and happy slaves in the southern U.S. before the Civil War (Tinubu, 2019, April 25). Uncle Remus was one of many portrayals of Blacks that served the trope of the "Magical Negro," the creative narrative device of the Black person as a guide to helping a white protagonist become a better person, through wisdom, strength and, perhaps most significantly, a gentle subservience. Recent portrayals have ranged from Will Smith as Bagger Vance in *The Legend of Bagger Vance* and Michael Clark Duncan as John Coffey in *The Green Mile*, to Mykelti Williamson as Benjamin Buford "Bubba" Blue in *Forrest Gump* and Robert Guillaume as Rafiki in *The Lion King* (though an animal-populated cartoon, it becomes clear in viewing the movie that the protagonists are "white," and Rafiki, with his heavy accent, is Black, supports the protagonists and so fulfills the role of the "Magical Negro"). As the sociologist Zuleyka Zevallos noted, the "Magical Negro" is a "narration device that seemingly subverts racism (after all, it portrays Black characters as virtuous). In fact, however, this character is centrally about maintaining historical power relations.… African-Americans … cannot be complex and flawed human beings, either in fiction or in public life" (Zevallos, 2012, January 24). There has also been a move among critics and writers to dispense with the concept of the "Magical Negro," because the "superhumanization" bias—the belief in a super-strong Black man—can lead to people being killed, as has been seen in the continuing number of police killings of men of African descent (Peterson, n.d.), the outcome being that the trope is *too real*, and too believable for too many people.

As far as Disney goes, it was in a bit of a conundrum—how to continue to market movies that were considered "timeless classics" while admitting that indeed, they were racist. What to do? You can't erase the past, but you can (in the case of Disney) add "racism warnings" (viewers can't fast-forward past them) to your movies:

> As part of our ongoing commitment to diversity and inclusion, we are in the process of reviewing our library and adding advisories to content that includes negative depictions or mistreatment of people or cultures. Rather than removing this content, we see an opportunity to spark conversation and open dialogue on history that affects us all... On Disney+ the following advisory will appear before identified titles: "This program includes negative depictions and/or mistreatment of people or cultures. These stereotypes were wrong then and are wrong now. Rather than remove this content, we want to acknowledge its harmful impact, learn from it and spark conversation to create a more inclusive future together. Disney is committed to creating stories with inspirational and aspirational themes that reflect the rich diversity of the human experience around the globe" (The Walt Disney Company, 2020).

According to the *New York Times*, media studies academics felt that the warnings would be useful to help children understand stereotypes, especially in the context of media literacy education (Pietsch, 2020, October 18). Jessica Laemle of Gettysburg College noted in an essay examining Disney's portrayal of women and People of Colour that continued deconstruction of negative cultural messaging is essential:

> It is difficult to escape Disney's influence on society. Under the Disney business model, any culture or message can be sold if it is mass-produced and marketed properly.... Disney is socially responsible for setting the standards of how female characters and those with diverse backgrounds are represented in films, and they need to do their part to challenge past (and present) stereotypes (Laemle, 2018, Fall).

In some areas, the company is showing continued insight and progress; for example, in Los Angeles, Indigenous-owned production company Skoken Entertainment is working on projects for Disney, and CEO James Pratt, a member of Saskatchewan's Cote First Nation, has "plans to shake things up by redefining the role of Indigenous people in the entertainment industry" (Benjoe, 2020, November 3).

Questions

1. How sincere do you think Disney is in applying racism warnings to its movies? Why or why not?
2. What else needs to be done by the company to ensure that it is seen as an agent of positive change?

Exercise

You are working under contract to the Walt Disney Company in a public relations role. Develop a plan for the company to extend its reach in getting the message out that it is seeking to engage schools (at the elementary and high school level) and post-secondary institutions in a dialogue about its efforts to create opportunities for dialogue about race and discrimination, using its classic early films as a starting point for discussion. What will you recommend that the company do in terms of reaching these stakeholders? What will you say to the media about these efforts? Create a plan and also a 500-word briefing note that offers some creative thinking around this issue.

KEEPING FAMILIES TOGETHER IN A RACIALIZED WORLD

Dr. Samir Shaheen-Hussain, an emergency room physician and professor at McGill University, had a question: "why are government officials preventing caregivers from accompanying Indigenous children on medical flights?" For Shaheen-Hussain, the practice of preventing parents from staying with their children on medevac flights from remote areas of Quebec amounted to a pronounced continuation of medical colonialism, the kind of colonialism that tore children away from their families during the era of residential schools and the Sixties Scoop.

Shaheen-Hussain offered up an answer to his question—and a solution—creating, in January 2018, a campaign entitled #aHand2Hold to address the issue, noting that it zeroed in on "child- and family-centred care, ethical considerations, standard of care, and the historical context of Indigenous children being forcibly removed from their families" (Shaheen-Hussain, 2019, January 31). The "ask" was simple: allow Indigenous family members to accompany their children on medical flights to the south. The provincial government flip-flopped on an answer, saying yes to the proposal when public pressure grew, and stating that systemic discrimination did not exist, but not actually following through on the commitment to keep children and their parents together during these hospital flights. When Quebec Health Minister Gaétan Barrette was later recorded at a news event suggesting that there would be cases where parents were denied access to the flight due to either aggression or intoxication, public anger rose, with critics accusing the cabinet minister of stereotyping Indigenous citizens; officials continued to skate around the topic, stating that systemic discrimination did not exist. Eventually the practice of allowing Indigenous parents to say with their children while being transferred for medical treatment would take effect, with (in contrast to predictions by the Quebec government) no negative outcomes. According to Shaheen-Hussain, in "consideration of the social and structural determinants of health, the government must take a hard look at its policies and practices, to root out racist and colonial thinking." But, as we saw in previous chapters, the problem of colonialized medicine continues, and an article in the *Canadian Medical Association Journal* about systemic racism in medicine (focusing on the racist attitudes of Canadian medical giant Dr. William Osler, and jointly written by family physician Dr. Nav Persaud, health care professor Heather Butts, and Dr. Philip Berger) underscored the history of systemic discrimination in North America, and the severe lack of recognition for Doctors of Colour who made significant contributions to western medicine. Response to the article was rife with accusations of presentism being tossed at the authors, and mainstream medical resistance to the change necessary to address the issue. According to the research of Persaud et al., Osler hated Latin Americans, warned against the "swarming" of Canada (then part of the British Empire) by "brown and yellow men," and felt duty-bound to ensure that Canada remained the domain of white people.

A century later, White men still head prominent medical institutions and there is a dominant view of the history of medicine that stars the likes of Osler. As statues of once-revered individuals who participated in racist crimes are being removed around the world, we should change Osler's place in medical curricula and explicitly address racism in medicine. What effect did Osler's racist behaviours have on his devoted trainees and the many others he influenced during and after his life? (Persaud et al., 2020, November 9).

Shaheen-Hussain told the *Toronto Star* that the glorification of doctors like Osler, with their racialized views (and the subsequent dismissal of physicians of colour like Black doctors Anderson Abbott, Alexander Thomas Augusta, a

Civil War hero, and Indigenous physicians Dr. Oronhyatekha and Dr. Peter Edmund Jones) serves to underscore and perpetuate the inequities in today's medical system (Oved, 2020, November 9).

Questions

1. What are the public relations consequences of official health agencies engaging in systemic discrimination?
2. How should public relations practitioners working on the communications side of health care manage issues of systemic discrimination?
3. If you worked in health care communications, what advice would you give a panel of medical staff with respect to changing the system?

Exercise

You are a public relations practitioner handling communications for a hospital in a small town, tucked into a rural area and with a substantial First Nation population. In the past, the hospital has been the subject of media articles on discriminatory practices against Indigenous patients, from misdiagnosing ailments based on suppositions of alcohol abuse to not taking Indigenous health concerns seriously. The hospital president wants to take a renewed approach, focused on relationship-building with the local First Nation, and you have been asked to work with the local Indigenous community on drafting a plan that outlines the ways in which the hospital will maintain open and fair dialogue with the First Nations community—and the mainstream—on all of its practices. Develop a 500-word plan that will take your organization through the basic planning stages for this initiative.

KEY TERMS

Cultural appropriation: the adoption, by people of privileged social status, of cultural identity markers that originate in communities of People of Colour.

Identity politics: politics that are focused on social, racial, cultural or ethnic identity, with a particular aim of promoting the core group's interests over those of other people or associations.

Islamophobia: dread and hatred of, and unfounded prejudice against, Muslims.

Magical Negro: A narrative device in which a Black character with strong moral values and wisdom provides guidance to a white character who is usually the story's protagonist.

Presentism: the seemingly smug, self-satisfied moral superiority with which present-day viewers look upon past people and events.

Sixties Scoop: the removal of Indigenous children from their homes, often without the consent of their parents, and their subsequent adoption to non-Indigenous families during the 1960s.

Virtue signaling: the attempt to demonstrate high moral values through the expression of opinions targeted to specific audiences, without necessarily being sincere.

REFERENCES

As It Happens (2020, October 16). N.S. fishermen's union head quits, says lobster dispute is 'too much of a toll' on his family. CBC Radio. https://www.cbc.ca/radio/asithappens/as-it-ha ppens-the-friday-edition-1.5765309/n-s-fishermen-s-union-head-quits-says-lobster-di spute-is-too-much-of-a-toll-on-his-family-1.5765312

Asmelash, L. (2020, September 4). A White professor says she has been pretending to be Black for her entire professional career. CNN. https://www.cnn.com/2020/09/03/ us/jessica-krug-gwu-black-trnd/index.html?utm_medium=social&utm_co ntent=2020-09-04T10%3A02%3A03&utm_term=link&utm_source=fbCNN&fbclid=I wAR3irPpp-EMsGo_lXaO8IdgVVzwx7HTgKahrlv-yPjbmtN1ScglIb36ZMVk&fbclid= IwAR2987FHEnH4MWeORvXhrKUBfM-EGkFp0xBWTZ0fl_wcsmgjhk8we1dWwFc

Aten, J. (2019, December 5). Peloton's latest ad was bad, but its response to the criticism was far worse. *Inc.* https://www.inc.com/jason-aten/pelotons-latest-ad-was-bad-but-its-response- to-criticism-was-far-worse.html

Basu, T. (2014, October 15). What does "Islamophobia" actually mean? *The Atlantic*. https:// www.theatlantic.com/international/archive/2014/10/is-islamophobia-real-maher-har ris-aslan/381411/

Belam, M., and Partridge, J. (2019, December 4). Peloton loses $1.5bn in value over 'dystopian, sexist' exercise bike ad. *The Guardian*. https://www.theguardian.com/media/2019/dec/04/ peloton-backlash-sexist-dystopian-exercise-bike-christmas-advert

Benjoe, K. (2020, November 3). Sask. man working on project for Disney wants to redefine how TV and movies portray Indigenous people. CBC News. https://www.cbc.ca/news/canada/sa skatchewan/jacob-pratt-indigenous-disney-1.5786518?fbclid=IwAR1aD_7gif4yH-HG62 IcGaj4MR2OvYIb0tvWiA0zHTZS5O0gYeNGao-9oJI

Bleich, E. (2011). What is Islamophobia and how much is there? Theorizing and measuring an emerging comparative concept. *American Behavioral Scientist*, 55 (1581). DOI: 10.1177/0002764211409387

Boutilier, A. (2020, October 20). Ottawa urges calm as fishery row simmers. *Toronto Star*, p. A8

Brown, D. (2004). Human universals, human nature and human culture. *Daedalus*, 133(4): 47–54. http://www.jstor.org/stable/20027944

Cambridge Dictionary (2020). Virtue signaling definition. Cambridge University Press. https://dictionary.cambridge.org/dictionary/english/virtue-signalling

Canadian Encyclopedia (2020). Indian Act. *Canadian Encyclopedia*. https://www.thecanadianencyclopedia.ca/en/article/indian-act#:~:text=The%20Indian%20Act%20is%20the, reserve%20land%20and%20communal%20monies.

Canadian Press staff (2020, February 24). 'Deep disappointment': Trudeau revisits blackface in Black History Month reception. Global News. https://globalnews.ca/news/6591552/trudeau-blackface-black-history-month/

Canadian Press (2015, March 11). Stephen Harper doubles down on niqab debate: 'Rooted in a culture that is anti-women.' *National Post*. https://nationalpost.com/news/politics/stephen-harper-doubles-down-on-niqab-debate-rooted-in-a-culture-that-is-anti-women

Canadian Press (2015, October 8). Government has tarnished views of Muslims, says Zunera Ishaq. *Maclean's*. https://www.macleans.ca/news/canada/government-has-tarnished-views-of-muslims-says-zunera-ishaq/

CBC News (2020, Sept. 21). Man charged in stabbing death of mosque caretaker followed hate group online. CBC News. https://www.cbc.ca/news/canada/toronto/mosque-stabbing-suspect-1.5732078

CBC News (2020, August 29). Activists topple statue of Sir John A. Macdonald in downtown Montreal. CBC News. https://www.cbc.ca/news/canada/montreal/defund-police-protest-black-lives-matter-1.5705101

CBC News (2019, September 19). "The progressive reputation of Justin Trudeau is in ruins": A sampling of international reaction. CBC News. https://www.cbc.ca/news/world/trudeau-brownface-reaction-international-1.5289870

CBC News (2015, October 6). Niqab ban for public servants would be considered: Stephen Harper. CBC News. https://www.cbc.ca/news/politics/stephen-harper-niqab-ban-public-servants-1.3258943

CBC Radio (2016, March 18). The allure and the dangers of "presentism." CBC. https://www.cbc.ca/radio/sunday/the-past-is-not-the-present-do-food-animals-have-rights-alberto-manguel-s-curious-mind-the-great-hunger-1.3497315/the-allure-and-the-dangers-of-presentism-1.3497463

City of Toronto (2020, October 6). City of Toronto 2020–2021 winter plan for people experiencing homelessness. City of Toronto. https://www.toronto.ca/news/city-of-toron

to-2020-2021-winter-plan-for-people-experiencing-homelessness/

Colour of Poverty (2019, March). Racialized poverty in housing and homelessness. Colour of Poverty/Colour of Change. https://colourofpoverty.ca/wp-content/uploads/2019/03/cop -coc-fact-sheet-9-racialized-poverty-in-housing-homelessness-2.pdf

Coren, M. (2020, October 22). Pope Francis endorsing same-sex unions a historic moment. *Toronto Star*, p. A19.

Cousins, B. (2020, August 12). Canada's rate of homelessness may be higher than reported: Nanos survey. CTV News. https://www.ctvnews.ca/canada/canada-s-rate-of-homelessness-may-be-higher-than-reported-nanos-survey-1.5060801

Crowe, C. (2020, March 22). It's time to think of homelessness as a public health emergency. *Maclean's*. https://www.macleans.ca/opinion/its-time-to-think-of-homelessness-as-a-publi c-health-emergency/

CTV News (2018, November 26). Bollywood bhangra blunder?: India not impressed with Trudeau's dancing. CTV News. https://www.ctvnews.ca/politics/bollywood-bhangra-blun der-india-not-impressed-with-trudeau-s-dancing-1.3816130

Daschuk, J. (2019). *Clearing the Plains*. Regina, SK: University of Regina Press.

Day, E. (2017, October 25). Canada's prime minister has spoken out against a burqa ban. *Emirates Woman*. https://emirateswoman.com/canadas-prime-minister-spoken-burqa-ban/

Dictionary.com (2020). Definition of cultural appropriation. Dictionary.com. https://www.di ctionary.com/browse/cultural-appropriation

Flaherty, C. (2020, September 14). More on CV Vitolo-Haddad and Jessica Krug. *Inside Higher Ed.* https://www.insidehighered.com/quicktakes/2020/09/14/more-cv-vitolo-haddad-and-jessica-krug%E2%80%8B

Flaskerud, J. & Strehlow, A. (2009, July). A culture of homelessness? *Issues in Mental Health Nursing.* https://doi.org/10.1080/01612840802319688

Fred Victor Mission (2020). Homeless in Canada: Important facts about homelessness you need to know. Fred Victor Mission. https://www.fredvictor.org/2019/06/07/homeless-in-canada-important-facts-about-homelessness/

Gallant, J. (2020, October 15). Heritage minister in no hurry to update profiles. *Toronto Star*, p. A8.

Global News (2020, September 19). Trudeau addressed his blackface controversy for a second time. Here's what he said. Global News. https://globalnews.ca/news/5925495/trudeau-apo logizes-to-canadians-over-blackface-controversy-heres-what-he-said/

Gollom, M. (2020, September 19). Why wearing blackface or brownface is considered 'reprehe nsible.' CBC News. https://www.cbc.ca/news/justin-trudeau-brownface-blackface-1.5289259

Gopnik, A. (2015, October 9). Freedom and the veil. *The New Yorker*. https://www.newyorker. com/news/daily-comment/freedom-and-the-veil

Haven Toronto (2020). The rise of COVID-19 and the fall of our community. Haven Toronto. https://www.haventoronto.ca/single-post/2020/09/08/Poverty-And-The-Pandemic?gclid=CjwKCAiA-f78BRBbEiwATKRRBMoHNXC5_Q2VqA9qcGJXLB0riM6TMZ6pXQbUw8q-e7gxnaAWB5Us5hoCEN8QAvD_BwE

Holladay, S., and Coombs, T. (2013). Public relations literacy: Developing critical consumers of public relations. *Public Relations Inquiry*, 2(2): 125–146.

Homeless Hub (2019). Racialized communities. Canadian Observatory on Homelessness. https://www.homelesshub.ca/about-homelessness/population-specific/racialized-communities

Hussein, S. (2007, November). The limits of force/choice discourses in discussing Muslim women's dress codes. *Transforming Cultures eJournal*, 2(1). http://epress.lib.uts.edu.au/journals/TfC

Ingram, K. (2019, October 16). Response to Trudeau's blackface scandal reveals a societal sickness. *The Manitoban*. http://www.themanitoban.com/2019/10/response-to-trudeaus-blackface-scandal-reveals-a-societal-sickness/38304/

Innes, R. (2020, August 13). John A. Macdonald should not be forgotten, nor celebrated. *The Conversation*. https://theconversation.com/john-a-macdonald-should-not-be-forgotten-nor-celebrated-101503

James, T. (2016, November 22). Homelessness action plan aims to house 150 homeless people by 2019. *Saskatoon Star-Phoenix*. https://thestarphoenix.com/news/local-news/homelessness-action-plan-aims-to-house-150-homeless-people-by-2019

Jones, R. (2020, October 23). AFN chief calls for resignation of RCMP commissioner as N.S. fishery dispute continues. CBC News. https://www.cbc.ca/news/politics/afn-chief-rcmp-commissioner-resign-1.5774499

Jordan, B. (2020, October 14). Statement regarding Sipekne'katik First Nation and commercial fishers. Facebook. https://www.facebook.com/BernadetteJordanNS/posts/1581531498720700

Kambhampaty, A., & Carlisle, M. (2019, September 19).Justin Trudeau admits to also wearing blackface 'makeup' in high school following TIME report. *TIME*. https://time.com/5680868/justin-trudeau-brownface-photo-apology/

Katawazi, M. (2020, August 19). Toronto police investigate after mosque faces sixth vandalism attack. CTV News. https://toronto.ctvnews.ca/toronto-police-investigate-after-mosque-faces-sixth-vandalism-attack-1.5069227

Kelly, E. (2020, October 21), in *Margin of Error* [television documentary broadcast]. TVOntario. https://www.tvo.org/transcript/129909X/margin-of-error

Kiambi, D., & Shafer, A. (2016). Corporate crisis communication: Examining the interplay of reputation and crisis response strategies. *Mass Communication and Society*, 19(2): 127–148.

Laemle, J. (2018, Fall). Trapped in the Mouse House: How Disney has portrayed racism and sexism in its princess films. *The Cupola,* Gettysburg College. https://cupola.gettysburg.edu/cgi/viewcontent.cgi?article=1769&context=student_scholarship

Lopez, (2017, August 17). The battle over identity politics, explained. *Vox.* https://www.vox.com/identities/2016/12/2/13718770/identity-politics

Mabhala, M., Yohannes, A., & Griffith, M. (2017). Social conditions of becoming homelessness: Qualitative analysis of life stories of homeless peoples. *International Journal for Equity in Health,16*(150). DOI 10.1186/s12939-017-0646-3

Maloney, R. (2020, October 19). RCMP 'let down' Mi'kmaw fishers, Indigenous Services Marc Miller says after violence In Nova Scotia. *HuffPost.* https://www.huffingtonpost.ca/entry/lobster-dispute-indigenous-nova-scotia-rcmp_ca_5f8de7ecc5b62dbe71c567fc?lvk=&ncid=fcbklnkcahpmg00000001&fbclid=IwAR1giy5YcakjJCKsvtXhisuEp6XJqOrlW-p_bD-M2CEEv_cwKbVfuGZs2YQ

Mastracci, D. (2017, June 27). How Canadian media normalizes Islamophobia. *Canadaland.* https://www.canadaland.com/how-canadian-media-normalizes-islamophobia/

McKinley, S. (2020, October 16). "This truly is systemic racism," chief tells PM. *Toronto Star,* p. A6.

McKinley, S., and McKeen, A. (2020, October 15). Attack on Mi'kmaq fishery sparks standoff. *Toronto Star*, p. A3.

Merriam-Webster (2020). Identity Politics. Merriam-Webster, Inc. https://www.merriam-webster.com/dictionary/identity%20politics

Montpetit, J. (2019, April 25). Quebec City mosque shooting. *The Canadian Encyclopedia.* https://thecanadianencyclopedia.ca/en/article/quebec-city-mosque-shooting

National Museum of African American History and Culture (2020). Blackface: The birth of an American stereotype. Smithsonian Institution. https://nmaahc.si.edu/blog-post/blackface-birth-american-stereotype

Neff, B. (1994, April 8). Multicultural, intercultural diversity—what do we call 'it" and how do these terms show up in public relations efforts? Central States Communication Association. https://files.eric.ed.gov/fulltext/ED384077.pdf

Noor Cultural Centre (2017, December). Islamophobia in mainstream Canadian media: "Muslims as Terrorists." Noor Cultural Centre. https://noorculturalcentre.ca/wp-content/uploads/2018/02/Islamophobia-in-the-Canadian-Media-Online-Version.pdf

Ojewumi, O. (2019, September 20). Justin Trudeau's blackface shows that being progressive doesn't exempt you from racism. NBC News. https://www.nbcnews.com/think/opinion/justin-trudeau-s-blackface-shows-being-progressive-doesn-t-exempt-ncna1057026

Oved, M. (2020, November 9). Sir William Osler's revered status in medicine shaken as racist views revealed. *Toronto Star*, p. A1

Persaud, N., Butts, H., and Berger, P. (2020, November 9). William Osler: Saint in a "White man's dominion." *Canadian Medical Association Journal, 192* (45). DOI: https://doi.org/10.1503/cmaj.201567

Peterson, J. (n.d.) Why we need to stop talking about the "Magical Negro." Perception Institute. https://perception.org/featured/why-we-need-to-stop-talking-about-the-magical-negro/

Pietkiewicz, I., and Kołodziejczyk-Skrzypek, M. (2016, May 24). Living in sin? How gay Catholics manage their conflicting sexual and religious identities. *Archives of Sexual Behavior.* DOI: 10.1007/s10508-016-0752-0

Pietsch, B. (2020, October 18). Disney adds warnings for racist stereotypes to some older films. *The New York Times.* https://www.nytimes.com/2020/10/18/business/media/disney-plus-disclaimers.html

Posetti, J. (2006). Media representations of the hijab. Faculty of Law, Humanities and the Arts Papers, 1822. University of Wollongong. https://ro.uow.edu.au/lhapapers/1822

Pullella, P. (2020, October 21). Pope says same-sex couples should be covered by civil union laws. Reuters. https://www.reuters.com/article/us-pope-film-homosexuals/pope-says-same-sex-couples-should-be-covered-by-civil-union-laws-idUSKBN276216

Rabble (2020). Niqab bans in Canada. *Rabble.ca.* https://rabble.ca/toolkit/rabblepedia/niqab-bans-canada

Renic, K. (2020, October 21). Court grants temporary injunction to Sipekne'katik band to end interference with fishery. Global News. https://globalnews.ca/news/7411240/court-injunction-indigenous-lobster-fishery/

Rivenbark, C. (2019, December 10). Commentary: Peloton ad is creepy but effective. *The Post and Courier.* https://www.postandcourier.com/opinion/commentary/commentary-peloton-ad-is-creepy-but-effective/article_89e86e14-1b81-11ea-a356-675222bdf812.html

Rubin, J. (2020, November 10). Indigenous communities join $1B purchase of seafood firm. *Toronto Star*, p. A6.

Samuels, A. (2015, July 19). Rachel Dolezal's true lies. *Vanity Fair.* https://www.vanityfair.com/news/2015/07/rachel-dolezal-new-interview-pictures-exclusive

Sapolsky, R. (2017). *Behave: The Biology of Humans at our Worst and Best.* New York: Penguin Books.

Saskatoon Homelessness Action Plan Steering Committee (2016). Saskatoon Homelessness Action Plan. Saskatoon Housing Initiatives Partnership. https://static1.squarespace.com/static/58dd630f3a0411286bd918ad/t/593ac2e59f745624fa053a4c/1497023216954/Homelessness-Action-Plan-Final-Print-Version-2016.pdf

Schneider, B., Chamberlain, K., & Hodgetts, D. (2010). Representations of homelessness in four Canadian newspapers: Regulation, control, and social order. *Journal of Sociology and Social Welfare*, 37(4): 147–172. https://homelesshub.ca/sites/default/files/attachments/Representations%20of%20Homeless%20in%20Four%20Canadians%20Newspapers.pdf

Shaheen-Hussain, S. (2019, January 31). It's time to ask what took so long to allow Indigenous parents on Quebec medevac flights. CBC News. https://www.cbc.ca/news/canada/montreal/it-s-time-to-ask-what-took-so-long-to-allow-indigenous-parents-on-quebec-medevac-flights-1.5000399

Sinclair, N., and Dainard, S. (2020, September 11). Sixties Scoop. *Canadian Encyclopedia*. https://www.thecanadianencyclopedia.ca/en/article/sixties-scoop

Statistics Canada (2019, April 15). The population living in shelters: Who are they? Statistics Canada. https://www150.statcan.gc.ca/n1/daily-quotidien/190415/dq190415a-eng.htm

Statistics Canada (2017). Canada Day by the numbers. Statistics Canada. https://www.statcan.gc.ca/eng/dai/smr08/2017/smr08_219_2017

The Walt Disney Company (2020). Stories Matter. The Walt Disney Company. https://stories-matter.thewaltdisneycompany.com/

Tinubu, A. (2019, April 25). Disney's racist cartoons won't just stay hidden in the vault. But they could be used as a teachable moment. NBC News, *Think*. https://www.nbcnews.com/think/opinion/disney-s-racist-cartoons-won-t-just-stay-hidden-vault-ncna998216

Trudeau, J. (2020, October 17). Statement regarding fisheries dispute in Nova Scotia. Twitter. https://twitter.com/JustinTrudeau/status/1317601144143777796

Walters, M. (2020, November 2). On the show "Does renaming restore or erase history?" *The Agenda with Steve Paikin*. TVOntario. https://www.tvo.org/video/does-renaming-restore-or-erase-history

Wedow, R., Schnabel, L., Wedow, K., & Konieczny, M. (2017, June 28). "I'm gay and I'm Catholic": Negotiating two complex identities at a Catholic university. *Sociology of Religion*, 78(3): pp 289–317.

White, C. (2020, October 21). Pope's latest affirmation of same-sex civil unions hailed as progress by LGBT community. *National Catholic Reporter*. https://www.ncronline.org/news/people/popes-latest-affirmation-same-sex-civil-unions-hailed-progress-lgbt-community

Willingham, AJ (2024, February 15). Rachel Dolezal, the White woman infamous for claiming to be Black, fired over OnlyFans account. CNN. https://www.msn.com/en-us/news/other/rachel-dolezal-the-white-woman-infamous-for-claiming-to-be-black-fired-over-onlyfans-account/ar-BB1ileu4

Wilson, J. (2020, October 23). DFO must respect Indigenous lobster fishing rights. *Toronto Star*, p. A17.

Winfield, N. (2020, October 22). Francis becomes 1st pope to endorse same-sex civil unions. Associated Press. https://apnews.com/article/pope-endorse-same-sex-civil-unions-eb3509b30ebac35e91aa7cbda2013de2

Young, B., and April, A. (2020, October 17). Southwest N.S. lobster pound destroyed by fire, man in hospital with life-threatening injuries. CTV News Atlantic. https://atlantic.ctvnews.ca/

southwest-n-s-lobster-pound-destroyed-by-fire-man-in-hospital-with-life-threatening-in juries-1.5149324?cache=

Zevallos, Z. (2012, January 24). Hollywood racism: The Magical Negro trope. *The Other Sociologist.* https://othersociologist.com/2012/01/24/hollywood-racism/

Zine, J. (2019, January 28). Islamophobia and hate crimes continue to rise in Canada. *The Conversation.* https://theconversation.com/islamophobia-and-hate-crimes-continue-to-rise-in-canada-110635

CHAPTER NINE

Conclusion

This wrap-up chapter, looking at the key points covered in the book, will provide the basis for thinking about the creation of a framework for understanding cross-cultural dialogue and public relations. In the conclusion, we will look at the following topics:

- Questioning the role of public relations practitioners;
- Some "lessons learned";
- The five big takeaways;
- Answering the question: "Where do we go from here?"

THE ROLE OF PUBLIC RELATIONS: ARE PR PRACTITIONERS APOLOGISTS AND RATIONALIZERS?

You will note in previous chapters that the most common phrases used in public relations focus on understanding, explanation, empathy, apology and a plan of action. This is standard fare for public relations, and often where it gets itself—and the organizations it represents—in or out of trouble.

As boutique communications principal Andrew Mckenzie says in "Is PR Evil?" the industry has not been treated well in popular culture, from Tony Curtis's portrayal of an oily press agent in *Sweet Smell of Success* to Colin Farrell's intimidating character of Stu Shepard in *Phone Booth*, and "I've always been uncomfortable with the stereotype of PR as made up of corporate apologists and fast-talking liars and spin merchants, especially since there are more than a few PR practitioners who quite happily fulfill these criteria" (Mckenzie, 2015).

The problem is that, outside of the provision of "just the facts" offerings (for example, corporate business pieces or the simple, straightforward responses of police department communications regarding acts of violence) too many PR practitioners may indeed be focused more on creating short-term "pretty narratives," "regret narratives" or "solution narratives" without thinking through to their long-term outcomes. Essential to remember is that "being effective in public relations requires making decisions that fall within appropriate ethical and legal boundaries. Ethical practices must consider the employer's self-interests, the public's self-interest, personal self-interest, and the standards of the public relations profession. Public relations professionals must also meet legal standards, as there are ways they can be held legally accountable for their decisions and actions" (Hatt, 2020). According to Allison MacKenzie, in "Ethics: Living your Professional Values," a 2007 survey of public perception of public relations found that more than 80 percent of respondents believed that the job of the public relations practitioner is to mislead the public on a client's performance (MacKenzie, 2015), which frankly sounds a lot like a combination of lying, bending the truth (sometimes ever so slightly) and leading people down a divergent path. Not a great thing to do. In cross-cultural dialogue, public relations practitioners—and the organizations for which they work—cannot simply "come up with" enough turns of phrase or apologies to knead the truthiness out of the truth, whether the truth lies buried in accountability regarding a police action against citizens exerting their rights to live their lives freely, transparency about the treatment of people in situations of racial discord or the expressed support for 2SLGBTQ+ rights in the workplace.

When it comes to engaging with diverse communities, as practitioners we cannot be passive, waiting for people to come to us—we have to reach out, and we have to be unafraid to move outside our comfort zones. We need to consult, learn about cultures outside our own, demonstrate patience, be non-judgmental, work directly with leaders within a cultural group, ensure the provision of a safe place for discussion and engagement and share ideas. In 2020, the Canadian Public Relations Society made a commitment to "take meaningful action to create a professional association that values and demonstrates diversity and inclusion." That commitment included a review of the public relations response to #BlackLivesMatter, a panel discussion at the society's virtual conference entitled "From Unconscious Bias To Conscious Communications: Strategies For Social Justice and Racial Equity" and the establishment of a "National Task Force on Diversity, Equity and Inclusion (DEI)" with a goal of establishing a DEI policy that would help drive internal organizational change as well as externally across the PR profession in Canada (CPRS, 2020).

It really comes down to doing a lot of learning; as Joseph and Joseph (2019) note in *Indigenous Relations* (in this case, in building relationships with Indigenous communities, but the advice is effective for other communities too), go to the website of the culture/community you want to learn about, "attend a public cultural event … research the protocol associated with the event … learn about the community's artists … volunteer in the community" (p. 17). There is a host of things that practitioners can do to increase their comfort level, and as most diversity experts will tell you, there are no dumb questions, and community members will welcome people to learn more about them and their culture.

Learning moments come in everyday ways. In 2015 I delivered a Black History Month presentation at the Whitby Public Library about a book I wrote (*Season of Rage*) concerning the activities of Hugh Burnett and the National Unity Association (NUA). Hugh Burnett was a Black activist in the southwestern Ontario town of Dresden, and his work with the NUA and with human rights activists from Toronto in the early 1950s helped to motivate the Ontario government of Premier Leslie Frost to pass two laws: the Fair Employment Practices Act and the Fair Accommodation Practices Act. The Fair Accommodation Practices Act made it illegal to discriminate against people in public access spaces like restaurants, bars and hair salons. It was flouted, openly and seemingly without fear of reprisal, by business people in Dresden, and this challenging of the law in particular triggered Burnett and others to stage sit-ins at Dresden restaurants that refused service to Black people (while at the same time the NUA was ensuring that Toronto media were present in the restaurants to record the events). Note that this was in 1954, a year before American Rosa Parks refused to sit in the back of the bus, and six years before the Woolworth's lunch counter sit-ins in Greensboro, North Carolina, both crucial events of the American civil rights era. So here I was in a library meeting room, a middle-aged white man keenly aware of my privilege and willing to talk about it, having written a book about a significant chapter in Canada's social, racial and cultural history and the people who played an instrumental role in it, in a room filled with about 30 Black and white audience members. Fast forward through the PowerPoint slide deck and discussion of the history of Hugh Burnett to the point, 45 minutes later, where I asked audience members if they had any questions. A Black woman sitting at the back of the room with her three children raised a pointed question: "Why are we talking about this history when right now Black people are being beaten up and sometimes murdered by the police? Things haven't changed!" I acknowledged her valid point, and responded that my book was about a chapter of Canada's civil rights history. I offered that I saw the point as being about not saying "things have gotten better" but that "we still have a long way to go." Then a white man who must have felt (as many white people with the best of intentions do) that he wanted to somehow make the mood in the room better, put his hand up and said that he gets along well with his neighbours, who are Black, and that his children have Black friends. "That's not what I am talking about," the Black woman said, and there was a pause. It was time for the "difficult discussion." The tension in the room was the crackling kind that puts people on the defensive—they wonder "which way will the discussion go?" I offered up to the group that this was the kind of dialogue we needed to help us work through, not around, issues of difference, and said that it was good to get these issues out in the open. I said that I agreed that things are as bad now as they were back in Hugh Burnett's day, and that we have a racism in Canada that is too often ignored but needs to be confronted. Other people added comments, and a long-time friend of mine, a Black woman and former school principal—someone with a calm assurance and a keen sense of empathy, caring and cross-cultural awareness—offered some words, in effect helping to moderate discussion, and with more commentary from people in the room the discussion reached a point of acknowledging that "this discussion is necessary" and the tension began to dissipate as we all agreed that the dialogue needed to continue, in different ways and in a spirit of working together. As we concluded the event, I paused for photos with people and signed a couple of my books, and the necessary discomfort of this conversation, I knew, was in the end very good. We didn't solve the problems that we faced, but we opened ourselves up to the opinions and feelings of others, and that was a very positive takeaway. It called to mind both Paulo Freire's concept of conscientização—the movement toward a critical social consciousness—and the words of James Baldwin, who said in 1962 that Blacks were not necessarily seeking acceptance by white people; they

> simply don't wish to be beaten over the head by the whites every instant of our brief passage on this planet. White people in this country will have quite enough to do in learning how to accept and love themselves and each other, and when they have achieved this—which will not be tomorrow and may very well be never—the Negro problem will no longer exist, for it will no longer be needed (Baldwin, 1962, November 17).

Every difficult discussion moves us a step closer to understanding, and the lesson I took from this event was that you cannot shy away, explain away, or walk away from uncomfortable conversations. The woman who raised the issue in my presentation on Hugh Burnett was right in what she said, had a right to say it and said it with her own sense of energy and caring, and the exercise of empathy and compassion was required by all in the room to bridge the "understanding gap" that existed in that space. We have to accept the discomfort that these conversations bring, welcome that discomfort and strive to use it to work toward a shared understanding of our cultures, our history and our society.

THE FIVE BIG TAKEAWAYS

1. As a practitioner, being proactive is essential—you cannot be passive; understanding other cultures, being sensitized to them, and being responsive demands an active role. You have to reach out beyond your own culture and homegrown worldview: ask questions, attend cultural events, volunteer for organizations, think tanks and committees and develop a sound knowledge base that you can build on.

2. You should take available training in cross-cultural dialogue; there are some courses that are offered for free. Additional training in Indigenous cultural understanding is also essential—Canada is undergoing a significant change in social attitudes, and undertaking legal agreements, adhering to the tenets of Reconciliation and developing new and exciting ways for people to learn about First Nations, Inuit and Métis. True, you can establish understandings in other, more experiential ways, and some of that will be hit-and-miss, but the best way to connect is through a combination of the received wisdom you obtain from experts combined with your own, roll-up-your-sleeves experience in the field of intercultural learning.

3. Ask questions of your organization—its position on cross-cultural issues that impact its day-to-day workings and dialogue, its messaging and its activities—and seek to influence it from within, by being knowledgeable about, and well-versed in, managing intercultural relations.

4. Think about the ongoing history of cross-cultural communications; as we have seen in numerous examples in the text, history does not always portray people in the best light, and 20/20 hindsight affords people a (sometimes too easy) chance to review what was said and by whom, and to ask if those messages delivered by practitioners (or crafted by practitioners for their clients) were reflective of the integrity of people who care about others, or

were simply mirroring an attempt to toe the dominant cultural line. Consider what you are doing now from the perspective of public relations a hundred years hence—how would you want to be seen? What would motivate you now to be the person that your descendants—both familial and industry-related—will respect?

5. Language. From the overuse of "I'm sorry" or "We're sorry" to the application of highly technical terms in attempts to gloss over the real impact of cross-cultural interaction, practitioners run the risk of becoming wedded to bafflegab and "smoke and mirrors" public relations. This also applies to terms that may have been "OK" in the past, but today we need to sit down and ask ourselves, "Are we communicating as clearly as possible, to the maximum number of diversified audiences possible, in language that is simple, direct, reflects our knowledge of other cultures, and doesn't offend?" For instance, Joseph and Joseph (2019) cite several terms, long accepted, that need to be dispensed with because of their offensive nature and disrespect for Indigenous communities, terms like "Circle the wagons," "Indian summer," "Low man on the totem pole" and "Let's have a pow-wow about this" (pp. 116–117). Figure out the language that is inclusive, that works for people, and keep yourself updated as to what is acceptable and what isn't; and don't fall into the trap of feeling that sensitivity to language is simply "political correctness"—that term in itself is a mocking insult used too often to let people "off the hook" when they make comments that are culturally offensive.

WHERE DO WE GO FROM HERE?

Where do we go from here? As practitioners, we go forth in a state of measured humility—we need to be able to *acknowledge our unknowingness* when necessary, and recognize that while we may be loaded with expertise on some subjects, we come to a playing field with our colleagues, our contacts, our stakeholders and our publics in a state of necessary learning. We need to recognize when we are falling into a pattern of cognitive dissonance, that state of being when the facts we see in front of us fail to align with our beliefs, causing us distress, and sending us scrambling to justify our (or our organization's) opinions. We "begin to justify the wisdom of our choice and find reasons to dismiss the alternative. ... As people justify each step taken after the original decision, they will find it harder to admit they were wrong at the outset. Especially when the end result proves self-defeating, wrongheaded, or harmful" (Aronson and

Tavris, 2020, July 12). Significantly, we have to be unafraid to ask questions, unafraid to admit to a lack of knowledge, but also strong enough to take a moral stand if necessary, for as the world changes—and the responses to the issues we face need to be sharper, clearer, faster and more contextual than ever—we need to remind ourselves of our rootedness in a commitment to, more than anything else, connect with people, get to know them, understand them, and work with them. As Paulo Freire said, "Knowledge emerges only through invention and re-invention, through the restless, impatient, continuing, hopeful inquiry human beings pursue in the world, with the world, and with each other" (Freire, 2000, p. 72).

REFERENCES

Aronson, E., and Tavris, C. (2020, July 12). The role of cognitive dissonance in the pandemic. *The Atlantic*. https://www.theatlantic.com/ideas/archive/2020/07/role-cognitive-dissonance-pandemic/614074/?utm_medium=social&utm_source=facebook&utm_campaign=the-atlantic&utm_content=edit-promo&utm_term=2021-01-02T17%3A32%3A00&fbclid=IwAR0zpdgmy-PbbsE3iDAynDpDM6Ow3BMsEQ-scyxsyGRAoUP7HJA-XY5NEb4

Baldwin, J. (1962, November 17). Letter from a region in my mind. *The New Yorker*. https://www.newyorker.com/magazine/1962/11/17/letter-from-a-region-in-my-mind

CPRS (2020). Our commitment to supporting anti-racism through diversity, equity and inclusion. Canadian Public Relations Society. https://www.cprs.ca/About/News/2020/Our-commitment-to-supporting-anti-racism-through-d

Freire, P. (2000). *Pedagogy of the oppressed*. New York: Bloomsbury Press.

Hatt, J. (2020). Ethical and legal practices of public relations. *Small Business Chron*. https://smallbusiness.chron.com/ethical-legal-practices-public-relations-57666.html

Johnston, B. (1990, Spring/Summer). One generation from extinction. *Canadian Literature*, pp. 10-15. https://canlit.ca/article/one-generation-from-extinction/

Joseph, B., and Joseph. C. (2019). *Indigenous relations*. Vancouver: Indigenous Relations Press.

MacKenzie, A. (2015). Ethics: Living your professional values, in Carney, W., and Lymer, L. (Eds.), *Fundamentals of public relations and marketing communications in Canada*. Edmonton: University of Alberta Press, 2015.

Mckenzie, A. (2015). Is PR evil? You'd presume so from watching movies. *IPRA*. https://www.ipra.org/news/itle/is-pr-evil-youd-presume-so-from-watching-movies/

About the Author

John E. C. Cooper is an experienced educator in the post-secondary school system in the areas of corporate communications and journalism, with a strong track record in adult education and curriculum development and delivery. A highly dedicated education professional with a Doctor of Education degree in Educational Research from the University of Calgary and a Master of Arts (Integrated Studies) degree in Adult Education from Athabasca University, he was a long-time senior communications manager with extensive accomplishments in all areas of government communications. As a knowledgeable journalist, corporate communicator, non-fiction and fiction writer and researcher, he has published eight books, including a textbook on crisis communications (*Crisis Communications in Canada: A Practical Approach*, published by Centennial College Press) used by teaching institutions across Canada. He has also received several awards for excellence in writing and communications.

www.ingramcontent.com/pod-product-compliance
Lightning Source LLC
Chambersburg PA
CBHW072049020426
42334CB00017B/1445